Two Walls and a Roof

Ireland born America bound
A book about Hope and Adventure
By John Michael Cahill

Copyright

Published by Rivermistmedia
29 Avondale Pk. Mallow. Cork. Ireland.
Email: rivermistmedia@gmail.com
Blog: http://johnmichaelcahill.com/wordpress/
Website: http://johnmichaelcahill.com/
Website: http://www.twowallsandaroof.com/
http://www.facebook.com/john.m.cahill.9

Table of Contents

Two Walls and a Roof...1

Copyright..2

Table of Contents 4

Forward...7

Introduction 9

The beginning...11

My Nannie..21

Three blind children. 30

Becoming a young salesman. 35

Christmas times 44

House fire. 48

The lost train set. 53

Our mother, none like her................................61

Two walls and a roof. 70

Lill's eel snake..78

Joe Hurley my best friend................................87

Fort Apache and other wars.............................92

Our father, a gentle Soul................................103

Pad Keely's school days..................................119

Big Kyrl adventures...134

The road to Charleville 158

Mad friends Disco days. 171

He better get sunscreen...................................194

Blessings upon you. 207

My Mallory days 223

Etta's years and our children. 235

Bobo 244

Local Radio. 267

Local Television. 282

Legal radio the fun ends. 289

JoAnn. Dream Maker. 297

The long lonely years. 312

Seville...   324

A new beginning...327

Dreams do come true. 344

Miracles we are...363

Dedication

This book is dedicated to my mother, Belenda Cahill, whose humour and optimism has always inspired me and gifted me with a great memory. My mother is one in a million.

It is especially dedicated to my American wife JoAnn whose chance remark on the internet began this work twelve years ago.

I am also indebted to my very good friend Laurie O'Flynn Rickard, who has helped me to turn my misspelled rambling notes into a book that I hope you will enjoy, one that offers you my belief in a very bright future for you and those that you love.

Finally it is also dedicated to my three wonderful children Lynda, Adrian, and Kyrl, and to all those others who have entered my life in a good way, I thank you all.

John Michael Cahill.
March 31 2012

Forward

I have written this book for one reason only and that was to get it out of me. For most of my life I have been involved in the media in some form or other, ending in radio broadcasting as well as owning my own video production company, Rivermist Media. However I have been primarily a storyteller for as long as I can remember. I have always loved talking to people and have no fears at all of speaking in public. This comes naturally to me because I came from the era of no television, no video games, and little radio; where your imagination was your real entertainment. They were times where you told numerous stories and listened to others telling theirs back to you, and it was all free.

My uncle Michael was also a writer, spending most of his spare time writing articles for the newspapers. He lived off his writing for much of his life. Michael loved his writing; I believe it relaxed him and, unknown to me at the time, I seem to have inherited his love for the written word and the magic of making pictures come alive from my mind to a page or a screen. I am sure that my sister Eunice has the same love and ability too, and it's as if Michael's writing till all hours of the night has infected the both of us, and why not, as we lived in the same house with him and his mother, my Nannie.

This book has come from my aging memory and the truth is everything to me, but I do not wish to offend or hurt anyone living or dead by my words. To this end I have done my best to disguise all those mentioned by changing their names and sometimes their places as well. Some people who have read the draft have been brought to tears, but most have been overcome with laughter and could see the funny side of our mad lives, especially mine, and I ask that you do just the same. Above all strive to be happy because I truly believe that…

"You are a child of the Universe, no less than the trees and the stars,
You have a right to be here".

John Michael Cahill

Introduction

Our house was an alleyway that had once been walled up front and back, and then roofed, probably in the late eighteen hundreds. It was a tiny house in a tiny town called Buttevant on the tiny island of Ireland, five thousand miles away from Missouri in the United States of America, and my life would bridge that gap in a truly miraculous way.

Inside that house, almost on a daily basis, an extraordinary drama was played out between a father too fond of the drink, an inspiring mother, and their six ordinary scrawny children. Like numerous others of that time, those six children were destined for a big fat nothing, but, that was not how it turned out. All six of them amounted to a wonderful something, and while each of the others have their own story to tell, this story is primarily mine. My brother Kyrle and I were our mother's Devils, who constantly got her and us into all kinds of trouble, while our father, a gentle soul, took to his bed or hid in a bottle of Guinness when trouble or work came knocking at his door, leaving our mother to face it all alone.

This book has been trying to come out of me for over ten years. I honestly believe that there is a book in each one of us because we all have our own individual story to tell, and it should be told, even if it's only to provide entertainment for those who come after us. This book was not written so as to hurt anyone, and I am thankful for all those who have touched my life this far, even if some of their actions brought me sorrow at the time. It was all worth it in the end.

As you read on you will surely see parallels between my life and yours, and if so, I ask that my story inspires you to believe in yourself, your Inner Self, the Real you, because after more than twelve years of study while writing this book, I have learned a great secret and it's this: Whatever you truly long for is supposed to appear in your life because it is not you that is doing the longing at all, it is the Inner you, the Real you, and It can and does work miracles, as this book will show you.

I earnestly hope that, after reading this book, you will believe in your own ability to create a magical life for yourself, and not do like I did, which was to wait for sixty years to find proof that it's possible.

John Michael Cahill.

Mallow, Cork, Ireland and Steelville, Missouri, USA. February 14 2012

The beginning.

The madness began on a cold March day in 1950. I came into the world some weeks late I believe, and actually arrived on the thirty first, barely ahead of fool's day. I used to think my mother held a great secret from me all my life and that I arrived after midnight, but of late she swears it was not so and she should know I suppose.

I was the result of a marriage a year earlier between a young woman of nineteen years, and a much older man who was thirteen years her senior. My mother had been 'matched' to my dad because her mother, the Nan, felt that 'he had prospects' and would take a useless fun-loving girl off her hands, such was the Nan's opinion of her own daughter. On the other hand, my paternal grandmother known as Gracie was dead against the match. She saw her favourite son as a businessman with great prospects, soon to be lumbered with a useless fun-loving girl, a description of my mother held in common by both of my grandmothers. Gracie only finally consented to the marriage after being convinced that my mother had a large dowry which she would bring to the marriage table, and which would later enhance both families. So Gracie agreed to hide her doubts inside a future bag of O'Mahony money. She was to be sadly mistaken on that account, as my Nannie was stone broke at the time, and the penny only dropped after the honeymoon was over, when Gracie began asking for her share of the loot. My Nannie had conned her counterpart, getting her son to take a useless daughter off her hands, and from that day on, they became black enemies, with my mother and us in the middle.

When it was my time to be born, my father Hugh Cahill had a dance band and he had become very successful both as a musician and as a band leader. His band used to play music all over the country in the style of the great Glenn Miller. In fact he called his band The Hugh Cahill Orchestra, mimicking his idol from America. Because of his profession, it was quite likely that when it came for my time to be born, he would probably be en route to a dance hall or to a pub, though he was anything but a drinker at that time. In either case it was unlikely that he would be at home for my birth, and so the matchmaker, my maternal grandmother, took charge, and Gracie wanted nothing to do with my birth whatsoever.

My Nannie was one hell of a tough woman, and you did not cross her ever. When she made up her mind about something that was it she would not change it, and in her mind, mother would need her and she would take care of the new child, because in her mind a useless funloving daughter obviously could not take care of it. My parents lived just across the road from my Nannie's house on the eastern side of the town on the main street. Their little home was originally an alleyway to the Awbeg River, where coach horses used to be sheltered before someone decided to turn it into a house in the late eighteen hundreds. I believe this happened around 1890 and the people were called Coughlans. To turn an alleyway into a house, they added a front wall and a back wall and later a roof, and in so doing they turned this right of way to the river into the smallest house in Buttevant. I call it 'Two Walls and a Roof', because that's what it was, with the other two walls being the gable ends of our neighbours' houses. The gable end on the church side was owned by our very good neighbour Eily Paddy Murphy, and on the other side the gable end was from a parish house where various Catholic priests lived over the years.

Some time later in my life, this little house would become my magic place. It would be an escape from the Nan - the matchmaker, and her black moods, a place of fun, madness, great discussions, chess games, a workshop for inventions, numerous chemical experiments and also home to most of the rest of our family. Above all though, it was a place where I could always count on a smile from my mother and a gentle feeling coming from both her and my father. In still later years, it was my place of chips fried in dripping with an egg, or French toast on a good day, but those good days were few and far between.

When I finally did arrive into this world, I was quite delicate, being two weeks late, underweight and miserable. My most striking features were a squint in my left eye, and a tongue which stuck out like a small snake, not the very best way to start off in life, but I had arrived at last, even if it was barely ahead of the fool's day. My long tongue, with its snake-like properties, was a great cause for concern and embarrassment to everyone, especially my Nannie, who spent all of her time trying to get it back in my mouth, and more importantly, keeping it there. It was a terrible battle and she only won in the end by dipping my dummy, known as a 'gollie', into some kind of sugary stuff which I loved, and this kept my snake inside. I'm quite sure that this concoction was very bad for my teeth, but it was either that or I'd never be shown off in public. The Nan did finally succeed, and at long last I could be displayed to the world, albeit at the Nan's whims, and that was where the first troubles began.

From the moment of my birth I was being held captive by my Nannie. My father only saw me at her behest, and mother saw me just a little bit more. Nannie got away with this by using the excuse that, "Sure he's delicate and ye can't mind him anyway. He's out all the time (referring to my dad), and you're useless Belenda". The Nan would refer to my father as 'he' in her way of demeaning the man, and she called my mother Belenda whenever she was angry with her. Most other times she would not use her name at all, preferring to imply my mother's existence rather than acknowledge that she might have borne a 'useless' daughter called Belenda.

I'm quite certain that my captivity in the Nan's abode continued for some months, probably two or three. Of course this soon became intolerable, and my father demanded me back from the Nan, telling my mother to do the actual demanding. He was much too afraid of her himself to do any such demanding and I suppose he pressed mother to 'take her on'. When she did ask for me back, Nannie flatly refused to give me up, telling mother to, "Clear out of my house and don't darken my door again". Mother left Nannie's and reported back to her husband, and who knows what they planned to do next. It's likely that they decided to just sleep on it, both being really afraid of the Nan because of her terrible temper.

Somehow the mother's demanding must have been playing on the Nan's mind, and in a fit of rage which was typical of the woman, she wrapped me up in a blanket, took me across the road in my basket, and then she left me on the street outside their door. There was no knocking or calling out, she just dropped me at the door and walked off across the street to her home. At the best of times this act would be a strange kind of thing to do to a baby, but considering I was only a few months old, it was three am in the morning and there were no street lights, it was quite insane and

13

showed her raging temper. At that moment she didn't care if the rats or the roaming dogs got me. As far as she was concerned, they could have me back.

My screaming must have woken my parents from their sleep of decision-making, and I was saved from the dogs, the rats, or the cold. I do know that both my parents were truly happy to have me home at long last. I would also guess that at some deeper level, even as a baby, I too felt very glad to be home with my real parents. Next day my father rose early, hell-bent on proving to his mother-in-law that he was a good father and could earn lots of money for his new son. Unfortunately, while he was gone and while mother was washing my one and only napkin, she saw from the corner of her eye, a dark figure glide up her stairs, come back down and then disappear out the front door. It was my Nannie of course, with me under her black shawl, stolen by sheer bravado from under her daughter's nose, and I would never return as their firstborn again.

Later that evening father arrived home with his money, full of joy, clutching his first ten shilling note for his boy. Straight up to my cot he went, but no John was inside it. He got a terrible fright and ran down the stairs shouting, "Belenda, Belenda, he's gone, he's gone. Our child is gone, where is he gone". Of course mother had to tell him where I was gone and how, and there and then their marriage seems to have ended. I feel he gave up on it all, not being man enough to go after his child because he was never a fighter, and my mother having being reared by this tough woman had no chance at all of ever getting me back, and so they resigned themselves to losing me forever. Father, not a drinking man in those days, took consolation in Arthur Guinness, and mother, always the optimist, felt sooner or later maybe her mother would give me up, but she never did. I was destined to be reared by my tough grandmother while my real mother only lived a few yards across the street, but she may as well have been living on the Moon.

For my part I became conditioned into believing that this woman across the street was a stranger, and that Nannie was my real mother, though I knew instinctively she was not. Nannie was a master at mind games and from the beginning she tried to alienate me from my real mother, though I have no doubt that it was done

14

because she loved me herself. Pretty soon Nannie began to treat me as if I was her own child, and I accepted this. I slept in her bed, was fed by her and adored by both her and her son Michael, my uncle. He used to call me 'chicken' and I have incredibly fond memories of him lifting me up high and taking me round on his shoulders, while Nannie would be roaring at him to, "Put the child down, don't you let him fall". Like my mother, poor Michael was also considered by Nannie to be worse than useless, a favourite word of hers in those days. But today I know that her 'useless' son Michael had sacrificed his life and his dreams so that she would have a roof over her head and food on the table in her old age, and few sons will do that today.

More than anyone else, I believe Nannie truly loved me. She did this loving with a kind of jealousy that's dangerous. She did her best to alienate me from my father also: not in a direct way, but subtle and crafty. She was a terrible woman for holding a grudge and would plot and scheme for years if necessary to get even with any wrongdoer, and she used this psychology on me and later on my sister Eunice who would also begin living with us. I suppose, considering what we know today about psychology, it's not surprising she acted like she did, as she herself had lost a child earlier in life and I was to be his replacement. I'm sure too that my mother, who was always a giver, even gave up her own firstborn out of sheer love for her own mother, and that takes some doing, but that is my mother.

As I got older, the fun started. I believe I was about four years old when I found the lemonade bottle full of paraffin oil on her stairs. I sat and drank it all down, not sure of the taste, but it seemed to be good at the time. Nannie spotted me and went into an immediate panic, shouting at Michael to get the doctor, "Quick, quick, he's drank the paraffin, he'll die. Run for the doctor will you". She used to use this paraffin oil to light the fire and I had drunk it. I remember feeling no discomfort of any kind, and the excitement seemed to be great. She was hugging me and saying, "Don't die, don't die on me, please God spare him, save him dear Lord". I don't remember what they did next, but I do know that I was sure determined to drink more of this oil stuff at the first chance I got, just because of all the affection shown to me by them all. Michael was blamed for letting the oil on the stairs, even though it was the Nan that lit the fire each morning, and this blaming became a pattern for all of his life. He was always blamed for all things she did wrong, and praised for nothing good he did right, yet we would all have been lost without him.

Even though my Nan presented a stern exterior to the world, she was a deeply superstitious, God-fearing woman of the old ways. She came from farming stock in Tipperary, and being from the country she knew all about faeries and pishogues and was scared to death of both of them, especially the 'Evil Eye'. Armed with such knowledge, it has always surprised me that both she and my mother would ever take me to an area that was bounded by a faerie fort. They used to go for a walk down the Charleville road to a dog track that was run by a family friend, a man called Thomas Nash. There they would sit and chat for hours, while I played around in the field with a ball, but the field bounding the track happened to have a large faerie fort in it, and it was even known as the 'Faerie Field'. Looking into this Faerie Field you could clearly see the large circular moat or lios that no one would dare to dig in, or excavate. This field was sealed off from the dog track by an old iron gate that had some bars criss crossing it, and I would say that it had never been opened.

As a curious child I used to go over to that gate and peer through it every time I was there, wondering what was over across in the tall ditch that was the faerie ring. However, Nannie had me warned never to go through that gate, but I remember being curious about the place. One beautiful summer's day, when I was about four or five years old, I was given a rare opportunity to partake in some real Irish myth and folklore at that field. We were at the track and I wandered off to the gate as usual and stood looking through it. No one will probably believe me, but when I looked through the old gate I distinctly remember seeing a small man dressed in a green coat and black breeches. He had a wide belt with a large shiny buckle tied across his middle, and he looked exactly like a faerie should, just as our folklore would describe them today. But at my age I had no idea about folklore or anything else either and I had never seen anyone like him before. It looked like he was very old: grey-haired, craggy-faced and bearded, with a small hat that

16

seemed to flop over on the side of his head. He was smiling and beckoning for me to go to him. He used a gentle hand movement, beckoning and calling to me all the time, but I heard no sound in my ears, and I somehow just felt this calling. I believe I liked him, and even though his wrinkly face frightened me a bit, his smile was drawing me to him for some reason, and so I began to climb through the gate. Then the panic started. I heard Nannie screaming, but I ignored her. There is a scene in the film *Close Encounters of the Third Kind*, when the child is drawn through the cat flap to the alien ship outside the door, and that's how it felt to me. I was powerless to stop myself from going through the gate. Nannie had seen me begin to climb through, and she instinctively panicked and started running to pull me back, shouting at Thomas Nash who was much closer. He caught me just as I was about to run to the faerie and pulled me back inside. We left immediately. I kept on telling them about the small man and how he was calling me and why couldn't I go to him. This was really frightening Nannie and I do remember that both Nannie and my mother became very agitated. There seemed to be a real sense of dread going on between them, but no one told me why they got so upset, nor why I could not go to the small man. They never again went back to that track, and I was always warned, even as a teenager, to keep away from that place, without being given a single reason why.

It was rarely discussed at home and if it came up, (it was usually me that brought it up) they always fudged the issue. I could never get either of them to talk about it much, and later on in life when I would persist, all Nannie would ever say in a dismissive kind of way was, "Ahh sure you just imagined all of that John, but tis better you stay away from that ould place anyway". Then her frightened fidgeting look would give her lie away, and besides that, I know I could not have imagined what I saw on that day, because I was far too young to create such a picture.

Apparently, had the faerie man managed to catch me, I would soon turn into a wrinkled, sickly baby and quite quickly die as a very young child. It was common enough in those days apparently, and I think the folklore people would have called me 'a changeling baby'. No medical reason would have been found to explain my untimely death, and I suppose I would have been seen as a victim of the old Roman saying, 'Those the Gods love, die young'.

17

Somewhere I read later that when the faeries don't get you, they leave you with a gift. I have no idea what gift they gave me, and after researching my life for this book, it may well be that they gave me the gift of a kind of protection from all the harm that nearly befell me over the years. This I do know; so far, their gift has not been that of gold coins.

My next memory of early childhood was when I was about six or seven. I had begun to read avidly. The first book I can remember having an effect on me was 'From the Earth to the Moon', written by Jules Verne. This book was all about men landing on the moon for the first time, written at least ten years before they really did land there. It was inspiring to my imagination and from it began my love of science, space and my fascination with fire.

Nannie's house was a two-story building: a ground floor, a middle floor and the attic where we all slept. I slept with the Nan in the back room, and in the front room, Uncle Michael had his abode. Nannie long suspected that he smoked in bed, but she could never catch him at it. She had this genuine fear of being burned alive, and she was terrified of a fire in our home, simply because we had no escape from the attic of that house.

We always had loads of books in the Nan's house, and I was greatly encouraged to read even though it had to be by candlelight, as we had no electricity in the attic at that time. I'm sure it didn't help my eyesight, but that's another story. When it was my bedtime, Nannie would send me to bed and light the candle, warning me not to go near it. This candle was stuck inside a milk bottle which stood on an old table that had a small drawer in it, used for her secret stuff. She used to make a big pretence of looking for things in the drawer each night, and early on I realised that she was hiding the matches there. I filed this away for future use, as even at six or seven, her craftiness was already having an effect on me. As if to give her confidence and protection in the night, she also had a heavy, toy snub-nosed revolver sitting openly on this table. It was clearly a toy, but she used to say that if we were ever being robbed, "He's useless (referring to Michael), and it's up to me to defend us, God help us all". I thought, even at my young age, that this was a bit optimistic, and I knew I would get far more fun from the gun, but she absolutely forbade me ever to touch it.

Our bedclothes were an under sheet, which was old and rough, and our coverings were a number of heavy wool blankets that would eat you alive with the scratching. Sheer exhaustion was the only antidote for the itching, and I'm not even mentioning the nightly attacks from the savage fleas who, because of the Nan's over use of DDT, had become immune to it. The survivors were hell-bent on giving us the plague by their bites.

One night I was reading my moon book and it vividly described the rocket as it crossed the Moon. It told of a flame shooting out from the back of the rocket and how this flame was the power behind the flight. It fascinated me totally. Pretty soon I saw the resemblance between my candle and this rocket ship, especially the flame coming from the top of the candle. There and then I began my first adventure with fire, and it still fascinates me today. I reached out and took the candle out of the bottle and began to fly it about as I read. Soon the book described the hills and the craters, so I made my own ones by raising my knees, and continued to fly in and out between my legs. I got the odd singe of burn, but it was only when my ship went well behind the hills that disaster struck. The candle flame somehow set fire to the hairy wool blanket and in the flickering light I saw the first signs of a fire. I dropped the candle in total fright, which only added fuel to the fire, and jumped from the bed in terror. It was then almost pitch dark except for the glow from the bed, and to my great credit, I grabbed our piss poe and threw its contents onto the fire.

It almost went out, but not fully. Then my last line of defence came into play. I clearly remember getting back onto the bed and standing spreadeagled over the spluttering glow and pissing like a petrified donkey down onto the fire between my legs. It went out, and then shaking with fright, I got the matches from the drawer and relit the candle.

I surveyed the damage and to my utter relief, the burned area was quite small but very black and charred. However, the bed was saturated. Of all the things I could do to infuriate the Nan, wetting the bed was the worst of them all and I was sure to be killed by her for doing it. Then her craftiness came forth in me again and I got a brainwave. I decided to take off my blankets and swap them over to Michael's bed, and this I did. Then later, sheer exhaustion set in and I fell sound asleep, still dreaming of the moon.

Nothing happened for almost two days; then the row began. She was tearing into poor Michael, calling him a pig and an animal: saying that his smoking almost cost us our lives and that he was going to go, he was definitely going to go, and she's not burning alive for his smoking. All this roaring and shouting was played out in front of me, as I was her sounding board. Poor Michael never said a word in his defence and he never broke faith on me either. He simply took her tongue lashing. She ranted and raved for an hour and her last words as he left were, "And don't you come back. I won't have you pissin' in the bed, I wont. I'll not have it I tell you".

The total insanity of her empty threats was that at that time, our only source of income was her widow's pension and whatever few bob he earned from shoe mending and his writing for the newspapers. If he ever really took off for good, both she and I would be out in the street. Of course he returned later in the day and she didn't mention the smoking again, but I kept far away from the candle after that.

My Nannie.

My Nannie came from the small village of Cullen in County Tipperary. Her people were farmers, and up until recently I believed that she came from fairly well off people, but that was not so however. Her mother, known to me as the Grey Nannie because of her white hair, always looked stern and old. The Grey Nannie had been married to a farmer who had been very wealthy once, before he took to the drink. His bad habit became worse and worse, and he proceeded to actually drink out their farm, leaving them totally broke. His family then bought them a second farm out of pity. By then the Grey Nannie had two young children, both of them girls. My Nannie was one of them and her sister Katie was the other. Their father soon drank the second farm out, and at that stage his people bought him a ticket for America, and he disappeared out of their lives. Katie was dispatched to a nuns' convent, probably against her will, and ultimately she too ended in America in a convent in New York or Boston.

By then, penniless and homeless, the Grey Nannie began working as a servant girl taking care of an old lady who owned the farm known as Gortnabearna. When the old lady died, she left a codicil in her will stating that the Grey Nannie would always have a room in that house till she too died. It said nothing about her daughter, my Nannie, having such a room as well. So a great comedown had befallen my Nannie and her mother, and they were left in a very precarious financial position, when out of the blue her husband returned from America. My great grandfather, the drunkard, now returned from America after doing well for himself, and begged his wife to go back to America with him. Twice bitten, twice shy, and even with no proper home for her and her daughter, she heard him out in the back seat of the local church before calmly telling him to clear off. He did and was never heard from again, but unknown to us all, somewhere in America I may yet have lost relatives named Ryan.

Nannie grew into an attractive girl in Gortnabearna and life

21

seemed to be getting better when she dropped a bombshell on her mother by falling in love with a British soldier stationed in the area. At a time of great political unrest and during the forthcoming Irish Rebellion, to fall for a British soldier was very bad news indeed for the Nan and her mother. It was especially bad news when the house they lived in, in sufferance, was also an IRA safe house, and her relatives had actually begun our War of Independence. This was not the thing to do, but love is blind and before it all came to a head, the soldier was shipped off to Flanders to fight in the First World War. He was soon wounded and shell shocked and sent home to England. Nannie found out about his plight and decided to go see him against the wishes of her mother, the Grey Nannie, who told her that if she left, she could never return. Nannie showed her spirit and temper, and even though she was still a young girl, she took off for England and found her man. He told her to forget him and to go back to a homeless Ireland, which she did. To this day, my mother believes that Nannie's heart was broken because she had lost her one true love in life, and it would never be the same with any man from that day on.

On returning home, as predicted, she was thrown out of her home by the Grey Nannie because of the shame she had brought on her family. She was ostracized by them all and a cousin actually threatened to kill her, and he meant it. She left the area and went working as a barmaid in a small village called Hospital in County Limerick. There she was befriended by Jack Mahony, a shoemaker, who quickly took a great shine to her and I believe after three days he proposed marriage and she accepted. As they were both misfits, I am sure she accepted his proposal probably out of sheer desperation, hoping that love might come later. He sold a house that had been willed to him and they decided to go to America to make a new life for themselves in the land of dreams. They bought their tickets and began their trip to Cobh and to the liner taking them to New York. My grandfather, Jack Mahony, who had been born in America, just had to say goodbye to his brother who was stationed in the British Army Barracks in Buttevant. They agreed a day's visit and no more. The town of Buttevant was only a minor diversion, but leaving for America was a very final act, so an emotional parting began. The two brothers drank and drank, and before Nannie could do a thing, her husband

22

sold their tickets promising to go later, but by then it was obvious that they were staying in Buttevant. When I look back on all of that drama, I think of how close I came to being born an American, and from then on a link with that great country was genetically forged, even though I did not even exist at the time.

They started a shoe mending business and Nannie soon bore her husband four children in quick succession. Tragedy struck early on though, when Jack developed a heart condition and he died a very young man, leaving her as a widow, with no social welfare and no one to work the business. By then she had not alone lost her husband, she had lost one of those four children earlier as well. Today I look back on my Nan's life and think of how tough it was for her always. Her pride was what kept her going. She also believed in secrecy. "Tell no one your business John, ever". That was always her motto and she lived by it every day.

She had few friends. Han Motherway, a widow like herself, was one, and a few others such as Nellie Garvan from next door. Nellie was the shipping agent for the liners to America, and it's no accident that for the formative years of my life, every day I saw a large cardboard cut out of the Statue of Liberty and the American flag in Nellie's window, as well as a selection of tickets for the boats on the White Star Line.

When my Nannie ran short of money, I would be dispatched across the road to Peggy Corbett's drapery shop with a note. It would read as follows: 'Give bearer the loan of a pound until Friday'. She would not demean herself by saying please, she never used my name in it, and never said thanks. Nor did she use her name on it either. My Nan made it feel almost like we were doing Peggy the favour, but religiously she paid back the pound from her pension on the Friday. When she needed a top up, she resorted to her secondary bank, the Bank of Liz Connell who came from the butcher shop across the road. Again, she always paid Liz as well. It was an admirable system that worked very well, but I still hated taking the notes, and I always felt like I was a beggar.

As I got a bit older I noticed how frightened she was of lightning. When we had a thunderstorm she would cover every shiny object in the house, especially the mirror, and start throwing the holy water around so much that it was drier outside than inside. I had no fears of lightning and would be driving her mad with my bravado taunting God to strike us if He could. This would make her go crazy. She would scream at me in rage, "The Devil is stuck inside of you, and if we survive this day, you're out, you're out I tell you, out of here, God forgive you. You'll burn in Hell for this yet". Then the storm would pass and the Nan that I loved so much would cry and say, "Why did you do that to me John, you know I'm afraid of the lightning. Tis only by the will of God and my prayers that we survived at all, now do my head, and be a good boy".

To make up for my actions and feeling sorry for this poor old woman, I would then have to sit on the window sill behind her as she sat on her old chair and begin running my fingers through her wiry greying hair, while massaging her scalp. This would bring her such relief that she would break into song, "Overhead the moon is beaming..... do more John, do more for your Nan". I didn't mind massaging her poor head, but if she brought out the ball of wool for her knitting, I was out of there faster than the lightning she feared so much.

Almost every year Nannie would return to her homeland and the Gortnabearna farm. I had cousins at that farm: Brid Anne, Mattie and Gerry Ryan, all somewhat older than me. Whenever the Nan would make her sortie to Gortnabearna, she would bring me with her. This trip was by train to Limerick Junction, as her people lived nearby. Then we would be picked up in their car and taken home to the farm for our holiday. I remember seeing a beautiful piano in their parlour, but we were never allowed play it. I suspect no one ever played it, but it stuck in my mind and that picture is as clear as day to me still. Each morning we would have the most amazing breakfast. Rashers made from hairy fatty bacon, fresh eggs, and loads of butter lashed onto brown bread just baked in the bastable. That brown bread was the only healthy part of it all. I can still smell the aroma and hear the bacon sizzling in the pan. To my utter amazement as a child, the Grey Nannie would take that bacon down from inside her huge open fireplace. It was black and obviously being smoked, and I just thought this was great fun eating the black meat.

When I was about eight years of age I began to rebel against the

Catholic religion, and even though I had got First Holy Communion by then, I was no lover of divinity and hated any kind of ritualistic praying. In the Ireland of the fifties, especially in rural areas, it was the custom to say the Rosary every night and this I hated with vengeance. So when we would all have to kneel down and begin saying this chant, I would be bored to death. The floor was a stone cold slab and our kneeler was the sugaan chair that we had been sitting on. I absolutely hated this praying, seeing no honesty in it. As I saw it, all we were doing was repeating verses in a tiresome monologue and I got nothing at all out of it. I also feared it because each of us had to say a decade of the Rosary, and God help me if I had to say the Our Father as I could never remember it, nor did I care to. I used to count the threads in the sugaan ropes out of sheer boredom as my knees stuck to the floor with the cold. All this time, Nannie would be glaring at me for my lack of answering. When it came to my turn for the decade, I would mumble along and as we were the guests, all the rest of the family prayed louder to help me out. Later on Nannie would drag me aside and threaten to kill me if I didn't learn these prayers better, but she never taught me either. When the praying ended, my favourite part would begin. The whole family, including the servants or workers, would gather around the huge open fireplace and start to tell stories. There would be folklore and ghost stories told for some hours as we sat by the warm turf fire in the flickering light of an oil lamp. I believe they had electricity then, but all I can remember is the lamp casting shadows mixed with the light from the fire, and it was a beautiful warm glow. I believe that it was in those days that I began my love for the art of storytelling, and I would listen intently as each person added his own version of some event he knew of. It was sheer magic to be allowed to sit in the inner corner and work the bellows as it pumped out air under the glowing turf until bed time.

Usually on the night before we left, someone would call for a concert. Nannie would be hinting at it all evening so that she could show off her John and his great singing voice. I hated this singing even worse than the Rosary. I would have to sing the only song I knew which she had made me learn over and over. It was called Doonaree. A most pathetic song all about 'love and kissing and girls' or so it seemed to me then.

The concert would take place in the kitchen with all the people sitting in their chairs forming a half circle facing the stairs. A curtain would be set up under the stairs and this area then became our stage. Mattie and I didn't get on at all, and he would be gouging me and pushing me from the back before the curtain ever went up. Brid Anne was older and seemed to have no fears of the concert, and neither did Gerry: both of them were a lot nicer to me too.

My last memory of those concerts was unforgettable. The curtain went up and Brid Anne introduced the show and called on Gerry to say a poem or something like that. Then Mattie had to do his bit, but I can't remember what he did. Then the finale was always my part and a big show was made of the 'special guest'. "John Cahill from Cork will now sing Doonaree" I peeped through the curtain and saw Nannie beaming with pomp and pride in her John as my name is being called out. Then I was shoved out from behind the curtain by Mattie, and I fell over a chair. After pulling myself together I began to sing. "Oh to be in Doonaree where the ......" I could not remember the next line. Total silence fell on the room; stage fright had hit me. Mattie sniggered from behind and I raged inside, then I tried again with Brid Anne trying to prompt me. " Oh to be ..... " This time I got a bit further along, based on her prompting. Nannie was glaring at me and had put on that dark face which I knew meant a good hiding was on the way at the very least, but it could mean death was a possibility also. Again, total stage fright hit me and I froze a second time. Mattie shouts out from behind, "Up Tip, Tip for the All Ireland", and even though not a sporting type myself, that slur on Cork was too much for me and I lost control. Figuring that I was going to get killed anyways by the Nan, I ran round the chair and began punching him in the head and kicking him like a mad man. He fought back and uproar was all the go. We fell on the ground and he was trying to bite me. I kneed him in the 'mickey' and he roared out in pain; all this happened in seconds. We were soon dragged apart. Nannie ordered me to say sorry and I refused, bang, a clatter across the head changed my mind. "Say sorry I tell you now, and shake hands with your cousin". As we were both in trouble, we reluctantly shook hands, but he tried to stick me with his finger nail as we shook. Later that night Nannie threatened me with never taking me there again, and as I did love the place, especially the stories, I felt bad all night long and couldn't sleep. Of course we did go back and Mattie and I made it up, but there were no more concerts after that night.

My brother Kyrle was born about a year or so after me, and I guess he became my parents' first child, or at least that's how I felt about it always. Kyrle had beautiful hair as a child and mine was a dead loss, getting worse the more the Nan tried to fix it, and it's the same to this day. She resorted to using what I called her 'crocodiles'. These were definitely antiques I would say from some time of torture in the Middle Ages. They were shaped like half moons that opened out into jaws which had jagged, razor-sharp teeth. I assume the way they worked was the jaws grabbed the hair and the teeth held it in place, and ultimately a smile or a 'wave' would form; waves were all the go then. Kyrle had curls and apparently looked great and my hair was flat and straight with a 'cow's lick'. But Nannie determined that now, I was going to have waves too.

The normal way these crocodiles were used, when not for torture, was that the person put them on some time before bed, then removed them before sleep. Not so with the Nan though. She felt sure she would get better results if I had them in all night long, and to make sure they stayed in, she would almost stick the bloody things into my scalp. She definitely had two of them, but more likely she had four. For God only knows how long, she tortured me with these implements of pain. Every night I would be yelling, "No Nan, not the crocodiles again tonight." The cries fell on deaf ears though, and then I had not alone to contend with the scratching from the fleas and the blankets, but I also had the tearing at my head as well. Aside from that, all seemed good to me then. I was becoming her idol and could do no wrong. Her comparing me to Kyrle also began about then, and of course I was way, way better in her eyes. Mother never bought into this crap and just felt the Nan was the Nan. Time rolled along.

Nannie was a great one for the walking and she and my mother would drag us off for long walks in the country for no apparent reason. We would be starved when we trudged along but it made no difference. We had a saying that the 'hungry grass will get us yet', and I was very often actually weak with the hunger, and Kyrle too. I don't know what was expected of these walks as I felt I'd rather be hungry at home, rather than face a long journey with my belly rattling. Nannie had no sympathy and would say, "Trot along there now and be good boys, sure twill make men of ye yet". We used to pick mushrooms for food on some of these occasions, and to this day I hate them because of those memories. I suppose she and the mother would be wondering where our next meal would come from, and a few mushrooms was a start at least. If we went for the blackberries she told us "Stop that, they'll fill ye with worms", it's no wonder I love jam because I craved sugar, and we rarely had any, and instinctively I must have felt it was in the berries.

After walking miles they would soon sit down on a wall or on the grass and start fixing the world, especially my dad's world. Despite his failings Nannie never really gave out too much about my father, she had a soft spot for him I think, as he was always struggling and she saw an affinity with him in this also. She would say "Ahh sure he's useless, quite useless I tell you, but then he's a Cahill what do you expect from that lot" In later years I found it hard to reconcile her words, because Nannie was the one who had made the match between my father and mother. As usual though, mother just agreed with her for a quiet life.

My Nannies arguments with Michael were legendary and sometimes violent. She would steal his money and fags. She did this for the mother while he slept, and in the morning there would be a big row about the theft. Nannie had a poker face and would swear blind that she knew nothing of his 'fags' or his money either. When this failed she would go on the attack and tell Michael to clear out of her house and to get a real job.

She used to 'steam open' his letters to read any personal mail and to see if his 'writing' payment had arrived. This was a terrible thing to do and even though I was young, I felt it inherently wrong to read other peoples mail. This steaming of mail was a black side of her, which I felt dishonored the woman's amazing integrity, which she undoubtedly had in all other ways. Poor Michael had no chance at a love life either as a result of her steaming. If by some fluke he managed to get a girl to write to him, Nannie could almost surely sense it, and she would immediately put the kettle on. As she read the letter, I can still see her muttering away to herself" "Sure I'll give her love, that bitch, that confounded bitch, sure she's only a tramp, not good enough, no no..not good enough at all" and yet another letter went into the fire. Michael never got married, he just couldn't because of Nannie constantly sabotaging his women. He lived to support her all of his life until he finally died from a stroke at a very young age. I think just like Eunice, Michael was never properly appreciated by my Nan. She always felt I did more for her which was untrue because, Eunice took care of her, and Michael fed her, life often treats worst those who deserve better.

Three blind children.

My sister Lill came next into our world and all I remember of her early childhood was that she was always asking Uncle Michael for a penny for a pop. He was always great for the nicknames and he called her Nell Pop, Kyrle was known as the Gaggyman and I was the Chicken or Gengen. Lill was a small chubby little girl and she always seemed to have a far away look as if she was searching for something, or so it seemed to me as a child. Because we lived in different houses, my other memories of her are dim, and those I do have are of her smiling a lot but looking hungry too. Later on of course, she became the butt of many tricks me and Kyrle would play on her as she was always a gullible victim and believed all we told her.

I would say about nineteen sixty one or two, times seemed to have gotten very much tougher for us all. I think the reading by candle light took its toll on my eyesight and I'm sure it was the same for both Lill and Kyrle, as by then, we were all having trouble seeing the blackboard at school. Mother had to get us examined, and in those days you had to go to Cork to get an eye examination. My mother and Nannie seemed to me to be carrying the whole brunt of all the bad times together, and any kind of new financial expense would be really bad news for the two of them. My memories of my father then are that he almost always seemed to be in bed either drunk or sleeping. It was as if he just was not there at all, and he had no spirit to fight or help his wife and family in any way.

To get to Cork we would have to go by bus and cross the city to the Eye Ear and Throat Hospital on the Western Road. The fare and some food were the big problem. Both Nannie and mother were at their wits' end and no way could they see how this could be done, especially getting the bus fare. As we seemed to be getting worse in the eyes, and desperation set in, my mother took the only resort open to her. She would join the really really poor of Buttevant and go to the Government office for help, better known as visiting 'The Poor Man'. This was as demeaning as it gets for proud people, especially the likes of Nannie, so of course she wouldn't go herself; she would send my mother instead.

My best guess is that mother was in her early thirties then, a good -looking, soft-spoken, and once upon a time fun-loving, happy girl, now walking down the town to beg for a hand out. It pains me so much today to know she had to do this, but worse was ahead for her.

In the dark and dingy old room, a few people worse off than herself sat waiting on hard chairs. Her name was taken by some clerk, and sitting down, she chatted quietly to the others who were waiting in line to be called. 'Next' was the dreaded word.

From inside an inner office a harsh and unfriendly voice boomed out, questioning some misfortunate girl in angry and loud words, removing her last vestige of pride by repeating her plight so loud that all outside could hear. "And you're telling me you're having a baby. Huh, you are so, be God, ...and I'm expected to feed it too is that it...and the others as well, be God, and he sends you no money from England...am I to believe that am I? Get out of me sight will you, I'm not made of money, ...Next ."

She came out in tears, brushing past the newest victim on the way in. One of the women, a Mrs O'Brien, decided she could not take it any more, and said to the mother, "Belenda I'll be off now and come back tomorrow when he's in a better mood". Mrs Gilliam went in and took his booming and ranting, and got what she wanted, and as she came out she whispered to mother, "He's not so bad today Belenda, you'll be alright."

"Next.... O'Brien....O'Brien," There was only silence as she had left. "Cahill so. Come on, I haven't all day, and be quiet out there will ye." Mother entered and stood respectfully at the desk. " Sit down will you, what do you want?" She told him that she had three small children who needed to go to Cork to have their eyes tested, and could she have money for the bus fare and a bit for food for the journey. Without looking up he scribbled a note, and throwing it across the desk says, "That'll get ye there. The State doesn't pay for those who don't work", a clear dig at the father's idleness.

She took her paper, glad of the fare at least, and headed back to Nannie's. Most likely the Nan borrowed the money for food from Peggy Corbett who was a true saint if ever there was one, and next day we are on the bus. What an adventure. Our first time on a bus, and imagine my delight at getting on it outside of our own door. This was great. The bus to Cork always stopped directly outside

31

mother's house. There was no shelter at all for the patrons and our shoot leaked as well, so you could be soaked while waiting. Many a time mother had given total strangers a cup of tea to ward off the cold or the rain. Now it was our turn to board the bus. Little did we know what she faced that terrible day. It drove along the winding roads of Cork and we just delighted in every twist and turn. I saw the Blackwater River in Mallow, the town, and even a train racing the bus. All three of us seemed so happy, and even mother seemed to brighten her spirits as we got closer to Cork, our ohh's and ahh's, and "look look" becoming more and more excited as the miles went by.

The fine mist that fell across the city did nothing to dampen our total amazement at the tall buildings, the great shops full of goods, Woolworths and the 'huge' River Lee. Mother wore a scarf to ward off the rain and I'm sure we had coats, and that's all I know. The journey out to the hospital was about a mile or so, but it was filled with new scenes for every step we took, and it seemed to fly as we trudged along in the rain. Lill held mother's hand as we walked, and Kyrle and I trailed along behind stopping and gawking into the windows until mother would shout back at us to, "Come on quick will ye, or we'll be late for the doctor".

At the hospital, all I can remember is the old dark waiting area which seemed like a long dingy corridor. I was the first to be called into the even darker doctor's office and there, an old, cold-faced man asked me to look through what seemed like binoculars and make a butterfly go into a net. I suppose I also read a chart, though I'm not sure of it. This man seemed to be totally disinterested in me and never once smiled. "Next....." It was Kyrle's turn and then the same for Lill. All the while mother sat patiently awaiting the results and our glasses, promising us a trip to Woolworths later. When those results came, they were shocking indeed. He coldly told her not to be bothered too much about the glasses, or returning there again, because within six months it was likely that all three of us would be blind.....and further, not to waste his time in the future. If this was the Ireland of freedom, we were far better off under the British. Mother left in a daze. As we began walking back into the city, she was distracted with grief and burst into tears somewhere along the Western Road. To this day I hate that part of our city. Not one, but all of us were going into the darkness, and so soon too. As she sobbed openly, none of us knew why, or what had happened. I clearly remember that Lill clutched on to her as Kyrle and I stood wondering what was wrong.

Such is the measure of my mother's optimism that instead of giving up like our father would have done, she determined that she would give each of us a memory so great, so grand, so awesome, that we would be able to conjure up this picture even in the darkness of blindness. She would show us a huge ship and the sheer size of it would stick in our minds. The emigrant ship Innisfallon was moored in Cork Harbour and this would be our picture. We trailed along in the mist, and after what seemed like forever, we got to the ship. It really was huge: black-bodied, grey and white. I saw the windows of rooms, portholes, and men working along its decks. The gangplank rested on the quayside and I wondered what Huck Finn would have thought of this ship. Was it as big as the paddle steamers on the Mississippi, and was it ever going to the sail that great river? I also saw a cone attached to a mooring rope, and spent a long time trying to figure out its purpose. Mother tried to describe the ship and the oceans with her limited knowledge, but her heart was not in it and she sat with a far away look in her eyes.

We played on the coils of rope, the crates, and the open quayside. Lill sat with mother on one of the small crates and she seemed to be able to comfort my mother when she cried on and off. Soon a man came by and saw us and mother's upset state. I think she must have told him her troubles. This stranger consoled her, probably thinking suicide was on her mind, though it was not, and after he left she seemed a little relieved. By then the hunger was getting the better of us all, so we headed back to Patrick Street and the shops.

I believe there was a small café located right on the corner of the river on Patrick's Bridge. Its name escapes me now. We traipsed in there, tired, excited, and hungry, but not so our mother though. It's as clear as day to me still, as I see how my mother just stared at the small menu for a long time. I remember that we all had chips, and I suppose an egg with bread and butter. Mother had a little pot of tea, just that and nothing else. That was our first bit of food since breakfast and she still did not eat. It struck me as very odd too that she was not eating, and the far away look in her eyes had returned.

Like all good mothers, she gave the food to her flock and went hungry herself, all the while being lost in the thoughts of her terrible news. I, being the eldest and about twelve, sensed that things were very wrong somehow. I know too that we eventually went to Woolworths after pestering her continually, but I don't think we bought a single thing there. Home on the bus in the dark and into Nannie's we all went. We sat around the table eating bread and jam while they talked.

The closeness of their heads and the low murmuring confirmed, to me at least, that there was a serious problem with the day. Nannie would every so often exclaim out loud, "Have sense will you Belenda, he's wrong, he's totally wrong I tell you, God help us all". Her way of dealing with this problem was to get angry at the news, and I think I have actually inherited that trait from her today. Soon they all left and I went to bed, still reading with my candle.

Somehow we all got glasses, though Kyrle threw his away early on, and thank God none of us ever went blind. On the contrary, some forty two years later, Kyrle, while working as a vision supervisor during the millennium celebrations for Ireland's national television service, RTE, had the great honour of transmitting the first pictures of the dawn of the new era from Newgrange. When the first rays of the new sun shone straight into that Megalythic tomb, the pictures that millions of people were seeing all over the world were the ones created by my brother Kyrle. He was seeing those images first, then beautifying them before they went out to the rest of the world. To Kyrle it was just another job. To me it was an occasion of immense pride, knowing my brother was doing this work. Watching too that same day was Lill, then a specialist nurse and top of her profession in the Isle of Man. She too took great pride in her brother's achievement, and mother no doubt waited for the credits to roll and his name to appear. When it did appear, she knew her so-called 'blind' son had made that unique broadcast happen, and surely she thought that cold-faced old eye doctor got it very wrong. I know I did.

Becoming a young salesman.

My Nannie was the driving force in my universe, but even at a very young age my Uncle Kyrl was becoming the one I really looked up to because he had a kind of charisma that was infectious, even to a very young boy. For some reason though, neither Nannie nor the mother liked him, and I never understood why that was nor would they tell me either.

Strangely enough both Kyrl and my Nannie, the two figures I looked up to most, were instrumental in creating what I believe was the most traumatic event in my life.

My earliest memory of Uncle Kyrl, who we called 'Big Kyrl', was that he was always out to make money. He epitomised the entrepreneurial spirit which I am sure I inherited from him. I admired Kyrl immensely as he neither drank nor smoked, unlike my father who did both to excess. Kyrl always had money and believed you had to invest to accumulate. He also had a great saying which he instilled into me. That saying was this, "The end always justifies the means". He had added the word 'always' to emphasise his belief that no matter what you did to achieve your aim, it would be worth it in the end, and he proved this belief to me often.

One of the things I loved most about him was his futuristic thinking. He brought the first cinema to Buttevant, later turning it into Cinemascope by curving the screen around the audience. This new movie experience was the talk of the age in Buttevant, being the forerunner of the Imax of today. Later on he ran dances to entertain the people, and later still he taught himself music, though he was never as good at that as my dad was. He knew all there was to know about engines, and radio and electronics fascinated him. He ended his years owning a very successful monumental works, where he erected thousands of headstones all over Cork and Limerick. Unfortunately for me though, his belief in the end always justifying the means was to have a traumatic effect when I was about eight or nine years old.

I think he either bought or owned a house at the top of the town. This he had rented to a local guard, a sergeant I believe. I'm not sure of his name, so I'll call him Ryan. Guard Ryan was married with a young family and I believe he felt settled in Kyrl's house. He paid the rent regularly and all went along well for a while, until Kyrl needed to sell the house to raise money for the upcoming cinema business he was planning for Buttevant.

In those days it was very important that one did not get on the wrong side of the local guards as they could make life very difficult for you, especially when you needed a dance licence or other legal permission of some kind. Kyrl was then in a bind because he had no reason to ask the guard to leave. He could not legally evict him even if he wanted to because he had paid his rent, and more especially when his tenant was a local guard.

By then father and mother were living in their little 'two walls and a roof' house, and I was still being held captive by the Nannie across the road. My brother Kyrle was about seven and our sister Lill was young, but my parents still had plenty of room. There was nothing critical about their housing situation. However, Kyrl felt that if father and mother were prepared to exaggerate their 'desperate housing situation' and put it before the guard, then he might be persuaded to vacate the house so that Kyrl could 'give it' to his brother. This was a typical ploy of my uncle Kyrl and showed his way of thinking about life. It was cold, calculating and mercenary. He did not give a damn about the guard or his young family, all he cared about was selling his house and that was the end of the matter for him. It's quite likely that Kyrl had also promised father a considerable amount of drink money to convince my mother to go along with his plan. But as I saw it, the bottom line was that he had no notion whatsoever of ever giving that house to his brother, or my mother either, he just wanted Ryan out of his house at any cost.

It appears that a row took place at home and my mother would have no part in the eviction of a husband, wife and young family, and took grave exception to being used as a pawn in Big Kyrl's game. What's more, I am sure that she went up the town to the house and told the guard's wife all about it. Obviously the guard went mad, and from that day on Guard Ryan had it in for Kyrl.

Over the following five years or so, bad blood flowed between both Kyrl and Ryan, and a deep level of distrust built up between them.

By about nineteen fifty eight or nine, the economy seemed to have deteriorated and no one had any money, not even Nannie with her regular pension. She too seemed to be in desperation most of the time. Uncle Michael used to mend shoes and hated every minute of it, but at least he earned some money from this work. I can clearly see him now, sitting at his little bench in the front of Nannie's house, flaking away at an old shoe balanced on his wooden last, and smoking his fag at the same time. I see too, on a shelf behind him, the little red Pears Encyclopedia that I read so often and where I got my first taste for America.

At that time it was customary for the people to bring their shoes in for repair during the week, and collect them again on a Friday night. At least that's how it worked for those with a wage or with money. For those other customers who did not call on the Friday night, probably because they had no money, I would be dispatched by the Nan on Saturday to deliver their shoes to them.

My Nan would go out of her way to warn me sternly not to give up the shoes without the money. "John, tell them 'no money, no shoes'. Bring their shoes back no matter what they say, sure they'll never pay if you give them the shoes. Off with you now, there's a good boy, ... and put on a coat". And off I'd go with my canvas bag of shoes, traversing Buttevant in all kinds of weather, collecting the money and battling the elements as best I could.

The hardest part of this job for me though was refusing to hand over the shoes. I used to feel terrible saying no, especially when I knew the people well, and often I did know them well because they were usually my school friend's parents. Many a time a school friend would answer the door and be standing there talking to me when I'd have to pull back the shoes from his parents' outstretched hands. Then I'd see that sad look in their eyes before they would say, "See you in school Cahill", before going back inside. It seemed so wrong to me to have to say no, I'm sorry, I can't give you the shoes because my Nan says I have to be paid first. When this happened, there would be this long pause as the woman looked at me and played the dignity game. Then she'd say, "Ahh sure tis all right so, tell her I'll collect em meself later on when he's home with the money". As we looked at each other we would both knew that 'himself' was probably in the pub drinking their money, or he was over in England working. In any case, she would not be calling in later. At that stage I'd leave with their shoes, and with no money. It was clear to me even at my age that no one was benefiting from such transactions, but that's how it was, and I would be killed by the Nan if I succumbed to their stories and handed over the shoes. There was many a time when I just could not pull the shoes back and I'd give them up, later facing the wrath of the Nan and her wet dishcloth. "Didn't I tell you not to give them up, didn't I?" Whack...... across the head. Those days were the beginning of my longings to be rich. I, John Cahill, wanted to be rich, but I wanted everyone else to be rich too. Then there would be no more use of that hated word...no,... just a lot of good times for us all.

Around that time, Michael became an agent for what was known then as 'The Pools'. These pools were a kind of weekly lottery, and I believe the proceeds were used to fund some kind of national charity. It was like an early version of our Lotto·today, and in desperate times, people grasped onto desperate measures, so Michael tried to become a sales agent for those pools, and he succeeded. He worked on a commission basis which was small, but it was 'better than a kick from a donkey', and I know too that he had initially gathered a very large number of customers, due to his popularity in sport and politics.

Like all lotteries, if you had a big win on the pools, all your worries were over, but of course it cost you a shilling each week to be in with that chance and a shilling was twelve pennies, which was a lot of money then. The pool money was to be collected on a Saturday, the day Michael would be busiest on his shoe mending. He couldn't do both jobs, so it was not long before a new job was added to my shoe delivering one. I was now going to become a 'pool money collector' as well as a shoe delivery boy.

Some pool customers were great and would happily hand over their money with a smile and a chat, but they were mostly the shopkeepers, or the so-called 'well off' of the town. I would give them their pool sheet, which showed all the winners from the previous week's draw, and pocket the shilling. Others, however, would say, "Is it all right if I pay you next week? Will you tell Michael to put me in this week, and I'll definitely settle it all up next week". In practice what this meant was that they would probably try and get away with not paying again on the third week, hoping for any kind of win, before finally not answering the door on my next visit. After that happened, we had lost them as customers. I noticed that this was beginning to happen more and more often, as did my Nan.

Just like with the shoe delivering, Nannie began to exhort me to try and get the money out of them at all costs. It was almost as if she believed I could do magic, and money would appear for the poor people on my visit. At the start I hated that pool collecting job and only did it because I had to, as I knew what it meant to her. The pattern was this: as soon as I arrived back with my shillings, she would give me the same money and send me up to May Sheehan's shop for her few groceries, so I knew that the commission was actually buying the food for us all.

Each Saturday I made my sweep of the town, going up one side and then down the other, returning to Nannie with my monies and the inevitable bag of undelivered shoes along with sheets from the latest lost customers.

For many reasons, the number of pool customers would ebb and flow. Some would drop out for financial reasons, but after a big win more would join. It was constantly changing, but I felt like the Nan, that on average, we were beginning to lose more and more people every week. People simply did not have the money because times had become so hard. One wintry Saturday, Nannie seemed to be particularly depressed. She was very low in herself and had a very sad look in her eyes all morning. Before my sortie to the street, she sat me down and said gravely to me, "John you're getting to be a big boy now, and today I want you to go out and call to every door. Don't miss a single one. You must try and get us some new people to 'join' our pools. You must do your best to get us new customers". I clearly remember her using the words 'join the pools' but somehow in my mind, I felt that they were being asked to 'buy' the pools. In my mind, I was now becoming a salesman as well as a delivery boy, and while I didn't like it, I sensed the urgency in her voice. Something was troubling her greatly and it felt like a big bill was due. This I did not like at all. She seemed very downtrodden that day and I felt very sorry for her. So once again I set off with my bag of shoes and my pool sheets, and a few coins in my pocket for change. After calling to a lot of houses and getting many refusals, I would have the odd success and I'd make a sale, and feel great about that. Soon I began to realise that 'selling' was not so bad after all. In fact I began to feel that it was quite alright to be told 'no' a lot of the time, as long as now and again you got told yes as well. Besides that, it seemed to be a far nicer job than pulling shoes back from my friends' parents' outstretched hands.

I collected and sold, and moved slowly along up the street, going from house to house and shop to shop, and all the time heading for the top of the town. By then it had begun to mist and turned cold and windy. My sheets were getting wet and I still had more than half the town to do. I wanted to go home, but the thought of the Nan's sad face kept me going. I had got us some new customers and felt I could get a lot more if I tried, so on I went.

My tactics for selling were simple. I'd have a pool sheet in one hand and a handful of coins clearly visible in the other. That way it looked like many people were actually buying my pools, and what's more, it seemed to be working for me. With my shoe bag slung over my shoulder and my pool sheets and coins showing, I looked like a regular little mobile shop. With each new sale I grew happier and more confident in myself, and on I went. Despite the miserable weather, I began to feel really great, thinking that if one half of the town had given me this many customers, then surely the other half would do the same, and that would be brilliant indeed. I began to imagine Nannie's face lighting up, all happy and smiling again when I arrived home, 'loaded' down with new pool money.

I passed the Convent of Mercy. No point in going in there as they never had us mend their shoes, and they didn't need to gamble for their dinners either. Then I arrived at the Mill Lane,
and there in the leeway of the high wall I took shelter from the biting north wind and the rain. I was almost at the halfway point and it was time for a review of my progress. I counted out my money and adjusted my pool sheets for the final assault on the top of the town. I can't recall just how much money I had collected,

40

but I know that at that moment I was very happy about it all, so on I went determined to be a success at this pool selling business, and to hell with the shoe delivering.

A few no's later and I got to what I think was a grey door, and there I knocked. No one answered, so I knocked again, this time a bit louder as I could hear loud voices coming from inside and a child seemed to be crying as well, so the people were at home. Whether it was from the shouting or the child crying, I don't know which, but as I knocked again, a strong feeling of unease came over me and I felt it would be better if no one answered the door.

Then suddenly the door was flung open and the doorway was filled with this huge frame of a man. He towered above me. He was big, heavyset, and unfriendly, with a large red head on him. He glared down at me and spoke gruffly. "Yes… yes, what do you want". I held out my pool sheet and said, "Would you like to buy a pool…, I'm selling a new lot today sir".

He looked at me for a moment with a puzzled look on his face, as if trying to recall something, and then he said. "You're Cahill aren't you?" Then feeling rich from all my successes, I proudly announced, "Yes sir I'm John Cahill, pool seller, selling a lot today". Suddenly I felt a very sharp pain in my face, then a kind of blackness came over me, and the next thing I remembered was being sprawled on the wet ground outside his door. I was dazed and confused while looking back up at the closed grey door. I recovered quickly only to find that all my sheets and my coins were then scattered all over the street. That towering man was Guard Ryan. He had lashed out and hit me straight into the face, but not a punch for sure, as I was not bleeding in any way. It was a very hard slap, and that, coupled with the shock of it, had knocked me to the ground. Adding insult to injury, he had slammed the door shut on me and gone back inside. There he left me to search for my coins, for my soaked pool sheets, for my pride, and my self worth, which remained on the ground in Buttevant that day.

As best I could, I gathered up my papers and the scattered coins, breaking down into floods of tears as I did so, feeling greatly ashamed of myself for no apparent reason. I know that I cried uncontrollably as I crossed the road, feeling glad of the safety of the other side of the street. I am quite sure that no one ever saw

41

what had just happened to me, but perhaps they did. In any case I got away from that place as fast as I could. I slunk off down the street to Nannie's house in a terrible daze, all the while trying to understand what had just happened and why it had happened. I could not figure it out. All I had done was try to sell him a pool, so why had he struck me? What had I done so wrong?

When I got in home I threw what money I had collected down on the Nan's table and told her angrily that I was never again selling pools; then I immediately went upstairs and began to play with my toy soldiers as if nothing had happened. I never shed a further tear that day, nor did I tell a single soul about it later in life. It was as if by not talking about it, I could deny its reality, and I hoped that the memory might one day go away, but it never did and never has because it's as vivid today as it was all those years ago. In the end I learned to accept it, but in writing this account of my life I have realized an extraordinary thing. In all the years that have since passed by, and in all the times I had later to pass that house, I never once actually walked on the pavement and passed that door again. In over fifty years I have never stood on the spot where it happened. Subconsciously I chose to walk the road or the other side of the street rather than the footpath. One day I will face down my fears and walk that footpath again, …but not just yet.

Nannie never again asked me to sell pools. I did have to collect them though. Without ever knowing the truth, she felt that I was no salesman. In her mind I was a Cahill, and what else could she expect out of that lot, sure they were all 'useless'. Even her John, and their father, who was stuck inside in bed, was the worst of them all. Many years later, and by a sheer accident, I was to overhear the real story behind Kyrl's house and the rows with the guard, and it all made sense to me then.

Until recently, my mother never knew what her well meaning act had done to her eldest son, but I think she would still have been against Kyrl's unnecessary eviction. Today, I believe the memory of that single incident was, and still is, the greatest impediment I face to becoming rich. Since it happened, I have always associate selling of any kind and taking money into my hands with unexpected pain. To this day I still hate that area of my town. It's all changed now of course and I'm sure that the guard has long since passed over, and may he rest in peace. With all that I now know about life and who we really are, I have learned that the only real way to release such pain is to forgive the perpetrator, and of course I have done that. He was probably having a domestic argument when I arrived and he just lashed out at the seed and the breed of someone he understandably hated, and I was in the wrong place at the wrong time.

The real downside for me though has been that from that day onwards I developed a terrible fear of asking for money, no matter how hard I work for it, or how much I deserve it. I know now that it's very unlikely I'll ever be a salesman of any kind, and that is a terrible pity, because on that Saturday I began to really enjoy the challenge of convincing a customer to buy my pools, and I was already preparing my mind for a second go at the 'no people' the following week. Fortunately traumas like this are not hereditary, and all of my children have an uncanny self confidence and belief in their real worth, unlike their father, who had it taken from him many times as a child.

I honestly believe that Guard Ryan was just like myself, a pawn in the great chess game of life, who unknowingly provided me with personal challenges I needed to face throughout my life. It is said that hindsight is not an exact science, but had I known earlier what I know now, my whole life would have been very different. Then, instead of you reading about struggles, dramas, and dreams, you would surely be reading about a life mirrored on that of my greatest of heroes, Richard Branson.

Christmas times

Each year the approaching Christmas was met with a combination of excitement and dread by us all. I think to this day I still feel the same way. Of course it's insane now at this age of my life, but that's how it is for me. Even though we are going through the worst economic period in our history, where our little country has been bankrupt by greed and corruption on all sides; by comparison to the late fifties, we live almost in Heaven. It's a wonderful experience to go back in my memory to some of those Christmases even though some of those times were quite bad.

My earliest memory was one year both Kyrle and I got the gift of a set of boxing men each. They were worked by a small rubber pump in the shape of a ball. The boxing men boxed each other as long as you pressed the pump, but that was the entire extent of their movement. We could not even have a boxing match between us, because each toy had its two men on the same pump, so we could not fight each other. Pretty soon I wanted to know how they worked and I prized off the little rubber ball from its connecting pipe. I blew into the pipe and the men moved. Kyrle did the same thing. After a few minutes of this blowing we got tired of it, but then the pumps would not go back on the pipes and our toys were ruined and useless. That was all we got that year and the present lasted a whopping ten minutes.

Another year we got a Christmas stocking made from some kind of mesh stuff. This was great. It had card games of Ludo, Drafts and the inevitable and brilliant Snakes and Ladders with a little dice for throwing. I think also it came with a bar of chocolate and a catapult. We got immense satisfaction from these simple toys and I always loved the Christmas stockings ever since. Today of course it's more like a Christmas sack that kids get, and it's filled with electronics of unimaginable entertainment, yet I bet most real children get more fun from the box than the gift inside. One year we got an amazing toy. It was some kind of small round plastic pole that had an elastic band inside attached to a propeller. As you wound it up and let it go, it actually flew way up in the air. I loved it and so did Kyrle, but I only remember one of them. We played with this for hours, maybe days even, before it flew up onto the roof and may still be there for all I know. I tried to make one of these flying machines later but could never get the propeller right. Since then, flight has fascinated me. Just how did this twisted plastic shape grab the air so well as to be able to lift itself. This was a question I asked everyone over and over and never got a convincing answer either. Eventually I would find the answer in what I called my Knowledges. These were a weekly magazine that became an encyclopedia when all one hundred or so were collected. Uncle Michael religiously gave me the shilling every week to buy my book and they taught me almost everything I know, and on Christmas there was a double issue which was the best of all gifts.

I would say I was about eight when that particular Christmas we got a big toy fire engine between us. It had a long ladder and a little fireman who would climb up the ladder by magic. The only problem was that it was one fire engine between two boys and who would be allowed drive it. Mother had some kind of lino on the kitchen floor and we soon discovered that if you raced the engine along the lino, it would somehow gather speed and fly across the floor. We couldn't figure out how it did this. For a good bit of the day we played back and forth, but in the end the curiosity got the better of us and we decided to rip it up to see what made it go. Father had a drawer in the back kitchen where he kept all kinds of little tools. It didn't take long before we got at the body of the engine with screwdrivers and a pliers, and soon we had it in bits. It was never the intention to destroy our wonderful toy, we just wanted to see what made the wheels go. We kept stripping until soon we were down to the mechanism. This mechanism was a kind of box of cogs, axels and a big heavy wheel. We studied it up and down and soon an argument developed as to what the heavy flywheel did. I was sure it was the driving force and Kyrle thought I was wrong. So I said if we take it out and it still works then I'm wrong. More ripping took place and suddenly the wheel and a load of cogs flew out all around us. I think there must have been a coiled spring buried inside the box, so now we were in trouble, because nothing we did would get it back together again. I blamed him and he blamed me and tempers flew. We started to really argue and a punch up began. At some point in the fight he grabbed the heavy flywheel which had caused all the trouble, and threw it at me. I ducked and it went clean through the glass pane in our kitchen door. By then it was definitely time for me to beat a retreat over to Nannie's, because this was going to get very bad. The fire engine was in bits, being hardly a day old, and the window was broken. I don't know how Kyrle got out of it, but I'm sure he blamed me, as mother came over in a rage to complain me to Nannie. I had spun my own tale to her and she told mother to, "Clear out of my house and don't darken my door again," her usual retort to my mother when she wanted to be rid of her.

Another year the father had taken up teaching music to some children. He had been at this for some months prior to the Christmas period, and it gave him some extra spending money, keeping the Guinness family in funds via Kit Roche's bar. I have no doubt at all that he was a great teacher, because he was. He had an infinite patience, capable of going over and over the children's mistakes until they got it right. One such child was a farmer's son who could never get it right, no matter how long he played for. Even I got so fed up listening to the same scale being played wrongly over and over again that I used to shag off when that boy would arrive. Mother too would be out on purpose when that child arrived and we all wondered how the father stuck him, but he did.

Probably in preparation for the dreaded Christmas dinner, mother made a deal with the boy's father to pay our father with a goose, not cash. That way she was at least guaranteed the Christmas dinner, and perhaps the thought of a goose for the feast was the real reason father persisted. The weeks passed, and in those days she used to do part time work as a barmaid in the same Kit Roche's pub that father was supporting so well. By then it was almost owned by my father because of his drinking habits. A few days before the Christmas, the farmer arrived with his goose in an old canvas bag. The goose was alive and was flapping about, probably suspecting what lay ahead. Mother was over in Kit's working and father was out, and as no one was at home, the farmer just dropped the bag inside the door and left. Father arrived home first, saw the goose in its bag and totally ignored it, and retired to his bed. Much later, the mother came in as well. Her arrival scared the poor goose from its sleep and once again it began flapping about in the bag. Being no farmer, my mother thought, "Oh that's too cruel to the poor goose, sure I can't leave him like that," so she took it outside to our yard and opened the bag so that it could 'get a bit of fresh air'. It got air alright and I think the goose could not believe its luck, because first chance it got, it flew off over the back wall. Our Christmas dinner, and father's infinite patience, had literally flown away. Later still when she was taking father a cup of tea, she railed on about the farmer and how cruel he was to the poor goose. She's telling her Henry all about giving it air and opening the bag in the yard, when father realizing the disaster says, "What did you say, did you say you left him out in the yard? ...Well he's gone now for sure". They rushed down to see, and sure enough the goose was literally gone. That year the children of two walls and a roof had a chicken from Gracie, and were very glad of it too. No one ever blamed the mother, there were no recriminations only laughter. In spite of our adversity, somehow we could all see the funny side of what had happened and the ability to laugh at adversity has remained with us all even today.

House fire.

My next experience with fire happened during a very bad winter. I had been forced into the 'altar boy business' by Nannie. I think the local Canon had gone around to the schools picking 'suitable' boys for his altar service, and neither I nor Kyrle were initially chosen, probably because we came from the poorer class, or we didn't look good enough for the Church. Obviously he had his own reasons and method of choosing his boys, but Nannie took it as a personal insult on us Cahills and she marched up to his door and made such a stink that he changed his mind. We were soon reluctantly seconded into his flock, against my will at least. There we were forced to learn how to answer Mass in Latin, and as I was already well into my anti-religious phase since about eight years of age, this was not going down well with me at all. It was a damn nightmare in fact, and even at that time, it did strike me as odd that this priest would have some of the boys sit on his knee as he examined their Adeum qui le tificat gibberish, but I never saw him do any more to them. The more I saw of this Church the falser it felt to me, even at that early age, and I believed everyone was being conned by that particular religious organisation, which was an astute observation, as time has since borne out. I was by then beginning to read all about the real world in my Knowledge's, and the more I read the more I asked questions about life, and no one could give me any real answers to my probing questions, even our all-knowing father. Everything about our so-called Catholic religion seemed to be 'a mystery' which you dare not question. Oftentimes I would persist in questioning these mysteries only to be told, you have to believe them, and this irked me a lot because I felt no one knew the answers themselves. I felt that Huck Finn, my hero then, never learned Latin or went to Mass, and why should I have to do it, especially if none of it made any sense to me. I suppose too that getting the odd clatter across the face or the head from that old priest when I missed some verse was both a punishment for the missing and a revenge for the Nan's attack on him, and it did not endear me to a Church that preached love and dished out violence. Left with no choice, I tried my best to learn the strange language of Latin and I eventually served his Mass for a number of years, but I always hated doing it. I was not alone in this Mass hatred either. One of the other boys used to be so sick of this Mass going that he began slugging down some of the altar wine each morning before the priest arrived. He said it was great stuff and that I should give it a go. I was too chicken to try it, thank God, and years later I heard that he became an alcoholic and died a very young man from the drink. I can still see him today in his white altar outfit, holding the bottle up to his head and guzzling away, offering it to me now and again, "Ahhh give it a go John, you'll love it boy, tis great stuff. Sure he'll never miss it, the ould bollix".

As time passed, my hatred for both the early morning risings and the Mass serving grew worse. I took it as a sign from God when one morning about seven am the Nan came tearing up the stairs shouting, "Get up! Get up will ye, the house is on fire. Get down out of here quick, tis on fire I say, hurry! Up, up!" I was in the last year of sharing a room with Uncle Michael, and after Nannie shouted those words into our room she took off back down the stairs again, screaming, "Fire, fire, get up will ye, get up I say!" We ignored her completely, but I did try to sniff the air for smoke, with no success. Within minutes she's back up again shouting as loud as ever. "Get up, the house is on fire, tis on fire I'm telling ye".

Her screaming had absolutely no effect on either Michael or me, as she usually did a similar screaming bit on a Sunday morning, though usually from the bottom of the stairs, and she never shouted the words fire before, so this was a new development for her I thought. I tried to go back to sleep, but I had become a bit unnerved by her screaming, as she did seem to be in a genuine panic.

In those days I was sharing a bed with Michael, and after a few more air sniffs I did think I could smell smoke, but I wasn't sure. Michael, who was tired out from his writing late into the night, and probably thinking it was a Sunday morning with her up to her usual tricks, just covered up his head and said, "Ignore her

Chicken, there's no way there's a fire in this house. Sure we hardly have coal, how could we have a fire?"

But very soon she was back up again, and this time she's trying to tear me out of the bed. By then it's obvious, even to me, that the room was rapidly filling with smoke, and I knew by her panicked look and the smoke around us that this was no trick. I'm out of bed in a flash shouting at Michael to get up, which he ignored, and I grab my pants, running for the stairs. So is the Nan, but before she starts down, she gives one more roar back in at Michael, "Awright so, go on then, burn if you want, but I'm not burning to save your lazy arse, and neither is my John," and she pushed me down the stairs before her. In the middle floor and one floor closer to safety, I'm hopping around trying to get my pants fully on. I have one leg in and I'm clutching the other when I see this really terrified look on her face. She was even scaring me then, and I ran for the lower stairs to freedom, while still trying to keep my pants pulled up. The smoke is acrid and choking us as I almost run down the lower stairs followed so closely by the Nan that she pushes me in terror and I fell down the last few steps into the kitchen, still clutching my pants. Initially I got a terrible shock, because looking up from the floor I could see that our ceiling was really on fire, and I'll never forget it.

After I recovered my nerves a bit, I noticed that while the ceiling was burning it was only doing so in one corner. It looked far worse than it was and I felt there was no more need for a total panic. The flames were slowly spreading outwards from the corner and some lighting papers and cardboards were falling onto the table below. It was a cardboard ceiling that Nannie had painted years earlier and so it was always a good candidate for a fire. While I'm getting into my pants and taking all this in, Nannie ran back up the stairs once again. Then, having 'saved' me she decided to have one last go at saving her 'useless' son Michael. I took that opportunity to make sure that my case of altar clothes, which was on the table, was fully opened and I moved them directly under the falling lighting papers. If anything was going to burn for me, it had to be the altar clothes. From the many lighting bits of paper and card that were falling, I felt sure that the hated altar clothes would soon catch fire, and that would be the end of my Mass going days. Then with no panic at all, I got an old plastic pan that we used to wash our dishes in, and ran out into the street to the nearby water pump. I was almost stark naked except for my pants, which was still only on at half mast, but that didn't deter me. I filled up the pan shouting to everyone passing, "Help! Help! Fire inside the house, fire, fire, help, help us!"

No one took a blind bit of notice. I ran back inside and threw the whole pan of water straight up at the ceiling, hoping that none of it fell back down on my own personal little fire below in the case. Out I ran again and filled the pan a second time, with more calling for help, with exactly the same result. No one even looked inside the door, let alone offered to help us. Once more I lashed the water back up at the ceiling. A quick check confirmed that all my altar gear was happily smouldering away and the ceiling fire looked like it was going out, so no more need for water. The fire finally did die out completely, and Nannie arrived back down followed this time by Michael in his night shirt. He was rubbing his eyes from the smoke and looked like a figure from poorest India as he stood on the stairs surveying the damage through the smoke. The Nan saw my altar clothes were well on fire by then and began to beat at the flames with her wet dish cloth. Then Michael says, "Good man Chicken, you did a great job there I see. Looks like there was a bit of a fire after all". The Nan glared at him with her black face as she beat out the fire in my old case, but thankfully not fast enough to save my clothes. Then she turned and really lashed into Michael, shouting and roaring like never before. She said that it was his burning the briquettes that had caused this fire. She screamed that she had specifically told him not to burn the briquettes, and that he was useless, that she had always known he was useless, and that a child had to save us and the house from the 'Fires of Hell'.

As it so happened, this time she was actually right. Michael had been writing late into the night as usual, and because it was a particularly bad winter, Nannie had lit the fire in the middle floor parlour, a very rare thing indeed. During the night Michael got cold, and when adding fuel to the fire, a smouldering briquette must have slipped down through one of the many holes in the flagstone. This briquette then set the cardboard ceiling below alight. Everyone knew that the fireplace in the middle room was dangerous, and that's why she never lit a fire there, but that year the Nan had splurged out because of the sheer cold in the kitchen. I

51

know for certain that before going to bed she had warned Michael not to be adding coal or briquettes to the fire in the night, but as usual he ignored her. We could easily have all burned to death that night but for the Nan's early rising for my hated Mass service.

After it all settled down, I was delighted at my calmness and heroism and felt surely I deserved a day off from school for saving us all. However, the Nan would have none of it, and she said to me, "Off you go now John, and tell no one about this fire. Tis bad enough that we both know he's a fool, (pointing at Michael) without the whole town knowing it as well. You saved us from the fires of Hell while he's stuck inside the bed. Now run along to school there's a good boy". No arguing did any good. She was adamant I was going to school, so I did. The only consolation I had from that whole affair was that I knew my Mass going days were over. No way could she afford to buy me more altar clothes, so there might be a God after all, though I still had my doubts.

The lost train set.

May Sheehan was a small, frail little woman who owned a grocery shop across the road from our house. She sold the newspapers, groceries and butter. The butter had to be delivered from the creamery and would not keep well - fridges being an unheard of machine in those days, so she didn't carry a large stock of it, and relied on the odd delivery from a local who might be passing the creamery. This was not an ideal arrangement and she often ran out, so she needed a delivery boy. Almost every few days, she needed a new supply and I was to become that delivery boy. I don't know how I actually got the job, but when I was about twelve years old, I began working for May collecting her butter. The deal was six pence a load and a load was about ten pounds I suppose, maybe more. I do know that I used an old shiny biscuit tin to carry this butter from the creamery to her shop. She paid me faithfully every trip and it was great having real money of my own to spend as I liked. A sixpenny bit was made of silver and had a shiny dog on its face, and it felt so good in my pocket. With such an amount of money, I could easily buy lots of slab toffee and even a bar of chocolate if I was to go really mad. Each time she paid me, I would be over the moon with happiness and I often bought a slab of toffee for both Kyrle and Lill as a surprise from my wealth.

The biscuit tin weighed quite a bit, but the creamery was only down at the bottom of the town, so my journey was not too long and I used to rest my tin on strategic window sills on the way up to her shop. It only took me about twenty minutes, and for that I earned a full six pence every few days. Things were surely looking up for me at last.

I do remember one day passing Peggy Corbett's drapery shop just some weeks before Christmas and seeing, to my utter amazement, a beautiful train set in a box in her shop window. I stood transfixed, staring in at this amazing sight. I had dreamed of having a train set for a very long time, hoping for one at Christmas some day, but never telling anyone of my dreams because this would be a really expensive toy. And I didn't want to add more stress to my Nan, knowing Santa did not exist for us Cahill's. But there it was. It was very unusual to see toys in Peggy's window as it was a drapery shop, and she never had toys in it, but that year she seems to have decided to try a new line of business to make money.

Peggy Corbett always seemed to me to be a tall gentle woman, always soft spoken and never gruff or ugly to me, or to anyone else either. She had never married and lived up the street with her parents. And what's more, she never seemed to age at all. She sold cloth, wool, some children's clothes and Communion outfits, and of course she was also the Nannies' primary bank. I think because of my many borrowings for Nannie, Peggy got to know me well, and I'm sure she liked me, and I liked her too.

After staring in at the train set for a long time I became determined that I would have it one way or another, and so in I went to Peggy. I enquired about the train set, how much it would cost, and did she have many for sale. I had a lot of questions that day.

She said that the price of the train set was seven shillings and six pence, an almost gigantic sum then, and she only had the one train set. When one considers that before the May Sheehan job I was only getting the odd penny now and again, it would have been totally impossible to buy that train set ever, as seven and six was 90 pennies. But, by then I was 'working' and I made up my mind that I would have that train set by Christmas. As a rough guess, I worked it out at about fifteen butter trips and I felt sure it could be done, and with time to spare. I asked Peggy if I could take the train set by paying her in small amounts and she asked me how small. "Sixpences", I say. Peggy seemed to know my heart was set on it and said, "I'll tell you what John, you save up your money and I will put the train set away for you till it's paid for, how about that?" I asked her, what if some rich person sees it and buys it before I can get all the money, and to her amazing credit she said, "No John, I'll put it away for you in the back of the shop till you have all the money". As I'm nodding agreement I'm already playing with it in my mind. When I'm leaving her shop she reached into the window and removed my prize; the train set was safe.

Now my money collecting would begin in earnest.

I went across to the Nan's and got a jam jar, then washed it all out clean and dry. Next I cut a slot in the lid to take the money, and so as to avoid temptation from the slab, I rolled loads of sticky tape around both the lid and the jar. Not even I could easily rob my jar now. I then got a small notebook, put a date on it, and set to thinking what I would do next. If memory serves me right, I already had some coins from my last butter job and they were the beginnings of my jar. The amount was noted in my book and the jar was then hidden under the floor boards under my bed. I knew full well that there might be others besides me who would be tempted to rob my jar, so it had to be kept safe from those hands too.

I worked it out that if I deposited every single sixpence based on the previous jobs, then I would have enough for the train set by Christmas week, and there was always the other money I might get from Michael, or Big Kyrl, my other uncle. Gracie's egg collecting might add a few coppers too, and all in all, I was sure I would make it happen for my train set. I began to imagine just where I would set it up on Nannie's table upstairs. I could move my toy soldiers around, and if anything, it would add to my playing with them. In my mind I played with the engine and disconnected the carriages, I added brick bridges, some of my little soldier men could fit in the goods wagon, and it could be used to transport my toy tanks as well. This was going to be great, just great. I also felt that secrecy was my best friend, so I told no one of my deal with Peggy, not even Kyrle, who I could also see playing with the train set later on.

I collected and collected, and the coins in my jar grew. Each deposit was a reason to celebrate and look at my jar. My notebook kept record of the odd extra coins that I got outside of my 'regular job', and I was quite ahead coming up to the Christmas period. Then the weather changed. It became bitterly cold. Times were particularly bad that year for us all as well and I could feel the tension rising as both Nannie and my mother got into their close talking huddled mode more often than usual. I knew from old that this always spelled trouble. It was as if by talking low while huddled together in Nannie's kitchen, they could somehow shield us from the bad news that was coming. I hardened myself to their situation and would not even contemplate a single thought of helping out with my little stash. I felt sure that they didn't even know I had one, so it was quite safe and so was my train set. Of course that was a great mistake. Parents nearly always know what their children are at, especially so in those days. It was easy too to see me carrying the butter tin every few days, and I was not buying sweets any more either, so I had to be stashing the money someplace.

During another of Nannie's borrowing sessions to Peggy, Peggy came right out and asked me if I was still collecting away for the train set, and I proudly pulled my notebook from my pocket and showed her the amount collected so far. I was almost there, and with time to spare too. Peggy seemed genuinely surprised and delighted for me, but probably she could not reconcile me and my stash with my Nannie's borrowing note. I asked for a look at the box and she brought it out from the back. There it was in my hands. It was too beautiful for words. It had a jet black engine, a green goods wagon saying 'P and T' on the side of it, a coal wagon with some plastic coal inside it, as well as the passenger carriages. To my surprise I noticed too that it also had an engine driver and a fireman with a small shovel inside the box. These were details I hadn't noticed on the window. I almost asked her for it there and then, but I was still a bit short and I was way too shy anyway. I believe now that had I asked Peggy that day, she would have trusted me with the balance and given me my box, but I didn't. I took the borrowed pound over to Nannie's and headed up to May Sheehan's for my tin box and that day's butter load.

Unfortunately, Peggy's latest pound didn't go far enough and that day it began to snow heavily as well. Mother had some trick with her little fireplace where she would wet papers and stick them into the back of the grate with cinders. This pushed the few new lumps of coal to the front of the grate and reduced the coals needed to keep the fire alive. She always tried to have a block of wood to the back too, but that was not always possible in those hard times. I don't know to this day how she managed to keep a fire going like she used to. It was sheer ingenuity on her part. Fortunately for her, our little living room was tiny and easy to heat, but of course the rest of the house was always like an icebox. Nannie on the other hand had an old black range which would burn anything, and she did so as well. Once it got hot, the cast iron stayed hot all day, so after she used her paraffin oil to get it going, we were set with kettles and pots boiling away all day long, but just as in mother's house, you also froze in Nannie's if you left the kitchen.

As the weather worsened, the mother's supply of coal ran out, and Nannie was just barely ahead with her bit of coal. They shared what they had for as long as they could, and it seems to me that my other grandmother, Gracie, was not willing to help in any way, or they were too proud to ask her. In any case, it would have been up to the father to do the actual asking, and he was not going to do that because he spent most of his time in his bed. In those terrible days, while my mother and Nannie bore the full brunt of our misery, my father found it easier to opt out from it all and go up the street to his mother's where he got fed. I never understood this mentality, but he was my dad and of course I forgave him for it all in the end.

Since birth I seem to have been gifted with very good hearing and this has stood to me well over the years. By that Christmas I had been given my own room, the 'haunted' one, and this was located just above Nannie's kitchen. The day came when I could clearly hear from my room upstairs my poor mother begging Nannie to ask me for the money from my jar. I became enraged immediately. Nannie was saying, "I can't ask him, I just can't. You ask him, I won't". I remember lying on the bed, dreading the next words I would hear... "John, John, can you come downstairs for a minute... please". It was the Nan and she was saying please, and Nannie never said please to anyone. This was surely going to be very bad indeed and I knew what was coming.

From my bedroom I roared back down, "Yer not getting my jar, it's for my train set. I'm not giving it up to ye.... Go away, leave me alone". I was wild with rage, but beginning to have my first doubts that the train set would be mine by Christmas.

"Please come down John, just for a minute so we can talk". It's the Nan again, this time she's pleading and using the 'please' word again.

In dread, I go down the stairs and there they are, sitting in their huddled way beside the old black range. Both my mother and the Nan are looking genuinely distraught. As I crossed the floor, mother looked down at her hands where she looked so very poor to me, wearing the scarf around her head that I hated. Nannie had this awful pleading face on her. This was far from the face of the proud woman she let on to be, and I hated what I saw before me in her as well.

"John, tis very cold. It's even snowing outside now and your mother here has no coal for the fire. The lads are all cold across the road and things are very bad," says the Nan. Across the road was her way of referring to 'two walls and a roof'. I try to lie and angrily tell them, "It's spent, all gone, tis all gone I tell ye. I have no money, only my old jam jar". Nannie ignores my lie and mother still has her head down in her hands not able to look up at me, and she seemed to be sobbing. Nannie presses me, "Look John, tis only till I get the pension on Friday, and then I'll pay you back, I promise you I will. Then you can still get your train set". Now she was actually lying to me….making me a promise I knew she could not, or would not keep. But my angry protesting was no use, and I did not believe her when she said she would pay me back either. I knew damn well that she had not even paid Peggy for her last pound yet, and there was only one pension left before the Christmas, so how could I get the train set before then. Still more pleading went on from the Nan, and in the end I could take it no longer and I just gave in. By then my poor mother was openly sobbing softly and looked even more miserable than before.

I honestly believe that something broke inside of me at that very moment, on that awful day, and I went back upstairs and got my jar half full of money. I began crying bitterly as I handed it over to her. Then this so-called tough woman, my Nan, was also openly crying as she gently took the jar from me, and by then it was all over. She opened my jar with the bread knife and then, trying to ease my pain, she gave me back a shilling saying, "Start again John won't you, you're a great boy". I ran upstairs, throwing my jar and the shilling inside it onto the bed. I cried for a very long time until I literally ran out of tears and finally gave up feeling sorry for myself. I knew then that no matter what work I did, I would not have my train set by Christmas, or probably ever have it, and resigned myself to its loss.

Next day I went across to Peggy. I put on a real brave face on it all, but deep inside me I felt so ashamed and so poor as I told her these words, "I want to say that I won't be buying the train set. I have changed my mind on it. Sell it if you like". I secretly hoped for a miracle where she might say 'I'll keep it for you till later.' She stared at me in disbelief, "What are you saying John?" I then tell her vehemently that I'm not buying it and to sell it to some rich boy. She went in to get it, as if to convince me to change my mind, but I can't stay there to see it, and began to leave while trying not to cry. As I left for Nannie's, I just had to glance back and saw her placing my train set back in the window. By the next day it was gone, and so were my dreams.

Many years later, when I was married and going out for a day with my family, I saw a genetic echo happen before my eyes. My son Adrian and I went into a shop to buy an ice-cream. There in a box in a glass cabinet was an almost identical train set to my dream one. Within seconds Adrian had spotted it and he began to pester me for it, and he was never one to pester me at all. I saw before my very eyes myself in my young son, and his dreams seemed like a mirror of mine many years before. There was no way that I could shatter his dream, and even though I could ill afford it that day, I bought the train set for him and we cancelled our day out. We crossed the road to a picnic area and set up our train set together and played for hours.

Many years later, on my fiftieth birthday, my sisters and brothers bought me my own train set at last, making up for the lost one. They presented it to me at a surprise birthday party in Mallow. However, Kyrle the bastard, as a joke and unknown to me, had hidden some of the tracks on the night. I was so excited with my gift that I left the party early so as to have a play by myself at home. But when I got home, half of the lines were missing and I could not make the track form a ring. I was raging, figuring out that he had tricked me, but the next day he gave them to me and we all sat on the floor and laughed and had a good play after all the years.

The really strange thing about this whole story is that my mother has no memory of it at all. I believe that it was either too hard for her to take and she has erased it from her mind, or that it was just one of the many other incidents of poverty lost among more dramatic ones in her life. In any case, it did me no harm other than make me very frugal, fear Christmas times, and hate jam jars with a passion.

Our mother, none like her.

What can anyone ever say about their mother. Our mother was, and still is, probably the most unselfish person I ever knew in all of my life, and before the readers will say that I'm biased, let me remind them that I was not reared by my mother, so I can make a fair assessment. For most of her life she was poor. She rarely if ever bought something truly for herself and it took almost 60 years before she got to fly on a plane, or even got to visit another country. The farthest she had ever travelled was to the Isle of Man to visit her daughters Lill and Eunice, who live very happily there now. Even with free transport in the latter years, she never had enough money to go on a holiday on her own. And what's more, I never heard her once say she would like to just get away from it all.

She bore six children in very hard times and welcomed each with equal affection, yet I'm sure shock set in too when the news broke that she was once more with child. She has always had a fantastic sense of humour and a real unusual laugh. It's a characteristic of hers I feel. I have early memories of my mother, who I always called 'Blend' as a child. This must have hurt her, with her firstborn not even calling her mother, or ma, or whatever, like normal families would do, but that's the price we paid for my Nannie's abduction.

When mother was pregnant she would always suffer from her teeth. She had good teeth, but it was something I remember her saying - that she would be in agony with toothache and have no money for a few tablets or the doctor. The father would seem to be impervious to his wife's pain and this was the other extreme in our family, as he was probably the most selfish of individuals - drink money superseded all else. They were at opposite ends of the spectrum when it came to caring for their children's needs, yet he made up for a lot of it by being kind and gentle to us always.

Mother became an epileptic as she got older, and I am one hundred percent certain that it was not a hereditary complaint. I had always felt it was due to sheer uncontrollable stress, and I noticed a pattern. She would get an attack at times of great stress and Nannie would unkindly say, "Ahh sure she's only putting that on for sympathy". This was very hurtful for me to hear, but to my shame I sometimes believed it, though I watched for the pattern. It took years for me to realize that the pattern was nature's defenses in action.

I never knew how she carried on. Every day was potentially a terrible day. It has to be soul-destroying for any mother to see her own children go hungry, or have but little food to give them: to know that there was no prospect of tomorrow being a better day, though she always told us it would be. For most of her early life, she lived on 'tick' or her 'book' as we knew it. This was the usual way then to get credit from a shop for a week's groceries. One had a little book and the shopkeeper wrote into it your purchase and the amount. By the weekend you were expected to pay your total and then start again next week. The shopkeeper also had his record, and the system worked great as long as you paid on time. This tick book was very common in the Ireland of those days. Quite often though, the book would remain unpaid for a week, then another, then you played catch up if the grocer was nice. Much more likely though, you didn't pay at all because you had no income. Eventually the patience of the shopkeeper ran out and your food supply totally dried up in that shop. The usual answer then was to move on to another shop and begin another tick book. To a great extent I was sheltered from this book thing, as Nannie always paid on time and usually she used her pension to buy groceries on a Friday because she had the regular, though small, income from a widow's pension.

When all books were run dry for mother, particularly when father just could not find a job anywhere, she relied on our paternal grandmother, known as Gracie, for reluctant handouts.

Gracie had a small sweet shop at the top of the town and was a good businesswoman. She always seemed rich to me, but she had a very mean streak in her as regards her grandchildren. Whenever mother sent Kyrle or Lill up to her for a loaf of bread, they invariably came down with mouldy bread - so mouldy that she actually fed her chickens better bread. I know this because Kyrle and I used to have to feed her chickens and try to steal their eggs. I often saw mother cut out the mould and butter or jam the rest of it, and it's no wonder we never needed antibiotics.

Finally things got so bad that my father just had to go to England, like many before him. The day he left was a miserable, cold, cloudy day. He had a small brown suitcase which was old and raggedy, and as he waited for the bus to Cork, mixed emotions came over me. In one way I felt that now, at last, we might get money, but at the same time I felt very sad inside because he looked so lonely and miserable himself.

When the bus arrived, I never saw him kiss my mother goodbye. Maybe he did, but it was not obvious to me. On the day he left, he was to take the same Innisfallon immigrant ship that we had seen some months earlier, when mother was told all three of us were going blind. He left, and on the hope of British money, mother got more tick and we seemed better off for a time. It's a strange and sad affair, but I saw almost a carbon copy of this very same situation in the film from Frank McCourt's masterpiece *Angela's Ashes*. No money came: then, still later, no money came. Mother lived on what Nannie could spare from her pension, and from Michael's shoe mending and writing business.

What we didn't know until many years later was that our father had been sending his mother, Gracie, money from the very beginning. This money was to pay back the fare he had borrowed from her for England. He didn't seem to worry much about his wife and children, who were both cold and hungry, and who lived just some distance down Buttevant's main street. Or maybe he felt Gracie would help, but she did not. These acts, while forgiven, were never forgotten in my mind.

What my father did in England is a mystery to me. He did send money rather sporadically, eventually, and I think he worked in a petrol forecourt as well as playing music in London's clubs for a time. In spite of the frugal nature of our life then, for me this time was the first time I ever saw a light at the end of the tunnel. We were getting better off, just marginally. Kyrle began working for Big Kyrl in his cinema hall, and I suppose he got a few bob for it too, so his life was also improving.

In spite of all our misery, my mother would laugh at least once a day at something completely stupid, in our view. We would be arguing and discussing some world event at teatime or dinner time and all hell would be breaking loose, but we always waited for the mothers clanger, which would come sooner or later, and she would say, "And what about the nul-c-ar bomb?" pronounced just like that. It was in the middle of the Cold War and she was constantly saying the Russians would blow us all up. We would collapse laughing, as it was all she would ever contribute to the debate, no matter what was its subject. We never once told her of her hilarious mispronunciation either, and to this day she still says it wrong, and still does not know why we used to laugh.

Mother was always on the hunt for an extra few bob, and over the years I heard many stories related to that task, but one in particular deserves a mention. One evening a very distinguished looking man and a woman arrived outside our door, and waited for the bus to Mallow. The evening was turning wet and the people seemed to be very early for the bus, so as usual mother invited them in for a cup of tea. They accepted and arrived into our kitchen where father greeted them cautiously. While mother was boiling the kettle and scrounging around for a few biscuits, the guests informed father that the man was an African Bishop, and his woman was a Nun as well.

That bit of news changed everything. Mother called father aside and insisted that he go across to Coleman's shop for some ham and cheese to make the 'special guests' feel welcome. In those days her tic book was being held in Coleman's shop, and a strict budget was in operation regarding luxuries such as food, but no limits were ever placed on the amount of cigarettes to be bought, as they felt the fags were their only pleasure. Father protested the obvious budget overrun but it did no good, a Bishop was in the house and a Nun too, so he left for the food. While he was gone the guests chatted to mother and told her all about Africa and their Missions, and she was delighted to have such important guests in her little home. Time passed and father had not returned when the bus arrived, but the guests assured mother that they could easily stay on for another few hours, especially in such pleasant company. That was not what mother had planned, but it was a Bishop after all, so she would be happy to listen away to their stories of desperation and African poverty.

Father finally came back after telling all those in Coleman's shop about the Bishop and his Nun friend, and on the way back he dropped into Kit's bar and cadged a pint on the strength of his famous guests. Mrs. Coleman was so impressed with these guests that father got even more tic from her, and bought far more ham than they needed. When he sauntered in mother glared at him, suspecting he was in Kit's bar all of the time, but she could not challenge him in front of such important people, so the tea was made again for a second time. I was told that the special guests ate all round them, so much so that, father didn't even get a bit of the extra ham, because they savaged it all down, praising the Lord and blessing all round them. However after many hours of their 'Mission' talk and more pots of tea, the mood became a bit strained. My memory of the story then is that mother decided to take the guests across to bless Nannie. This would at least give father a break from their constant praising of the Lord, and their veiled begging for Charity from my parents who were people, who actually needed it.

The Bishop blessed Nannie and heard her Confession, and after this was all done, he assured her that the Gates of Heaven were already opened for her, and that all of her Sins were now forgiven. Poor Nannie was so impressed with his Blessing that she asked him what did she need to do to be sure she was saved and quick as a flash the Bishop says "Yerra give me and the Lord a tenner, sure you have nothing to worry about, you're going straight to the Lord whenever he calls you, and sure that won't be for years". Nannie was beaming and felt that ten pounds was a very small price to pay for Eternal Salvation, so she paid him in cash. They all left just in time for the last bus to Mallow.

Before the Bishop got on the bus, he again thanked mother and gave her his most personal and powerful Blessing for free. He said he was doing this because of her kindness as a Good Shepherdess. Mother was delighted and swore she felt the power of his blessing, but then she thought no more of it and went in and challenged her Henry, who thought he had escaped.

The Bishop arrived in Mallow and over the next few days he said Masses, and heard Confessions as well, and generally did what celebrity Bishops do, he became the talk of the town. He collected money and prayed and so did his cohort, the Nun and this continued for some days I believe. In the meantime, mother was working in Kit's bar and a farmer that she knew well came in for a drink. They began chatting and he told her that his wife was not well, and if only she could have been there when the Bishop was in town, he might have been able to make her better. Mother then got an inspirational idea for making a few bob, and told the farmer that she herself had been given a most 'Special Blessing' by his Holiness the Bishop, and that she was sure she still carried the power of it on her forehead. The farmer asked how that might help his wife, and my mother said that if he paid her a half crown, which was about a quarter of a pound, that she would rub a newspaper on her head and the power would go into it, and he could then rub it on his wife to make her get better. I call it her 'theory of transference'. The farmer agreed and they went over home and she made him some tea. Then she rubbed her head with a bit of the Cork Examiner tearing off a corner of it and giving it to the farmer. He paid and left, and two days later he assured my mother of the great improvement in his wife. He said that he had told his wife all about my mother's story, and that after hearing it she got immediately better the moment the paper touched her skin. Mother was delighted at that news. A few days later, the Bishop and his cohort were arrested in Mallow as confidence tricksters. I fell around the place laughing when I heard about this, as mother kept on trying to assure me that she could still feel the power, 'now and again'. What an amazing instrument our mind is and Science has often shown the power of the placebo, but I would have to question how a piece of The Cork Examiner could carry anything other than news.

She always had a 'fag'. No matter what happened, she had a 'fag' at hand or a part of a one, known to her as a 'butt'. She had this crazy habit of lighting it with a big string of paper, which she would stick in the fire in the kitchen. She would tear off the paper, roll it into a kind of string, light the fag, then throw it back into the fire. She set the chimney on fire many times (to the father's horror) by doing this, and she also burnt his accordion by the same method. But what I remember most about her string lighters was her insane gas incident.

She had a gas cooker in later years and as usual it was a fire hazard, but my mother herself was worse than any hazard. Numerous times we all saw her light the gas cooker with her string lighter. Her method was insane. She would first turn the gas full on in the oven, then go into the kitchen and light up her paper, then calmly open the oven door and stick in the lighting paper. There would be a bit of a small explosion, but the oven would light and all would be well. This continued for years and years, and we all gave out to her for doing it. It made no difference, she just continued as usual until the day when a knock came to the door. She had turned on the gas as usual and hearing the knock, out she went to the door and forgot about the gas being turned on full. After a considerable chat at the door, she realised that she had forgotten to light the oven. By then our back kitchen was a potential bomb. Unthinking, she lit up her string paper and opened the oven door to a massive flash and explosion. A large burst of flame shot out and she fell back on her ass. It blew off all the hair on her fringe but no other personal damage was done, but I believe the oven door blew off as did a bit of the wall. The only reason she escaped at all was because our back kitchen was more akin to a sieve than an airtight room, and most of the gas had already escaped. Even though she got a really good fright, she soon returned to her pyromania and it remained so until she rose to an electric cooker.

I'm sure the love every mother feels for her children is almost universal, and when you have money, worldly goods and security, it's easy to give your flock a good time. But when you have nothing, when you don't know where your next meal will come from, when there is no social welfare worth mentioning, then the true test of a mother's love begins.

Even though my Nannie did help my mother, it always seemed to me to be a begrudging help, never really given with love or compassion at another's misfortune. This made it all the worse for the mother when she had to ask for a few shillings from the Nan. Today as I write this account, I only now begin to realise the stress my mother endured and never once complained. I can only imagine how she must have felt daily for years and years. Life was very cruel to such a woman, but still she never gave up on us, her children. She lived for the day when we would be able to fend for ourselves, which of course did eventually come. Looking back on her many gifts to us now, I realized that one of her greatest ones was encouragement. She was always willing to encourage us, even if she didn't understand a bit about what we were doing. One of her best sayings for me was, "John do all that you can when you are young, because when you're old, all you will have are your memories". I think it's the best advice a parent can give to a child, and even though she preached it, she never allowed herself to do much.

My mother never hit me or beat me once in her whole life, nor do I remember her hitting any of us even though I used to drive her crazy while arguing and fighting with Kyrle. She often threw me out and would say 'get back over to Nannie's', so as to keep the peace, but she had a way of getting you to do what she wanted without violence, and I loved that in her. My father was the very same.

In our school days, she never once had a negative view on how well we did. All she would say was, "Do your best and that's enough". I don't think she was ever a great scholar herself, and because of that she was at a loss to understand or help us with homework as we got older, but we never minded. When we could, we would try to draw her into a discussion or more usually an argument, just to hear her 'Nul-c-ar bomb' clanger. Her humour was paramount. Even in bad times she would laugh, and she had numerous stories of her life with our father, usually referred to as 'her Henry'. I always got great pleasure from these tales, no matter how often I heard them.

One story she told of her courting days with my dad fits the two of them well. She and 'her Henry' went to Cork City for a day in a home-built car. This car was a total wreck. It had a Guinness label pasted to the windscreen as a tax disk. This was very fitting in hindsight based on the amount of money father had paid over to Guinness at Kit's bar. As they drove down Patrick's Street, the floor on her side literally fell out onto the street. She had to continue with her knees up on the dashboard and see a huge hole appear in the floor. I heard that the floor of the car was actually made from a metal sign advertising cigarettes: 'John Player' or such like. Later on the same day their back wheel flew off and passed them out as they rounded a bend on the way home. As she told us this story, it was as if she took pride in surviving this potential death trap and she would then continue with yet another story of life with Hugh Cahill.

She was so tolerant to all our devilment. She would feign being mad at us, but we saw through it. I think it's this freedom to express our true selves that has helped us all in later years, and the mother never denied us that freedom. In fact she encouraged it every day in her tiny little house on the main street of Buttevant.

Two walls and a roof.

My mother's two walls and a roof was comprised of a ground floor, a first floor and an attic. The front of the building had an area we called the shop, though it never was a shop of any kind. This shop had a settee that was pushed up against the wall on the priest's side of the house. In the early days I remember the priest was a very kind friendly man. He was big into the choirs and singing, and all my memories of him are very good. Father Shanahan was his name and sadly I heard he died a young man some years later. When he died we were given a cold-faced old priest called father Hennigan. I never liked him. He just seemed to me to be resentful of us as neighbours, and generally was unfriendly to us. Our shop front was about eight feet long by six feet wide and here we played marbles and darts, depending on the mood. The dart board had to be nailed to the front door, which was an old wooden affair that was rotting on the bottom due to the rain from our leaking shoot. It was the rule that when we played the darts, we had to bolt the front door or else you could quite literally get a dart in the eye as you entered. This almost happened to father more than once as he made his return from Kit's Bar.

Travelling on in from the shop we had a door with two glass panels leading into our so-called living room, often referred to as the kitchen. One of the panels was broken and had a pot mender holding the cracked glass in place: a remnant of our earlier fire engine incident. The living room was tiny, about five feet wide by seven feet long. It had a table pushed up against our neighbour Eily Paddy's wall, and there was a fireplace on the priest's side. A small window faced east and would freeze your ass off with the draft before father added on a back kitchen some years later. Beneath this window father had his throne. It was his favourite place in the whole house outside of his bed. The throne was made from an old car seat stolen from Big Kyrl's shed down the street, and beside this chair mother had placed a tiny little table with a shelf underneath for papers and books. The window ledge behind father's head was deep and two small curtains hung from a wire strung across the window as a decoration. These curtains, together with papers and books as well as an old valve radio with no back, were father's defense against what he called the 'East wind'. After a session in Kit's he would arrive in home saying, "Jekus Boys, tis the East wind again tonight, God help us all. Sure we're frozen with the cowld, put on the ould kettle there Belenda for a sup of tea". Then he would have a poke at the tiny little fire that mother would be carefully hoarding all day. This usually led her to say, "Henry will you leave the fire alone, that block has to last me all night," to which father would almost always answer with the same retort, "Boys o'boys, O'Brien has nowhere to go". He would say this with a kind of drama which we all loved and knew he was joking. Mother would smile and put on the kettle for tea, and on a good night, a rasher as well. Then the chats would begin and we would all argue and talk for hours until it was late. Finally, as if on queue, someone would say, "And what about the Last Supper?" Then father would rise up and go out to the back kitchen and fry up another few rashers if we had them. He would arrive in with the food on a plate for us all to share between us and I clearly remember the great taste of a rasher in bread washed down with a cup of the mother's tea. One time father fried these rashers in a cream that mother had been using to cure varicose veins. That night we all saw the bubbles on the rashers but ate them down anyway, and it was days before we found out what he had done. In his defense, father swore the cream was in a butter tub, so he was blameless, and it's a wonder we are all still alive.

This little living room also had the stairs going up to the first floor. It had a ninety degree bend on it as you went up, and even a small person had to bend down low or bang their head on the wall. Father always maintained that if he made that hole in the wall any bigger, the whole house would fall down.

The first floor had two bedrooms and a further even tinier stairs went up to the attic. Originally our granduncle, Johnnie Cahill, lived in the house and later moved up to this attic. His bed was a big four poster affair and he had a beautiful writing bureau in the back corner. The front room was the place where he cooked and lived. It had a little fireplace with a stone flagstone which was solid, unlike Nannie's cracked version.

In his latter days he would pay me and Kyrle to get him his few groceries and empty his cinders up Nannie's lane. Again the memory of me taking his bag of ashes up and dumping them has stayed with me always. He would be cooking sausages on a Saturday and often while he did this, we would smell them downstairs, then get hungry and venture upstairs so as to rob one or two from his frying pan. We knew him as 'Old Johnnie' and I'm sure he knew we stole his sausages, but he never complained.

Johnnie was a beautiful hand writer and loved to write history. He was a master stonemason by trade and built part of Belfast City Hall when it was not a time to profess Catholicism. I loved talking to him and would do so for hours and hours.

Johnnie was a wonderful storyteller too, and he spent many years writing the history of the Cahill's. He had done so much of this that it had filled two foolscap copybooks and it was his pride and life's achievement. I would see him writing away at his bureau and then, whenever he took a break, we would talk about what he was doing. He said he was writing the history of the Cahill clan and would give it to us one day before he died.

One time as I sat with him I asked if these Cahill's had ever done anything famous. He said that the only famous Cahill his research had ever shown up was the one at the 'Battle of the Little Big Horn' or 'Custer's last stand'. I almost fell off the bed with delight, as by then I had read many accounts about that great battle. I began to bombard him with questions: what had the Cahill man done, how did he die, was he brave, and how did Johnnie know all about this Cahill man?

To my amazement, Johnnie told me that this Cahill person had not died at the battle. Far from it; he had survived simply because he had fought with the Indians. Now I was totally on a high. I loved the Indians and always felt they got a real bad deal, and to think that a namesake had actually fought with them was just incredible news. Johnnie was so certain of this that he burned it into my mind, and I became fascinated with trying to know more about that battle and the famous Cahill who fought in it.

Johnnie was true to his word, and some time before he died he came downstairs one day holding his life's work: his completed history of the Cahill clan. By then he and mother were not getting along and he presented her with his gift saying, "Belenda, I am old now and have nothing to give to your children but their history and here it is. It's my life's work". She took it and threw it up on the window sill. She had seen the Cahills at work, being married to one of them for some years and they had not impressed her, so in a moment of unpardonable temper, she threw his two foolscap copybooks into her fire, thinking that she would at least get heat from their history, because she certainly didn't get any money from it. And so ended a treasure that I have always regretted. At the very least I would have seen in my granduncle's beautiful handwriting the actual account of the Big Horn Cahill. I would also be able to pass onto my own children an old man's work of over eighty years. It was a gift so priceless that it's always been the only thing I have had difficulty in forgiving my mother for. Of course she later regretted it, but what's done is done and today my younger brother Hugh in Australia has taken up the research into our family history together with my niece Charlotte in the Isle of Man.

Long before we were born, Johnnie had been married to a seamstress called Lill, and they were the original owners of our two walls and a roof house. They were very happy and loved each other a great deal, but they had no children. My sister Lill was named after his wife and Johnnie took this as a great honour. To his credit, he allowed father and mother to live on in his little home rent free until he died at the great age of ninety six. He always drank Pearl Barley when he got sick and swore it cured all ills, and after living to the great age of ninety six years, something tells me that he's right about the Pearl Barley and I should drink it myself.

Coming up the stairs from the shop and turning left you were in the mother and father's bedroom. It had a big holy picture on the wall, and two of the bed legs were broken and held up with books and a brick. A large part of this bed frame was made of iron and later on, in our 'radio transmitting' phase, we connected an earth wire to this frame to give us a better signal. We were totally unconcerned that this wire and the iron bed frame it was attached to could become fully live and potentially lethal, depending on how we plugged in our two pin plug further upstairs. Father would not even feel the shock if it became live as he seemed to be always immune to them, and we felt what the mother didn't know would not trouble her. Literally speaking, every night that she hopped into the bed she had a fifty fifty chance of getting shocked, but we were careful not to plug it in the wrong way and she never knew. Eventually father spotted the wire coming in the back window and made us remove it.

Father loved to read and he had a small little florescent bulb on a switch nailed to the wall above his bed. As his eyesight failed he brought this light closer and closer to his head so that in the end he was in danger of setting his hair on fire, but he didn't care as long as he could read about Rome and Egypt and Alexander the Great.

In the front room our sister Lill used to sleep. She also had a little fireplace in her room, but it was only lit once ever, and that was nearly the end of our father. That account became known as the 'bullets incident' at home and was told and retold so often that, even though it is burned in my brain, I still find it hard to believe. Father told me his version of the events often, and he would use it to say with a smile that our mother had tried to assassinate him many times, but that one time was the closest she ever got to pulling it off. He had begun a hackney business and was due to return from a run to Shannon airport with the famous horse trainer, Vincent O'Brien, who was a friend of his. He and the father knew each other very well and he was always good for a sizeable tip. This particularly freezing day father was on the way back from an early start and the trip to Shannon, and mother knew that the large tip would soon end up on Kit Roche's bar counter if she didn't take some kind of action to prevent it. So she decided to light a fire in the front room and have a really nice warm bed for her Henry, far from his East wind in their back room. She felt that she could save on the coal by only lighting this fire at the very last minute. The theory was that father would arrive in and she would encourage him to have 'a rest' in the warmer front room because she would soon be lighting the fire there, and while he was sleeping she would remove the tip from his pockets and save the money. It would all have worked out perfectly except for the little matter of some 303 bullets that, unknown to all, were then also resting in the same fireplace. The Cahills had all been enlisted in the Local Defence Forces and Big Kyrl had been the quartermaster in charge of guns and ammunition. He had an endless supply of 303 rifle bullets and so did the father. It was not uncommon for them all to do a bit of shooting, as by then Big Kyrl was a law unto himself and did whatever he liked in the town.

Over time, it appears that some live 303 bullets were left on the mantelpiece above the fireplace in this tiny front room. When cleaning there, mother would throw any papers she found into the grate and, probably in the middle of a spring cleaning session, she also threw in the bullets, knowing a fire would never be lit there, or maybe she didn't know they were live. One can argue the sanity of this forever, but I won't be the judge of it now. God only knows how much time passed by between the cleaning spree and the day in question, but father arrived back in frozen and tired, and her plan worked perfectly. He headed for bed and a sleep. After tucking him into the bed, she lit the fire and went off down the stairs. Father's bed lay against the wall opposite the grate, and at that point there was only a gap of about three feet between him and a most untimely death. Suddenly there was a tremendous bang, followed quickly by another one and then some more in quick succession. No doubt the whole street must have heard the shootout in Cahills house that day. To the listeners it must have seemed like the OK Corral shootout was being re-enacted in our house in Buttevant. Father began screaming and shouting while at the same time trying to burrow himself deep into the mattress, covering his head with the pillow while the bullets hit the walls all around him. The coals and the papers were blown out of the grate, and then the bed he was hiding in actually caught fire. Then from the safety of her kitchen the mother shouts up the stairs, "Henry, will I get Big Kyrl?" Father told me that he was quite sure he was going to die that day, and that he had accepted it, but all he really wanted to know was how many bullets had she thrown in the fire. We all feel that three at most was all it could have been, but father always swore there were more. He stayed under the pillows until it looked like the shootout was over, and then he beat out the fire on the blankets and made a run for the door. Running downstairs for water, he ran back up again and quenched the fires that were about to burn down the house. There was an inevitable shouting match of course, and then I think just sheer relief that he was alive. No one would believe that a tragic accident almost took place in that room that day, and I am sure that had my parents decided on some amorous activities, then one of them would surely be dead, but fortunately they didn't and all lived to tell us the amazing tale.

It was no secret that the ghost of Johnnie's wife Lill was often seen in that same room. She was seen there leaning on the mantelpiece smiling down at my sister Lill. No one was ever afraid of her, but I never saw her myself. Maybe she was the angel who saved father from his 'assassination' and mother from a jail sentence, as what judge would believe such a story was simply a tragic accident.

The back kitchen, as we called it, was a tiny little room about eight feet by six feet. It had a metal roof and a cardboard ceiling much the same as Nannie's one, and just like hers it too, was a fire hazard. For all I know, father may have made both of them. For many years, the toilet was also located inside in this little back kitchen. It was a walled-off section, once again made out of hardboard and painted blue. Mother hated this toilet with a vengeance, and constantly wanted a toilet outside her cooking area. Eventually she did succeed, and when father was building it he swore that she made yet another assassination attempt on him. The back kitchen had a cooker and an old stone sink for washing. There was a big window above the sink facing the river and Sheahens field, as well as looking down into our little back yard. Our back yard was about thirty feet long and about ten feet wide. It was surrounded by high walls on both sides and a shed belonging to Eily Paddy sealed off the bottom of the yard. On the left side was another shed owned by the priest, and it had a big aerial pole attached to its roof. We were to put this pole to good use later, and at a young age both Kyrle and I began climbing these walls just for the fun of it. Soon we were like cats with no fear of heights at all. Every time mother saw us on high, she would be fainting with fright and go complaining to the father. His words were always the same, "Belenda, will you have sense, sure if they got up they will get down". Then off in he would go and sit on his throne.

After constant pleadings, rows, and threats, father eventually built on an even smaller shed and attached this to our back kitchen, extending the roof and putting in a plastic sheet to allow light onto his throne. Here he located our 'new' toilet and mother's sunken bath. She had always wanted a sunken bath, the forerunner of a Jacuzzi, and after she finally got father to make it, we all discovered that it was almost impossible to get out of it once you got in because father had not added a rail to cling onto, and you literally had to roll over on your knees and crawl out onto the floor. It was such a disaster that it never got used.

The addition of the bathroom sealed off the East wind and finally made our little living room into the coziest room in the house. Mother had a fantastic collage of family pictures hanging on Eily's wall. Father had tried hanging this collage originally with a six inch nail, and the nail went right through into Eily Paddy's house next door. She came running out complaining, and after father pulled the nail back he became convinced that we would never again have a secret, because Eily could hear everything we said. He became paranoid about filling the hole and later hung the picture on what was a rarity for him - a much smaller nail. The collage had amazing photos in it, and I loved to look at it. Across from this picture hung a huge wooden mirror and it seemed to be held up by a mantelpiece resting over the fire grate. The mirror and mantelpiece held all of mother's little knick knacks, ornaments, and post cards. As she rose to a television set, we put it in under the stairs, which by then father had redirected to the front shop. She had a little cabinet under the stairs as well as the television set, and that completed our two walls and a roof home.

Lill's eel snake

My brother Kyrle took up fishing when he was about twelve and tried to get me interested in it, but that was a complete waste of time. I had no patience for it at all and never caught a single thing, and as far as I know he didn't have much luck either because I never saw him arrive home with an actual fish. A lot of fish talk was heard, but never an actual fish was seen by me.

Our sister Lill, who was a few years younger than us, was always a potential victim for our practical jokes, and we would play one of our best jokes on her using the one thing Kyrle did actually catch. On one fishing expedition to the river, Kyrle caught an eel: not a fish in my view, just an eel. It looked like a small snake and even I was unwilling to touch it as it wriggled on the line. We didn't have the heart or the courage to kill it, unless it suffocated from being out in the air, and it did seem to be alive all the time. We did not know what to do with it either, and I'm sure it was Kyrle's idea to put it in Lill's bed and scare her. I admit to concocting the story we used as we walked back home from the river. Our story would hinge around a zoo truck transporting a load of dangerous snakes through Buttevant on the way to a zoo. Then after an accident, a crate of the snakes would have burst open and they all escaped. Where else would this happen but just up the street from our house of course. As we walked home with our eel well hidden, we worked out every detail and how it was to be played out. We would nonchalantly ask mother (in the presence of Lill) if she had heard anything about the crash up the street, and then drop the subject completely. Then later the crash was to be resurrected again with a detailed description of the deadly snakes and a lot of questions being thrown at father to add validity to our story. The snakes were deadly Black Mambas obviously, and using my 'Knowledges books' we would, if necessary, prove how deadly a bite might be. Our knowledge of antidotes was going to be used (and of course the lack of them), and details of how slow and painful death would be if bitten. I was in Heaven playing out this scene in my head with Kyrle. Lill would inevitably go to the father and start asking about these snakes on the quiet, if our plan was working.

I checked out the lie of the land while Kyrle snuck the eel into the house in an old bag with his fishing gear. No sign of anyone, so he took the eel up to her room and placed it under the covers at the end of the bed. He told me that it was still wriggling away as he left it there. After a long time Lill and mother arrived, and after the tea I says to Kyrle, "I wonder if they found em all". Mother says, "Found what?" Kyrle, feigning disinterest says, "The snakes, didn't you hear of the crash?" Mother seemed not to hear, but Lill did and goes, "What snakes, I hate snakes, I'm scared of them". I say to her in my older brother voice, "Don't be worried Lill I'm sure they got them all". "What do you mean all? How many snakes, how did they get there? Where did it happen?" She flooded us with questions, now looking really concerned. I said I had to go home to Nannie's for my dinner and left Kyrle to handle her questions. We didn't want to over do it.

He played a blinder so that when I came back later that night she was in a state. Father had arrived in and Kyrle was asking him about Mambas, and which type were the worst. I piped up that I knew already which were real bad, as I had just been reading about them in my 'Knowledge books'. I knowingly explained that the black type were the most vicious and deadly. I also confirmed that they don't like cold and would seek out warmth always, even at the cost of being discovered. Poor Lill was beside herself with impending terror. Then once again we changed the subject and began playing chess. Lill could not get it out of her head though. She kept asking about the mambas and I kept telling her they were well gone, and that the zoo people just do not allow deadly snakes to escape. Kyrle says, "But they did escape". Mother told him to shut up and not to be frightening his sister. This only made Lill even more scared, as by then she felt that something was definitely up and we were trying to play it down.

I'd say she was about eight years old then and used to be sent to bed early, and as it neared her bedtime, I was having difficulty holding in the impending laughter. I knew that one look at Kyrle would blow it all, so I said I had to go out the back to the toilet. Lill clings on to the mother and begs her to make sure the door is closed after me in case the snakes come in. I arrived back in trying to look shaken but deliberately doing a bad job of hiding it. Kyrle asks what's the matter, and I say, "Nothing, nothing at all". He keeps hounding me, and Lill is listening intently as I get real close to him and whisper out loud that I thought I saw a mamba out the back. She shrieks out and clings onto mother again. At this stage she is refusing to go to bed unless father checks the room, which he does. I was sure it was blown, but he only gave a cursory look, probably suspecting we were just playing tricks on her.

He takes her up to bed and again checks the room for her. She got in bed, and still there is no sign of the 'snake'. He had hardly got down the stairs when we heard this unmerciful scream. "Ma... ma..... I'm bit.... the snake, the snake, I'm bit I'm going to die ahhhhh ma maaaa!" Lill came tearing down the stairs screaming in terror and crying her eyes out, clutching her mother while all the time pointing to her foot. I fell off the chair laughing. Kyrle almost collapsed with the laughter as well. Father jumped up and ran to her, telling her to stop, that there were no snakes in Ireland. She kept screaming and pointing at her foot. She seemed so sure that she was bit in the foot that father takes a look and saw some kind of mark. At that stage I thought I would be sick from the laughing. He quickly gave her to mother and ran upstairs, and found the eel. He got real mad and I hightailed it home to Nannie's fast. I do think in hindsight that Lill might have been bitten. She swore that she was, and I suppose it may have left a scar on her mind ever since, fearing snakes still, but Kyrle and I laughed at it for weeks and weeks. I was not welcome over there for weeks either, as I believe Kyrle convinced the mother that it was all my idea, and that it was I who put the eel in the bed. Eventually all was forgiven but not forgotten. Lill was saved from further jokes for years after that as I think she did get a terrible fright and we felt sorry for her. Besides, soon after that we had Eunice and Hugh as new victims.

Lill was close in age to Kyrle and me, and as such, when we were all small she felt like 'one of us' though we usually just used her for testing out our practical jokes. We all began to grow older together and soon we three became teenagers.

My two other sisters were many years apart, with Eunice being born in such hard times that she was gladly handed over to Nannie to rear, unlike me who was stolen by the Nan. Eunice became a virtual slave to Nannie and ultimately became her great confidante in later years. She loved her Nan in a way that my mother loved her: selfless, forgiving and everlasting. In Eunice's schooldays she was a bright girl, being constantly harassed by Nannie to be even better than she was, and no matter how well she did, it was never good enough. Michael loved Eunice and called her 'Wally'. I have no idea where he got that name from. Years after I was well gone they would both be in cahoots against the Nan as she got older and crankier and fought the two of them daily. The Nan's house then was almost as dramatic as my mother's place.

As I got older and became addicted to Pink Floyd's *Dark Side of the Moon* I needed a sound system that did justice to that amazing album, so I built my own version because I had no money to buy a professional one.

This strange extravaganza was built into a wooden box, and for effect I added a lot of red indicator lamps which gave off a good red glow in the dark. I had placed my system under my bed for extra effect and the Nan believed it was just a matter of time before I became incinerated. She would not have liked that, but she was vehemently against joining me in the conflagration. My room was very small and was directly below the Nan's bedroom, and she had to pass through it to go upstairs. Every night she had this ritual of looking under my bed, expecting to see flames and threatening to have me out the next day if my system was not gone out before me.

With the sound system under my bed I could easily reach down and turn up the volume or change the tape without getting out of bed, and this was the ultimate in pleasure for me. She was constantly hassling me about the volume and the red glow under the bed, and no matter how much I tried to assure her of its safety, she would say, "You're a Cahill and fire follows that crowd, and I'm not burning for you, so turn that thing off, now". In her mind, useless Michael would probably escape because he would be writing late into the night below in the kitchen, but not her and Eunice. It was a constant battle and the Floyd had to win. When she got really mad though, I would simply pull the plug to the light in her room above, as I had originally wired it. What she didn't know was that her light was far more likely to set the place on fire than my sound system due to my poor wiring skills.

My sound came out of two old car speakers that I had mounted on either side of my bed on the wall, and this sound, coupled with the red glow in the dark, was amazing to me. I used to come in late from an outing with my friends and immediately start up the *Dark Side*. For those who know that music, the 'Heart Beat' at the start would be vibrating the wall, and about then the Nan would be shouting down to me to turn it off, "Or you're out, you're out in the morning, I tell you". This was her usual meaningless threat and I would be waiting in suspense for the 'alarm clocks' part of the music to go off and drive her totally demented. I loved it. Each time it happened the result was almost predictable. Nannie would then demand that Eunice go down and, "Tell him tomorrow he's out, tell him Eunice. I said he is out for sure, tell him that I said it, that I have spoken". Then she would exhort poor Eunice to, "Turn that thing off so we can get some sleep in the name of God". This ritual happened quite often and Nannie would always lose out in the end because after the whole album played out, it would automatically switch off leaving only the red glow lighting my room, and by then I would be sound asleep myself while the others higher up would still be seeing the imaginary flames coming up the stairs to cremate them. I was a bastard I have to admit, as I was addicted to that music and didn't care a bit how they felt about it. Eunice was so brainwashed by the Floyd that she can still remember the words of some of their songs. Oftentimes Nannie would become so convinced that the place was 'on fire' that no matter how cold it was, or how late, she would make Eunice get up and go down and check out my room, which was 'haunted'. No one ever told me that till I had a very frightening experience there some years later, and even then they denied that it was haunted, but Nannie would never sleep there herself.

Recently, while researching this book, Eunice told me that when I began working, Nannie also had other rituals that she insisted were applied to me. I was always to be given the 'second' cut of the bread, "Because John is earning now, and he is to get only the best'. My inedible dinner was to be kept warm on top of a pot of boiling water so that it didn't dry out, and Eunice was warned to present me with this dinner on a special tray kept especially for me. And finally, I was to be given all this attention while sitting on the warmest chair by the fire because I had just come in from the cold. It's a wonder that both Eunice and Michael didn't hate me. In my defence I don't remember asking for any of this attention, but Eunice swears I demanded it. One time, in a rage, Eunice took the second cut of bread for herself, and Nannie saw her do it. She beat her while shouting at her, "Don't you dare take John's bread again, you little bitch". Poor Eunice was indeed a slave twice over, and like mother, never once complained.

Across the road Tishie was about to be born on March the sixteenth, the day before Paddy's day, and I clearly remember that particular Paddy's day because I had just made a microphone from carbon granules and an Andrews tin, and we could hear the parade on it as it marched up the town. That same day Lill was cooking a chop for the father, who had just returned from Kit's bar and from a drowning of the Shamrock escapade, while our mother was in the Mallow hospital having our new sister Tish. Lill, knowing no better, only cooked the chop on one side, and the other side was bloody and raw. Father, always a squeamish man at the best of times, but by then full of porter, sat down and began to eat his chop cooked by a ten year old child. Suddenly he saw the blood and flew into a rage. He threw the whole chop out the back as he puked all over the place. I find it so strange how some memories stick in us for an eternity, and other ones vanish in hours.

My sister Tishie, who is actually called Patricia after the Paddy's day birth, is an amazing girl. Like Eunice and myself, she seems to be very spiritual in outlook. Since writing this memoir I realize that Kyrle, Lill and Hugh are quite the opposite, being totally science driven, living by logic and reasoning, while we others tend to live by emotions and feelings. In my view neither side is right or better, just different, but it does cause some amazing arguments when we all meet, which is way too rare these days.

Tishie was the father's pet I think. He loved her as did mother, and all of us saw her grow into the girl that fell into much better times than we had, and we were all so glad of that. She went on to university and got her degree, and there she met her husband-to-be, John Stack. They live happily in Scotland with my nephew Hugh, a Downs Syndrome boy with great artistic talents. Eunice lives in the Isle of Man with her husband Seamus and their three girls Bree, Carrie and Ciara, while my sister Lill has two children Peter and Charlotte. Lill married a Manx man, Philip Faragher, and she too lives very happily on the Island of Man. It's all too rare that we Cahills meet up now, but thank God our mother, the focal point of our family today, is still alive and well and she also lives on that beautiful little island.

Uncle Michael nicknamed my youngest brother Hugh as 'The Congo'. He did this after a number of Irish soldiers were killed in a fierce battle in the Belgian Congo in Africa around nineteen sixty when Hugh was born. When he came into the mother's world he was probably the least wanted of my parents' children, but who am I to know this for sure. I feel he came at a real bad financial time, but no doubt he was loved by our parents like the rest of us were. However, I suspect deep down he sensed that he would be better off arriving a year or two later when things were beginning to improve.

I think Hugh grew up alone. He used to sleep with Kyrle, who was nine years older, and they fought like dogs: worse than we ever did. Hugh literally had to live by his wits and survive all by himself, and to my shame I just remember him as being almost invisible, yet I loved his smile.

Mother had got bad epilepsy by then I believe, and I think another child to feed was just too much for her to take. Her poor mind cracked and she began to get what we called her 'fits'. I only ever saw her in one of them and it scared the devil out of me. Poor father was kneeling beside her, comforting her and telling her that she was ok. That really scary event was the one time I saw him show total love for his wife. You could feel his concern as my mother jittered and moaned, looking desperate as she lay on our floor with father kneeling beside her holding her hand and propping her head.

Of course Hugh was totally blameless for the fits and for arriving in bad times, but I am very sure that a child, especially a very young child, can sense the feelings of those surrounding it, and if all you ever feel is fear, then you become defensive and a survivalist. You learn to live by your wits and Hugh became a master of that art right down to this day.

He was always on the defensive about everything, always trying to prove himself better and more right than Kyrle and I. I didn't care about this at all and I would just argue for the fun of arguing, but I never took it personally. Kyrle did though, and would fly off the handle in an instant. They were always arguing about something. They once had an argument that went on for days about the principle of a draught and why and how a fire actually lights, and what is the purpose of a chimney. I still laugh at this as even today after their numerous 'proofs' bounced off me, I am as confused as ever and still don't know the principle myself.

Hugh was caught in between two sisters and two older brothers. He must have always felt alone and unloved I believe. This was wrong as we all do love him, but we were useless at showing it. Yet he has grown up with one of the most balanced personalities I have ever met. He makes friends instantly and easily, and has a great personality and sense of humour. He is very outspoken and is always battling the system. He's a modern day Robin Hood who will argue for the sheer mental exercise of it, and it's a brave person will take him on.

He was certainly a bit of a womaniser growing up too, and I still meet women today who ask how he is and where is he now. He lives in Perth where he is very happily married to Celestine, the love of his life. They have three wonderful children: Tara, Tirna and Nieve. All of them are full of life and adventure, and I can't wait to hear of their exploits as they become adults. Hugh has, in my mind, the most inventive brain of any of us Cahills. I believe he can think laterally as the norm when most of are barely able to think at all in a crisis. I know this is true because I saw him do it in Hong Kong some years ago, but that's another story.

My brother Hugh started to study the problem of DVT (deep vein thrombosis) better known as 'blood clots' on air travel, and as a result he has come up with the ultimate solution. Together with his long-time best friend Gerard O'Connor (another Irishman) and myself, we have lodged patents in the USA on Hugh's invention. At the time of writing, a number of them have been granted to us and a final one is close to grant.

According to Hugh, our invention will save thousands of lives in the future, and not alone on planes either, but in offices also, especially in America. Only time will tell where that project will go, but I am in no doubt of its success.

Joe Hurley my best friend

For as long as I can remember, Joe Hurley and I were fast friends. He lived just down the street from us. His father, Tadgh Hurley, owned both a furniture shop and a grocery shop, and later still he brought television sets to Buttevant for the first time. Like Big Kyrl, Tadgh was a true entrepreneur and I always liked him. Mother had an account in his grocery shop for a while until they got fed up with her lack of payment and stopped giving us groceries. When she had been paying, she used to splurge out now and again: usually on a Sunday. This great splurging out amounted to her buying a tin of fruit cocktail on a Saturday night for the Sunday dinner. Times were getting better and we could now afford the odd tin of fruit, even if it was on tick. What she didn't know was that each Saturday night me and Kyrle would punch a tiny hole in the top and bottom of the tin at its edge to drain off the juice and then drink it. This was a regular occurrence and the minute we knew a tin was ordered, Kyrle would be itching to get the father's hammer and nail ready. We simply loved that juice and to this day I often drink it, but thankfully I don't need a hammer these days. On the Sunday as mother opened the tin she would get raging mad, seeing no juice once again. She would dispatch Lill down to Hurleys shop demanding a new tin saying, "Them Hurleys are trying to poison us all and I'll not have it". We did this drinking the juice for a long time before the Hurleys decided enough was enough, and her credit was stopped. Mother then moved on to Connor Corbett's grocery shop with a new tick book, and no doubt leaving an unpaid bill at Hurleys.

Joe Hurley always seemed to be rich to me. He had all kinds of toys which he didn't care about, and I had a magnetic attraction to him. No matter what he told me to do, I would almost certainly do it. To this day I don't know why this was so, but he had great charisma and he made me laugh all the time. All he had to do was give me his certain look and I would burst out laughing, and for as long as I could remember we had been friends.

We played in a field up the ball alley lane which I am sure belonged to the Murphy family. Old Tom Murphy had a hardware shop literally across the road from Joe's people and for some reason Joe hated them all with a passion. Tadgh Hurley owned a small field on his side of the lane behind his shop, so it was not surprising that Joe claimed the field on the opposite side of the lane as well, as that was how Joe was, but everyone knew it belonged to old Mr. Murphy…except Joe.

Young Tom Murphy, (Mr. Murphy's son who was hated by Joe) was always openly claiming the opposite, and often there would be a shouting match between them from the safety of their front doors. This arguing led to a number of scraps with Tom, but all were mostly a bit of pushing or name-calling events except for one memorable day.

It was coming up to Cahermee time and the travelers, known to us as the tinkers, had stationed their horses in the Murphys' field. Cahermee is a famous horse fair held in Buttevant each July the twelfth. Joe and I were both about eleven or twelve years old then and up for any kind of devilment, especially Joe Hurley. We were standing in the field studying the horses huddled and tethered together in a corner when Joe says, "No one told them tinkers to put them horses in my field. Let's get rid of them Cahill". Of course Joe had to act the tinker as well and give them the odd lash with a long stick he had found. Tom Murphy must have seen us and arrived, shouting at us to get out of his field. Joe, who was by then an expert at bad language, told Tom to, "Fuck off out of my sight". As Joe's disciple, I told Tom to fuck off as well, me trying to impress Joe with my tone and bad language.

Tom would not go and Joe says, " Murphy, I'm giving you fair warning now, get the fuck out of here or you'll be sorry. Isn't that right Cahill?" I says, "You'll be sorry, Murphy," as I glare at Tom trying to look and act tough too. Still he would not go, so we made a run at him, and being two big bullies, we knocked him to the ground. Then Joe says, "Lets throw him to the horses," winking at me evilly. I grab Tom's legs and Joe, being stronger, grabs his hands. Poor Tom, who was younger and weaker than us bullies, struggles and kicks out, but it's no use. We pull him over near to the horses and start to swing him. Joe says, "Who owns the field now Murphy?" "My father does," says Tom. Hurley says, "If you don't say who really owns it quick, you're going into those horses". More swinging and Tom still refuses. All the time Joe is swinging and counting, "One… Two… Three," we both let go on three and Tom sailed through the air into the horses who were already agitated. I saw all the trampling and took off, as did Joe. Poor Tom got trampled I believe and ran off home in a terrible state to complain to his dad. Old Mr. Murphy was the gentlest man I ever saw, but he later arrived over at Nannie's house to complain about me and he was very angry. However, she would not hear of a bad word said about me and she told him to get out, that her John would never hurt a fly, definitely not his son. He left and she then tells Michael, "Don't get any more paint from the Murphys, go on up to Colemans instead. I'll not have this carry on, he's lost our business". One would think we bought loads of stuff from him, but all she ever got there was a couple of tins of paint every four years for the Corpus Christ procession. In her eyes though, her order to Michael to withdraw her custom would have dire economic implications for the complainer, and at the very least, he would go bust in the future. Then when I snuck back home she attacked me with her dishcloth and told me to keep away from Hurley, that he was the Devil and bad news followed him. This only cemented our friendship all the more, but I always regretted the incident as Tom was truly outnumbered and didn't deserve what he got. Me and Hurley chatted about it in our camp in the trees in Murphy's field later, and he blamed me saying that I was not supposed to let go of Tom's legs because he had winked at me. It was just a prank that went wrong and I don't think Tom got really hurt thank God. We never attacked him again though to my knowledge.

We were going to the national school at that time and had a woman teacher. I think we called her Margaret. Hurley began having fantasies about girls' panties or 'knickers' as he called them. He decided that Margaret must wear pink ones and these were his favourite fantasy. Joe tried various ways to see if he was correct. He would be dropping his pencil or copybook trying to look up her dress. He had no luck and complained almost daily to me about it after school. He seemed to be almost obsessed with seeing her underwear. The fact that Margaret was probably in her fifties made no odds to Joe. If anything, it made it even more intriguing.

Margaret used to give us 'the stick', the term used for a good hiding, if we did poorly on the lessons and this was her weakness according to Joe. One day he decided to fail everything on purpose and also to give her back cheek as well, such was his determination to see up her dress.

He had seen her flake one of the Knockbarry boys on the arse across her knee for back cheek, and he felt this would be the way to go. Joe had no work done at all and smarted off at Margaret when she asked why that was. Sure enough she got real mad and pulled him across her knees and flaked him hard across his pants with the stick. As she swung into action he roared out in pain, then another whack and more roaring, then I saw the funniest sight I had ever seen. There was Joe spread across her knees getting his ass beaten while he's clearly bending his head and looking up her dress. Then he looks down directly at me and gives me a big grin with the 'thumbs up' sign. She did wear pink after all. I thought he was taking the whole thing far too serious, but that was Joe.

When I was about thirteen, Hurley gave me my first sex education lesson. Joe seemed to be an expert on the matter, as in all other things then, and one day I asked him what 'it' was like. I believed, wrongly, that he had 'done it' as that was the term used then to describe having sex, because he was constantly alluding to this great thing called 'doing it'. On the day in question we retired to our camp in Murphys' field and inside the bushes Hurley told me the great secret. It amounted to this quotation and I never forgot it. "Lad, see this mickey?" He opened his pants and proceeded to show me his small little penis, "Well tis like this lad, what you do is you stick this in her hole and if she bleeds you better get out of town fast coz she's pregnant and you're in big trouble". That was the entire sex education. Where he got this great information from, besides his vivid imagination, I never knew, but I believed him. Then he asked me to show him my mickey, but I was too shy and kept it inside. Hurley just laughed and said, "Lad it's ok if it's too small now, coz when the right 'bitch' comes along twill get real big". For a long time Joe had been referring to women as bitches and every time he saw a schoolgirl go by he would go, "Look at the fat arse on that bitch Cahill. I bet she loves it," then he would slap me across the back and say, "One day soon you'll know what I mean". After Joe's sex lesson I remember becoming really confused and was about to ask him more but decided to leave it for another day in case he pressed me to show him my mickey again, so we went off playing hurling instead.

We had numerous scrapes and adventures. He tied a donkey up to an old gate and invited me to ride on his back just so that I could, 'Feel like a real cowboy,' according to him. He assured me it was safe as the donkey was tied up. I climbed the gate and got on the donkey's back and it all seemed great to me for a few seconds. I was hardly on board when Joe released the rope and gave the donkey a huge flake with a stick. The donkey reared up and took off down the field with me clinging on for dear life. It felt like I was 'breaking the horses in' in the cowboy films, but I was terrified. The donkey bucked me off and made a run at me. I ran for the ditch, barely getting over it before it trampled me. I was terrified, but Hurley was literally crying with laughter. I punched him right in the eye and left for home. Joe came after me still laughing and saying over and over, "Sorry Cahill, sorry lad, but you should have seen yourself on his back, you'd have died laughing too". I shrugged him off and told him to fuck off, but secretly I was beginning to see the funny side of it myself, especially now that I was not on the bloody donkey's back. But by then I was back at Nannie's door and Joe knew that was forbidden territory for him. I think it was never the same with us after that. We were still friends for years after, but something broke the friendship that day. I got a terrible fright thinking I was going to be trampled to death and all Joe could do was laugh at all that was happening to his best friend. I had enough of Joe by then, and we drifted apart until our secondary school days with Pad Keely, when once again Joe would be Joe, only worse and Nannie would be proven correct.

Fort Apache and other wars.

Big Kyrl had begun to show films in a hall he was hiring from the British Legion. He was always an amazing entrepreneur and my idol in Ireland, as distinct from Huck Finn in the US. We had free entry into the cinema as teenagers and even earned some money as ushers now and again. These films were to become our inspiration for all kinds of adventures. At this time we had become friends with a very gentle boy called Martin Sweeny. His people lived up on New Street and his dad, Ger, worked for Cork County Council in the roads division. Ger had a big shed out the back and it was full of all kinds of items that we were to use later on like paraffin oil, tar, tar barrels, sheets of galvanized iron, long metal pipes and an endless supply of wood. The shed was an Aladdin's cave for adventurers like us. Martin was a few years younger than us and his people had a television set when it was almost unheard of in those days. Martin's parents seemed to be very happy that we would play with him each evening and at weekends, and we three became like the Musketeers and actually acted them out at times with great swordfights.

Pretty soon we began to act out the films shown by Big Kyrl. Initially it was just the usual cowboys and Indians stuff, but soon we progressed to submarine warfare. We actually built a big submarine in a field next to Martin's house. It was made from tar barrels, sheets of iron and boards, all taken (or stolen) from Ger's shed. Inside our submarine we had an old wind-up gramophone with one vinyl record, the French National anthem: La Marseillaise. I got so sick of hearing this that I started to have nightmares from it, and to this day it is not good for me to hear it.

Kyrle added the real touch of class to our sub when he somehow managed to get a barrel with no top or bottom, and this became his conning tower. I see him as clear as day, standing in the barrel or conning tower, giving orders and surveying the sea field with his hands as binoculars. In winter we lit a fire inside the sub and burned the old felt used for roofing. The fumes were terrible and it's a wonder we are still alive considering what we were breathing. We had a library and charts and seats inside, and it actually was almost waterproof. Our sub lasted through a good number of attacks from the townie gang and others. They were all jealous of it and us, and constantly plotted its destruction.

As we saw each new film, we would build a set and get to re-enacting our own version of events. One of these almost ended in tragedy for Martin. We had seen a film called *Fort Apache* I believe, but I could be wrong. In any case, the fort was attacked by the Sioux and burned. This was inspiring stuff for us. It just had to be re-enacted. Kyrle was going to be a Sioux warrior which he pronounced as 'see-uxx'. It took him years before he realized his mispronunciation. I had no idea either and just followed his version until Uncle Michael mocked him one day, and I knew then how to say the word, but I never told Kyrle: I just sniggered at his ignorance.

We had to first make a fort and then I would decide if I was a Sioux or a cavalry man, depending on the fort and how it looked, though I was far more partial to the Indians. To make sure this fort would burn, we were not going to use iron sheets but cardboard soaked in oil. To get this cardboard, we resorted to our old faithful supplier: Tadgh Hurley's drapery store at the bottom of the ball alley lane. Tadgh always had cardboard packing boxes that he used to protect his furniture out in his back yard, and we were always stealing them from him. We stole a large number of these cardboards over a few days and soon were ready to build the fort. It was made by beating stakes into the ground and nailing the cardboard to the stakes so that it formed a square. My guess now is it was about ten feet or so along the sides. The gate was a section of cardboard which could swing on a stake. At this stage I had become completely on the side of the Indians even though Kyrle had already become 'Chief'. I opted to join the war party and do some burning, and the excitement was building inside us all. Martin was given no choice but to be a soldier in the fort. He had a rifle and he liked being in the safety of the fort, wrongly as it turned out. The Plains would be far safer if only he knew what was planned for his fort. What Martin did not know was that Kyrle really intended to burn the fort. Martin had never seen the film like us, so he didn't know the danger he was in. To ensure success,

93

Kyrle got a drum of paraffin oil and doused the cardboard walls liberally with the oil. Then the battle began.

Initially we ran round the fort with our bows, hollering and whooping just like the real Sioux did. Martin fired volley after volley, and now and again one of us would fall to the ground dead or wounded. This went on for about ten minutes before Kyrle gave the command, "Light the arrows". He had stolen some firelighters from home and broken them into small squares. We tipped our arrows with the spongy materials and soon he had his one lighting. I lit mine off of his and we began the attack, circling round and round. "Fire arrows!" Zinggg…his arrow went into the fort, followed by mine. Both aimed at the walls and not at Martin, thank God. Not a thing happened other than Martin shouts out, "Ye missed and John you're dead".

I feigned death and lit another arrow from the small fire of papers Kyrle had now lit as our fire source. So did he, and this time we sent two more flaming arrows straight into the wall. I saw the oil catch fire and a black smoke began to rise. "Yippee, they're done for," says Kyrle, "Fire more arrows". By then all pretence of circling was gone and we just stood there like two Robin Hoods and fired arrow after arrow into the fort. Soon it was really blazing and the whole area was filled with black acrid smoke. Martin stopped firing and shouting. In fact we could neither hear him nor see him at that point and I got a bit worried. I ran up to the blazing gate and called out, "Martin where are you, you in there, you surrender yet?" Only choking and coughing came from inside and the heat beat me back. By then Kyrle was at the fort too and he called out as well. The fire was so hot that we both got scared. I felt we had to save Martin, so I ran across the field and got one of our long pipes and poked at the burning wall of cardboards. Now I could see Martin on the ground choking and coughing and clutching his throat. Kyrle ran back with his 'Quix bottle' fire extinguisher which was useless, and after pushing down the burning wall, I ran in and pulled Martin out to the air. He was ok but red-faced amid the black smoke and choking for air. The fort burned out as the three of us watched it. Martin said the most unforgettable words, "Next time I wanna be with the Indians".

On another occasion we had seen the Romans capturing Troy or

Egypt or someplace and they had been using huge catapults firing rocks as big as cannonballs at the enemy. By then our little gang had a lot of enemies in town. There was the Knockbarry gang, the Townies gang, Charlie Mack and Joe Hurley (a born ringleader), as well as the crowd from the area known as the Quarters. Usually we were well able to defend ourselves with our small catapults, fire tipped arrows and our secret weapon: the 'weed killer bomb', which was still not used in battle but under development.

We heard a combined attack was being planned for a Saturday with the aim of destroying our submarine once and for all. As luck would have it, some weeks earlier we had seen the Romans in action and I felt that we should use the sapling trees on the ditch in front of the sub as our catapults. These would be our first line of defence. We all agreed, and soon we had ropes attached to the tops of the young trees and were bending them down to the ground, where the ropes were attached to some iron stakes driven into the soil. I believe we had three of these systems ready all along the ditch prior to the attack.

Kyrle got some canvas bags and filled them with rocks and stones, and we tied these to the tops of the trees now sprung back and ready to fly forward. Unfortunately we had never tested these new weapons.

Saturday came, bleak and overcast, and we waited and waited. All of a sudden there was a yelling from Joe Hurley, the self appointed ringleader of the combined gangs, and he and a few others began climbing over the outer wall of a nearby field, shouting and roaring at us and firing their catapults as they advanced on our submarine. "Launch one," Kyrle shouts at me and I cut the rope holding down the first tree. Whoosh, up went the sapling with its bag of stones and it flew right over their heads, breaking into shrapnel all over the road. From what I could see, the gang still on the road took off, never having seen such a weapon, but the others, now numbering about five or so, cautiously edged forward, firing all the time. "Launch, launch, launch," Kyrle screamed at Martin and me while he fired his arrows. More stones flew off and again they went over the gang's heads and the wall. This was not working at all. The trees were too good and we had fired too late. Hurley's gang was almost upon us, and now becoming desperate, I gave the order, "Catapults ...and aim for the eye," and I did just that. I aimed for Joe Hurley's eye. The stone hit him on the forehead and he reeled backwards in pain. We sent a hail of stones at them as their hail zinged all about us, and even though a stone or two hit me and the lads, we were winning. Hurley was bleeding badly from the forehead and ran back over the wall heading for home. I ran out after him to make sure he got the message, and was caught in an ambush by Mickey O'Rourke who punched me into the nose and tried to kick me to the ground as well. I was now bleeding too and made a dash back for the camp where Kyrle and Martin came out to save me. As for the others; with their leader gone they lost the will to fight and soon all became quiet. I remember us all shaking hands and cheering because our sub was safe. We were never attacked again either. After that incident Hurley became Kyrle's arch enemy with no possibility of forgiveness ever.

We had become experts in bomb-making after Kyrle was given the secret from a friend of his: a spy in the Knockbarry gang. He was told that if you mixed sugar with weed killer powder you would get an explosion. The problem for us was he did not know what the proportions were. The weed killer was sold as a white powder in the chemist shop or hardware shop I believe, and I don't know how we got a load of it, but we did and were soon in the bomb-making business. The first attempt did not explode at all but burned fiercely. The next attempt did almost nothing and we did a lot of experimenting before we began to use science to help us. I figured that we should stop wasting this powder, and start measuring the amounts we used and keeping a record of it until we got the mixture right. Pretty soon this began to show a pattern, though for the life of me now I can't remember what the proportion was for a bomb, as against the intensely burning proportions of a rocket. One was the direct opposite of the other, I do remember that. It was not long before we blew a good size hole in the ditch and then, having perfected the explosive side of things, we advanced to making rockets.

President John F Kennedy was coming to Ireland and he had already given the go ahead for the landing on the Moon, so we became utterly fascinated by the Americans' work on rockets. We decided to make our own very large rocket and try and impress the great man. Maybe we might later be given a job in NASA, but to ensure success we would build our version of a Saturn 5 Missile and shoot it up in the air in front of a military chopper, hoping that the pilot would see our abilities and report the great news to the President.

We stole the lower section of a drain pipe, probably from Tadgh Hurley's shed, and mixed a load of the powders as rocket fuel. Kyrle beat in the top of the drain pipe to make it into a point or nose cone. I added a stick and wired it to the side of the tube just like you see in today's fireworks and I think we painted the words Cork on the side of the pipe as well. We were ahead of our time except for the Americans and Chinese.

The real worry for us though was that this rocket was huge and very dangerous. We knew that if we had got the proportions wrong, simply because of the amount of powder being used, it could easily become a bomb rather than a rocket. Each of us knew the danger and it was scaring us, but there was no turning back then as everyone was talking about the President and we wanted to really impress him, just in case he needed a forward base to keep the Russians in check. We drew straws to decide who would light the fuse. This fuse was a string dipped in paraffin oil, the good old reliable in plentiful supply in Ger's shed. Kyrle and I both hoped that Martin would win the honour, but he didn't draw the short straw. That left it between us: I cheated and made Kyrle do the fuse work. He knew I cheated and I knew that he did, but I made him do it anyway. The plan was to launch this missile some distance in front of the chopper, as it always took the same path over the town, and hope the pilot saw it fly up in front of him, when he would later report to the great man.

Our launch pad was a little domed hill inside the local quarry behind Sadler's shop on Buttevant's Main Street. We would set it up on the hill, then climb up the side of the quarry face and tell Kyrle when it was coming from a distance. He would light the fuse, allowing him time to get back up the cliff face too so that we could all watch as it flew off directly ahead of the chopper. I was about thirteen, Kyrle was twelve and Martin was nine. We figured on immediate fame, never thinking of the consequences if it actually hit the helicopter, as we were sure it would not. At the

97

very least we might be recognized as rocket experts and meet the great Irish American President.

Soon Martin and I are on the cliff top watching and hearing the chopper approach. I roared down, "Light the fuse and get up quick, tis on the way". Kyrle lit the string, and to this day I don't know how, but the flame seemed to jump ahead of itself. Maybe it was petrol we had mistaken for oil. Kyrle saw this too and ran like hell for the cliff face, but he never made it up. Suddenly there was a huge flash and a massive bang, and he vanished in a white cloud of smoke. I got a terrible fright. I was sure he was dead and I had cheated him, and it should have been me dead not him. I tore down the cliff shouting, "Kyrle, Kyrle where are you?" After what seemed like an eternity, we heard the voice from the bushes and briars way down below at the base of the hill. I could not see him still. Then he emerged from the nettles and briars as black as night with two white eyes staring back at me and says, "The bloody thing blew up, the fuse, the fuse ran too fast. Pull me up will ya, I'm stung alive". Somehow we dragged him up. He was covered in scratches and his clothes were singed, as was the back of his hair which had turned black. I think I laughed out loud with great relief that he was alive. As we climbed back up, he says to me "I know you cheated". I felt really ashamed but continued to deny the undeniable. That was the worst experience we had in our bomb-making phase, but it was not the only one. I often thought later in life what did the pilot really think when he saw that flash. One thing was sure though, President Kennedy never did meet us, and on the day he died, what I remember most was how close we had come to meeting him and the deep sorrow that filled my heart for the loss of such a great man.

At an early stage we took to making 'gillies' or what are called go-carts today. The aim always was for maximum speed. We had few parts: usually an old pram, a few boards and the father's endless supply of six inch nails. A six inch nail became our friend. We called it a 'six incher'. It could be used as a nail, a hook, an axel, a u-bolt even a drill when reddened in the fire and used to bore a hole in a bit of wood. The father swore by those nails and always had a collection in his tool drawer in the back kitchen. He had a wrench that he called a geegaw. This was an adjustable spanner with two big jaws and where he got that name from I have no clue, but somehow it appeared fitting and he used this wrench constantly. He had a small twist drill, but it had only one bit and if that was the wrong size we resorted to the red hot 'nail drilling' by the fire.

Gillie building was becoming a fad and I think we were the forerunners of today's boy racers. We had an arch rival gillie maker known as Charlie Mack. He lived up the street from us and his brothers, being mechanics, always had loads of wheels, axles and excellent parts. They were also geniuses at anything mechanical and Charlie began to make gillies like us. One time he told us that he was making a Henry Ford Model T and that it would blow our ones off the street. Kyrle took exception to this insult, and he discussed with me how we could build a gillie based on some Roman film that had a sea battle in it. In that film they had built ships with battering rams and they sank all round them. He called it his secret weapon. He felt we should ram Mack first chance we got. That meant us building a battering ram gillie, but how to make the ramming part was the problem.

I immediately began building the frame, but kept seeing Kyrle searching day after day for what he was calling his 'secret weapon'. I had no idea how he was going to make the weapon, but I built away and finally got the frame completed. It had a wooden base with a cord steering rope, and it turned on the inevitable six inch nail. The back axle also was held by the nails and I was all for taking it for a spin, but no, not Kyrle.

He said he had seen Mack's Ford and it looked awesome. Charlie had used a large wooden tea chest for the body, and it even had a roof and was painted black, or so Kyrle kept telling me. When I finally saw it, I thought it was awesome too. That day Mack had sped past us gaining speed from the slope on our street and as he did so, Kyrle says, "That's it, I got it, I see his weak point". He made off down the town to Big Kyrl's shed and arrived back with a length of two inch iron pipe. Big Kyrl used these pipes as rollers for moving headstones where he cut them into sections and Kyrle had stolen one of them.

Kyrle began to hacksaw like mad. Then I realized what he was doing; he was making a battering ram just like the Romans did, but it would be made of iron and far more dangerous. He kept at it, sawing and filing till it was like a spear, and then using the usual six inchers, we mounted this spike onto the front of our gillie. All this work was taking place down our back yard safe from the prying eyes of Mack.

Another check on the street showed Mack once again passing and enjoying his driving. He passed us again as we stood at the door and gave us a smug wave and Kyrle says to me, "Ok that's it, get me up to Fitzs', I'm ramming him next time". Out comes our new gillie and we pushed it all the way up to Fitzs' shop on the highest part of the street. Then Kyrle challenges Charlie to a 'race'. He had absolutely no intention of a race; he wanted a war. By then Charlie was staring at our pointed spear and I'm not sure if he was scared or not, but because of Kyrle's taunting he agreed and lined up his Ford beside our battering ram.

I can't remember who pushed him off, but off he went down the street. Kyrle had whispered to me, "Let Mack off first and then keep on pushing". As Charlie sped away, I gave a mighty push to Kyrle and ran along pushing as hard as I could. We are rapidly gaining on Charlie and Kyrle starts shouting, "Julius Caesar, Julius Caesar", and when he's almost parallel with Charlie, he suddenly turns sideways and the spear goes clean through Charlie's wooden tea chest. How he wasn't impaled I'll never know. At the bang I tripped and fell, and last thing I saw was the two of them locked in a mortal combat, with both gillies careering across the road glued to each other, and Kyrle is now waving his fist in the Roman salute. Mack's 'boat' had been sunk. How they escaped the cars beats me too, but in those days there were fewer of them. They disentangled outside May Sheehan's and Charlie threatened us with his brother for wrecking his Ford, so we laid low for a while.

It did not take long for us to rise again though, and this time Kyrle wanted to build a 'super gillie'. He had the idea that if we used huge wheels on the back and tiny wheels on the front it would have to go faster and it would look like a Roman chariot as well. We managed to find two big bicycle wheels in the dump and once again we were modifying the battering ram gillie by adding the big wheels at the back and much smaller ones for the front. The word was out that the Cahills were building a 'super gillie' and planned to race it down the Ballalley lane. I was a good bit worried at this test run, as the Ballalley is very steep and ends on the main road. Besides that, it's quite a short run too, so how were we going to stop it at the bottom of the lane. Kyrle dismissed all this as nerves, and he just wanted the speed. I wanted a good few plays on this new gillie myself as it looked like a chariot without sides, so I really did press him on how to stop it: all to no avail. We planned a Saturday test run and a good crowd of lads gathered on the top of the lane, including Mack and Joe Hurley, who was still not speaking to me then due to the donkey incident being fresh in my mind. Everyone was amazed at our design. Doubtful heads were huddled in discussion, Mack among them. Our hands were being shaken and more lads were nodding that it was the best gillie ever seen in the town. Even Joe Hurley, my ex-best friend, tried to make peace with me, hoping for a go on it later, but I refused. We were the local heroes, even if only for one day.

We had agreed that Kyrle would do the test run as he said it was his gillie, and in truth it was. I still maintained that we should have some way of stopping it though, and then inspiration dawned on me. I got the idea that he should use a big concrete block attached to a rope as a brake.

The plan was that he would push the block out behind him as he was nearing the main road and the gillie would stop due to friction. We got the block from Hurley's wall, with Joe protesting as usual, and we tied a strong string to both the block and the back of the gillie. All was then ready for the great push off.

I'll never forget that day, it was so exciting; it was like launching a rocket. I so wanted to be part of the speed that at the last minute and without telling Kyrle I planned to jump on behind him and sail down the lane with him, then use my foot as a brake if the block failed. That was the plan at least, but it didn't quite work out like that though. By then, Kyrle is all tensed up and keeps telling me to, "Come on, come on, push me off will you", so I do. I gave him a huge push off, but I jumped on board as well. A huge cheer went up from the crowd as we both sped down the lane. Almost immediately I tumbled right off the back of the 'chariot' because it was going so fast, and there was too little room because of the block. Kyrle was really speeding up and as I picked myself up I saw this amazing sight. Here he was frantically trying to shove off the block as he's chased by a load of lads all cheering and waving at him. The whole crowd was running past me and it all felt so great, but Kyrle was panicking, trying desperately to push off the block. When he did, it suddenly snapped the string before it could do any good. I saw him fly straight across the road with his hair flying back and no doubt a panicked look on his face. He crashed straight into Hutchins' wall. As the ram hit the wall, he actually catapulted up into the air, hitting the plate glass window and collapsing back on top of the gillie, which was by then totally wrecked. I was running across the road and by the time I got to him I was furious. He had mangled the new gillie before I even had a spin on it and I kept on shouting at him, "Why didn't you steer for the lane, the lane? I'd have steered for the lane". As I saw it, he could easily have turned slightly to the right and gone on down Hutchins' lane where I felt he might be able to slow it down using his leg as a brake. Of course I was not the one travelling at twenty miles an hour, then heading for the main road, so it was easy to be critical.

Poor Kyrle was dazed: probably concussed. He had this blank look in his eyes and he didn't argue back as I was shouting at him, and that was very unusual. I think I must have realised then that he was hurt somehow, and helped him home. I think someone stole the chariot that day, as we never used it again and I have no memory of ever bringing it back to base either. It's a likely bet that Mack or Hurley used it for 'parts' but I don't remember any more gillies being built after that famous one. Kyrle recovered and still laughs at his escape even today.

Our father, a gentle Soul.

My father was a small man of just over 5"5'. In my mind he always seemed to be poor and I never saw him have a wad of money in his life, yet before he was married he was fast becoming wealthy and would be considered a yuppie by today's standards. His real love was for music. He was self taught and many is the time he recounted his long hours spent in the attic practicing on a piano accordion bought from a local man called Herman Weedle in Mallow. In later years he learned the saxophone and I have been told many times that he was a real expert on that wonderful instrument. Every time I hear a sax solo I think of my dad.

I was told too that everyone liked my dad, and I never met anyone in my life that had a bad word to say about him. His personality was very gentle, and he was full of old sayings, stories of his youth, and later still accounts of his mad life. He had a very broad mind and could be seen to discuss almost every subject ad infinitum. It was very rare that he lied about anything, and the only time he did tell lies was to cover his tracks with our mother when he had been spending money he should have been handing up to her. He was especially interesting in the days before television, when we would spend many hours discussing electronics, space and all kinds of science subjects as well as the Roman Empire and Alexander the Great's feats. He seemed to know everything. I loved talking to him, except when he was drunk. Then all he did was repeat over and over again the same old stuff we talked about ten minutes earlier. When he was like this I would listen away to his repeats and pretend it was all great news, but secretly I longed for his sober discussions. I can honestly say too that my dad never raised a hand to me or to any of my brothers and sisters. He would get a mad look on him if he drank whiskey and change his personality, but if he got too mad, mother would threaten him with the poker and say, "I'll guzzle you if you don't stop this carryon". This rarely happened anyway because whiskey was too dear and went down his gullet too fast, unlike a Guinness which he could make last all night when needed.

My father seemed to have no ego at all and, after marriage, no drive for fortune or fame either. In a crisis he always took the easy non-confrontational route and perhaps that's why he had no enemies, because he was never a threat to anyone. All he ever wanted to do was play his music. His life was hard but very interesting and he seemed to me to be more of a friend than a father. My earliest memory of him is of me being a very young child and both of us sleeping together in the same bed in the front room where my mother almost shot him in her bullets incident. On that occasion I remember him holding me and asking me if I was warm enough, which I wasn't. I was feeling strange, as by then Nannie had me conditioned into believing that it was she who should be holding me.

He was a man too fond of his drink. I never understood if he drank from desperation or just as a cop out, but in truth it was probably a combination of both, beginning with Nannie stealing me from him and my mother. He always had a listening ear though, and he would give an apparently 'all knowing' opinion on how something worked. I always listened with great pleasure to his infinite knowledge, especially of electronics.

I think Lill was his first favourite followed closely by Tishie, who ended up being his number one, but Hugh always secretly loved him the most I feel. It's impossible to ever know what my siblings thought as we grew up, and all I really know for sure is how I felt at the time, and most of the time I was not happy with how he drank. Eunice and the father had a somewhat stormy relationship I felt, as like me she had no time at all for the bottle, and yet he loved her like us all and he told me so on many an occasion.

My father was a jack of many trades but he was primarily a musician, later a painter, a hackney driver, and finally a general driver and handyman. There are times when I try to remember something good that we all did as a family, but I can't remember one thing. Even though he had a hackney car, he never took us once to the seaside. We never went as a family anywhere together. I never remember him and my mother going out together for an evening as a husband and wife, certainly not in the early days. I do remember one terrible incident though, an incident that remained with me since childhood. It happened at a time when Big Kyrl had decided to start up his cinema hall in Buttevant. Advertising boards did not exist then and Big Kyrl, in keeping with his mantra, saw nothing wrong with turning our mother's little house into one large advertising display for his upcoming films. He wanted to put his huge movie advertising posters up on our front window. Naturally mother absolutely refused to allow this, and as father had been promised money for a few pints of Guinness, he insisted on putting the first poster up, so up it went, and from then on, any passer-by on the street would be immediately transported to Monument Valley and the Wild West or Humphrey Bogart's Casablanca. It took up the entire front window and our front room suddenly became as dark as night. Our two walls and a roof had then been reduced to a billboard. When this happened I was a very young boy of about six. I saw my mother go wild and her temper boiled over. In a fit of rage she climbed up onto the window shelf to tear it down, and to my horror and to my father's eternal shame, he got a bucket of cold water and I saw him throw it up at her. She slipped and fell back, tearing the poster to bits as she fell onto the old couch. To this day that single act made no sense at all to me. Why had he thrown water up at my mother? It made no sense. He was not as strong physically as she was, and his nature was gentle, but the need for alcohol overcame all on that day, and I suppose this bucket of water was his only method of retaliation. It was a shameful thing to do and I have never been able to forget it. I got so upset that I ran across the street to my Nannie's house and ran upstairs to my room crying. It was my earliest experience of domestic violence, but was by no means my last. Sometimes there was the usual shouting and roaring between mother and father and the occasional threatening of a guzzling by the mother, but for the most part I was sheltered from it by living in Nannie's house, and many homes were far more violent than ours. There were times too in Nannie's house where violence happened as well. On one such occasion Michael couldn't take any more of Nannie's ravings and he threw a kettle of boiling tea at her. It spattered her and did no more damage, but it shocked both him and me so much that I think it never happened again.

Father's great love for music bubbled over and it was inevitable that he would form a dance band known as the Hugh Cahill Orchestra. This was a 'big band' in the style of the Glenn Miller Orchestra and he played the same kind of music as well. His band was a huge success. Father played from one end of the country to the other, but he seems to have avoided the cities, concentrating on rural Ireland for his livelihood.

I know that his only lean times were during Lent, when the Catholic Church in their infinite wisdom felt that Ireland's population should have no entertainment and dances were 'forbidden'. It did not seem to worry them how the musicians might feed their families at that religious time, but that was how it was in those days. Then pop music appeared on the scene.

I vaguely remember the pop music era beginning and the father's band feeling the pinch at the time. It must be difficult for anyone to accept your time has passed, but when it's your livelihood that's also passing, then it's all the more terrible. My mother was no help either, and if anything she was totally destructive as regards the band. She didn't like the idea of the band boys arriving in late at night and then dumping their instruments into the front room of her home, but this was a normal event for a band. They were out all night, slept all-day and rose up at 4 p.m. for a new day's gigs, but unless you understood this you could be driven mad because no normal housewife routine fits that pattern of living.

Mother almost takes pleasure in describing how destructive she was to her husband's livelihood. One day she was rolling up her blinds on the 'Wild West window' when she stepped back into a drum kit and wrote off the base drum. It was so damaged it could not be repaired and father had to buy a new one.

She next wrote off his piano accordion on another day with her crazy form of matches that we christened 'string lighters'. At the fire grate she lit up a stringy bit of paper so as to light her 'fag'. Then she threw this paper back into the fire, except that it didn't go back into the fire, instead it landed on father's accordion which he had been airing near the grate. It fell on top of the ivory keyboard and up went more of his living in a blaze. There was absolutely no repairing of that instrument either.

On yet another occasion she decided to clean his saxophone, and

106

not having any idea about instruments, she threw all the black pads for the keys into the fire, thinking these were dirty things. Father was not much better for letting his instrument become so filthy. That cost a fortune to repair, but at least he didn't have to buy a new saxophone.

He was booked to play for a very important Hunt Ball in Bandon town, and on the day of the ball, she burnt a hole right through both legs of his only black striped trousers, by leaving the iron on it too long. Father then had to go and borrow a black pant's from Kyrl, who was at least a foot taller, and roll up the extra length inside the legs. It might well have been a Hunt Ball, but fathers pants now looked more like jodpur's, and one could believe he was taking his gig far too serious. It certainly was not the fashion for the Leader of the Band. She tells that story with an almost evil pride and smiles as she does so. I think she must have hated his dance band despite it being their livelihood.

The father was quite a humorous man too. He was not a joke teller but enjoyed a good story. His lifetime friend was a man called Arthur O'Lowery. Arthur was a brilliant mechanic and he and the father were drinking buddies. Father told a story of a time when Arthur and he were testing a motor bike that Arthur had just repaired. They went for a spin down the Charleville road at high speed and the bike seemed to drive just fine, so they retired to Herlihy's pub where they got 'langers' drunk. Later on and by then totally blotto, they mounted up for the return journey to Buttevant. After a few attempts to get the bike started, it spluttered into life and once again they took off at high speed, heading home to Buttevant. As they neared the town something happened to the bike. Father used to say it was the petrol pipe came loose, but in any case the bike actually caught fire, and a flame soon shot out from under my father's legs. He had to stick his legs out like a butterfly's wings so the fire wouldn't burn him. The bike had now become a rocket as Arthur sped up to burn off the fuel, fearing an explosion. Father was roaring at Arthur to stop, but Arthur was just roaring drunk, and had already decided to keep going. They tore straight through the town with hair and flames flying behind them, and headed on for Mallow. At Ballybeg there is a small lake just in off the road and it was here that Arthur took serious action and drove their bike straight into the lake. They fell off into the water, but the fire went out without the expected explosion. To me, that was one of the funniest things my dad ever told me. I could see the two of them racing through the town with a flame going out from behind them, both sozzled drunk, panic stricken, and heading for Mallow. It's like a thing you'd see in the movies, except it was almost the norm for those two mad men. The whole town was talking about it and Nannie said to mother, "Didn't I tell you that fire is following them Cahills. No matter, sure they are all useless anyways".

The flames were following these two all their lives. They had a business blasting stubborn trees and old hay barns for farmers. Arthur had numerous boxes of gelignite and other explosives in his workshop in the centre of the town. One evening he and the father were fixing some engine in the workshop with the gelignite stacked in boxes nearby. When suddenly the engine malfunctioned and it burst into flames, not panicking this time as they were sober, they got a crowbar and stuck it through the blazing engine and lifted it out to the back yard where it burnt out. Little did the innocent people of Buttevant realise the escape they had that day, or know the dangerous life they lived when those two maniacs were at work.

The father had many personal stories. He either had an attraction for trouble or he was prone to bad luck. Some things he told me about were so funny that I used to question if they actually happened, and in a strange way my own children have asked the same question of me in relation to my mad life.

One story stands out for me. It was at a time when my father was about 28 years old. He used to visit Gracie, his mother, each day, and even though he was married by then, he would stay with her till late at night helping and chatting, and I suppose trying to cadge the money for a pint.

Some distance down the street an actual certified lunatic was living. His name escapes me, but he took a great liking to the father. I'm sure my father liked him as well as he always spoke warmly of him even though it was often in jest. One night around midnight as the father left Gracie's, it began to really lash down with rain. Lightning flashed and thunder rocked the town and everyone ran for shelter, especially the late pub drinkers. Everyone ran except the father. He never ran anywhere. In all my life I never saw him run once. So he walked briskly down the main street without a coat or hat. As he walked home he passed pubs and closed shops and onlookers at the lightning. When he got to the lunatic's door, who should be standing there but none other than the lunatic himself, gawking out as well. Seeing his good friend getting drowned, he shouted to the father, "Hey Cahillo, Cahillo, wait for me. I'll give you a shelter with my new umbrella". The father, being polite and also being afraid of the lunatic who was a lot bigger than him, decided to humour him and stood in the rain. In seconds, out ran the lunatic dragging his umbrella behind him. Then in a real suave gesture he proceeded to open it out and raise it above their heads. Then with his arm wrapped around the father's shoulder like bosom buddies, they proceeded to walk slowly down the street. This would be normal enough except for the fact that there was no cloth on the lunatic's umbrella - not a stitch, just a series of bent spikes sticking out in all directions. As they continued on down the town, the lunatic kept telling the father how lucky it was for him that he had his best umbrella handy. The lunatic continued to ignore the peals of laughter coming from the onlookers, and father used to say that he thought he would never get home. Father was too embarrassed or scared to say anything, and the lunatic refused to run, so on they went arm around arm with the lightning flashing, the rain lashing, and a whole town of bowsies laughing their heads off at the 'two' lunatics.

Father told me that his last memory was of seeing the lunatic walking back up the town, umbrella up spikes out, and him impervious to all the jibes from Buttevant's revelers. The scene is, for me, all the more funny because at that time the street was only lit on one side, and the lunatic was walking back on the darkened side. He would be almost invisible until a flash of lightning came along, then suddenly he would appear from the gloom like in a horror film, only to disappear once again just as fast. He was supposed to have been certified as sane from the mental home, but he was most definitely insane, and for a time their walk of fame was the town's big news. I believe from then on father came home earlier and crossed the street to avoid his friend.

He told me too of another actual event which he witnessed and which was sad and hilarious in a strange way. This was during his hackney days and he had been given the job of taking a fare to a local wedding. This fare was a poor man who had a terrible speech impediment and stuttered a lot. The man was travelling alone to the wedding and confided in the father that he hoped for a miracle by finding 'a loose woman' at the same wedding. His idea of 'loose' was simply a woman who was unattached, lest I give the modern impression of the term, and at an Irish wedding, a woman on her own would indeed be a miracle. The father was all encouragement as he liked him and tried to build up his courage and confidence. As it happened, by a total accident, there was indeed a single girl there also, and again by pure coincidence she too had an impediment almost as bad as the father's friend. To make it even worse, the father actually knew her but his fare did not. As the day wore on, Frank the fare laid eyes on her early and fell in love immediately. She too spotted the similar loner to herself across the floor. Father could see a disaster looming and when Frank began describing his plans and looking for more encouragement, the father tried his best to persuade him against such a meeting. But it was no use and he told the father to, "Ffffuuckk off," saying maybe he was just jealous and wanted a go at her himself. The dancing began and the lady was left standing by the wall. Off went Frank across the floor, all fired up from the drink. He made a bee line for the woman and says to her, "Woood youuuu likkke to to dddance?" With that she drew out her fist, gave him an unmerciful clatter across the face and says back to him, "Dddon't yoou ddaree mmooock mmock mme you fufkkken baa baa bassstard". All hell soon broke loose and she burst into tears. Then the more he tried to explain in his stutter, the worse it got. The father, initially seeing the humorous side, waited to see what would develop, but soon he felt sorry for both of them and he went across to explain the sad fact that they were both in a similar situation. I never knew if they hit it off later on in the day, but hopefully they did and had their own wedding. The father wasn't invited if they did, as he would surely have remembered it.

My father could tell these stories for hours at a time and as a young lad I could listen as long as he told them. Our lives were so much simpler then and happy too, but this was usually in the middle of the week, when he had no money for the demon drink, and the weekend was far far away.

Even though he tried and tried to succeed in life, drama and misfortune seemed to follow my father. He had saved some thousands of pounds from the dances he was running and he ventured into the hackney business. He bought a big American station wagon which was to act as a band wagon, a hackney car, and a car for pleasure. It really was a beautiful sight apparently and he only got to use it for a short time when, as usual, a fire disaster struck. He was taking May Sheehan, my butter woman, to Fermoy town, and just outside the village of Castletownroche the back wheel flew off. I was told that the previous night Big Kyrl had been out with a woman and he had gotten a flat wheel. It was raining hard and he rushed the wheel changing business, leaving the nuts too loose. So it was no surprise that when father rounded a bend at the Grotto, off flew one of the back wheels. The car tilted down at the rear, and in typical form, this was on the side of the petrol tank. The car had no petrol cap and they were using an old rag stuffed into the tank's opening as a cover. The axle began scraping the road and showering the back of the car with sparks. Sparks and petrol are a deadly mix and the inevitable happened. Father, seeing a fire coming from the back of the car, realized the danger quickly and screeched to a halt. He ran round the car and pulled May out quickly, just as the tank and the wooden car exploded in flames. They were very lucky to escape with their lives. The car rapidly burnt down to the chassis and as he had no insurance, he watched as his thousands were gone up in smoke. I really believe that my father never did fully recover financially from that disaster. He saw his livelihood go up in smoke before his very eyes, and considering the value of money then, it's easy to see why he might never recover, but as was typical of my dad, he never blamed Big Kyrl. He would only say, "Ahh sure twas an accident". For Nannie though, once again it confirmed her belief that fire definitely followed 'them Cahills'.

Castletownroche was also the scene for another more serious drama though. His band was playing in Fermoy and it had been raining for days. The Awbeg River was in full flood and it passes through the little town. On the night of his gig, part of the bridge

111

was after falling into the river and they screeched to a halt just before crossing it. The band members objected to crossing it, not wanting to drown in the flood, an understandable fear and a bit of a row developed with Kyrl calling them all "A pack of ould women". The compromise was reached when father decided to drive across the bridge by himself first, and if he was not swept away then they would trust the bridge and walk across it later. This took guts I believe and father was terrified, but he used to say to me "John the show must go on, no matter what". I think Kyrl had also indoctrinated my dad with his mantra of the end justifying the means. In any case father crossed it and so did his band but they came home by some other route. That bridge is only yards from where he burned his station wagon car. I often cross it myself today, and I always think of my dear old dad, every single time.

As we grew up I noticed that father would always try to find enough money for a pint or two by doing some handyman job. Mostly he succeeded, but not always. On one occasion he was asked to fix a Hoover vacuum cleaner. He knew nothing about them at all but the motor had stopped working and he did know about motors. Mother told me that he worked on it all day, such was his drive for a pint. Eventually he got it going after much poking, soldering and cleaning. The father seemed to have got a brainwave during the job as to how to double his money.

He decided to offer to clean Nannie's chimney using the repaired vacuum cleaner. She was good for a 'fiver' at least, and he knew that she was always afraid of a chimney fire.

He arrived at Nannie's house and started to describe just how dangerous the chimney was looking, and he put the wind up her so much that she was petrified of a conflagration and almost begged him to do something about it. Quick as a flash he arrived back in with his new chimney cleaning device and soon he began to stick pipes and hoses into the chimney breast, then turned on the machine. His head was buried in her chimney as he poked and sucked the soot with the hose. The noise was so loud that he could hear nothing and he was impervious to the drama being playing out just behind him.

Nannie had been sitting on her couch just behind his 'Hoover' when he started up the motor. By then she was getting feeble and moved slowly. Father had forgotten to put the cover properly on to the machine, which accounted for the noise, but he had not fitted a bag to it either. He had never seen a Hoover in his life and the customer had removed the original bag before she gave it to him for repair. Within seconds a whirl wind of black soot and dust covered Nannie. She looked like a black person from darkest Africa. He kept poking the hose up into the chimney and she kept being coated in soot, all the time roaring for him to stop and trying to pull herself off the couch to escape. But he couldn't hear her over the noise and soon she was totally encased in soot. Poor Nannie just couldn't get up fast from her couch due to her age, and every time she roared at my father, even more soot went down her throat, choking her as well as coating her.

After a desperate struggle she managed to rise up and took off out of the kitchen to the front door, gasping for air. Then from the safety of the kitchen door she kept shouting in at him to, "Get out, get out will you". He still didn't hear a word she said so she started throwing books at him. Still he kept going till the machine mysteriously stopped working. When finally father came out of the chimney, he realised the disaster he had caused and one look at Nannie's face meant no fiver was coming. He gathered his machine and left for home, all the time Nannie was tongue lashing him heavily for his utter stupidity and deafness. But to make matters worse, the soot had so clogged up the motor that it had burned it out completely. By then it hadn't been a good day at all, and he retired to his bed cursing and swearing at his ill luck for ever having had any dealings with the Mahonys.

His immunity to electrocution was proven many times. On one occasion mother had asked him to hang up a curtain line over the East Wind window. Father's answer to every problem was a six inch nail, so he got two of them and his little hammer and got to work. These were driven into the wall and a wire line was strung between them. He went to bed after that exertion saying he had done enough for one day. Then when mother proceeded to put up the curtains, she got a massive shock from the wire line but couldn't believe it, and so she went back to try it again. More violent shocks followed, so she went upstairs and told her Henry that she was getting 'electrocuted' from the curtains. He told her to cop herself on. "You're never happy. It's impossible to get shocks from curtains, now let me sleep will you", and back he went to sleep.

Sometime later she again tried with the same result, and even then she was beginning to question her sanity, especially when the father tested the line with his wrist, which was his version of testing for a live wire. Of course he felt nothing and pronounced it all to be safe, then he hung up the curtains convincing the mother that she was as usual imagining things, or simply going insane as he suspected, and that it was she who was driving him to the drink. Months later the mother asked Kyrle to test the wire line and when he did, unsurprisingly enough, he found the line to be fully 'live'. The father had driven a nail into the live wire buried in the wall beneath the numerous layers of wallpaper. Then he attached the wire line to the nail, and during his hand test felt nothing as usual.

Nothing was ever 'earthed' in our house either, as we never had an earth rod buried in the yard due to its high cost and father's belief that the earth concept was just trouble in the making. We had the earth wires always connected up to the sockets so it looked safe, but they ended up going nowhere. Father always said earths were not needed and only blew fuses, that they were nothing but trouble, and that it was impossible to get electrocuted. He believed we were all like him (genetically immune) except for the mother, who was a Mahony after all, which explained why she got the shocks and we did not.

Father was never a gambler. In fact I think none of us ever were, but my brother Hugh told me of the one time when father would most definitely have made a killing on the horses, but he drank the bet instead.

It was just after the war around 1948 and I believe petrol was still being rationed at the time. My father had a hackney business and as such he had a supply of petrol coupons which he sold to the great horse trainer Vincent O'Brien at face value: an unheard of act at the time. This was the same Vincent O'Brien that father had taken to Shannon on the day of my mother's assassinated attempt on him with her bullets incident. As a result of father's kindness at helping out such a great man, Vincent seems to have given him a guaranteed winning tip for a horse called Cottage Rake, who was unheard of at the time and was a huge long shot. Father told his good friend Arthur O'Lowery of the tip and drank his bet before ever putting it on the horse. The horse won the Cheltenham Gold Cup, and from what I can gather, half of Buttevant also won huge amounts of money including Arthur on the race. Father used to say wryly that his best friend built a house on his tip while he drank my mother's money in Arthur's pub, such was his bad luck.

One of my fondest memories of my dad was us being together on the night of the first Moon Landing. Space travel had always fascinated me. I suppose it came from my candle flying days or readings about it over the years. But I will never forget that day when the whole world was watching television, except for my mother and the Nannie. Mother had no interest in it at all, and Nannie denied the whole thing, saying it was a con job by the Americans to fool the Russians, her belief turning into a well documented conspiracy theory some years later. However, myself and the father were glued to his small screen under the stairs for the whole event. We sat transfixed as the black and white images flashed before us. When those magical words, "The Eagle has landed", came over the speaker we both shook hands and father said, "Tis a great day to be alive, John, and never forget it. Boys O'Boys the Americans have done it". I said, "Yes, yes they have," and I got so excited that I ran out into the main street looking up at the moon and began shouting, "They are up there, the Americans are up there. Horray for the USA". A bowsie from Kit's looked on at me and shouted something at me, but I don't know what it was and cared less as I stared up at the moon. I just jumped up and down on the road. Father came out to the door and then both of us looked up at the moon in awe. I felt an amazing closeness that day to my dad, and longed to see America. Standing at our door I told him so. I said, "Da, one day I will see America". I was nineteen years of age and it would take me just under thirty years to realise that dream. My father just smiled as I spoke, but it was a doubting smile. I think he felt such a great country was beyond the reach of us Cahills.

My father was diagnosed with cancer and when I asked him what the doctors had said, his exact words were, "John, tis all up, I'm going to die soon. Look after your mother". I felt a terrible sadness creep over me right then. All my many criticisms of him were gone, and all I could think of was, 'I'm losing my dad faster than I ever imagined I would'.

Father's last days were very hard for him and our mother, as well as for all of us. Mother found it terribly hard to see her Henry suffering and wasting away before her eyes. Fortunately, even though abroad, my sisters all helped out and came home to visit him at various times. He was adamant that he wanted to die in his own bed, in his own 'two walls and a roof' and mother respected that wish. He gave her a few frights when she thought he was going, and on one such time (a Sunday actually) she rang me in a big panic telling me he was finished and to get home quickly. Within five minutes she was back on again saying he was okay, the panic was over. That night I went home to see him. He was sitting up in his bed reading the paper as if there wasn't a thing wrong with him. I castigated him for scaring us to death in a nice jovial way, and then he pulled me aside and said, "John, I'll be gone by Wednesday," and he was. It was an extraordinary statement and has remained with me since in mystery. That same night he asked me to buy him a bottle of Lucozade, a non-alcoholic drink, which I did. On taking a big slug from the bottle he announced to my surprise, "Jekus Boys that's real good stuff, John". I told him rather insensitively that if he had reached that conclusion forty years earlier, we would all have been far better off, but he just smiled and didn't reply. There was no need to state the obvious at that late stage of his life.

That same night my daughter Lynda, who was a very young girl, began filming my father talking to me. We all knew, especially him, what we were doing. We were trying to preserve him after he had gone. We did the small talk and skirted around his passing and it got too sad for Lynda who broke down into tears. I have that tape of my father, just hours from his death, making funny faces at my child so as to make her stop crying, such was his good side. That tape is beyond price and now and again I see my dad at his very best.

After some very hard months of bitter but resigned suffering, my poor father died, heavily dosed with morphine. My sister Tishie and brother Hugh couldn't make it. They rang him at the final moments. Tishie was snow bound in an airport in Scotland, and

116

Hugh was holed up in a friend's house in Australia crying his eyes out. Father seemed to be waiting for Tishie to arrive at his bed any minute. She had made every effort to do it, but the weather had snowed in the airports and she was not going to make it and told him so on her last phone call. When father realised that his Tish could not be there, but that she was safe, he quietly slipped away from us all in body but not in spirit. I truly believe that as long as his stories are told, as long as we speak of him, as long as we laugh at his jokes and his life, he will remain with us till we ourselves are gone too.

I will always thank most sincerely the Marymount Hospice Movement in Cork, especially the nurses, for their most wonderful kindness to my father and to the many thousands of others afflicted by the terrible ailment of cancer. It's no accident that many years later, both me and my son Kyrl, would be indirectly responsible for raising almost two million euros for cancer treatment in the hospitals of Cork, Marymount among them. I feel privileged to be part of the 96FM radio team who have made all this happen and I know that my dad is very proud of us all for doing this work because I can feel it.

In a moment of weakness, I had earlier promised Hugh that at the funeral Mass I'd read out a fax from him on the altar, thinking I'd modify his words and shorten it when he sent it to me. When it did arrive, it was so beautifully written that I secretly cried while reading it, and at the church I completely broke down on the altar in front of the very large crowd of people attending the service. I struggled and stammered along, tears flowing down my face, and I felt so ashamed for my stuttering, especially in front of people from my home town. It was so terribly hard to do that I almost gave up on the reading, but somehow I continued on to the very last words. Hugh's fax had described in a beautiful poem what his father had meant to him. It showed a love that was palpable, it showed his sayings, his use of the words 'Jekus Boys' and his humour. It was written by a son too far away to come home, but with a memory that described his dad in a way that showed how much he was loved.

A simple promise made by me on a phone call to Hugh had turned out to be the most difficult task I had ever to perform in my life. The task, though terrible for me personally, was eased by the wonderful Buttevant congregation, who gave me a standing ovation when I finally finished. Father's many friends knew him as Hughie Cahill: a musician and a handy man, perhaps a man who drank too much, but one who did not have a bad bone in his body, and they showed me their respect for my dad that night.

His funeral had a great turnout on a terribly cold and dangerous night. Friends of ours came from miles around to pay their last respects to a great musician and well loved friend. He had thousands of faults and certainly was not the ideal role model for a father, but yet when he was good, he was very good and we all loved him in our own way. Father was a very religious man, and I spent many a day arguing the existence of God with him. Now that he's gone, I am quite sure he got a warm welcome when he finally met up with his own version of his Deity. I'm equally certain that he is smiling at us all right now, and probably saying, "Jekus Boys tis a terrible summer, and O'Brien still has nowhere to go even in Heaven. Sure I'll put on the ould kettle and make a drop of tea". He sends me double rainbows when I think of him, and I have had the most awesome proof that he is still around, but that's for another day.

Pad Keely's school days.

I think I was about twelve when there was yet another row between Nannie and the local Canon, the same one from our altar boy days. In some kind of protest she withdrew me and Kyrle from the Buttevant National School, which was run by the clergy. We were then sent off to the local secondary school known as the Sacred Heart College. It was run by a friend of Michael's and at that time you had to pay a fee to be taught in a secondary school; the equivalent of an American High School today. I have no idea how Nannie planned to pay this fee for the two of us, but when her temper was high she never looked at the consequences of her actions. Almost overnight we began our second level schooling in the College at the bottom of the town. It was right across the road from the old British Army Barracks which had earlier been burned by the IRA. In our time it had been converted into a local hurling field, and there we played hurling during our days in the Sacred Heart College.

The school had just two rooms, one which actually had bars on the windows and still does today. The main room had two classes in it for a time, with two teachers and two classes of boys sitting back to back without any partition between them. This meant that each teacher could hear what the other teacher did, and also notice how the boys were answering. In hindsight, this had to have been an impossible situation for both teachers and students. Later the headmaster, Pad Keely, a long time friend of Michael's, had made another small classroom out of a room in his house, which connected to his kitchen. His house was in effect the actual school, as he was using rooms that were part of his home as classrooms. I know that it was an ingenious act on his part to allow for a fourth classroom to magically appear, by making yet another tiny room into a classroom for fifth year students. The only students in this 'new' classroom when I was there were myself, his son Brian, and his daughter Molly. It was so cozy that I often felt like one of the family. I am sure now that, just like us all today, Pad too was only trying to make ends meet and being able to tell the Department of Education that he had four classes must have added to his grant from them, if he even got one.

There were swords on the wall of the main room, which we played with now and again, and a very long blackboard on the western wall. This room also had a kind of podium next to the window where Pad would stand and read the paper or keep notes. It was also where he kept his bamboo stick for punishment. Living today in a time of political correctness and public exposure to the sadistic treatment meted out to innocent victims, especially those run by religious orders, it's very important for me to point out here and now that we the students were never victims of sadistic acts by Pad or his staff. Neither Pad Keely, nor any of the other teachers he had in his employment ever acted sadistically towards us. I can say that in all truth, but they were often at times incredibly cruel and violent. Pad especially believed in literally beating the knowledge into our heads by brute force if necessary. His wife, known to us as Ma, also taught there, and she too was well capable of meeting out strong punishment by the use of the same bamboo. This stick was about two foot long, shiny and with knots along its length. It hurt like hell when you had a strong man or woman behind it, and they were swinging it down with full force. Today I wonder what frame of mind one has to be in when you are choosing a bamboo stick for the specific purpose of inflicting pain on another human being, especially a young one. How do you find such a stick, and what are you thinking? Is it long enough, is it strong enough, how many knots per inch etc? It's no wonder that we have a fucked up society, and the only surprise to me now is that we are not even worse than we are. I started in a school where the Catholic nuns beat us; then later on I went to a National School where we were also beaten by most, but not all of the teachers. One man I absolutely loved as a teacher in our National School was a man called Martin Kearney. In all of my days at that National School I never once saw Martin raise a hand to anyone, and what's more important, he managed to teach me more than all the others combined. Now that has to say something. So on reaching Pad Keely's college we were well used to being beaten, but not so hard and not so often.

In the Ireland of those days, our people were browbeaten and the parents were conditioned into believing that it was normal and expected that their children would get a few flakes at school, but not so my mother. However, she never knew about our beatings until years later when Kyrle 'spilled the beans' and refused to return to Pad's school.

Early on, Pad laid down the rules and we went from the odd flake to an almost daily ritual of beatings and insults of all kinds. Pad taught me maths, Irish, Latin, and later on science. Those were my terror subjects, especially algebra and (God help me) calculus: the scariest of them all. He should never have been a teacher of students of my IQ, as we just were not good enough for him to teach. I believe Pad understood maths like I later understood electronics. In my opinion he instinctively grasped the concepts and simply could not understand why we couldn't grasp them as well. The philosophy of fear kicked in and he tried to make us learn from fear of his stick, or his fist. Of course this had the opposite effect completely, and the more scared we became the less we could possibly learn. I remember being dragged up to the blackboard one day to explain Tan, Cosine, and Sine and getting beaten across the head for each one I got wrong, which was all three of them. In the end I resorted to playing the odds, and started guessing the answers. I guessed very wrong most of the time, with painful consequences. That beating gave me an everlasting terror of algebra and especially calculus. I get very angry now when I think of what happened to me that day because later on, when I had to do my electronic engineering exams, I had to teach myself maths all over again. Then I had to face down the fears of those memories and learn calculus all by myself. I discovered that it was a beautiful science, used in surveying, engineering astronomy and architecture, and that it was very old indeed. I discovered the most amazing thing, which was that I could measure the height of a tree without climbing it, and all I needed was a square of cardboard, a ruler and a basic knowledge of geometry. Had Pad been kind enough to give me that simple example, I know I would have loved that subject instead of having nightmares about it for years.

Pad's school was an 'all Irish' school as well. Basically whatever subjects that could be taught through the medium of the Irish language were taught through it. This meant that I initially hated the Irish language but eventually lost my fear of it, though having the grammar beaten into me didn't help. Ma taught us geography, history and French, and I can't remember what else. I know that she loved to teach history and was a real expert on it, especially European history, and she gave me a love for it that has remained with me today. To be fair to her, she was a far better teacher than her husband Pad, and you could tell she loved what she did. The one time she did beat me, which sticks out in my memory, was for the geography of Spain. I just could not get the names of the Spanish rivers right. The Guadalquiver was my downfall. No matter how I tried I could not remember its name. She gave me such a hiding for that failure that, even though only sixteen then, I promised myself that not alone would I never forget it again, but one day I would stand over it and spit into it. Many years later on a trip to Spain I kept my promise. I went to Seville, walked out to the middle of the main bridge and spat in the river saying, "I won today, and I'll never be beaten for you again". That day too I fell in love with Seville, so there was a good end to my ignorance and the hiding I got. I was a total dead loss at French though. It seemed to me to be a sissy's language. All that pronouncing and polished accents just didn't appeal to me at all. I was killed on a regular basis for this language too; so much so that I think in the end she just accepted that I could not learn it and gave up on me finally.

Monday morning was usually our worst day with Pad. He would arrive into the classroom singing, and if he had his old gown on, we knew we were really in for it. It's also a fair bet that the man might be sick with a hangover, but he never showed it. He would say, "Ceimseata," and, "Amach ar an line," the most dreaded words possible. 'Ceimseata' was the Irish word for 'geometry' and 'amach ar an line' meant 'out on the line'. It felt like we were waiting to die as we all formed a line heading for the executioner's examination of our work. Prior to this I would have arrived early at the classroom looking for a 'cog' from anyone better than me, which was easy. Unusually the better guys would arrive later though, and so the few boys who would even allow a cog were like gold. The way it worked was like so: the two of us needing the cog would sit on either side of the good student's workbook. This worked best for geometry as one would copy the drawing and the other boy would write the explanation of the drawing. Then we would swap sides and reverse the process. That way two students could do a cog at the same time with one of them holding the page up between them. This was of course totally forbidden by Pad, but he knew we were doing it and was always trying to catch us out.

One day Noellie Ryan from Knockbarry and I were sitting at either side of a copybook cogging away, when Pad arrived in early. It became a scene of utter confusion as the coggers scrambled to shut books and dash for their correct seats. "Cheimseata, agus amach air on line", and so it began. The line moved slowly along towards Pad who sat in a chair in front of the blackboard. I had been doing the proving part or the text part while Noellie had been doing the drawing, but neither of us had been finished when Pad made his surprise entrance. Now it was too late and we were both in big trouble, so we kept trying to sneak back along the line.

By the time Noellie got to Pad he had no text, just the drawing; the opposite of me. Pad asks him to explain the drawing, which should have had the text with it. Noellie has no idea and gets thumped around at the blackboard for a long time. Pad of course knew a cogger had been at work and became determined to make an example of the coggers that day. He called Noellie a Dunk and a Foolah and beat him around as he tried to explain his triangular drawing on the blackboard with no success.

Joe Hurley was next in line, as I had managed to scoot behind him in the confusion of Noellie's clattering. Hurley had got his cogging so wrong that he had only half of either side done. Pad was really furious by then, figuring that there were at least two obvious 'coggers' at work and he laid into Hurey. Joe got a real good hiding that day, but he was used to it by then, being useless at almost all things and swearing that he was immune to pain. And then it was my turn. I had been working on a plausible lie for Pad, getting ready to say that I had done the drawing out roughly at home and was meaning to add it later to my page, but I never got a chance to tell it.

Pad sees my perfect explanation of the theorem without any drawing at all: the most vital part, and knows of the third cogger. He holds up my copybook for the whole class to see. "Here we have the genius Cahill.... Cahill's such a genius that he's even better than the great Pythagoras, because our Cahill needs no drawing at all, isn't that so boys". The class confirms my skills with one voice. "Yes sir".

"Yes Cahill, you're the boyo alright. You can prove this teoragan without any drawing at all, isn't that so, you Dunk?" The word Dunk was his shortened version of donkey. I was trying to remain out of reach of his fist when suddenly I saw stars appear inside my brain. He had given me such a box across the head that I actually did literally see white stars flashing around inside my head. The force of the clatter was so strong that it also knocked one of the lenses out of my glasses, and that lens flew across the floor rolling under a desk. Pad then laid into me too, and I never forgot it. While he was beating me with his fist and his stick, I had just one lens in my glasses. These glasses were being held together by a 'band aid' across the nose, one of the legs was soldered permanently to the frame, and now a lens was gone too. I felt so poor, so vulnerable as the whole class looked on, glad it was me and not them. After the eternity of pain and humiliation, he threw my copybook at me and says, "Get out of my sight you Foolah, you'll only ever have a shovel boy, a shovel I tell you". Then I had to try and find my lost lens. I clearly remember going down on my knees in front of the class and creeping along the floor searching under the nearby desks, while Pad looked on. Typical of Hurley, who was by then sitting down at his desk in the front row and game for a laugh, he had put his foot over my lens hiding it from me. My friend Denis the Menace told me of this and I angrily jerked Hurley's leg from over it. The whole class, including Pad, laughed and my temper boiled up inside me. Then I needed to get my lens back in the glasses while Pad moved on to his next victim, giving me the odd sidelong look as he did so. As I struggled with the lens, the burning rage inside me grew more and more, and without warning I caught my copybook, held it up in front of me, and tore out the blank drawing page from it. This act of defiance I did right in front of Pad and the whole class. Then I balled it up and stuffed it into my bag. Pad stopped his examination of the latest victim and glared down at me. Standing defiantly, I glared back at him, as if taunting him to do his worst. He looked puzzled and then said sternly, "Cahill, sit down you Foolah, you'll have a shovel yet boy, I'm telling you so". I sat down and swore I would have revenge on him for that day.

It was not all black at that school though, but I could count on one hand the good days. One such time happened when Pad decided we should go on a school trip to beautiful Connemara. Connemara was the home of James Joyce and Padraig Pearse. These were people we learned about at school and Pad figured that it would be very educational if we went to their homeland and also had a day out for a change. The journey was by train to Galway and then on by bus to Salthill where we stopped to look around and have a walk by the sea. I have no idea how Nannie got the money for this trip and I can't remember Kyrle being there either, but Joe Hurley was for sure. Me and Hurley snuck off around the little town and in a lane we found a shop selling water pistols. I do know that I had some money because I suppose I had been collecting from all as usual, so Joe and I bought a gun each and headed back to the meeting place and the bus. We filled the guns somehow and began to squirt all the lads. Pretty soon these pistols became all the rage and we told them where to get them, which was not far up the street. Even though the bus was about to leave, there was an immediate exodus back to the shop and soon almost the whole class had these guns, all loaded and ready for action. We had delayed the bus and Pad was raging. No sooner were we in the bus than the war began. Joe and I were near the back and squirted the rows up ahead. Pad and Ma and another teacher I believe sat at the very front of the bus. To their credit they ignored the usual shouting and laughing that went on during such a trip, but this was getting out of hand. Pad came back and of course all the pistols vanished. He gave the usual orders in Gaelic, "Ciuineas buachailli ciuineas," meaning 'quiet now boys'. After a time the shooting began again, though somewhat reduced to sniggering and the odd outburst, as each boy fired then ducked and weaved behind the seats. Within a short time we had run out of water and I suppose Pad guessed that would happen, so he was ignoring the laughter again. True to form, Hurley says to me, "I'm gonna piss in mine, you up for it Cahill?" Of course I was, as we were being drowned by the Knockbarry gang at that point. We unscrewed the corks in the guns, got out our mickeys and tried to piss into the small hole: a very difficult job on a moving bus, and on the bad roads of

Connemara. I think we lost as much on the floor and over our hands as we got into the guns. As we are both pissing and hiding down behind the seats, we both looked across at each other and burst out laughing at the badness of what we were at. Then loaded and ready again, we see two of the boys' heads cautiously peer over the seat in front of us, both gawking in amazement as we try to stuff our mickeys back inside our pants. Joe fired immediately straight into the nearest boy's mouth and I missed my man. The stream of piss arched up over his head, drowning the guys farther up the bus. Someone shouts out loud, "Hey hey they're pissin in the guns lads," and he shouted this out so loud that Pad heard it and came tearing down the bus.

"Gimme, gimme those guns now...." No Gaelic this time. We surrender our weapons and he drew a swipe at Hurley who ducked and he missed him. Then Pad went to a vacant window and threw our guns right out into beautiful Connemara. No worries about littering in those days. The day went on and we saw an incredible seascape as the bus drove the coast road. An Spiddal was awesome and I tried to cheer Hurley up. All he would say was, "Fuck the scenery, I want my gun. Fucking Keely is a right ould bollix". Poor Joe just wasted the whole day sulking. We went on to the Gaeltacht and spoke Irish in the little village of Carraroe, then on to Maam Cross and the area of the 'Quiet Man' and my cowboy hero John Wayne. Huck Finn had by then almost disappeared from my mind, as the Wild West and Monument Valley had overtaken him. Later still we ended up back in Galway city where I bought my first and only chemistry set with the remainder of my money. It is as clear as day to me still how it looked. The box was red and had a great picture of glass tubes, a Bunsen burner with a flask, and some glass pipes with steam coming out of them. The box was sealed and when I got home it did not have any Bunsen burner or a flask either, but it did have a line of little glass tubes full of chemicals. Copper sulphate, iron filings, and some kind of red cobalt stuff which I never used because it looked like it would be too expensive to waste. I took this box around with me for the rest of the journey and Pad sees it and asks me "Cad e thu a Shean?" meaning 'what's that John'. I told him "It's a chemistry set sir", knowing no Irish for that stuff. He took the box and studied it carefully and seemed genuinely interested, giving it back to me with a look of disbelief. I think he felt it was wasted on a donkey or road worker with only a shovel, but he didn't say any more. That chemistry set began a love of science that remains with me to this day.

Pad too took up science a little while later. He built a science room in a shed at the back of the school. I believe my little chemistry set sowed the seed in his mind. This was my favourite place in the whole school. He had all kinds of gear in his lab and I loved it. Pad was more into physics than chemistry though, which was bad for me, as despite Pad's hidings, I was still poor at the physics maths but brilliant at chemistry. I loved the way mixing two dangerous substances such as chlorine and sodium could give you a bit of harmless table salt. I loved making hydrogen using a battery and some water and watching it pop as it burned. Everything about the subject fascinated me and I knew it was not Pad's strong point, so he taught physics more often than chemistry. He gave me a great hiding one day for getting the maths wrong on a 'latent heat' experiment. I almost developed a fear for physics after that carry on, but that fear is now long gone, replaced by a love for all things scientific.

Joe Hurley, as usual, got up to devilment in this science room. He managed to set fire to the lab and almost gassed us all in the process. During one of these rare chemistry classes, Pad was showing us a jar of phosphorus or potassium, I am not sure which now. It was either kept under water or oil, but I know it would burn fiercely in air. Pad took a tiny piece of it out of its jar with a metal tongs and showed it to us. It suddenly burst into flame, creating an acrid choking white smoke. Pad railed on about how dangerous this chemical was. Of course the word danger was an automatic 'file to be used later' signal in Joe's head. Joe, who was sitting near me, says, "Hey lad that's some stuff isn't it". Pad is glaring at us and shouts out, "Shut up ye Foolahs. Look below at the two Dunks, knowing it all". Hurley puts his head down and pretends to be writing, but gives me this sidelong look which he knew would make me laugh; it always did. I had to look away quickly or we would both get killed. Pad then left the room for some reason and seemed gone for a long time. Hurley decided he would teach the class in Pad's absence and mock Pad at the same time. Up he goes to the front of the class where he starts calling us all 'Foolahs' and

'Dunks' and 'Street Urchins'. "Get down off the tree boy, and get a shovel you Dunk". All were well used phrases of Pad Keely. Joe soon began marching up and down in front of the class, imitating the great man so well that I hoped he would never stop. The whole class collapsed laughing as his imitation was so good. He shouts out, "Cahill, come up here you Dunk, and show us this phosphorus stuff". I say, "No way, I'm not going near it, no way". "Get up here you stupid Foolah or I'll tan your arse so bad you won't shit for a week." This was Joe's original saying, and he's then playing the part of our teacher to perfection. It was hilarious. He had the face of Pad, the glare of Pad, the correct wording of Pad and then he made a drive down to my seat, and pulled me out by the ear. We could see if Pad was coming back as he had to cross a yard, and I saw Joe give a cursory glance out the window as he was dragging me up to the front. I'm shouting, "No sir, no sir, you're hurting my ear sir". "Stand there you half eegit. I'll get the phosphorus and you'll demonstrate it to the class, isn't that right boys". "Yes sir," they all shout out. I had a bad feeling about all of this as Joe was by then laughing, and he had his 'evil' look on his face. When he got that 'evil' look I knew it always meant trouble. In a big show of 'Padism' he grabs the phosphorus jar from the shelf, but just as he did so he spotted Pad returning across the yard. He shouts out, "Pad's back," and tries to put the jar back on the shelf as I make a run for our desk. In so doing I knocked Hurley aside. The inevitable happened and the bloody jar fell on the floor and exploded. It's then like the Fourth of July in the science room just as Pad comes in the door. We are all choking and coughing and trying to get out, and he starts shouting, "Out, out, get out, get out". He pushed his way in towards the fire, and just as fast he rushed back out again. The smoke or the fire beat him back. He is shouting for us to get water, but we don't lift a finger. Everyone just looked at each other. We didn't give a damn if the whole lab burned down, with all of us quite happy at Pad's misery. Total confusion reigns, as by then the whole room has filled with the acrid white smoke which began pouring out the door. The room was either on fire or filling with gas. We always felt it was on fire, but I suppose in truth it was not so bad, and just looked worse than it was. In any case we were quite happy with the events that were transpiring before us. While all this was going on and the class was standing around in the yard (or hiding in the sheds like me and Hurley), Hurley sees a big mound of potatoes over to one side. He says to me, "Hey lad, look at Pad's spuds. I'd love to piss on em. Can't do it now though, he'd see me for sure, but I'll do it tomorrow". This was Joe at his very best. Not alone had he almost burned down the lab, but he saw yet another opportunity for fun, and was already planning it. I think he was still out for revenge for his water pistol on the Galway trip. The excitement was soon over in about twenty minutes, and Pad then began the inevitable post mortem. He lined us all up in the yard and marched up and down the line. "Who did this?" he shouted. No one made a sound. Hurley began fidgeting and looking around and Pad spotted him. He made a drive for Joe, who then felt it was all over, and he took off running straight out the main gate with Pad on his heels. He never returned to Pad's school. It was the talk of the school for ages and Joe became everyone's hero; fame at last. Expulsion was automatic. Nannie was right once again and I was warned to stay away from Joe Hurley as the Devil was stuck inside of him.

That school had such an effect on me that even after I had long left it, I was having nightmares about it for years. I would wake up sweating, thinking I had no homework ready, then realise that I was gone from it. I did get my revenge in the end, but it was a pyrrhic victory.

Some years later, when I was almost eighteen, I was asked to join a public speaking team in Buttevant. By then I had been well gone from Pad's school and had a huge chip on my shoulder from those earlier days. By a fluke, the subject I was asked to speak on was 'corporal punishment'. That was one I knew only too well from personal experience, as did all those others who had gone through Pad's school.

The first heat of this public speaking competition took place in a small hall in Dromina, not far from Buttevant, and the hall was almost full on the night. I was to speak for four minutes, then take questions from the judges. I had written a speech which was greatly critical of this form of education, and as I was sitting listening and waiting for my turn on stage, who do I see arrive into the hall but Pad Keely. He sat some three rows from the back and my blood boiled over at the sight of him. Then remembering my glasses day and my oath of revenge, I saw that Pad still had his same smug look of superiority on him and the more I saw it, the madder I got. Temper and fury took over, and I could not wait for my turn to speak. I was last to speak and spent the time glaring down at Pad from the stage. He did not even acknowledge my presence. This 'Foolah' that he had taught now had a rage burning inside him, and was far from needing a shovel on that night. The chairman then spoke, "And finally we have John Cahill who will speak on the subject of corporal punishment in schools. Over to you John". I started my intro, "Ladies and gentlemen, my subject tonight is corporal punishment, and here I have prepared some notes..... but I don't need them." With those words I threw my sheets of paper out into the audience saying, "Because I intend to give you all a detailed description of just one of my schooldays in Buttevant". A lull suddenly came over the whole audience. This was not the done thing, and all could sense it. Something was going to happen here tonight. Pad was well known for his teaching methods, but no one ever dared to challenge him, but that night I was going to change all that.

Over the next four minutes, I described a random day from memory for me in the school. I described the fear of going to school, the beatings, the hatred for our national Irish language, and the stress of trying to do homework you knew was always half guesswork. I described the constant insults and browbeatings we were given, and I did all this in a way that showed my anger was rising. You could hear a pin drop in that hall as I was coming to the end of my speech. I finished by speaking directly to the audience saying, "And that, ladies and gentlemen, was just one day at Pad Keely's school in Buttevant where I was taught for five years, and Mr. Keely is here in the audience tonight. He is sitting there at the back of the hall, and I challenge him to call me a liar". He recognised me then alright. Pad got up and left the hall. A cheer went up. I got a standing ovation, first marks too, and we won the competition that night. The nightmares only got worse. That night I saw Pad like the Fourth Horseman of the Apocalypse coming for me. I awoke in terror, sweating profusely. The only plus that came from it all was that I have never had a fear of public speaking since that night, and that wonderful gift has stood to me well over the years. It's sad for me to say that I absolutely hated Pad Keely. I never hated anyone in life like I hated him. I told everyone of the type of teaching he gave to us, or the lack of it. I have to say that I took personally all that had happened to me in that school, and I deeply resented all that he did to us. I specifically resented the fact that Pad never entered Kyrle or me in the Young Scientist Exhibition, which we would easily have won, especially in its early years. At that time we were making electronic projects so far in advance of our age that we were light years ahead of those students who were actually winning the event. It would have given us a scholarship and a future in science, and also brought great prestige to his school. Pad never even asked us to take part, and I never understood why. It was as if he resented our obvious abilities in that area. Most of all though, I hated to be beaten in front of my brother Kyrle, who would be sitting in the class with their backs to us. It was a terrible feeling of shame indeed.

Kyrle did bring honours to the school, or at least in Pad's eyes he did. He got more honours in his Intermediate Certificate than anyone ever before, including Pad's own children. Pad was so proud of his teaching methods that he decided to personally deliver the Certificate to the mother. A big mistake indeed, as by then Kyrle told her the truth about the beatings and the name-calling and how he was known as a 'donkey' and a 'street urchin'. When Pad called home, father met him and he too knew of our school days by then, but he also knew that mother would be better able to handle it. He told Pad that mother was over at Kit's doing her bar work, and she would love to get 'the good news'. The bar was full when Pad walked in. He had such a presence and was held in such awe in those days that when he entered a room, it was like the parting of the Red Sea as he moved to the counter, and to the mother. She saw him and her temper rose. "My dear Mrs. Cahill, I am the bearer of great news. Your son Kyrle has achieved the highest honours in my school, and I bring you his certificate". There was a long pause as mother just looked at him at the bar counter. He hands her the certificate and she takes it gracefully, still not saying a word. The pause goes on and on until Pad finally says, "My dear aren't you happy? What do you have to say about this great news?" Mother looks directly at him and says, "Well Mr. Keely, I'd like you to answer me just one question". "Yes of

131

course my dear, what do you want to know?"

"Well you're a very educated man Mr. Keely, so please tell me this. How could my son Kyrle, a donkey and street urchin, possibly get such a great result? Can you answer me that...can you?" Stunned silence followed, but Pad said nothing. The whole bar waited in shocked silence as everyone expected some answer from the great man, but none came. Pad just turned on his heels and walked out. As he left, the cheer that went up from the bar was ringing in his ears. Neither Kyrle nor I ever returned to his school. Instead, we were headed for Charleville, and numerous other adventures there.

In the end, after years of nightmares, after trying everything I knew to get even and finding that nothing worked, I came to the simple conclusion that all I had left was forgiveness. He was doing the best that he could do to drum knowledge into ignorant students, as he saw us. I am totally sure that he never took any pleasure from the hidings he gave us, unlike others of that era. I believe he himself was an incredibly intelligent man, and was just so frustrated at our inability to learn what was simple for him that he resorted to fear and violence as a last resort, believing that we were just too lazy to learn. The only time he ever let down his guard and showed any kindness to me was during a carol singing session on one Christmas Eve. Every year he would make the whole school learn carols and sing them as we marched around the town at Christmastime. This particular year he decided that we should also play music. We were all going to became flageolet players. This was great in theory and we learned the Adepter Fiddles in the comfort of a poorly heated school in early November. However, the reality of the Christmas week cold with biting freezing winds and no gloves was a different story. We were to do two nights of caroling. After the first night of freezing and singing, most of the students decided to either give up the whole business, or did not bring their flageolets at all on the second night. In fact the only music being provided that night was by myself and his daughter, who played the accordion. When we were gathering to begin the march, he arrived, and seeing no one with instruments except me and his daughter, he looked at me and smiled saying, "Math an fear a Shean," meaning 'good man John'. I was so pleased at his remark that I played my heart out that night and noticed him smiling at me proudly now and again. It's a sad thing to go through a school for five or six years and only remember one happy word from your headmaster, yet there was no badness in the man, but it took me years to discover that fact.

I was visiting the Nannie one evening and we heard the funeral bell toll above in the church. Nannie said, "John close the door, and you should go to that funeral. Pad Keely is dead". Rather curtly I told her that I'd rather dance on his grave than honor him with my presence in a false display of sorrow. She just shook her head and said, "Sure he educated you, didn't he? And anyways, what harm did it do you?" Her words stuck in my head all the rest of the night, and later I could not sleep, tossing and turning in bed all night long. It was then that it hit me, and I realised the power of forgiveness. I spoke to him in my mind and he came to me in my thoughts asking me to forgive him, which I did truly and honestly from my Soul. From the very moment I did this forgiving, I felt a huge weight lift from me, but strangely too it seemed to lift from Pad as well. I could clearly feel him smile at me again, just like that Christmas many years earlier. He thanked me and said he was sorry, and then he disappeared from my mind never to return until now. Was it all in my imagination, did I just dream of him? I am sure not. Since that night I never again had a nightmare about Pad or his school, and now only think of him and that Christmas when he tried to make musicians of us all. As he would say himself of another friend passed over, 'Ar dheis De go raibh a anam ailis, may he rest in peace'.

Big Kyrl adventures.

I think I was born curious. I believe most children are naturally curious, but it's driven out of them by many outside factors. The obvious one is parents who unintentionally instill fear rather than self-confidence into their children. They do this by almost daily telling the children what they can't do rather than convincing them that they can and should do everything humanly possible to enjoy the gift of a wonderful life. My mother had a great saying, often quoted by me to all and sundry. She would say, "John, do everything you can when you're young because when you're old, you'll only have your memories". I absolutely love that advice and as a family we were so lucky to all receive it. The other area that parents could help is in encouraging their children to read, read, read, at all costs. Father would say a book is the entrance to another man's mind. Naturally then our houses were always full of books even though mother only ever read one full book in her life. She had this mad idea that if you read a few pages of the front, a bit of the back and some random bits in the middle, then that's the book read. Her method was pathetic, and that's why we relied on father for almost all of our knowledge of the world, and on mother for our security and love when that same world beat us up. Our 'video games' were numerous old books with tattered pages, comics and the odd magazine, with drafts and chess for added excitement.

Naturally these books prompted numerous discussions and arguments, and all these arguments would lead us to develop huge egos. This, I believe, lead us rightly or wrongly to an odd kind of self-confidence. We developed a self-confidence based on the book knowledge we had, and insecurity from the poverty we lived through. I know that even today my mind still swings between those two powerful memories.

My first memory of anything electronic was seeing an old triode valve lying sideways on the mother's cabinet in our back kitchen.

This cabinet doubled up as a place where she kept her cutlery, her cleaning cloths and the little food she could muster. One of the drawers was always dedicated to father's collection of small tools, and his never ending supply of six inch nails. I would say I was about twelve or thirteen when I saw the valve, and I took it in to the father and asked him what it was. In his unique and gentle way, he explained to me what this valve was and what it did. I know now that everything he told me was technically correct, though at the time it seemed like sheer magic to me.

Little did he know that his words would set me on a career that has brought me amazing adventures, earned me a great living and would eventually lead to many electronic ideas, inventions, and two US patents on a device to prevent the killer condition known as deep vein thrombosis. I got so fascinated with father's words that I spent hours with him questioning and trying to understand this awesome electronic magic. He never once got tired of my unending questions either. After spending a whole night interrogating the father, my head was about to explode with excitement. I think that day and night I exhausted all my dad's knowledge on the subject, and there was nothing for it now but to find some books to extend my overwhelming curiosity on the subject known as 'electronics'.

By a great stroke of good fortune, Buttevant was to be given a stop for a mobile library. The mobile library was to me the single greatest asset that the government had provided for rural Ireland. It used to come around every two weeks and would park outside the local bank. A borrower could take out only two books from the adult section, and I think one from the children's section. By then Kyrle had also been bitten by the electronic bug because we began to think that we could use this knowledge to build a radar early warning system to save our submarine from future attacks. So the day the van arrived we went straight down and joined, hoping for books on electronics or 'radio' as it was known then. The librarian made it clear to us that we were not old enough for the adult books, where we had seen a great collection of American radio books. So we ran back home and got both mother and father to join and we picked the electronics books for them to take out for us. Obviously this was spotted by the librarian who was utterly amazed that two children should be planning to read such advanced technical books, but he had no choice but to allow it. We then had four radio books to read. It is a fact that before the week was out we had read then all from cover to cover, and both of us were beginning a second read on the second week.

I know I literally absorbed the knowledge. I soaked in this magic and Kyrle did the same. We could not wait for the next visit and more books. After about a month of this tricking with father and mother, the librarian just said one day, "Lads just take whatever books ye want, it's ok". We became quite friendly with that kind man, and he always did his best to have the most modern radio books available for us, ultimately ending with television books before the mobile service ceased and we had left Buttevant.

The minute I would read about a circuit I would want to build it, just to see how it worked or even if it worked. Kyrle did too, but he was always more patient than me and would always have some purpose before he began to building anything. Our main problem was that we had almost no parts, and early on we began to search all the local dumps for old radios. No place was safe from us then, as we searched everywhere: sheds, lanes, and quarries. Big Kyrl had his cinema going by then and he had two Vortexon amplifiers driving the sound into his picture hall. He had some spare Mullard valves which we stole, as well as a load of carbon rods for other experiments, and our stock began to build.

The very first thing I learned in electronics was the colour code for resistors and how to read the values by the little coloured bands painted on the components. It was at about this time that Kyrle and I began our arguments on how circuits worked. The books were by then all read many times over, and it's amazing how we could get different views on how things worked from a book. In the end, father became the inevitable adjudicator. All the arguing ultimately did was to hone our skills and we both developed different ways of doing things. Whenever we decided to build a new circuit, each of us did it in different ways and Kyrle's method was the correct one for sure. He would not start to build a thing until he had every single correct component ready. Then he would slowly and carefully build it, and it would virtually always work first time. I'd be far too impatient for that, and in my case, the minute I decided what I was making, I'd be off building immediately. It did not matter to me what components I had, or what I was missing; I'd make do and just build away for the sheer fun of it. Virtually none of my yokes ever worked first time while Kyrle's always did. It's not surprising as electronics is an exact science. But these failures never upset me for some reason. Often Kyrle would be gloating and snickering at me, and many times we ended in a punch up, but the unwritten rule was no damage must ever be done to our parts. It was from my struggle to get devices working that I learned most, and oftentimes my solution made the circuit work even better than the original, or my device turned into something completely different. Those years of building and 'doctoring' as I called my method, were to serve me greatly over the coming years.

After we built many sound amplifiers I got tired of it. I wanted to build an oscillator, which is the heart of a radio transmitter, but I could never get one to work. I tried and tried for weeks with no success. My building method was the problem of course. In the end, and close to desperation, I convinced Kyrle that we should do a joint effort, with me promising to do it his way. He agreed and our parts collecting began again. We both knew the circuit inside out, especially me after my numerous failures, so it was down to getting every component correct, and winding the coils properly and exactly. Eventually he got it made, despite our many rows in between, but when he powered it up I was sure it would work. What we had finally made was an oscillator which was in effect a low power radio transmitter. When it was powered up, I tore down the stairs from our attic to the radio below in the kitchen to see if it worked and it did, as Kyrle had managed to wipe out Radio Eireann, our national station. I let out a huge yell. "It works, it works, Kyrle it works", I shouted wildly as I ran back up the stairs, bringing the father's radio with me as proof.
Kyrle had this strange look of disbelief as I plugged in our radio and waited for the valves to warm up. We stuck in a bit of wire as an aerial and blotted out Radio Eireann once again. Both of us shook hands, and it reminds me of Harry Potter and their code of honour. Now that we had a transmitter, what would we do with it next?
Father was called immediately. We knew it was a waste of time showing mother, as she had no idea what we had done, and father

says, "Boys o'boys, that's great. Now bring the radio back down, I want to hear the news". I looked at Kyrle in disbelief because I saw the significance of the device, and Kyrle said, "Sure he's sozzled, he don't get it at all. Better take down the ould radio though". I went home to Nannie's that night with my head spinning again. I felt deep inside me that an extraordinary event had taken place; that we had done something truly amazing which would have a bearing on my future, but I couldn't fully grasp what that might be. I know that I couldn't sleep when I was in bed. I spent most of the time going over and over just one question. How far would this radio wave travel? Next day in Pad's school I could not concentrate at all: a dangerous game in that place. All I could think about was how could we make it work better.

In those days we used to have our hair cut by the local barber, a man called Batt Thornhill. He was a very famous sportsman in Buttevant and was a good friend of our family. I suppose every month or so we had to get our hair cut and I know we never paid him for it. I know too that neither of us had a clue about sports, and no matter how Batt tried to get us interested, it never worked. In the end he just gave up, and no doubt from then on saw us as two non-paying customers wasting his time on a busy Saturday. I think he could never get rid of us fast enough, and would chop like mad; dragging and tearing at our heads just to see the back of us faster. Beggars can't be choosers, and we were often the laughing stock of school friends after such a cutting, but I'm sure there were other reasons for their mirth besides our hair, such as my round glasses making me resemble the cartoon character Magoo. In any case we both decided that we needed to get even with Batt whose Sunday games were his weak point. To a lesser extent we felt that the evening news was also a weak point, and that turned out to be far more serious for us. We decided to silence both the news and the games on Batt's radio. The fact that it would also silence father's radio downstairs was of no concern to either of us at the time.

A debate began about how long the aerial wire should be for the radio signal to cross the street to Batt's house, and to be sure of success I insisted that we run a wire all the way out to the aerial pole on the priest's shed next door: an easy task for us who were like two cats at the climbing. We did this work and all was soon ready. News time came around and we had the kitchen radio turned on, tuned to Radio Eireann as usual. Kyrle powers up the oscillator and sure enough the news disappeared from the radio in the kitchen; just a swishing silence remained. We left our oscillator on and went across the street to Nannie's house, passing Batt's shop on the way. As cool as a breeze we wander in to Nannie's, and there is Michael in a panic tuning the radio like mad. He had no news either, and he was a good distance further away from our attic. I gave Kyrle the knowing look, and Michael says to me, " Chicken, any idea what is wrong with the ould radio? T'was working grand a few minutes ago, and I want to hear the news". Nannie pipes up immediately and says, "Yer not touchin that radio, I forbid it, leave it as it is". She knew that we were well known electronic experimenters by then and didn't want her radio broken. I feign a bit of knob twiddling and says, "Tis probably the valves are gone," hoping she might still say to take it away and we would have even more parts to play with, but no, she just told me to leave it alone. We left and headed for Batt's shop to see if we could hear the news there, but he's standing at the door looking up and down the street and seems a bit perplexed. So now we are sure that our plan was working and we have taken our first steps at revenge on Batt for his rough scalping. About a half hour passed by and we turned it off; then Radio Eireann mysteriously returned to all. We sat in the attic just giggling and talking low and looking forward to Sunday's match. I don't think it was an All Ireland Final, but we silenced it just the same, as well as knocking out the odd news bulletin for the next few days. Over the next three weeks or so we just enjoyed the whole thing and blotted out programmes at random. I suppose initially people just felt it was that the radio service had gone off, but when it became a bit too regular, people complained to the Department of Post and Telegraphs and they sent out two tracking vans with rotating aerials to investigate the problems unique to Buttevant.

Unknown to us they were zeroing in on our transmission, and by the luck of God Kyrle spotted one of them slowly driving up the main street as he got fags for the mother. He ran in and tore upstairs shouting all the time, "Turn off, turn off!" He was as red as a tomato as he pulled out all the plugs, shaking like a leaf. "We're caught, we're caught, the van, the van's on the street...tracking" I ran over and looked out the attic window and there it was, stopped right outside Batt's shop where we can see Batt chatting to the engineer about some match, or his lack of a radio service.

Of course that ended our silencing days. What we did not know at the time, but heard much later, was that our little oscillator on its very big aerial had not just silenced Batt's radio, but it had in fact also wiped out every radio for about a mile around. Basically the whole of Buttevant had no radio service when we were 'on the air'. Fortunately for us we were never actually caught, as the father would have been taken to court and fined. We were too young to be prosecuted, but after a while the word leaked out that it was 'them mad Cahills' that had wiped out the radios in the town. Many years later that local story was to be remembered by one of four businessmen who were starting a pirate radio station in Mallow, and who were having no luck technically: until they called on me. That call would change my life, but first I had a lot of living still to do.

Even though I loved electronics, it was not my only pastime. I also loved films, playing hurling and handball, but from an early age I think I loved playing practical jokes on people, and hated being the butt of such jokes played back on me. I almost always got into some kind of trouble over these jokes as well, but it never stopped me from taking an opportunity when it arose. On one occasion while on a visit to my Aunt May's house in Waterford, and being about fourteen years old then, my practical joking got a bit out of hand. That incident was the cause of me being violently thrown out of the cinema in Waterford city. I think it was called the Ritz and I'm sure it is now probably long gone. It happened to be showing a horror film about some kind of a hand that was choking people to death. I can't remember the name of it right now, but this was supposed to be a great horror film and I wanted to see it for weeks. I got to go see it on a Sunday matinee, but I had the great misfortune of sitting behind two girls who never stopped talking all through the film. I was sick of telling them to shut up, but I was getting nowhere with them. Worse still for me was the fact that one of them had already seen the film, and she kept telling her friend of all the good scary parts coming up. I was livid by the time the intermission came round, and so I decided action was needed. I went out to the shop and bought two 'iced lollypops' and held them in my hands so as to freeze my hands and turn them into iced claws. Even though in pain, I was waiting patiently for an appropriate 'good part' to arrive. It was summertime and the girls were wearing dresses with low cut backs: sitting ducks for my master plan. During a scene where the hero was driving through a forest in a thunderstorm, and where the claw was making its way across the seat and about to choke him; I suddenly dropped my lollies and 'clawed' both of the girls on the back of the neck. The shock they got was incredible. One of them literally leaped about two foot clean out of her seat and into the air. The other girl almost fainted. Then the screaming started. It was way beyond what I could have expected. A panic took over the crowd, and it got so bad that all the lights soon came on. The girls were shaking and clutching each other, trembling all the time. They were so scared that those beside them became frightened too. Some people were trying to console them and some were leaving the cinema in terror. It was mayhem and I had caused all of this. By then it was damage limitation time for me, and as I was trying to look innocent. I kept trying to kick the damn lollies down under the seats in front; hiding the evidence so to speak. At the same time some fucker kept pointing at me and shouting, "He did it, he did it, I saw him". The bouncers were very mad and roughly dragged me by the scruff of the neck clean out of my seat and kicked my arse all the way out to the front door. There they literally threw me out onto the street. As I pulled myself up from the pavement I was cheeky enough to go back into the ticket office and demand a refund, saying I had only seen half the film. The ticket seller shouted back in to the bouncers, "He's back, he's back," and when they made a drive for me, I felt I'd forget the refund and took off running. I could see from the expression on their faces that I was in for a real hiding if they caught me, as by then loads of people were leaving and demanding their money back. I had managed to ruin the film for all concerned, but I still blame the girls for it.

It was also during one of my many trips to Aunt May's in Waterford that I had another one of my many near death escapes. Aunt May lived in Sallypark, a housing area on the northern side of the River Suir. The main road into Waterford ran along in front

141

of the houses and then crossed over a railway bridge going into Waterford's railway station. This bridge was very dangerous as it was very steep and the road made a sharp zig zag as it crossed over it. Each Sunday my cousin Michael and I would be dispatched off to Mass, crossing this bridge via the narrow footpath. On this particular Sunday, Michael and I were walking alone to Mass and had got to the middle of the zig zag part of the bridge when an old-style milk tanker came rapidly around behind us. It was closely followed by a small car full of Mass goers. The tanker had its tanks arranged in rows, unlike how it's done today, and the speed of the truck and the zig zag pattern of the road caused the rear tank to roll off the back of the truck. It missed me by literally a foot and then it squashed four of the five people in the car travelling close behind it. They were probably killed instantly, and the milk and blood washed over my legs as I was that close to it all. I'll never forget the screams of agony of the old lady I saw crushed before me that day. In shock, we just continued on to Mass and thought no more about it until later that day at dinner time when Aunt May said, "Did you lads hear of the terrible accident on the bridge?" I piped up and said, "Yeah sure we were there right when it happened, we saw it all happen," and I went back to eating my dinner. Silence descended on Aunt May and her husband Barry. My Aunt May then looked across at Barry and then slowly and gently they began to ask us about it, but they did not pursue it too much. Later that day Barry said he would take Michael and me for a drive, and as he did so, in a very gentle way, he wormed out of us all that had happened. I believe Barry is the reason I don't have nightmares from that terrible tragedy, as I was only about fourteen years old then and I had seen four people die violently just feet from me. I never forgot the scene as I glanced back at it. Almost all the car was squashed flat and was under the tank with milk still pouring out and running down the road under my feet. Fortunately, to my knowledge at least, that incident never affected me traumatically and shows that we are all surely protected throughout our lives. It was one of my early escapes from passing over, but by no means my last, and my next one would be caused by my Uncle Kyrl. Both Kyrle and I worked for him for long periods at various times in our early years, and on one occasion his work was almost the death of me.

He was in his monumental works phase and had been given the job of removing a huge headstone to have it sanded down, re-lettered and new names added. This idea of removing a stone was very unusual for him, as most of the times he would letter a new headstone in the workshop, or have it lettered locally in the graveyard using the father as letterer 'on contract'. Payment would amount to a few pints for my dad.

On this particular occasion though, we were taking the stone back to some isolated cemetery deep in County Limerick and it was wintertime. I know that it had been raining for days because we were supposed to return the stone some time earlier, and he could not do it because of the rain. Kyrl had a lot of handymen available as casual labourers and one incredibly good friend of his called John O'Brien, affectionately known to us all as 'Black John'. He got this name because he had jet black hair, looked scruffy always, and was as strong as a black stallion. On the day in question, Kyrl called in all his crew; myself included, though Kyrle was not around for some reason. Black John was there, as were two other men; one called Buddo Reilly and I think his son also, or it might have been Black John's son. So in the rapidly failing light, we five set off for the wilds of Limerick.

Kyrl drove a big horse of an old car which was attached to a huge trailer by a makeshift hitch. The massive stone and all our tools, plus a few bags of cement had filled the trailer to bursting point, and I had a bad feeling about the whole trip. We set off heading north to Charleville. I was in the back, wedged tightly between Buddo and the other lad, and both of them were smoking like chimneys. According to Kyrl, my job was to keep the World War Two jerrycan, which was filled to the brim with petrol, from spilling out and being 'wasted'. He did not seem to feel a cover was needed because he had me acting as a human cork, with my hand permanently jammed across the top of the jerrycan. The fumes were almost making me giddy, but I was scared to death that a stray spark from a cigarette or 'fag' would set us all alight. Every so often Nannie's words about 'fire following them Cahills' would surface and scare me to death. This almost happened when Buddo's companion, trying to look cool, flicked his cigarette butt at the open window. Even though I saw it go out, it flew back in again and landed on his lap. He started panicking and began kicking at the can, trying to prevent his mickey from burning. I too began panicking and screaming that he was going to knock it over if we didn't stop. Of course Kyrl just kept on driving, and both he and Black John exploded laughing at my panic. Black John then says, "Hey lad, your uncle Michael named you well, sure your notten but an ould chicken, bawk bawk," and more laughter ensued from all the gang. I got so red in the face that I almost set the damn petrol on fire by myself, and I still have no idea where the flying cigarette went. Kyrl never slowed down either, or seemed to care that we might all burn; me being the first.

The journey went downhill fast from then on, and we soon got totally lost. Kyrl never once used a map in his life. I don't think he could read one, and we drove round in circles, by then in the pitch black of a November evening. No one seemed to care about time though, as we were set on the idea that the stone had to be erected before more rain hit.

On we went, all the time discussing where we might be. Suddenly, out of the foggy gloom, I saw what looked like an old castle on our left with our road travelling on up over a large steep humpy bridge. I remember seeing the headlights shine like two searchlights going straight up into the fog as Kyrle drove on up the bridge. Almost immediately, and with total shock, I saw the lights dip right down into a huge fast flowing river straight in front of us. We were going to drown for sure. "Fuck, Fuck, Fuck," shouts Kyrl as he slams on the brakes, but the sheer weight of the big stone pushed us forward into the river, and with a huge splash, the front of the car went completely underwater with the lights remaining on. The whole scene felt very eerie as I could see steam mix with the lights in the fast-flowing muddy water which was fast entering the front of the car. In total panic we all scrambled to escape our impending death while Kyrl kept shouting, "Out, out will ye".

In total panic we all began to push open the doors and jump out into the raging flood. The minute I got out into the water it caught hold of me, and I could feel the current pulling and tearing at me as I had jumped out on the wrong side of the car. I felt no cold from the water, just a sheer terror and a desire to live come over me. The water was soon up to my waist, and to save myself from being swept away, I tried to hold onto the car door. Even though all this drama was happening fast, it seemed to me to be going on in a kind of slow motion and I saw the others all around me moving real slowly. I felt sure that my life was over, when Black John grabbed hold of my jacket. I grabbed hold of his hands, and both of us waded to safety clutching onto the car as we went. I know without doubt that he saved my life that night, and to my shame I don't ever remember even thanking him because I was so frightened.

To this day I can recall that sinking feeling that we were all going to drown there and then, and that I was too young to die in that place. I think the trailer both saved us and almost drowned us because the fast moving current just could not move the car while the trailer was attached to it, and by pure luck, the trailer was still on the road. After the initial shock wore off, which in Kyrl's case was after about five minutes, he says to Black John, "John, I think we need to take off the trailer and push the bitch out of this water. What do you think?" Never as much as 'that was a close one lads' or 'are ye all ok there, anyone been drowned' for example. No, not Kyrl. He had a stone to erect, and by God he would do it that night. Failure was not an option for him. As he saw it, no one had drowned and we couldn't stay there all night, so we had to do something. This was always Kyrl's way of dealing with any crisis: take immediate and decisive action. It did not matter whether that action was right or wrong, as long as you did something, it was all ok. I loved that way of thinking, as you always felt he would get you out of the situation somehow and he always did.

After a bit of a debate, it was decided that we had to risk being swept away once again, so we were going to have to go back into the water and push the car out from the front. As if to quell the obvious fear of the river, Kyrl kept saying, "Tis not a fucken river, tis a flood across the road. Under the water is the road, and it's as solid as a rock, so let's get at it lads". I believe he simply would not accept in his mind that there was a huge current of water crossing this road, and he just did not believe in danger of any kind. But I knew that I was not going back into that river no matter what he said. We detached the trailer and saw that the car only moved another foot or two in the current, but at least it did not get swept away. With Kyrl and Black John first in, despite misgivings, the rest of us followed and after a struggle, we pushed the car right back out of the flood. Kyrl then got at the engine and kept at it until it spluttered into life. Then with a big cheer we re-attached the trailer and headed back the road to some pub he had passed earlier. We went in soaked, cold, and hungry, and in my case trembling and still scared to death. There they gave us tea and drink as we told of our escape. Most of that part of the night is a blur to me now, as I think I was constantly shivering more with fright than from cold, and I kept thinking about what had happened earlier. They told us where the graveyard was and that it was nearer than we thought, so then at about eight o'clock at night, we arrived at the gates of the cemetery. Even though still wringing water from our clothes, we had the stone erected by midnight. I think I was about sixteen years old then, and all they could talk about on the way home was how I was so scared of fire when it was really water I should have been scared of. Peals of laughter continued over and over with Black John and Buddo later arguing over the name of the river that had almost drowned us all. I believe it was the river Maigue, and I often pass over it these days with a shiver running up my spine. When I eventually got home around two in the morning Nannie was waiting and distracted with worry, having had a bad feeling all day as well. I just told her it was a long day and that we got soaked. I'd say she felt it better not to ask about the job, as her John was alive and home and gone to his bed exhausted.

Uncle Kyrl had no sense of danger whatsoever. During the winter he used a home-made gas heating system to heat his picture hall. It was plumbed like a water system, and he and Black John had done all that work in an afternoon. That plumbing was so bad that it was always leaking gas, and the joke in Buttevant was that Kyrl Cahill's hall had the best pictures ever, because you got the 'real experience' in his hall. If Kyrl was showing a film about the gas attacks of World War One, then you got actually gassed in his hall as you watched. Even more likely though, and as if to add further realism to your experience, you also ran the risk of being blown to atoms by an impending gas explosion because of those leaks. Kyrl saw it differently though. He saw this gas leaking as a 'complete waste' of his gas, and it had to be sorted before the winter ended, so one Sunday he asked me if I had a 'good nose' on me. When I assured him that I did, he told me to join him in the hall for some gas fixing work. I was all for an extra few bob until he and his cohort, Black John, told me their plan was to turn the gas full on from the huge tank out the back, and then go along the pipes with a lighting cigarette lighter, all the while watching for 'the little' flame that would erupt at the gas leak. I thought they were joking at first, but no, that was their plan and I was supposed to go ahead with the 'young nose' and smell out the gas leaks before they arrived on with the lighter and the guaranteed explosion. I flatly refused that job, and after much ribbing I compromised and agreed to work the gas valve on the tank safely outside the building. With the back doors wide open, they agreed to shout out the 'on-off' commands to me and that was my compromise. They had to do without the 'young nose', as I intended keeping it on my head that day. They spent hours at this gas work, and actually did find all the leaks, or at least to a level that seemed to satisfy Kyrl regarding his losses. My predicted explosion never happened either. Black John assured me again that Michael had named me correctly as a chicken, and as he was leaving, Kyrl says as if to comfort me, "Ahh don't mind Black John, sure we might have blown up and then you'd have been right", such was his wit and seriousness at the same time. I never knew which was real with him.

Father had numerous stories about Kyrl and his lack of any sense of danger too. One time when Kyrl had become quartermaster, or somehow was in charge of a small local defence force known as the LDF, he took his platoon out on manoeuvres one night. As they crossed a big field, a very dangerous and prize bull took offence at their intrusion. The bull charged and Kyrl shouted to his force, "Stand yer ground I tell ye". It had no effect, as all the men began to run for the gate and the ditches in overall panic. Kyrl, who seemed unconcerned at this Pamplona event, kneeled down, pulled back the bolt on his 303 rifle, and as the bull turned on him and charged, he shot it dead within feet of where he was kneeling. There was a big investigation of course as it had been a prize bull, and the farmer was demanding compensation from the State and threatening legal action. Kyrl was brought before an investigating council and the judge concluded that he was on official business, had the right to bear arms with live ammunition, and as commander on the night, he took the correct decision to protect his men. All charges were dismissed and he became the talk of the town, being the man with the guns and no fear whatsoever.

I remember also that the attic part of his home was like an armoury. We used to play there among the rifles, bullets and Lugers. Big Kyrl didn't like it, but every chance we got Kyrle and I would sneak up to his attic and became gangsters. I'm sure that the only reason we didn't kill each other was that those guns were never loaded and we didn't know how to load them yet.

Kyrl was also a musician. He played with the father in his band purely to make money. He had no love for music much, and saw it once again as a means to an end. Michael O'Callaghan, a great local musician and dear friend of Kyrl's, told me one time that my uncle Kyrl was a 'mechanical player' unlike my dad, who was a true lover of the notes. Michael said, "Kyrl Cahill had taught himself how to read music by sheer determination, but only ever saw black dots on the page, not notes". As we chatted about his music he told me that if Kyrl was playing and saw a fly move cross the page, it was quite likely that he would 'play the fly', only ever seeing the dots; and he was serious about it.

There was a logical progression from music and dancing to entering the entertainment business, so that in later years Big Kyrl somehow managed to either lease, or ultimately buy the Old British Legion Dance Hall. This hall then became his main source of income. Both Kyrle and I soon became his part-time workers in the hall, and we had numerous adventures there over the coming years. Kyrle became his projectionist for the cinema and I was known as the 'ticket man', both collecting the tickets and ushering the punters to their seats with my flashlight.

After starting the cinema he realised that he could charge more for comfort, and set about doing that. He converted the stage area into what he termed 'The Balcony' and there he installed some softer seats at a much higher price. The plebs in the cheap section, known as 'ninepennies', got to sit on rows of old hard wooden seats from a disused church. My job also entailed not allowing the plebs to sneak up to the balcony after the movie began. I was like a yoyo going from side to side all night long and rarely got to see any film myself, and all this for a miserly sum each week, as his theory was that we were family and didn't deserve payment.

During the Buttevant Cahermee festival days when the town would have all kinds of revelry based around its famous horse fair, Kyrl would reconvert his picture hall back into the original dance hall. This would mean a total removal of all seats and the 'Balcony' would soon be turned into the stage area for the bands. He would hire out the hall to the local committee for a share of their profits from the many dances they held there, and to add to his profits, one year he decided to open an 'exclusive' mineral bar as an added attraction.

Kyrle and I were going to be working in this 'bar', which turned out to be a huge hole he had blown through the side wall of the hall. It opened out into a small alleyway that he also owned, and he put a sheet of iron across the top of this alley to act as a 'roof'. A large wide board was laid across the bottom of the hole to act as a counter, and inside on the alley side we stood on two butter boxes or old mineral crates to give us 'height' as Kyrl called it. He said ye better be higher than the tinkers or they will play 'mockie bawn with ye'. I had no idea what that even meant, but it sounded ominous to me even then.

Our mineral stock was stacked in the alley beside us, and it was just tough luck if it rained on us. He said he didn't care about 'a sup of water' landing on us as long as we made him the money. On the face of it, it seemed easy enough as all we had to do was stand on our boxes and sell bottles of orange. I thought the first night went very well, but not so Kyrl. According to him we had sold no way near enough 'drink', and his answer was to nail all the windows shut before the next night's dance. When I asked about how we would un-nail these windows later on, he said, "John, the end always justifies the means. Didn't I tell you that? Don't you worry about the bloody windows today, I need em sweatin tonight".

On the second night his window trick worked a treat, and sales were way up because the hall was like an oven causing sweat to pour off both the tinkers and the townies alike. Still he was not satisfied with the profits, so on the third night he took me and Kyrle aside and told us that we had to also collect the empty bottles, as the 'real profit' was in the returned bottles. What's more, he agreed that we would get extra pay for each bottle brought back inside the 'bar' before the night was over. For some reason he had got it into his head that people were taking home the bottles after the dance. He was also afraid of fights, as the bottles would then be broken. There was always a fight or two each night, so he saw a risk to his profits and we were to reduce it.

For me though, the thought of just going round collecting 'empties' was dead easy extra money, and so I set off first chance I got. I became eagle-eyed, studying the form of the dancers. Who was physically big, drinking fast, and dancing like a mad man? Who was trying to impress a fat woman, as she would drink more and he would buy her more. I had all kinds of possibilities going round in my head as I eyed up both the drinkers and the bottles alike. Soon I collected away and made a tidy sum that night. Kyrle served bar with one of Kyrl's many casuals and was adamant that he was also collecting the next night, having seen my extra stash of cash.

By the final night the money fever was up on me. I convinced Kyrle to let me serve for the first half, and then I'd collect for the latter part of the night. He was a bit suspicious, but I managed to make him believe that most fights took place in the latter part of the night, and he would be safer inside by then. In actual fact I had worked out that the place got like an inferno towards the end and that meant they drank far more. Kyrl also changed the door policy to ensure that you had to pay again on returning if they went out for a bit of fresh air or 'a shift', the term used for a million forms of sexual activity, so no one would be leaving at all that night and profits should soar.

Soon I was watching for each set change in the music, and the minute the dancers leapt up for another set, I would swoop in and grab their bottles. I became greedy and took any bottle that was about two thirds empty. It worked fairly well for a while, but then the inevitable happened. I took a bottle from under the nose of a very large tinker man and his even bigger brother.

Unknown to me I was spotted and no sooner was I back in the bar when they arrived at the hole in the wall. The tinker pushed his way through and grabbed me by the shirt and pulled me clean out through the bar opening, knocking over bottles of drinks and empties alike.

He had me up against the wall and was shouting and roaring that I took his drink, and he wanted it back. The only thing saving me was my youth. Very quickly Black John once again came to my rescue, and the tinker and his brother were quickly thrown out of the hall. Kyrl wanted to know if the tinker was right, and I had to admit that he was, so he says to me, "Well John twas not a bad plan and would have worked on the townies, but I'm not so sure about the tinkers though. Maybe it's just as well it's our last night huh". Smirking, he went off on his rounds of the hall and left me to serve away, still shaking from the fright I had got.

That night all of the windows in the hall were mysteriously broken. Next day I arrive for the cleanup and Kyrl says to me, "John, you should have left em have their ould drink. Now t'isnt nails we need to worry about but glass", but that was all he ever said on the matter again. That was a great side of him too that I admired immensely. There were never any recriminations for disasters; no need to state the obvious, and it was all put down to experience. Next year I would not be stealing bottles from the tinkers.

Even when a disaster was a costly one, he would not get really annoyed. I had been doing the headstone lettering in his workshop known as 'the shed' for a long time when my worst disaster happened. By then I had got quite cocky about my spelling accuracy and would letter a stone with almost sheer abandon. Kyrl's method was different, and he warned me to use his method as the customer was always right according to him. When a name was to be placed on a stone, Kyrl had a book which he would produce for the customer. Then he always, without exception, asked them to print out what they wanted on the stone in his book, and he just copied what they wrote. It worked with total success for him, and he kept telling me to make sure I followed the book. Of course I didn't need a book by then; I was invincible, or so I thought, because I was being taught by Ma Keely the master speller, and could never get spellings wrong or she would kill me, so I didn't bother to use the book after a while.

This worked ok for a long time until one day I was asked to print the name Ballymagooly on a new headstone. I lettered away and he placed the stone in the yard for the customer's usual inspection before we erected it. Then disaster struck. I had either added an 'o' or should have added one. In any case I spelled it wrong, and as the customer was arguing with Kyrl he dashes in and demands the book. I can't even find it at that stage as I had used it so little, and he rushes out again all apologies, telling the woman that he will make her a completely 'new' stone at no extra cost, and it will be spelled correctly next time. I hear all this going on and figure I am getting no wages for the next ten years, based on what he paid me. I am kicking myself for my arrogance. In he arrives and he is not happy, demanding we find the book. In the end it's found jammed down beside an old stone, and he gives me this look saying, "What did I tell you about the book?" All I can say is, "I'm sorry. I'll work it off till the stone is paid for". Then he starts laughing, "Surely you don't think I'm going to give that old skinflint a new stone, do you?" I say, "But you told her you would". He says, "John, there are tricks in every trade, and it will be a new stone, even if half of its gone. Am I right". I still don't know what he is talking about and look at him blankly.

He is smirking away as he tells me all this, then says, "Let's get the old stone back in and I'll make it a new one before your very eyes". We get it in, lay it on the bench, and he grabs his sander and begins to grind down the whole front face of the stone. He was one hell of a polisher, I'll grant him that, and in half an hour or so all my work is obliterated. Now he says, "This time use the bloody book will you, and learn two things from this experience: first you don't know everything, and secondly there is always a way to fix things," and off he went. I never again got a stone lettered wrongly either, and I did learn a wonderful lesson in humility that day.

Kyrl had two passions I believe, he loved cars, and he loved touring around Canada and America with his adopted son, John Collins. Aside from his numerous money making schemes, the buying of a car was the chief occupier of his mind when he was not abroad with John Collins. As he got older he would change his car each year, and for months he would be studying all the parameters such as engine size, colour, and internal attachments, and in this my own son Kyrl is a carbon copy. But the test drive was always the biggest event for him, and he would want to be fully satisfied before he parted with his cash. After he did make the purchase he would arrive on to my father and give him the test drive as well, though it was always Kyrl who did the driving. One time he had bought a very fancy modern car complete with radio and electric windows as well as an electric cigarette lighter. Father was taken off for the inevitable spin and as they drove along Kyrl demonstrated all the new gadgets in the car. It was a sunny day and Kyrl demonstrated the electric windows by winding them down. Father was amazed at this and soon began to relax in the comfortable new seats and so they chatted as they drove along. After some miles he became fully at ease with his domineering older brother, and asked Kyrl if it was all right to smoke in his new machine. He got the ok from Kyrl, and so he gets out his fags and reaches inside his pocket for the matches. Kyrl says, "What are you doing Hugh, you don't need matches anymore, just watch this, use the lighter. It will pop out when it's ready and you can light up then". At that Kyrl activates the lighter and in a short while it pops out. Kyrl says "It's ready now Hugh light up" My father can't believe what he is seeing and says "Jekus boys Kyrl that's a great yoke". Then he lights his fag and before Kyrl can stop him he throws the lighter right out the open window. Kyrl shouts "Noo Hugh" but it's too late, the little round device has gone in over some ditch never to be seen again and after about two hours of embarrassed searching they give up on it all. Kyrl drove father home in silence, and next day he changed the car, because he was so disgusted with what happened. My father got no more test runs after that either.

When I began researching this book I asked a great friend of Kyrls to tell me about the real Kyrle Cahill because he just fascinated me. I wanted to know the side of him that he showed to no one, or so I believed. The man I spoke to was Michael O'Callaghan a great local musician and Kyrl's best friend. I felt if anyone could describe my extraordinary uncle, Michael could. As it turned out there was no secret side to the man. He just lived a charismatic life and adventures seemed to follow him, but unlike my dad they were always good adventures. Michael did tell me of a day he would never forget though. Kyrl owned a stone quarry near a town called Doneraile about five miles from Buttevant. When he needed stone for his monumental works, he would organize about eight locals as helpers and head for the quarry to do a bit of rock blasting. My great uncle Johnnie who was a lot older than Kyrl and who was our master stone mason, was the so called expert on the blasting. Johnnie had concocted a kind of drill that would bore a small hole vertically into the cliff face then he would add the gunpowder charge and tamp all this powder down with a wooden pole. Later he added the fuse and all going well there would be a fine blast and a slice of rough stone would fall from the cliff face, later becoming someone's headstone. This normally worked well enough until the day when Johnnie forgot the tamping pole. Kyrl was insisting as usual that the day would not be wasted and a blast had to take place. I believe he convinced Johnnie to use an iron crowbar and gingerly tamp the charge while the whole crew looked on in amazement. The iron bar hit flint and the whole ground blew up, throwing Johnnie into the air, sending the bar into orbit, and landing the rest of them onto their asses on the ground, shaken but unharmed. Undaunted by this near death experience, Kyrl convinced Johnnie to do it all again after a tea and Guinness break, and this time they were rewarded with a good haul of rock for the headstones. Kyrls mode of rock transporting was to get his crew to load all this stone into a flatbed truck that he had built from scratch and this they did.

Michael O'Callaghan was a young boy of about sixteen then, and he was the newest member of Kyrl's crew. He was constantly asking Kyrl to let him drive and to teach him the skills associated with it and that day he got his wish. With the truck well overloaded with stone, tools, and the eight men, they headed back for Buttevant. The journey was uneventful except for the odd time when the steering wheel would come loose and the truck would head for the ditch. Then Kyrl would say "Mickey will you stick to the road and leave the fields to the horses" and go back to chatting about the days events as Michael struggled with the dodgy steering wheel.

Just outside Buttevant, the Doneraile road falls very steeply into the town, and arrives at a junction on the main street which is actually the main Cork Limerick road. As the truck came over the hill and began to descend, it got faster and faster despite Michael frantically pumping of the brakes. The brakes had failed, and while this came as no surprise to Kyrl, because he knew the truck was of Cahill construction, it became a great shock to the sixteen year old child who was then beginning to really panic. They were rapidly gaining momentum as Michael prepared for the inevitable crash into another vehicle, or if that didn't happen, they would go straight through the wall of Saddler's, shop. In either case the stopping was going to end badly and he began shouting and screaming at Kyrl to do something. Kyrl just told him to "Cop himself on and relax, this is a driving lesson". By then they were fast approaching a small bridge over the Awbeg River and fortunately there was a narrow gap in the wall between the road and the river. Michael said that he was terrified at that stage and quite sure that he was going to die, especially when he saw some of the men jumping out of the truck and rolling around on the road. Cool as a breeze, and at the critical moment, Kyrl grabbed the wheel and jerked it sharply to the right sending them all through the gap, and into the river with a huge splash. Michael said he was shaking uncontrollably and must have been as white as a sheet as he saw the last of the men pick each other up out of the river. Then Kyrl said "Are we staying here all day Mickey, back her out will you for Gods sake".

He did finally get the truck out of the river and they all retired to the pub except Kyrl and Michael who retired home and made tea. It was almost a typical day in their mad lives and once again Kyrls mantra of the end always justifying the means had paid off. Sadly both of them have since gone to their Eternal Rest and I would lay odds that during the Olympic Games they were watching Heavenly TV. In keeping with his mantra Kyrl would be insisting to Michael that performance enhancing drugs were perfectly necessary, and Michael would be playing the Irish National Anthem as our great athletes proved that they at least, didn't need them.

Father told me of yet another one of Kyrl's moneymaking schemes with that same truck. The Buttevant hurling team was playing in some very important final in Liscarroll, and the whole town wanted to go to it. It was during a time of petrol shortages and public transport was nonexistent then. It was going to be impossible to get to the match so Kyrl decided to turn his flatbed truck into a kind of bus, and take a load of supporters to the game. He added a temporary railing to the side of the truck, and he also added steps making it easier to board it. All was ready and on the day of the match he started selling places on his truck-bus. To get even more punters on board and so as to make even more money, he insisted that they all had to stand for the entire journey, a distance of about seven miles. This did not go down well, and there were those who actually complained very bitterly, but he didn't care a bit saying, "Take it or leave it, and pay up or shut up, your delaying us all". With no choice, and a line of already drunken supporters waiting to board, the complainers boarded and soon filled the truck to bursting point. Kyrl sat in and started his truck-bus, and off they went to the match. In order to save his petrol, father told me that Kyrl seems to have taken some kind of a short cut along the back roads of Cork, and as they came close to the village, they went up over a very steep hill and began to career down the other side, at an ever increasing speed. The supporters who were well into the singing and shouting by then noticed this too, and all their singing stopped suddenly when the truck-bus almost turned over on a sharp bend. Kyrl noticed this too as the brakes were having no effect, and he quickly realized that unsurprisingly, the brakes in his truck had failed yet again. But not alone had the brakes failed, so had the steering, as the wheel had come off in his hands when he struggled to guide them around the sharp bend. Father said that they must have been going about fifty miles an hour at the time. Kyrl then tried to use the gears to slow them down, but that too failed and he could not get the engine into a lower gear either, because in his panic he broke the gear stick off as well. The supporters were now panicking and clinging onto the railings and each other for dear life. With all control lost the truck tore on down the road and went right through an old iron gate and tearing away part of the ditch. Then it began crossing a field still at great speed. It finally hit a tree with such force that it toppled over, and threw all of his passengers out onto the grass in every direction amid screams, curses, and puke.

No one was seriously hurt though, and they all limped off to the match. Kyrl spent the intervening time righting his truck, and after the game was over he was once again waiting with his hand out for the 'return fare'. He tried to convince them all that their ticket had always been one way, and now they had to pay him again for the return journey. The situation got very nasty because his truck-bus had almost killed them, and they angrily pointed that fact out to him. Still he was insistent, and in the end I believe he just drove off and left them all on the road to find their own way back, and that would be typical of Kyrl. There were a lot of bad feelings towards him for a long time after that, but they needed him and he knew it, and all was forgiven but not forgotten in time.

Kyrl, like my dad, is buried in a cemetery which is on the road to that same village of Liscarroll. His unofficially adopted son and my cousin John K. Collins and his wife Agnes, erected a most beautiful headstone in his memory and it bears this inscription.

We are the story tellers. We are the music makers, and we are the Dreamers of dreams.
I know of no more fitting words to describe my amazing uncle Kyrl, the man we all knew as Big Kyrl.

The road to Charleville

I was about seventeen by the time we decided enough was enough with Pad, and Kyrle refused to go back to Pad's. We still had not finished our schooling, so Kyrle and I would have to go on to Charleville Tech to do our Leaving Cert, finish formal schooling and then hopefully get a job. That was the usual plan in those days. We had no chance of a university degree unless we got a scholarship, and even though Kyrle had the brains for it, Pad had torpedoed his chances early on.

Uncle Michael knew the head master in Charleville Tech, a man called Dan Fleming. He had been a famous rugby player and was also very high up in the GAA. The school was already over-booked, but Dan decided that he would take us in and the few others who had also left Pad's school that year.

Charleville is nine long miles north of Buttevant, with a devil of a hill at the mid-way point. We were going to have to cycle to school each day and back. In today's days of busses and cars transporting the children to school, it seems now inconceivable that our parents would let us off into the dark on winter mornings and return in the dusk after school, but that's how it was in nineteen sixty seven or eight. I know that neither I nor Kyrle had any kind of lights on the bikes, as the batteries were far too expensive and we simply could not afford them.

Four of us used to do that trip each day and we were all as tough as nails. We took our lunch in the schoolbag, ate it at dinner time, and headed back home at four in the evening without further food. I believe we used to cycle the nine miles in just under two hours. It was always faster coming home because of the big hill then in our favour.

The school was mixed with a big age range in it. It was a critical time in our development and we were brought into close proximity with girls or 'bitches' as Joe Hurley always called them. Up until then we would have had the odd foray down to the castle in

Buttevant, but it bore no comparison at all to the number of girls, and the type of girls available in the Tech. I felt this was just great. What's more, we were all older than most of the class, except for the senior girls secretarial class, and because of Pad's teaching, we seemed to be geniuses knowing ten times more than our fellow students. Pad had got something right at least.

One guy asked me what Latin was when I was describing our previous schooldays, such was the level of education we then found ourselves in. Soon the girls picked up on this so-called standard of genius, and we began to become a kind of magnet for them: mini celebrities in fact. I think at almost eighteen I would have been the oldest in the class except for one guy who had failed his exams so many times that his parents may as well have abandoned him. He was a farmer's son and almost bald because diesel fuel had fallen on his head when he was younger and it never grew back. He was big and burly, and after the diesel spill all he had left on his head was a wild tuft of discoloured hair which stuck out in all directions, but mostly from his left side with the right side being almost bald. He really did look like a Yeti and I christened him that privately. For some reason he took to me as his only friend and I liked him a lot, but I just can't remember his name which is a pity. This friendship resulted in a rather 'odd couple' moving together through that school. A four-eyed Magoo-like genius and a Yeti figure tagging along beside him, hunched over like Quasi Modo and hanging on every word the Magoo-like figure spoke. I'm sure we were the butt of many a joke as we moved among the throng, and Kyrle avoided us completely out of sheer embarrassment.

Looking back on those days, I know now that our class was a bunch of misfits, failures and delinquents in every sense of the word, and in Pad's view, a new pack of 'donkeys' had joined the student fraternity in Charleville. We were all 'strange' in some way or other and Dan had no classroom for us, so he made one out of the foyer in the school entrance. When you came in the front door, there we all sat in our temporary classroom, and no matter what business you had in the school, you went right through our class. It was so funny to see us all fold our chairs during lunch break and stack them away, and then when lunch was over, we had to redo the whole seats again and sit for the next class. There seemed to be some kind of store where we kept the seats and this was always a good spot for a bit of fun with the 'bitches'. That's all I can say on that matter.

Dan Fleming seemed to like us from the very start. He was a great teacher and while he shouted and roared a lot, you always got the impression it was only an act on his part. Our first test of his acting came when, after some weeks of being late for school, he called the four of us into his office which was in the small corridor behind our makeshift classroom. We marched in full of confidence and bravado, and I being the ringleader walked in first. He was sitting at his desk writing. I was just about to sit down when he shouts up at me, "Cahill who told you to sit down". I was a bit taken aback by this and I say, "No one sir". "Correct, so keep standing". He then tells us that he is sick and tired of watching us arrive in at any time of the mornings and it's going to stop. "It's to stop, or there will be hell to pay. Get it in yer heads, it's to stop. Now be off out of me sight and don't be late tomorrow".

We left sniggering, and already I had decided he was just bluffing as I don't think I ever saw a stick or anyone use a stick in that school so far. Besides, I was feeling like a man by then having survived Pad, and could now take on the world sure that I had no more Pads to deal with.

Next morning we were late again. Dan comes out of his office right into our classroom and as we are opening the bags he says, "What did I tell ye yesterday?" glaring directly at me. I say it was the wind sir, the North wind held us back. Dan looks out and says, "Tis a sunny day. Are you trying to cod me Cahill?" I say, "The wind came up and went down; that's what winds do," my cheek being obvious to all. He made a drive for me and I thought I was back in Pad's school, but he stopped short saying, "Ye are all on yer last warning". On the way home we decided that we better get up earlier and not tempt fate and Dan, so for the next few weeks we are on time and things settled back to normal. We would still miss the odd day but always got away with it until much later in the year when it was biting cold and every extra second in bed counted greatly.

This particular morning we were seriously late, by about half an hour or so. Dan is waiting in the yard for us to arrive. It had frosted real bad and I was frozen, as were the lads. I used to wear an old leather jacket with just a jumper and shirt, never a vest, as I always believed the body can correct for extremes of temperature. Dan is standing glaring at us all as we come flying in the gate. He says, "Put yer bikes in the shed and come out here to the yard". I thought, 'he's up to something for sure and I don't like the sound of it at all'. We trail back out and by then the sun is shining brightly. "Take off yer clothes, ye can leave yer trousers on ... for now". What could this be, I thought, as he yells his words at us with apparent anger. "I said take off yer clothes". The frost is turning his words into smoke and I don't get what he's up to. We all look at each other and he draws a kick at my arse and misses; I believe deliberately so. We start to strip off. I get to my shirt and he shouts, "Take it off Cahill," so I do. Kyrle has an old vest with holes in it, and he really does look like a street urchin. Maybe Pad, who used to call him that, had a point after all. Dan shouts at him, "You too, take that strainer off". The other two boys were now down to bare skin also and all of us began shivering with the cold. He says, "Stand there like men, I'll be back". I thought this was going to be like *Mutiny on the Bounty* and he's gone for the whip or the cat o'nine tails to flog us all. Pretty soon we see heads appearing at the school windows: senior girls' heads and tall boys 'heads; teachers' heads and even the caretaker Bill came out to watch. This was serious I thought. Kyrle is looking at me and the shed and I thought he was going to make a burst for his bike, not wanting a repeat of Pad's days, but Dan comes out without a whip.

"What did I tell ye about being late", he is marching up and down our line. "Stand up like men, and stop yer shaking. Yer not in the Arctic. I told ye there would be trouble didn't I? Well now ye'll get a taste of it. Ye are now going to do fifty laps of the school, and every time ye are late, ye will all do the same thing even if only one of ye is late, get it...."

I thought he was joking. He wasn't. "Cahill, you're the ringleader and you're first. Get running, ye can race if ye want," he says with a smirk. I knew then that I was in the presence of a very smart man, and a great teacher of life as well as of education.

We began running. It was like the movie *Chariots of Fire*. All we needed was the music and the sea. We circled round and round the school yard. The school's pupils were in hysterics, pointing and laughing at us through the windows. Bill was leaning on his sweeping brush and as we passed Dan grabs the brush and chased after us lashing out as he went. Even I began to laugh, warming up then, and so did Kyrle and the other two lads who could see the funny side as well. Pretty soon it seemed like great fun, but after about thirty laps we were wrecked and struggling. Dan had by then left again, a ploy on his part, as no one was counting the laps, and he wanted a graceful end to our running. We stopped at the door and gathered the clothes, donned them, and went inside. It had wasted about an hour of schoolwork, but it gave immense entertainment to all of the school, and embarrassment to us with a lesson to all that you don't ignore Dan. However, we were still troublemakers and remained a thorn in his side for a little while more.

I was to have a real Arctic experience soon after though. It was known then that one of the best ways to meet 'hot' girls, especially 'foreign' girls from Dublin, was to get to the Irish Colleges in Cork's Gaeltacht. Here you were taught to speak the Irish language for a few hours each day and later you had the evenings off to do the bitch chasing. Dances were also arranged for the students known as 'ceilis'. I was far more interested in the girls than any of the old Irish dancing because Nannie's concert days in Gortnabearna were still fresh in my mind. There she used to try to have my cousin Brid Ann teach me Irish dancing and I hated it, but dancing with 'hot foreign bitches' was another matter entirely. However, all of this fantasizing depended on me getting to the Gaeltacht, and the only way for that to happen was for me to get a scholarship by passing both a written and an oral Irish examination. This was where Pad's schooling would finally be of benefit to me, as I was well used to speaking and writing the Irish language in his school, so I felt I was certainly set for the Gaeltacht and the girls.

The weather was then becoming bitterly cold, but still we cycled on every day to Charleville Tech. The mornings became very dark too as we entered the winter months and, as usual, this had to be the time they decided to hold the Irish exams for the scholarship. I think Kyrle had no interest in the Gaeltacht because he would easily have walked the exams, him being a fluent Irish speaker, but he never said he wanted to go there at all. I got it into my head that I was going to the Gaeltacht come hell or high water, and as it was all free if you got the scholarship, Nannie had no problem with it either. She said, "Sure you might learn something at last, and it will surely stand to you later". Little did she know what I was planning to learn, and 'standing to me later' could easily be a poor choice of words the way I was thinking.

As it came nearer to the exam time, the usual exaggerated rumours began doing the rounds, especially from some of the guys who had been there the previous year. I heard tales spoken in hushed voices that sometimes the Dublin girls were so 'wild' you'd never be the same after an experience with one of the hottest ones. I also noticed that my friend the Yeti was very keen on the idea of going as well, but we all mocked him because he was so useless at Irish. Nevertheless, these stories intrigued me and I discussed my upcoming adventures with Joe Hurley. He was all advice based on his imagined 'experiences' of sexual passion. I knew by then that he was as innocent as me, and he was a total liar as well, so I ignored his ramblings, but he did make me promise to give him all the details after I came home from the place. I had not even got to do the exam yet, and Joe was already living his amorous adventures through me.

The morning of the exam came, and in the pitch black dawn Nannie looked out into the street and saw that it was beginning to snow. She rarely left me get off school, but that day she was adamant that I was not going, exam or no exam. I was equally adamant that I was going, and I dressed and made my own sandwiches as she refused to do a thing to help. On that day mother left Kyrle stay in bed because she was sure there would be no school because of the worsening weather, so determined to get to school I head off out the door on my bike. I wore my old black leather jacket outside a warm jumper which was knitted by the Nan, a shirt and a pair of her old gloves, and rode off straight into a blizzard. It was totally insane, but I knew that nothing was going to stop me from going to the school that morning. I had no fear whatsoever, just sheer determination and a burning desire for Hurley's 'bitches'.

Initially I followed the tracks of some car that had passed earlier.

Pretty soon the tracks vanished, but I kept going in the dark. I could barely see and clouds of snow blew across me covering my glasses. I took them off and still I kept going. To this day I have no idea how I made it. No doubt I was cold, but a strange thing happened to me after about three miles. I began to feel no cold at all. In fact I believe I actually began to get warm. I never fell off the bike either, despite the slippery road, nor did I stop on the road even once. I just pedalled slowly along. After some hours, I arrived at the gates of the school.

Bill the caretaker, who was always a cranky old geezer, saw me cycle in the gate, and by then the sun was shining. It had brightened to a beautiful but very cold morning. He got a terrible shock. I remember him just staring at me speechless while holding a shovel of snow. What I had not realised was that I had become a moving igloo. There was surely about a foot of snow caked across the whole front of my body, my head included. My legs were caked also, but not to the same extent. I think Bill just did not know how I had not died, as he knew the journey well. The poor man grabbed hold of me, shook me off, and took me straight into his boiler room. There he opened the door of the furnace where I shook off the last of the igloo. I felt no discomfort at all, not one bit. I had seen no school buses though, and no one seemed to be walking around either except me and Bill, and then he says, "Boy, why did you do it, you could have frozen to death for nothing. Sure there's no school today boy, there's not even a bus running, and I'm only here to keep the place warm". I was speechless. After all that, and now no exam either, I couldn't get over it.

He kept asking me if I was ok and was I getting warm. Then he says, "I think I should call you a doctor". I got such a fit of laughing at that, and then the two of us just began laughing our heads off. I think it was sheer relief on his part and then I saw the insanity of it all, so I laughed even more. When we finally calmed down, he says, "Have you any food boy", and I produced my lunch. He made tea for both of us and we talked about my wanting to go to the Gaeltacht so badly. I left out the part about the girls. He kept shaking his head saying, "Jazus, I never seen the like of it boy. Who let you out in that blizzard? Sure I never seen the like of it". He became human in my eyes after that day because he was genuinely concerned about me, and from that day on he would always address me as the 'Snowman'. As I'd arrive into school, or if he saw me in the yard he would go, "How's the Snowman doing today boy", with a wry smirk on his face, and I'd reply, "Still freezing Bill". No one even knew why we played this game, and it only added to the mystery surrounding the mad man from Buttevant. After my rest and our chat I ate my food, got back on my bike and cycled home. I never did the exam. It was cancelled till later and by then we had left the school. No one only Bill knew of my igloo, and while I suspect he told some people about it, I never once heard a soul ask me about it later on and few would believe it anyway. I was destained never to meet with the 'hot women' of Dublin, and Joe Hurley was disappointed more than me.

Around the late sixties, the country was beginning to prosper a little and the government brought out a scheme for giving out free books to the needy, provided your income was low. Our income at home was so low then that it was below the floor line, despite the growing economy. Dan arrived into the class with a paper describing the scheme and telling us all that to qualify, all we had to do was bring him in a letter describing the home circumstances. Pride is a terrible curse and after telling Nannie all about it she decided we were not beggars, and she refused to give me the letter. Neither did mother. The deadline for the books approached and Dan made this clear in a speech a few days before it closed. Still we had no letter. It was clear that anyone who went into Dan's office uninvited was carrying this 'letter of shame' as Nannie saw it. A few did go in at the start and a few more went in closer to the deadline, but not us of course, and we were probably the most deserving of any of them.

I think the deadline had passed when one day Dan comes out of his office and interrupted our class in the hallway, and says to me and Kyrle, "You two are trouble and I want you in my office at four sharp". He was glaring at us in front of everyone. I thought he was joking as we were then well accepted at the school. He doubles back as if hearing my thoughts and says, "I mean it, troublemakers. Four sharp". At four the class was breaking up, tidying back the chairs, and we knocked at the door and he calls out to come in. As we enter, Dan shouts out real loud that he is tired of us disrupting the school, causing trouble and still being late and it's going to stop, but he is smiling at us as he's shouting. I didn't get it and neither did Kyrle. Then he says, much quieter, "Sit down there lads. That's for the benefit of outside ears". He asks us why he has not got the letter he wanted for the books. I say because my Nan won't give it to me. Kyrle stays silent. Dan says, "But I'm sure ye qualify and tis a shame to waste these books, so I'm going to deal with it myself and get ye the books. No one need know, alright?" This was just the kind of man he was, and I'm sure we were not the only ones he helped with that scheme. Then he says, "Be off now". As we leave, he is back shouting at us again, "And if ye don't cop on, yer out of this school. I'll expel the both of ye and good riddance, Buttevant tulls".

He had used the expel word - the worst threat, and as all heard it, we rose even higher in stature. Dan got us the books and no one ever knew the how of it. I don't know what he did. I suspected he wrote two imaginary letters describing the situation which he knew must be the case, because I am sure that Michael had filled him in on it all at enrolment time. Dan Fleming was one of a kind and I could never praise him enough.

I have to say that I loved that school. It had a totally different teaching ethic to Pad Keely's place. In the Tech, the teachers did not care if you learned or not, but they did try their best to teach you. Dan had a saying that I never forgot. On the day that we joined, he came around to our class and said, "Now listen to this boys. Ye are here to work. This school has girls, and if they interfere with the work, give up the work," and he marched out. I was in a place where I could learn at last. We were both to bring great honours to that school later on in one extraordinary day.

The school had organised a writing competition in the school. There was no prize, just a competition where the best composition would be read to all the classes. By then I was well into my Communism phase and also into the belief that God was not necessary for life to begin on Earth. I had studied this and read of the famous Miller experiment, showing that amino acids would form in a flask if the right conditions were there, and these amino acids were the building blocks of life. I was trying to decide which I would write about when it dawned on me that I knew more about

Communism than the Miller experiment, so I went for that.

It took me two days of writing and re-writing, and in the end I had a great account of Communism and compared it to the Christianity Christ taught before the Catholic Church got at his teachings. Michael read it and was amazed at it. Nannie refused to read it when I told her Christ was the first Communist. She said the Russians would love to have me, and the Devil was still stuck inside me, brought in by Joe Hurley, and the both of us were Hellbound. I don't know who else read it, but when it got to the school judging panel, it won hands down. I was asked to read it at all the classes, even the senior girl's class, and this was for me the greatest thrill. I believed totally in all that I had written, so I was good at answering any questions that came from those listening.

Somehow the subject matter was brought to the attention of the local Catholic priest. He was an old stager and hated me already because I was clearly a rebel and troublemaker in the religious class. By then we were after coming up in the world and a bus used to take us about half way to the school, but we still had to cycle the other half. Later on, in a vindictive act, Pad had our bus stopped, and we were soon back to cycling all the way, but at that time we used to wait for our bus at a stop just across the road from the Catholic church where this old priest had his house. This area was, and still is, the main Limerick road, and is on a gentle bend, so I suppose it is a dangerous place to be at the best of times. I had always loved handball and one day, to kill time, I started playing ball up against the wall right on the bend. Pretty soon it became the place to play. There was little traffic in those days and we were not fools. If a car was coming it would be driving slowly as it was entering the town and obviously our game would be suspended till it passed. The old priest sees this going on and arrived across to me telling me to clear off with that ball or he will call the Guards. By then I didn't give a damn about the Catholic Church or their priests either, so I tell him no, I won't stop playing and he can do what he likes about it. I'm real happy with the cheek I'm giving him too. He demands that we do stop, glaring at us, but we all stand our ground. Then beaten as the bully he was, he backed off shouting that, "There will be trouble," and as he leaves I shout after him, "Fuck off to your ould Church, you ould bollix". He swung round glaring at me and we went back to the game, ignoring him. He had done his worst and got nowhere with it. Next day he complained me to Dan Fleming I'm sure, but that did him no good either. However, after I wrote about the Communism and showed how Christ was the first Communist, he went ballistic. He arrived at the school raging and demanding my head. I was 'openly' preaching Communism and I was to be expelled immediately. Dan called me into his office and told me all about the priest's threats and his demand that I be expelled. Dan said, "Of course I'll not expel you. What you wrote was brilliant, keep on writing. You do have a gift for it. But John, try not to play any more handball on the road. I'm responsible if anything happens to ye". He told me that there was a proper ball alley in the town and to use that. I didn't have the heart to say that it was always locked and we would probably miss the bus if we used it. Every time I pass that spot today, which has changed little, I remember those days, but we did stop the playing there, not out of fear from the priest, but out of respect for Dan.

By the time we went to Charleville Tech both Kyrle and I were after becoming real good at electronics, and this knowledge was to bring us a huge element of fame on one amazing day. It brought great honour to the school as well.   There was an annual countywide school competition being held, with the Lord Mayor of Cork presiding and handing out the prizes. Cash no doubt I hoped, and a certificate. Our school used to enter it every year and never get anywhere. The competition was held in the Munster Institute in Cork city, and as well as a projects event, there were also a question time competition and a public speaking competition.

We decided to enter all three. Kyrle would build a complete reel to reel tape recorder and I would build the test box I had designed in my head a hundred times. The school also had other boys entering, but all the hope was riding on the two of us as the devices we were making looked amazing to the school. In our school, we were up against guys who were entering projects such as 'measuring the temperature of eggs in a cock of hay, or where does rainfall come from', so I thought if that's the best they can do, then it's no wonder that they never win anything. I think it took us probably two weeks to make our projects. Kyrle built the whole machine and also the amplifier from scratch and it looked amazing. He needed a speaker and this he made in the woodwork class. I made my test box there as well. So as to cover the cone of his speaker and make it look nice, he cut a square out of the silk lining from inside the mother's only good coat. Of course he hung it back up, and as she was always saving it, she didn't notice her loss for months. I made my test box with ease and loved looking at it. It had a series of switches which would allow me to substitute different values of capacitors or coils or resistors into a circuit via two wire probes. I was also using a compass sitting inside a coil of wire, which was a crude form of voltmeter, and this alone was a genius of an idea if I may say so myself. It was not the most practical thing, but by using my box I could tell if there was a voltage in a circuit by how much the compass needle moved off North. I also had a bulb and a battery in the box to act a as continuity tester. All of these ideas are used today in professional versions of my box, but way back then, nothing like it even existed.

The day came for our trip to Cork and we all trooped into the bus, with Kyrle trying to lift both his speaker and tape machine. We had tested both inventions many times by then and we were very confident, as was the whole school, that Kyrle's was a real winner. Everyone was amazed at our talents and our reputation as geniuses would be confirmed if only we could win, and become the best in Cork city and county.

In the projects room there was a long line of judges sitting at long tables and you passed from one to the other displaying and explaining your project. The long table in front of them was a bit off-putting because each guy was talking and showing right beside you, and it was going to be hard to concentrate. Nevertheless Kyrle opted to go first in front of me. He started to show off the tape machine and his speaker and microphone. I saw all the judges lean forward and look at his big box, complete with reels of tape. The judge asked him to explain how it worked, could he show it actually working, and had he really built all that by himself. Kyrle said, "Yes Sir, if I have a power point I can plug it in. I did make it all by myself, well my brother here helped a bit too," and he smiles back at me. After applying power, he turned it on and the reels spun but no sound came from the tape. He didn't panic though, just did another test. Still nothing happened. The judge was very sympathetic and quite amazed that this young lad had actually made this device, even if it was not working. He was about to pass it on to the next judge when Kyrle says, "If I can use my brother's test box here, I can fix it I'm sure". Now all the heads turned round again. The judge was delighted to agree and we got at it. Within a few minutes Kyrle, using the substitution part of my tester, had it working and then it was talking perfectly, recording the judge and all those around him. I was totally delighted that I had been able to help him and in so doing it proved the value of my box too. I only had to explain the compass part which worked as a voltmeter and the end result was that I won first place, and Kyrle got second. We didn't know we had won though until the Lord Mayor made the final announcements and presentations later that evening at five o'clock. What I did know though was that later in the day, during the question time, I won first place out of all the technical schools in Cork. To add the icing to my cake, I also came first in the public speaking competition where I was lucky enough to be asked to speak on my favourite subject 'Corporal Punishment' or as I called it 'Pad's Punishment'.

As the Lord Mayor began announcing the winners, it was almost embarrassing the amount of things we had won for the school that day because our 'question time' team also won with our help. It was such an achievement that Dan gave us all a day off a few days later, and I remember our pictures with the presentations and certificates used to be hung on the wall of our foyer classroom for years, though probably they are well gone by now. My main prize, as I suspected, was cash. I was presented with thirty pounds, and on the way home I asked the teacher if the bus would stop and I could buy all on board crisps and lemonade, which I did. If there were any doubts about our fame, they were then well vaporized. Nannie was delighted and took the balance of my money immediately. I don't think she even gave me back a shilling let alone a pound, but she was very proud. Both Kyrle and I were on a high after that great day. I still have my little certificate stashed somewhere and the memories from that day will never leave me. It was then going to be impossible for that old priest to get rid of me, and Dan had been vindicated at last.

Mad friends Disco days.

When I was a teenager, we always seemed to have had long hot summers full of fun and all kinds of great adventures. As I look back on some of those days, I have to believe that some Force or Guardian Angel or Spirit had to have been watching over me because I escaped an early death far too many times to think otherwise.

Around nineteen sixty seven or so, our neighbours, John and Donie Connoly, and I were sitting on the banks of the Awbeg River one beautiful sunny day in July discussing how we would become famous. We argued back and forth on the best way to achieve this, and finally concluded that in a small town the only thing we could do was a Christmas day swim; an unheard of idea at the time. The swim would take place in the very river we were then looking into, all serene and peaceful like the 'gentle Mulla' in poet Spenser's *Faerie Queene*, with no currents and almost no water either. Of course the warm sun was also shining across our backs.

We decided to do it, shook hands on the deal and began to spread the word that we would swim the river the following Christmas Day. The general feeling among those we told was, 'well so what, anyone can do that,' and it looked like Buttevant was not ready to grant us fame for that event, but we had shook hands on it, so we had to go through with it, and we started to 'train' for the day.

Training for me was to wash every day from then on in cold water, not a difficult task for me as we rarely ever had any hot water. The months passed by and we kept spreading the word, hoping for an audience on the morning, but still no one gave a damn.

About ten days before Christmas it began to rain like mad. Within days the river began to flood, and one evening we went down and had a look at it all. I was petrified as I'm no great swimmer, and the water was already out in the fields with the very spot where we had made our pact under at least two feet of water. The lads were still all for going ahead, as Donie was like a fish in the water and afraid of nothing; not even God, and John was almost as good. Christmas week arrived and the rain, which had stopped for a day or two, began all over again, lashing down in buckets. Then we heard that 'the powers that be' were secretly 'confiscating' our swimming togs to prevent us from drowning, as Nannie was sure would happen. To get around their plan, I borrowed togs from a friend of mine. Christmas morning arrived; cold, dark, and miserable, but not raining at least. We felt that there might still be a crowd to see our swim. The Connollys were as determined as ever and their poor mother Liz, who was Nannie's secondary bank, was sure we would all die. She could not stop her sons or their mad friend from going, and so she begged us to at least have the Pope's blessing from the Vatican so that we would all go to Heaven when we drowned. To pacify her we had to kneel and pray as we got the Pontiff's blessing from Rome, curtsey of her television set. I remember not thinking much of the Pope, but genuinely praying a lot that we would survive. Then off we went after hugs, kisses, and tears from poor Mrs. Connolly and her family. Nannie had refused to kiss me goodbye, as she said the Devil was still stuck inside me because I was breaking the heart of an old woman and ruining her Christmas dinner. But secretly I believe she felt sure that we three would not do the swim because we had no togs, and we would all be too shy to go in naked.

We got to the river entrance with not one person to be seen as an audience; fame seemed to be eluding us. As I suspected, Liz Connolly had hidden her sons' togs, but that did not deter them one bit, and they announced that they were going in naked. I felt a bit odd about that initially, but soon the feeling left me, so we all stripped off stark naked and got out of the car in plain view of the road. We climbed up on the wall and stood there for a while examining the situation while shivering with the cold. By then most of the field was flooded, with a current coming from the river swirling out into the field. It looked very dangerous but I did not have a real bad feeling about it, thinking I could probably stand up in the current if needed. As we stood naked on the wall we began having some doubts about the current, but not Donie. We all shook hands, yelled something mad and jumped in over the wall, running right into the freezing waters. I can't honestly remember what happened next. I do remember the shock of the cold water, and it suddenly feeling way deeper than I had hoped for, but it did not go over my head. I think the current pushed us down the field to a shallow area by a gate. The next thing I remember was the three of us were walking naked back up the road to their car, shivering and laughing our heads off with relief. When we got to the car we shared my towel to dry off. I think the two lads brought no towels, feeling they might not need them after they drowned, or they cared little about drying off. We got dressed quickly just as the local policeman arrives on a pushbike. "What the hell are ye doing in there?" he shouts in the window. "Nothing Guard, we were just swimming". I sniggered and Donie and John exploded laughing. The guard, who was at a loss to know what to do next, just shook his head and left. I suppose someone driving past into Buttevant must have seen us on the wall, and rang the guards telling them of the naked guys about to jump into the flood.

We went home for the dinner full of excitement, full sure that now we would be famous, but alas, I believe no one in Buttevant even cared or believed that we had actually done the swim. All we have now is the memory of it. Over the years I told numerous people about it, but it hardly got me a look of surprise; certainly no fame came from it. Of course it's quite commonplace today with sea jumps, lake jumps and even river swims on Christmas day for charity, but no one ever that I know of jumped into a flood, and I still say it deserved more fame than it got. Now like the famous line from Titanic, 'it only resides in my memory now'. Perhaps the Pope's blessing did save us after all, and kept me alive for the many other escapades that were ahead of me, but I would have more faith in the gift from the Faeries.

In the latter part of the sixties, music became the outlet for teenage energy; at least it was my outlet and that of my friends. We were immersed in the acid bands of the era: Pink Floyd, Led Zeppelin, The Who and Deep Purple to name just a few. These bands were emulated by the new driving force in Ireland, a growing rock band scene. We liked The Freshmen and the heavier bands like The Plattermen and of course our all time favourite was 'The Taste'. This was the great Rory Gallagher's rock and blues band. He was a world class guitarist and lived in Cork City. Rory was the young people's hero, and mine certainly.

My friendship with Joe Hurley had faded quite a bit over the years and around nineteen sixty five or so I began to find friendship with three other lads. Kyrle had become friendly with them during my summer vacations in Waterford, and I just seemed to drift into that group as Joe drifted out.

We were all becoming avid rock music lovers. Two of the lads were Jerry Hayes and Liam Fowler; Joe Moloney would join us later. All of us loved the freedom portrayed by the rock music, the long hair, the tie dye shirts, and every form of rebellion possible. It did not take long for the town to brand us as Buttevant's hippies. I remember tying rocks and old rubber balls into my tee shirts while trying to dye them in an old pan down the yard. They turned out so bad that they actually looked real good. I wore them when Nannie was not keeping an eye on me, often changing outside the house. Pad Keely was not impressed with this carry on, but to his credit I don't remember him ever casting real aspersions on our hairstyles. He had plenty of other material to throw at us.

We four used to go for walks down the Charleville road and sit on the bridge dreaming of fame and what it would be like to live in America among the great musical stars of the day. Looking back on it now, I remember that Jerry Hayes had a kind of mystique about him, wearing really long hair and a moustache, and he always spoke with a soft gentle voice. I think women could not figure him out, and that accounted for their attraction to him. Liam Fowler, who was slightly taller, was good looking, fun loving, and a generally very likable guy. He also seemed to have some magnetism for the women as well. Joe Moloney was always deeper, quieter, and like me, he seemed to be searching all the time for the 'right' woman to come along.

As teenagers we had no way of seeing our favourite bands, but we could dream of the day when we would see them live, which we did often. Unknown to us, fate was about to step in and provide us with some transport. It came out of Jerry's passion to drive cars fast. Even though he could not drive at all at that time, he still wanted a car for the 'cool look' it would bring him. We were growing up fast into young adults, full of the joys of life, as Ireland was also growing economically into a time of new hopes and dreams. Unlike today, we were then living in a time of relaxed laws in Ireland when no guard really took it too seriously that you had neither a driver's license, nor an insurance certificate, so one evening Jerry felt that he would ask his dad for the loan of 'the van'. Jerry somehow persuaded his father, who was a local builder, to give him a loan of his work van; a dramatic mistake indeed. Then, even at a very young age, young Hayes had pretensions of becoming a rally driver, or more likely a Formula 1 driver. The minute he got behind any kind of an engine he became a complete lunatic. He just loved speed and driving fast had been his passion for as long as I knew him. It was the funniest thing to see poor Kieran Hayes, Jerry's dad, slowly crawl up the town, never going any faster than thirty miles an hour so as to 'save the wear and tear on his van', and knowing what speed his son would be doing in it later that evening. We would be watching this from the street and smirking away as the fever would be gripping Jerry at the sight of his dad's snail-like pace up the street. No sooner would he be into the van and out of sight of the house than Jerry's foot would be boring a hole in the floor, converting 'the snail' to 'a moon rocket' in seconds. He would be driving flat out at seventy or eighty miles an hour, and bends on the road made no difference to this speed; they were just challenges to be overcome. He had this theory that we, his passengers, were really only ballast, as when he would fly round a bend he would shout out, "Bank to the left," or "Bank to the right". We, like slaves in the belly of the van, would suddenly throw ourselves at the left or right side of the van while laughing our heads off. This weight transfer was often all that kept us on the road and on four wheels, and many a time he drove on just two of those. We became very used to this ballast work over the years and would almost automatically throw our weight at the sides without any call from Hayes. But any poor misfortune who didn't know the score got scared shitless, and would leave like a ghost having re-found religion during a short spin with Hayes. If Hayes happened to be giving some girl a drive, he became even worse going out of his way to impress her with danger; a rather poor method in hindsight. After we spent some years travelling the roads of Ireland with Hayes, we all believed that he was actually a most brilliant driver, and would trust him with our lives. Often we did, but one night he really scared us badly though to this day he denies its seriousness.

We were going to see a band called Chapter Five in Fermoy. I had been having no luck with the women for some time and I concluded it was my scruffy image that was causing it. Our idea of fashion then was non fashion: tie dye shirts, dirty torn jeans and a headband if you felt like it. The closer we looked to tramps the better we felt, and we all liked the look; after all we were Buttevant's brand of hippies. This was not the regular attire of the time though, especially for those who went to hear the unspeakable country music which we despised, but there lay the problem, as most women then went for that kind of music. We had to conform or stay inexperienced as regards the ways of women, so we compromised and dressed like tramps while listening to country music.

The night in question I had a master plan. I was going to go to this rock group dressed in a 'suit'. This meant I would stand out so much that I had to be noticed, and the 'innocent' girls there would be fooled into thinking I was a real nice guy because of the way I dressed. That was the plan at least. When the lads arrived to collect me they collapsed laughing at first, and they simply refused to be even seen near me, as the suit was a dark wine coloured affair with some kind of alien material whose origin I could never determine, but it was definitely not Irish. Hayes immediately christened it my 'pink suit' which only added to the lads' laughter. The Nan had bought it from the 'Jew Man' on tick, and that could possibly be one explanation for its odd texture and colour, as it was a cross between an Egyptian cotton and a Chinese silk. I never seen the like of it, and that night was my first time getting into it as well.

Hayes said that he couldn't soil his reputation by being seen with someone in a suit, let alone someone in a pink suit. He said it was just too much for him to bear. I refused all their threats and wouldn't take it off because I knew they would not go without me. In the end they capitulated with the compromise that I was not to queue up with them at the club, and off we went, late as usual.

Hayes was picking up a girl in Mallow, yet another poor victim, and I and Fowler and Joe Moloney were relegated to the back of the van acting as the usual ballast. Fowler was feeling sick from his grandmother's stew and kept moaning all through the journey to Mallow. Hayes was by then very late because of my arguments and him starting out late as usual, and he began driving even faster than ever. He picked up his victim and sped off at really high speed. He tore around the first corner and the victim started to protest loudly, but by then it was too late, and we were going to Fermoy on wings. I really became scared myself as Hayes was roaring the banking commands with a different frenzy. Soon the poor victim was beside herself with terror, and Joe was drumming away to himself, oblivious of the danger and banking automatically as usual. Fowler was roaring that he'd be sick if Hayes didn't slow down because he was being thrown from side to side. It was as if a kind of madness had gripped us all that night, starting with the laughter over my pink suit. After about fourteen miles of excitement, screams of terror, sick moans, and drum sounds, Hayes suddenly went flying into a zigzag bend. It was at a place where the road crossed a railway line almost at right angles. He shouted the commands, "Left, right, fuck," but we couldn't change sides fast enough and he lost control of the bloody van. It hit the ditch and sped across to the other ditch, going up on two wheels, where it also hit the kerb and began wobbling. Then, with Hayes fighting for control, Fowler was thrown right up in the air and landed on top of me. Moloney had suddenly stopped drumming with the realization of his death's proximity and he too started screaming, "Fuck, fuck, fuck Hayes," then he too fell on top of me.

Simultaneously Fowler puked his grandmother's stew all over me and my psychedelic shirt and pink suit. I was covered in vomit and not sure if I was still alive or not. There was a total panic for a short time, and it only took seconds before Hayes finally got the van slowed down, but not stopped. He was shaken but pretended it was our fault, and again speeded up as if to prove that he was not scared at all. The girl, who was by then crying and shaking uncontrollably, just got ignored. We all began to laugh our heads off except the poor victim who seemed to be in a state of shock. My suit was ruined and I was now pissed off at this disaster. Hayes said he had the answer: we would drive down to the river somewhere nearby so I could wash it off, and it would dry in the heat of the van. He was not seemingly worried that it was October

177

and freezing cold, and neither was I if the truth be. known. I just wanted rid of the stinking stew. Somehow he found some road to the river and down we went. In the moonlight we all fell out the back of the van and headed for the water. I believe Fowler actually drank some of the river water to feel better. The girl finally stopped crying. Moloney told some kind of a joke and we all laughed again. I washed my suit in the river, completely unperturbed by the girl who looked on in horror as I togged off. There, standing in my underpants, I wrung it out as best I could, then I dressed again in my pink suit which had by then turned completely black. Off we went again.

We got to the club and at the front door I got a lot of really strange looks, but we were well known there, and felt sure they would let us in. Hayes, who was feeling guilty for almost killing us, overcame his revulsion at being seen with me now in a black suit, and we all stood together. I smirked at my image, as I looked like a small priest with long hair, and a tie dye multicoloured shirt. A pink suit surely was better than that. After paying, in we went to the deafening music of the club.

The victim had disappeared, and we didn't know where she went. Hayes said she had no stamina anyways. As the night wore on, the heat dried out my suit slowly and in patches. Pretty soon I was wearing a psychedelic suit as the red was coming back into it, and my success at getting dances became extraordinary. The lads were fuming at this, as they were reduced to looking at the band while I careered all around the hall almost like a celebrity. Where I would always fail was when the girl leaned onto my shoulder to roar some comment over the music. When this happened she would suddenly feel the water squish out from some part of my clothes, usually my shoulders. This usually meant there would be a shriek of, "Ohh uckkk," and my girl would beat a speedy retreat saying, "I'll see you around creep". Then in defeat I would return to the friends, but in the end it did dry out, and later I did score with a nice innocent girl who let me take her home. The lads were so mad at this that they decided to sabotage my chances, and Hayes drove the van along beside us, taunting us all the time. The girl was not impressed and soon left after Fowler throws open the back doors and roars out loud, "Come on you old bollix, we're heading for the Majestic". The trip that had almost killed us had been a complete waste of time, but the night was still young and we were soon on our way back to Mallow's famous dance hall; the Majestic Ballroom, where we arrived just as the dance was ending.

While I was having the fun with Hayes and co, Kyrle had gone working to Dublin and was having his own adventures there. He would be gone for months at a time, and as mother never had a telephone in her life, she would be relying on me to pass on any news of her second son. By then I too had started working and I was not good at the visiting. Besides, Kyrle would only phone me at work now and again, so mother might go weeks without hearing any news of him. Often six months went by without her ever actually seeing him, and this used to drive her to distraction with worry.

Kyrle thought nothing of it though, nor did I. We all knew that we were alive, and that seemed to be enough for us when you're young. Eventually he would get lonesome and make a journey home, and it would be a cause for major rejoicing by mother. Father saw it as a reason for a different kind of celebration; an increased number of visits to Kit's bar. I remember one time in particular when the rejoicing turned sour. It was a Friday night and Kyrle arrived in home drunk as a skunk unexpectedly. He was wearing a black, heavy top coat that was covered in mud and he looked quite the worst for wear. Mother was both delighted and disgusted with him, while father saw him as his saviour and provider of many extra pints of Guinness. By a pure fluke, I happened to arrive home for a visit shortly after Kyrle and father had retired to Kit's pub. Mother began bitterly complaining Kyrle to me saying, "Jesus Mary and Holy Saint Joseph, he looks like a tramp John, and he's paralytic drunk as well. I think he got fired from his good job in the Post Office today". I ignored her worries and told her that she should have sense, that he was probably always drunk on a Friday night. I was wondering about his bedraggled state of dress though, and seeing the mud caked all over his coat, I felt that he had been in a fight that he lost. The curiosity was killing me and I wormed the answer out of him later that night after he and father fell in the door singing, drunker than ever. Mother had gone to bed in disgust, followed soon by my father. Then the two of us chatted on for hours while Kyrle sobered up, as usual, as the night wore on.

Contrary to being fired, he had actually been promoted that day and decided to celebrate by coming home for the weekend by train. The problem was that he took to celebrating early on the train and got sozzled drunk, then missed getting off in Buttevant. The train was pulling out of the station when he took decisive action and jumped from it as it left Buttevant. He fell into a mud ditch and that's what saved him from being killed. I couldn't believe it, but it was confirmed years later when one of his friends told me that he was with him on the train, and had tried to stop him from jumping.

On the Saturday we went walking down the castle and met old friends. The day passed uneventfully. Mother had gone mad getting food on tic and made our favourite dish; chips and an egg, as well as ordering a 'round of Galtee bacon'. This was the ultimate treat for us, reserved for very special occasions. Of course the prodigal son returning was as good as it gets. During the day she had cooked this 'roundel' as we called it, and had left it in her 'fridge' on the window sill. Mother's fridge was made from a large stone inverted pudding bowl sitting on a saucer, where the meat would be placed inside it and left overnight to cool. On the Saturday night we again chatted for hours and hours, with Kyrle then back to 'normal'. We discussed every possible topic and argued over quantum physics till we ran out of insults and ego running. Then about six a.m. the hunger took over and we raided the back kitchen for food, with no success. Then we both remembered 'the fridge' and the inevitable roundel of beautiful bacon sitting so lonely on the front window. This roundel of bacon had just one flaw: if you cut it, it always left a tell tale sign of the cut, and we knew full well that this bacon was for the 'Sunday Surprise' at teatime. It was like the turkey at Christmas and was almost as rare too. Kyrle felt that we should be able to cut a full circle off it and convince the mother that it had 'shrunk' in the night air. So we got at it and cut a ring off it, and ate it down. It was so delicious. However, we could not hide our theft, so we felt that if we cut a second thinner ring it might work better the next time. That just made it worse. Then while we were wondering what to do next, our nine year old brother Hugh arrived down the stairs to see what his heroes were up to. Here we found the perfect scapegoat. I offered him a chunk of the bacon, because by then all attempts at hiding our crime were in vain. "Here Hugh, have some bacon, tis lovely". He froze in mid-step half-way down the stairs, realizing the setup by instinct. "Ohh no way, I'm not being blamed for ye eating that bacon. No way, ye can shag off, and I'm telling". Then he hightailed it back up the stairs to his bed, so we ate the rest of the roundel and left some money in the fridge to soften the blow. Then, with my belly full, I went home to Nannie's and forgot all about our crime.

Sunday came and we headed for the river, and later that evening we were walking back down the street and saw the mother standing at the front door glaring up at us. "What's the matter with her John; she seems as mad as can be. She's still not mad over me drinking, is she?" We continued on down and her glaring got worse. I said, "Who knows why she's mad, sure I blame them bloody pills; they have her driven demented. It's either them or the moon". We both laughed out loud and that was the wrong thing to do, as she must have thought we were laughing at her.

"Where's the bacon? Ye ate the bacon didn't ye? Now we have nothing for the tea, not a thing to eat". I felt it might be time for a sortie across to the Nannie's, but I didn't want to leave Kyrle to face all the music on his own, so I said, "Mother we left the money for it under the bowl, I swear to God we did". "Don't you swear on a lie John, there was no money there, nothing". She was still raging on as we passed her, going inside to the living room. There we saw the father looking rather sheepishly at the television without his headphones on; a sure sign that he was only feigning interest in the TV. The real culprit was the father of course. He had also gotten a hankering for the bacon that morning, but finding it gone and our money in its place, he took off across the road to Kit's and drank the money instead. A big row then broke out, and finally Kyrle began threatening never to come home again if mother didn't stop going on about it all. That was too much for her and she was almost ready for the tears, so we all stopped arguing. I may be wrong, but I think we fixed the problem by getting a few 'chicken suppers' later that night. Mother still goes on about it, and being gifted with an excellent memory, I suppose we will never be allowed to completely forget the night we raided her fridge and ate the roundel of bacon.

Kyrle went back to Dublin next day, all forgiven, and I got the blame as usual. Probably Hugh ratted on me to the mother, and for some days she was not on speaking terms with me. Her mood was noticed by Fowler and Hayes when they called for me later in the week. "Hey man, what's up with your mother? She seems pissed off at you man".

I did not feel like reliving the bacon incident, so I said, "Ahh sure I blame them ould pills that the quacks keep giving her, she's never been right since she started taking them". Then Fowler looks at me with a twinkle in his eye and says, "I think it's the moon meself". In those days I used to blame the moon for every kind of mad event, and knowing that he had got me, we all burst into laughter.

We four were getting a reputation as hippies, lunatics and dangerous guys to be near in those days, and mothers were always warning their daughters to avoid us at all costs. Fowler had by far the worst reputation. He had a magnetic attraction for women and got into loads of scrapes as times went by. The strange thing was that the more the mothers warned against going near us, the more women we seemed to get - well Fowler did anyway. Music was our real love, and when we liked a band, we would head off to hear them in Hayes' dad's van. Driving a great distance was no problem for Jerry, as he loved every minute of it, but he had no license. Soon, being out most of the night was accepted by us all as the norm. And even after numerous adventures all over the county, I can say with complete honesty that we never harmed anybody despite all our antics, but we often nearly killed ourselves, usually because Hayes thought he could defy the laws of physics.

At a very young age, Liam Fowler was to lose his mother, his dad, his grandmother, and later his young sister Marie to leukemia. I know of no man who has suffered as much as Liam, and as if to show just how cruel life can be, he later lost his young wife as well. In spite of all of these tragedies, he has always had the most amazing personality, and is great fun to be with. He has, at long last, found happiness today with his childhood friend Betty who is Jerry Hayes' sister. But way back then in the late sixties he had become very alone almost overnight. For us his friends, his house became our meeting place, our place of planning for the future, and the place where we 'jammed' with sweeping brush guitars and chair drums. We used to listen to Radio Luxembourg as it was the only station playing pop and rock music. I well remember the night that Thin Lizzy became the first Irish rock band to enter the charts. It was with their classic 'Whiskey in the Jar', and we went wild with delight as it happened. We used to have great jamming sessions in Fowler's kitchen, each of us having his very own 'instrument'. I had a sweeping brush guitar, Joe Moloney had a chair with rungs as his drum kit, Hayes had another guitar (a smaller brush modified) and was playing lead of course, while Fowler was a rock singer, complete with imitation microphone.

As the music blared, we imitated the movements of the super groups, often with sexual connotations for the benefit of the imaginary 'groupies' who frequented the front of our stage. We pranced around the stage, which was in Fowler's basement kitchen, and I used to also double up as roadie, turning up and down our 'amps'. These amps were the drawers on Fowler's cabinet, complete with two broken knobs with pointy ends just like real amps would have. As we pranced around, and as the music intensified, Hayes would shout, "More band," which was my cue to increase the volume on Fowler's old radio.

None of us smoked, drank or took drugs, though I suspect we were supposed to be into all three at various times according to the do-gooders of Buttevant. We were just crazy young fellas mad into music, women and the explosion of life known as the sixties. The neighbours often complained to Fowler that we were way too loud at one a.m. in the morning, but it did no good at all. I would be instructed to turn up the amps even louder if I could manage it at all. I would do as instructed, so we just got even louder till they stopped complaining. Then I just turned down the amps again to a nominal loud level and peace was restored to the street.

Fowler's only worldly possession when his Nan died was a television set. We used to watch a series of four short horror stories each Monday night on Radio Teilifis Eireann. Hayes and I were terrible practical jokers, and as ever we would be gearing up to scare Fowler, who was a real nervous type. We would wait for a

183

real good scary part when he would be really into the terror and glued to the screen in a trance. Then at the appropriate moment we would leap at him simultaneously in the dark. It always brought the same reaction from him; initially total terror, then shrieking, and then roars at us to, "Get out, get out now, and don't come back, ever". He always calmed down after our begging for forgiveness and promises to be better in the future, which we never were.

We played all kinds of tricks over the years, but not just on Fowler. Hayes' sisters and their friends used to walk home from the pictures in Kyrl's hall, and as they would be coming up the long dark hill we would be waiting inside the wall with our four flash lamps at the ready. When they got really close, we would leap up in the air making the worst possible faces, which were not difficult for us, and scream at them. They would go into total shock, and then take off running and screaming like mad women as we fell around the field laughing. We did this for a while till the effect wore off, but then we decided to try the same trick on some ducks that frequented a lake near Hayes's house. He hated these ducks as they were squeaking all night long and used to keep him awake, so one night we crept up on them in the dark, and made a run at the lake with our lights blazing, leering and shouting like mad men. The poor ducks took off in terror and for months didn't return. Hayes was ecstatic and wanted a renewed attack when they finally began drifting back in one's and two's. However we declined, as there was no more fun to be had from it by then, and besides, a lot of the locals were missing the ducks.

One of the funniest things we did during those mad years was to become involved in what I believe was Buttevant's one and only 'streak' event. This came about when another Buttevant lad decided he wanted to join our 'gang'. His name was Anthony and he was a good bit younger than us. We really did not know what he could bring to our level of insanity, so we tried our best to put him off the idea. This didn't work so we then told him that he would have to do a test in order to qualify for membership. Anthony was up for any kind of test we might give him, and after considerable discussions we felt that if we gave him an impossible task then he could not be expected to do it; no face would be lost by anyone,

Anthony included. With that agreed, the task chosen was a 'streak' through the town in broad daylight, and it had to be done from the bottom of the town up to Fowler's door and inside. Surely this was an impossible task given the bad publicity streaking was having in those days. We felt sure he would never do this, especially when he might end up before the courts, but not so our Anthony. He was all for it. Still we thought he might be bluffing and planned the run with him for the following Saturday. Jerry Hayes had agreed to use his van as the base for the streak and would be located at the bottom of the town with Anthony getting ready inside it for his run. Anthony was supposed to race up the street, passing the mother's house, and on past the Catholic Church on the way to Fowler's door where he would fly inside to safety. I was to run alongside him taking pictures with my Polaroid as proof of the great event.

The Streak Saturday came round, and Hayes, Fowler and I arrived at Anthony's house where he was waiting fully dressed, but wearing a very long heavy black overcoat. It was a very cold day, but somehow I felt that this coat did not seem to be for protection from the elements. He jumped into the back of the van and actually started stripping off immediately, becoming stark naked within minutes. Then he wrapped himself in the coat and waited for me to leave with my camera so as to get ahead of him for the photos. All three of us looked at each other in disbelief as Anthony crouched down in the back of the van and began visibly shivering while waiting for the proceedings to begin. We three then got scared and felt a rethink was needed because he was obviously going to do the impossible after all. A rethink was indeed needed, so we drove up the street and parked outside the mother's house while we discussed our next plan of action. Anthony flatly refused to put his clothes back on and just waited behind us in the van while we argued back and forth about the merits or not of a streak. While this was going on, my mother came out the front door, and seeing us parked and talking, she pokes her head in through the open window. She says, "What are ye up to lads?" I think she could see naked Anthony in the back, but I'm not sure. In any case I say with a smirk, "Well, we are seriously thinking of doing a streak mother", and at that she goes completely mad. Jerry, knowing her temper and fearing trouble, had already got the van started and was heading for the top of the town. As we drive we see the mother heading for Nannie's, no doubt to complain me to her. All of us enter Fowler's house skitting and laughing our heads off, and once inside we try to get warm by all four of us standing around Fowler's one and only means of heat; a small little two-bar electric heater. I just fell about laughing as I saw Anthony open the front of his coat and take over the whole heater saying, "Lads me bollix is frozen, and when am I streaking anyway?"

The day wore on with tea being made by boiling the kettle on the same heater, and soon it got dark. We continued to chat about the streak and eventually one of us came up with the next bright idea; that we would modify the long streak to a shorter and much more exciting one. Anthony would now have to begin his run in a laneway right in front of the Catholic Church then run diagonally across the street into the relative safety of Fowler's house. I was again to act as official photographer, and the only other condition was that the run had to be timed to take place when the church goers were leaving the evening religious service. Again, to our surprise, Anthony agreed to do it while still shivering naked in Fowler's kitchen. It was pitch black as Hayes drove Anthony around the back lanes of Buttevant, ending up on the one right across from the church as planned while Fowler and I waited for a signal across the street. Jerry Hayes was to flash the lights on his van when Anthony would make the run and I would run to him to take the picture. They waited for the people to pile out from the church and then the signal came as the first of the congregation passed us on the street. Anthony let out a wild Tarzanian yell, threw off the coat, and with arms spread he began dashing across the road for Fowler's door as I dashed towards him with my camera at the ready. There was a traffic island in the street in those days and Anthony and I reached it at the same time as a car. I took the picture and a big bright flash lit us all up, with Anthony's nakedness being the main attraction. The approaching car almost crashed into the island as the driver's head shot around in amazement and disbelief at what he saw. There was also consternation among the old women on the street. In my run I saw hands fly up to mouths, hands pointing at us and others were just frozen in shock at what they were seeing. We ran in slamming the door behind us, leaving poor Anthony outside banging on the door and jumping up and down with both cold and fear. We soon let him in, and after Hayes arrived we began the congratulations with lots of handshakes and praise being heaped upon him. Then we waited for the 'proof' of his run to develop before our eyes, and it did. There he was: Buttevant's one and only streaker, complete in all his nakedness with arms outstretched, whizzing by the traffic island to the amazement of the people of his hometown, and all this was happening in front of the Holy Catholic Church. A hero was born that night, but he never joined our gang, and all his great run achieved was to finally convince everyone that we were definitely all on drugs of the worst kind.

Anthony used his photo to create a mystique about himself which he well deserved. I know that he was not shy about showing off his physique as one day when I got on a bus, he arrived on his motorbike and parked it by the side of the bus. The bus was loading its passengers and I had sat down on the outside of a very nice quiet local girl. As we chatted I heard his motorbike race its engine again and again. Looking out the window I saw his (or should I say my) picture slowly creep up the window just inches from the head of the shy girl. He had seen me get on the bus and was up for devilment. Fortunately the girl didn't look round and soon the bus took off, being chased up the street by Anthony still waving his photo. The girl didn't see it, but almost everyone else on the bus did, and I saw a lot of smirking and pointing going on as I tried to pretend I didn't know him. Over the years I have met him on and off and he is still as charismatic as ever, but I have never enquired about the famous picture. For all I know it's been framed on his bedside table.

Probably about nineteen seventy three or so the four of us decided that we should make our own entertainment based on a new phenomenon called Disco. I'm sure it was Hayes' idea, and how it actually came about is now a mystery to me. I would have been about twenty three then and had been working for a few years in a television shop in Mallow with a man called Larry Anderson, of which more anon.

Our disco would be called 'The Liberation Disco'; a name I disliked, but that was what we were going to be known as. Hayes would do any art work needed, and basically he drew everything, including our handmade posters. I would build all the electronic gear, the amps and the lighting control units. The other two lads would build all the woodwork needed to contain our 'equipment'. I had by then developed a sound to light electronics system, the first of its kind in the world I believe, and I think it was while showing this to Hayes and Fowler that they got the idea of making 'the world's first real' disco. Without a single penny of capital, we borrowed or stole the wood from Hayes' father and I was to convince Big Kyrl to let us use his dance hall for our testing. He reluctantly agreed, asking me how much electricity it would use. I said, "Sure tis only a few flashing bulbs Kyrl, how much could that use". It was much more like a few hundred bulbs though, but I felt it was wiser to keep that fact to myself, for a while at least.

We began building away goodo, but we needed a wooden base to hold the turntables and the amps, and that was becoming our biggest problem. Hayes' dad Kieran had nothing that we could steal that would do the job, so we were at a standstill. Fortunately my mother had persuaded Nannie to get Tadgh Hurley (Joe Hurley's dad and owner of the furniture store) to sell her a new table. This was delivered and was stored in the front of our house, waiting for a decision on the best place to put it. I noticed that it would be a perfect fit for what we needed, so we stole it and carried it up the street to Fowler's shed, which was our 'factory' for gear building.

Rather than have a big row over the theft, I told mother that evening that we just needed to borrow it for a few days to try out our new moneymaking idea, and that she would get it back perfect with a financial bonus as well. This pleased her at the time and the next thing we did was cut two huge holes in the table so that we could sink the disco decks and the amps into it. As we sawed through the new table, Hayes was having some doubts, fearing a backlash from the mother. We all agreed to buy her a new table from the first money we made, and because that made us all feel better, we then sawed off the legs as well and put the table on top of a tar barrel as a kind of plinth for good effect. Hayes later painted this barrel black and white in a zebra style. There was no going back then, and she was never getting that particular table back.

Next we built the light boxes which were made of a wooden

frame containing bulbs placed inside car headlamp reflectors. The front of the light box was covered in a plastic that Hayes had also painted in a psychedelic pattern. Jerry Hayes really was a great artist.

Our speaker columns were also made of wood, and initially these had just two big speakers; one that we bought and the other we stole from Big Kyrl's hall and replaced with a radio speaker so he wouldn't cop it. Later still I began to rob speakers from old radios at work and soon we were ready for our first tests in Kyrl's hall.

The night he gave me the keys, he told me not to burn the place down and wished us luck. We excitedly began to set up our gear on his stage; we were in the entertainment business at last. It was all so very exciting as it came together and I think the first record played was Dearg Doom by Horslips, an Irish Celtic rock band that we loved. The hall exploded into coloured light which exactly followed the music. It was awesome to see and we stared at it in awe as the music blared into the empty hall. The flashing lights began to attract the teenagers outside, as by then the whole town knew that we were about to launch a whole new idea in Buttevant. Soon a few people arrived in for a look, and later a lot more arrived and we had to shut the show down or ruin it as a surprise for our debut. We reluctantly turned it all off and cleared the hall, but the word spread. Over the next few weeks we refined the play list and the lighting and I added a series of switches that I would play like a piano to turn the lights full on, overriding the electronics. This was a great addition to the show, and later the lads would mock me because of the way I would go insane with my fingers flying across the switches following the music to a tee. It's important to also add a point of information here because when I was sixteen, I used to wire houses illegally. I had no qualifications then, but I worked cheap and had a vague idea of what I was doing. I had covertly begun a small electrical business in which customers asked me to add on an extra socket or light bulb here and there in their house or farm. I made a nice bit of money doing that work, but the wire was costing me a fortune. When Big Kyrl found out about it, he asked Kyrle and me to rewire his dance hall for him, and we agreed as long as he bought the wire. I felt that we could save a lot of his heavy wire by putting the cheap light stuff above the ceiling and not tell him about it, and we did just that. To fool him, we would run some heavy wire up the wall to a junction box hidden above the ceiling and then run the cheap flex across the roof until the cable came down the wall to the fuse board. Our view was that anywhere he could see the wire, we would use good wire, but for all else we ran the cheap stuff. He examined the work and passed it all and paid us. I believed that he would never go up into the ceiling area, nor would he suspect that we would cheat him either, but he was wrong on the cheating. Later I wired many a house using Big Kyrl's good wire and did it without a smidgeon of guilt. In my mind I was following his mantra that the end always justified the means, and I was just getting even with him for paying us pittance over the years.

Returning to the disco days, our first disco night was announced with a flood of Hayes' posters being placed all over the town. We knew that we were going to have a packed hall full of teenagers and even adults looking on to see this new light phenomenon. Big Kyrl had officially hired the hall to us, and at about midnight I took his rent down the town to his house and paid him proudly. He was genuinely delighted with his nephew's success and wished us well while also agreeing to keep renting his hall to us at a cheap rate. Then as was his custom, when I was about to leave, he walked me to the front door for the 'final chat', and we looked up the town to see his hall. We could see it alright and he saw it in a new way too, as did I. He always had a few rows of bulbs running up the front walls and around a kind of overhang that he had built across the main door. It was a nice feature, and because one could see it from the entire main street, when it was lit up, it signaled that a function was taking place in Kyrl Cahill's hall. That was how it normally worked, but on our disco night all of those outside lights were also flashing in time to the music. Even I knew that the only way that could happen was because the wiring was completely overloaded and the wires, especially those above the ceiling, had to be getting red hot. Big Kyrl spotted it too and went into an immediate panic, demanding to know just how much electricity I was using. I had no idea, but calmly I told him that I had made those outside lights flash on purpose so as to attract in even more people to the hall, and that seemed to calm him down. I was dreading that he might suggest a visit up to check, but he didn't. I could not wait for him to go inside so that I could run back up to the hall and turn off half the lights, preventing yet another fire in the history of the Cahills.

Our disco was a huge success; the whole town was talking about it except for those who saw it as 'a place of sinful intentions'. History has since shown that the very same Church that railed on against us and our morals had priests that were doing far worse to the youth than our flashing lights and darkened hall ever could. Still, this Church persevered in demanding that parents would not allow their children to go to our gigs, and Catholic Ireland ultimately won. We continued for a while with our crowds dwindling more and more until in the end we had no choice but to stop playing in Buttevant. Rather than be defeated by them, we took to the road. We then had Ireland's second ever mobile disco. 'The Liberation Disco' became 'The Liberation Mobile Disco'. The first one was in Dublin and soon would go bust, and by a twist of fate I would actually work on it in the distant future.

To become mobile and get wheels, Hayes would use his father's driver's license illegally to hire a big van from Kenny's Van Hire in Cork and drive it like a lunatic to Buttevant. There we would load all our gear and head off to Dungarvan, our regular gig every Saturday night. It was brilliant; incredibly exciting, and also very dangerous. Two rival gangs were our main punters. The bouncers would disarm them literally at the door, keeping the weapons in two separate boxes, and returning them to their owners at the end of the gig. There would be chains, knives, and knuckledusters, and I once saw a hatchet in the box. We had no stage either and only a barrier we made from long seats separated us from the gangs, but to their credit they never once harmed us. They did not need to, as after each gig they fought each other all the way round our van while we loaded our gear. It was a crazy, crazy, fun, happy and mad time, and we acted and felt like rock stars with the only thing missing being the groupies.

Our fame was growing also, and one night we were contracted to do a gig in a small village for a youth club somewhere near Mitchelstown. When we got there I was sure we were either in the wrong place, or it was going to be a disastrous night because the whole area seemed so quite. We began to set up when the first bus arrived. About a hundred kids piled out and lined up to pay. Then

191

more busses arrived soon after, and in a short time a huge line had formed with hundreds and hundreds of teenagers all excitedly waiting to hear The Liberation Mobile Disco. Perhaps the name was not too bad after all.

Fowler, our lead DJ, began the main part of the show with the classic 'Brown Sugar' from the Rolling Stones, and I saw magic happen. I believe it was our best gig ever, and one could feel both the excitement and enjoyment of almost one thousand kids in the hall that night. They danced and danced and loved every song we played. Fowler was never better, and Hayes and I worked the lights like demons while Joe Moroney had opened the show and whooped up the crowd to a great frenzy at the start. In the middle of Led Zeppelin's 'Whole Lotta Love', a piece we used to specialize in, all of the main lights suddenly came on and immediately the atmosphere died. I'll never forget it. This had never happened to us before on a gig, and I ran off down to try and get them turned off while the crowd looked on in amazement. In the box office the local priest, who I believe was a trustee of the hall, had decided like the Buttevant gang that we were corrupting the morals of the youth, and the show would only be allowed to continue if the hall was fully lit. This was totally unacceptable to us and no amount of pleading from us, or from the people hiring us, was going to change his mind either.

Fowler told the crowd of fiery young teenagers what was going on and first the booing began, then bottles were thrown at the windows inside the hall, and when that didn't work, some chairs were broken. Very quickly a riot almost happened. It was looking like the kids would wreck the hall. We stood and waited, and finally the old priest capitulated and the lights went out. We were back in business with 'Sympathy for the Devil' being blasted out to the cheers of the kids. It was a great night and we were on a huge high as it ended. It was a night when we would easily be able to pay the mother back for her table as well as buy a lot of new gear, but we were counting our chickens far too soon.

When we had loaded our gear and went into the box office for our take of the door, the caretaker informed us that the 'priest had taken the takings' and we were not going to be paid any money. Our share was supposed to be used as compensation for the 'damage' done in the 'riot'. It looked like my mother would have

192

to wait for her money.

We left dejected, disgusted, angry, and broken-hearted if the truth be known. Catholic Ireland had won yet again. I think we gave up on our Liberation Disco soon after that, because it's the last memory I have of those wonderful days. For the record, mother never got paid for her table, and for years after she would rise me about it. The only regret I have from those days was that we took the beating from the priest far too easy that night. Today a solicitor's letter would have settled his case quite quickly. That incident left me with a bitterness that I never forgot or forgave. The disco days were great fun, but we were all about to move on with our lives, and had grown into even older adults by the time they ended. We drifted apart and only meet far too rarely these days, but when we do, it's like as if forty years have not passed by at all and the laughter begins all over again.

He better get sunscreen.

In about 1967 a man called Larry Anderson called to fix the mother's TV set. She had it on rent for three shillings and six pence a week; the equivalent of less than twenty cents a week today. It was always in danger of repossession as she didn't always have even that amount of money to pay for it, and it did get repossessed on a few occasions. The father loved it though as did we, and it was the greatest of pleasures to be sitting in your own home watching 'Lincoln Vale of the Everglades', 'Mr Ed', or some other exciting or funny programme. It was definitely a lot better than standing in the cold outside Tadgh Hurley's window with the others who could not afford the magic box of light. The TV sets that were made in those days were very unreliable, and fixing them was like a black art. If you could fix a television set you were considered a kind of God, or at the very least a genius or magician. Those TV sets used valves or 'tubes' as the Americans called them, and these valves only had a limited lifespan. Each TV set had as many as twenty valves, all different sizes and costs too. Therefore they were always breaking down because the valves would burn out. If you were trained as a TV engineer, it looked like you were made for life, and as a late teenager I was about to go into that very business.

My Nannie had a large 23 inch Pilot set and my mother had a smaller 19 inch Philips set which was always in trouble. That meant that a man called Larry Andersen was a regular visitor to my mother's house, and to a lesser extent, to Nannie's also as he fixed both of them. He worked for a company called Buckley's Stores in Millstreet town, the location for a famous Eurovision Song Contest held there in later years. On one of these occasions the mother asked Larry, who she liked a lot, if he had any job going for a 'good lad'. She was meaning Kyrle, as we were both still going to Charleville Tech at that time, and she was preparing the road for her son. I had met Larry a few times when he was fixing Nannie's set, but I was too shy to ask him for a job even though I loved what he was doing. He had no job then, but told mother that he would keep her in mind if a job became available. She was determined that Kyrle would get a good job, and soon she had answered an advertisement for a job in the 'P & T' as it was known then. This was the state owned Department of Posts and Telegraphs, later to separate out into the Post Office and Ireland's national broadcaster now known as RTE. Kyrle went for that job and got it. He took off for Dublin where my aunt May was putting him up until he got on his feet and earned enough to move out on his own. When he began he worked in the phone service, and in typical form he began to study for promotion, which he got very rapidly due to his ability to learn with ease.

Kyrle had barely begun working in his new job in Dublin when Larry returned looking for him. He was already committed and I was 'volunteered' for Larry's job. I wasn't even asked if I wanted it. The Nan told me that I had to take it as it would bring in 'steady money'. Larry didn't mind, but I think he would have preferred Kyrle as he knew him better than me. The job had an immediate start, so I had to leave school without finishing it as Larry was opening his own business in Mallow, and he wanted a boy who was honest, who would work cheap and learn to fix TVs. That was exactly what he got. I was fed up with school anyway, and I didn't want to be poor all my life, so I gladly took the job and the tiny apprenticeship salary going with it. I can clearly see my first day at work just as if it were happening to me right now. Mallow is seven miles south of Buttevant and I had no transport of any kind other than my old push bike. On my very first day I got a drive to Mallow from a local man that the mother knew. He took me right to the shop and said, "That's it," and left me to my own devices. I was just 18 years old then and as innocent as you could get, despite the general belief by Nannie that I knew everything. However, I had two things going for me: I was inherently honest with money due to Nannie beating it into me earlier in life, and I loved electronics with a burning passion.

When I first saw the little shop I was not impressed at all. It had a big sign over the door saying 'Mallow TV Service', and Larry and his first wife Eileen were living in an apartment above the shop. I went in and knocked on a little frosted glass window that was in the middle of a wooden partition which divided the workshop part from the customer's front area. A small narrow door was also fitted into this partition and it had all the signs of a do-it-yourself job. If this was Larry's place, then I saw a similarity to how we Cahills did things and I relaxed a little bit while I waited for someone to answer my knocking. No one did, so I went in the little door and on my right was a narrow staircase going up to the flat above. My first real shock came when I saw Larry come running down the stairs stuffing his shirt inside his pants, and on seeing me for the first time close up, realised 'this is him'. I saw his shock too and thought this may not be such a good idea after all. He shook hands with me and said welcome, then he told me to do whatever I liked that day as he had to rush off to Millstreet because he was late, and straight out the door he went.

I was at a loss as to know what to do. I was in a small room converted to a workshop. It was about eight feet by six feet with its unfinished wooden partition dividing this inside office area from the outside world. The customer area outside was known as 'the shop' and it had a fair-sized window with a large shelf area facing the street. The entrance door was a divided affair with some small panes of glass giving light into the shop. There were TV sets strewn all over the place and some radios too. Confusion seemed to be the order of the day. The toilet was shared between us and a printing business, and it was located down a half-covered laneway beside our shop. The actual toilet itself was a small cubicle area with a red door, and aside from us and the printers, anyone else who knew of its location seemed to be free to use it. Quite soon I concluded that I better never get 'the runs' as I'd never make it down that lane in time, or it might even be occupied.

Back inside the little workshop, the walls had been covered with a big Pilot TV diagram and a shelf or two which held various bits of TVs and radios. There was a marble fireplace on one wall which was never used, and a long workbench ran along most of the back wall, except for a really tiny area to the right under the stairs. This little area was to become my workbench when Larry would be using the main bench. No one can imagine nowadays a little business like this unless you live in the wilds of China, but that business was where I was about to spend the next twenty years of my life. Those years were without doubt going to become times of incredible happiness for both me and Larry, but all that was ahead of me still, and on my first day I was petrified and disappointed with where I was. Larry told me to knock off at six just before he shot out the door and was gone like a flash, shouting back that he'd see me tomorrow when he had more time. I sat down in a kind of daze and looked out through the frosted window wondering if this was going to become my life from then on.

J ust under the window Larry had placed a table with a small green money box. This little table area, complete with its money box, was to be where I would take in any rent money and also the payment for repairs to people's television sets. All that was the theory at least, and all of my duties had been explained to me in the few minutes before Larry took off. As we spoke I began to like him immediately, within a matter of minutes actually. He seemed to be really a mad, nice guy, and I felt he wouldn't fire me easily, so I relaxed a bit as he spoke. Very soon he was gone and I was left all alone, now 'in charge' of the shop - his shop, and I had no idea how I was even going to get to this workplace tomorrow.

As I mused on what lay ahead for me, there was a shadow at the glass followed by a loud buzzing noise which scared the hell out of me. A customer was at the window pressing a buzzer which Larry had forgotten to show me. I slid across the glass pane and there stood a woman wanting to pay her TV rent money with a ten shilling note in her hand. I was so nervous that I took it, put it in the box and said thanks, then closed the window and sat down again shaking nervously. The buzzer went off again and I slid across the glass. The woman just stared at me and I stared back at her saying, "Thank you misses". Still she seemed not satisfied, then finally she said, "Where's my change, do you think I'm a fool or what?" Then I felt like the fool as I fumbled in the box, wondering what change I should give her. I had no idea, and in the end I had to ask her what change she wanted. She told me and left in a huff. Then I immediately counted the money in the little tin box not wanting to be accused of anything. I wrote the amount down, as I wanted all to be right by evening time. I made my own little ledger; Larry had none, and this was what I used for a number of days, carefully adding all the money each evening, and checking and double checking all the time to make sure that none had gone missing. I was terrified of loosing my job because Larry seemed to have made a big thing about honesty when he talked to the mother. As it turned out, he need not have worried as honesty had become a principle of mine by then.

My next shock came later that morning when I saw Eileen, Larry's wife, arriving down the stairs, because she too was from Buttevant and I knew her. She made me feel at home instantly and asked me if I wanted some tea. I was really very shy at that stage, especially with older women, and I refused politely even though I would have loved a cup of tea at that moment. Nannie had made me a few sandwiches and some milk in a bottle as my lunch, and so I resigned myself to that place for better or worse. It was not my ideal of a job, but it was a job nonetheless and I determined to make the best of it as Larry was nice at least. That morning I know that I did not have one single penny in my pocket. I know too that I decided there and then to save money so that I would not feel so broke in the future. I made that commitment to myself while standing at the door of the shop looking out onto the street and the rain, and it feels like it was just yesterday.

Lunchtime came round and I ventured off down the town. Mallow as a town was completely alien to me, and I knew Charleville far better from my recent school days. Of course, according to Nannie, Mallow was a 'den of iniquity', but she said it would do for now and would 'give me a start'. Twenty years later she was still saying it would do for a start. Even though I often told her that I was very happy there, she still felt I deserved better.

I always loved inventions. They are in my blood, no doubt coming from Big Kyrl's side, but of late I realize too that my mother also had the gift of a creative mind. She absolutely amazes me with some of the ideas she comes out with today, usually ones designed to make life easier, especially for old people. However, in those early years we just ignored the mother, especially when it came to anything requiring brain power, because according to Nannie 'sure she's useless'.

Larry Andersen would soon become the most inventive person I ever met in my life. His people were also inventors, and he told me that during the war his dad had made a car run on charcoal when petrol was scarce. Larry continued this fascination with energy later, especially with his ideas on 'perpetual motion'. I was destined to have a first hand experience of this energy work within days of beginning his employment. My second day with Larry was almost as bad as the first; again he ran out the door saying I did real good for the first day, and he'd see me tomorrow for sure. He was gone and again I remember feeling very much alone. I noticed that Larry's customers were mostly people who came in to pay for televisions that he was renting to them, but he had no system of records. Even I knew this was not a good way to do business and I planned to bring it up with him if we ever got to sit down together.

On my third day of work I arrived in finding Larry sitting down at the desk quite calmly for a change. It was a Wednesday and he told me that he always had that day off, and it was also a half day in Mallow. Now we were going to spend some time together. At first it felt very awkward as I was so shy, but I believe that he noticed this side of me and made light of it. As the day wore on and we chatted about what we liked to do in life, he came to the conclusion that both he and I were mad on inventions. As an aside we both also dreamed of becoming millionaires as well.

Soon I began to relax, and liked him more and more as the day wore on. He was funny, had a strange kind of moustache, jet black hair, and he laughed every chance he got. I figured too that he was a good practical joker like me, and so I felt that we had lots in common already.

We talked about energy-saving ideas, which were his favourite subject then, and as if on cue he says, "Wait till I show you my latest invention". He told me that it was a new kind of 'heater' based on the idea of using light as heat. I had my doubts about the concept, but before I could argue he says, "Watch this," and then he plugged in a wire leading to a large television cabinet under the bench. That might be a normal enough event in a TV shop, but in Larry's invention, that cabinet was full of very large 250 watt light bulbs.

The minute he plugged it in there was a big bright flash, and immediately the whole of our little workshop became as bright as the sun. I was blinded by the light, literally. He says, "What do you think of that John, isn't she great? That's our new heater. It's made of bulbs and they give off light which is heat, as you know". I didn't know what to say, believing that at a minimum I'd better be buying sunglasses, and in the worst case scenario, I would be freezing to death at work in the winter. With this kind of thinking, day three had me seriously worried, believing I might be in the wrong job with the wrong person after all.

While I'm trying to figure out what to say next, the buzzer on the counter goes off. Larry turns away from the light and slides the glass window across. It's an old woman wanting to pay her rent money. As he opens the glass window, I see her stagger backwards clutching her eyes, saying, "Jesus Mary and Holy Saint Joseph, what's going on in there? I only came in to pay me rent". Unperturbed, Larry says, "Tis all right maam, I was just showing my new man here our new heater," and with that he turns back to me and says, "Plug it out there John, will you, it might still need a bit of work done on it".

Then in the relative darkness, the old woman warily returns to the little counter and gets out her money, all the time cautiously staring back in at me. As she is paying, she says to Larry, "Is he going to be in there all winter with that light, because if he is he'd better be getting sunscreen," and then she bursts out laughing, confirming my worst of all fears. It wasn't just me that thought it was an insane idea.

When she's gone Larry says, "Well what you think of it," and then all excited he plugged 'the sun' back in again. Not wanting to be impolite on my first real day I say that I like the idea of saving energy, but can we block off the light as it was blinding everyone, including me. Larry looks at me in astonishment, and then says, "But tis the light that's the heat, don't you get it?" Our very first argument was about to begin, and after an hour or so of this debating back and fourth, Larry's compromise was to point the box at the far wall, lighting it up like Big Kyrl's cinema screen. It looked like the new 'heater' was staying and I better be getting a warm jumper for the winter.

T he heater was a failure because of the blinding light and Larry capitulated, but only partly. His newer version was a smaller, more individual heater. He decided that both of us would have our own individual 'box heater', as he called it. This was a strong cardboard box with holes cut in the front for our feet. We could literally stand into it, or sit with our feet going into our heater, and of course the heating element was once again his high power bulbs, now confined to a smaller area. This type would last us for numerous years, and though a real fire hazard, it actually worked brilliantly because if my feet get cold I am useless. I loved his 'box heater' so much so that all of my life I have made one, and as I write these words in January, my feet are stuck inside my own cardboard box, fed by an infra red chicken light. Larry's invention still lives on.

While I was initially getting a drive to work on a temporary basis, I used to have to hitch a spin home every evening. I hated doing this hitching even though it was quite common then. Since that time I have always hated to pass anyone who is hitching, and invariably I'll stop and offer a spin. It always amazed me how so many people would pass you, especially when it rained. I discovered years later they were afraid to get their cars wet. My temporary morning drive soon stopped after some time, and then I was on the road full-time with thumb out both morning and evening all through that winter. It was very hard going, and then my determination to get some form of transport set in. Though it would take a miracle with what I was earning, I believed I would soon get wheels.

I remember giving my first week's wages to my Nannie with a great joy in my heart. It was the large sum of thirty shillings; the equivalent of one Euro fifty today. She took it all from me as if to test me, and when I said nothing and began to leave, she gave it all back to me again. Then she asked me how much I wanted to keep. I clearly remember just wanting to buy my own lunch in the town, and not have to eat her inedible sandwiches, though I didn't put it like that to her.

We agreed a deal, and from that day on I always gave up my money to the Nan. I felt real good about doing so too, as it was the first time that Nannie had some stable money, aside from her little pension. The very first thing I did the following Monday at lunchtime was to skimp on my lunch money, and open an account in the Mallow Credit Union. I planned to save up for a second-hand motor bike and get me out of the thumbing business once and for all. Over the coming months Larry began to teach me about television and how it all worked. We argued incessantly about electronics and inventions, and laughed every day we were together.

Larry and I had so many things in common: we both loved science with a passion, electronics was a form of religion for us, and with the march of technology we were always presented with new challenges, not to mention our love of inventions. Larry also had a drive for millions like me, but his method was to get them by cracking the 'perpetual motion dilemma'. This was a life long dream of his and I'm sure he is still thinking of cracking it today. Perpetual motion was the search for some method of self-generating and perpetuating a movement of any kind, but this movement would have to be self-sustaining and continue for ever. There are very good scientific reasons why this is impossible; for example the laws of friction, or the law of the conservation of energy. These laws never deterred Larry. He and I came to believe that together we would crack it eventually, and we came up with many schemes to test the theory. All failed in one way or another. If they had ever succeeded, I would most likely be writing a book about how to suntan safely in Spain.

My days with Larry were the happiest ones ever. We learned to face every kind of technology with a love of the challenge rather than a fear of it, as some do today. We saw the advent of the transistor, the large chip, and in latter years the microchip. Larry was constantly on at me, as was my Nan, to do my exams or 'get my papers', as they called them. I had no interest at all as I was so happy fixing and learning new things, so why bother I asked them often, but always I was hassled by both of them. I decided in the end to give in and do the bloody exams. I had no money and no transport to go to Cork to study, so I decided to do a correspondence course as the study part, and then sit the exams as an external student in Cork.

From my schooldays with Pad Keely I had developed such a terrible phobia about maths that I could not do any kind of maths at all, and in electronics they were a vital part of the study. When my first course papers arrived I discovered that I had to take on an additional study programme for maths because of my terrible fear. I would have to teach myself the subject from the start, and this I did. After I cracked the maths, the electronics exams came very easy to me as I loved what I was doing. In the end I got exceptionally good results and even surprised myself with the level of knowledge that I seemed to have.

There was a nice twist to the day when I finally showed Nannie the many electronics exam results I had achieved. She didn't understand the significance of the results, especially the City and Guilds ones, but the Diplomas she did understand, and knew they seemed to be very good. She was sitting in her old chair by the fire as I showed the certificates to her, and when I was finished she says, "John, I suppose it's time I gave you this other certificate too". With that she reached up to the mantelpiece, and from behind her large plate that she used to cook the Christmas turkey, she took down my famous disaster of an Intermediate Cert from Pad's school. It was a watershed for me, and taking it from her, without reading it I opened the top of her range and stuffed my Inter Cert into the fire. As we saw the paper burn up, Nannie just smiled that knowing smile, and we never spoke of exams again.

After being with Larry for a year or so, he felt that I should now learn to drive as I needed to be out doing house calls. By then we had become fast friends and all shyness had vanished. I loved the idea of learning to drive and becoming a real service engineer, and out of the shop at last. He had a red Mini Minor car. It was a real crock of an affair, held together by his mechanical ingenuity as he was as good as my uncle Kyrl with fixing cars. The gear stick had a heavy weight taped to it, preventing it from hopping back out of fourth gear. The wipers didn't work, and the starter used to stick, so it had to be pushed often.

It had a suitcase full of valves and parts laid out across the back seat, and if you couldn't fix the TV, it was carried back to base in the passenger seat. On a bad fixing day there would often be as many as three television sets in this little jalopy. That Mini, which was affectionately known as 'the bomber', was a real fast car though. It could almost fly, passing out Mercs and Jaguars easily, and later I would drive it to its limits, getting numerous frights in the process. When Larry began teaching me to drive, we had a real close call because of my addiction to speed. Larry and I had been out doing TV calls for a few hours and it was getting late. We were also arguing about how some circuit worked while I was driving like a madman. I was really into the speed then, being fully infected by Hayes who was driving us around to dances at that time. Larry was constantly telling me to slow down, but he was equally engrossed in our argument. As we approached Doneraile town, I came upon a very unexpected bend of almost ninety degrees sharp. By then Larry was hawing on the windscreen so as to draw the circuit with his finger. I took my eyes off the road to see his drawing, and when I looked back up, the car was heading for a wall and very quickly too. Instinctively I sharply swung the steering wheel as Larry let out a yell and pulled on the handbrake so hard that it snapped clean off in his hand. I am certain that the car went up on two wheels as it sped all over the road. It was exhilarating and so exciting, and as it was happening I thought I should do this again, if we survived. All too soon it was all over though and it flipped back on the road with Larry cursing and calling me a 'bloody' lunatic, and worse things too. We soon recovered our composure and arrived into Doneraile. I tried to make him laugh by telling him that it was his fault for arguing with me, but he was quite shaken at our close call. We drove on to Buttevant in silence, and next day he told me to get a provisional licence as he had no intention of getting killed with me so early in his life. Up until then I had been driving with no licence at all, and no insurance either. It wouldn't happen today though. When I did get my first provisional licence, he gave me the keys and said to get going as the only way for me to learn was to either drive properly or get killed trying; the choice was mine, but he was not teaching me anymore. Soon I was whizzing around at breakneck speeds every day. Later on each evening, with great sadness, I would have to return the car and go back to hitching home. Sometimes as a curtsey, Larry would ask me to give a customer a spin home in the car if we had just sold them a new television. That way I could install it and show them the workings. I remember one time I had to take a particularly prudish and posh woman home with her set. The new TV set was put in the back and she sat into the passenger seat as I got into the driver's side. Our Mini had been through the wars by then and the bottom of the driver's seat had a large hole with the springs showing through it. Larry and I were well used to this and didn't care, but as we drove away the woman says to me all of a sudden, "Do you have teeth in your arse?" I thought I was hearing things and said back, "Excuse me?" She repeated her question, looking all serious and I answered, "No, not at all, why do you ask?" me turning bright red in the face by then. She says with a big smile, "Well I think you do, because your arse has eaten a hole in the car seat". I didn't know what to say then, and felt like telling her that Larry's arse had been eating it far longer than mine, but I just went silent instead and stayed that way till I got to her house. I would never have guessed such an expression would have come out of the mouth of that woman, and later when I told Larry, he got such a fit of laughing and told me that he thought it was her way of wanting to see if she was right.

During those learning years I had many close calls, getting almost electrocuted at least twice, but the closest one was completely outside my control. I was always guaranteed a spin home on a Wednesday from the father's best friend, Arthur O'Lowery. Arthur was a lunatic driver too, and he was always in a rush home, especially during his dinner hour. He was a mechanic in the local garage, and would take different cars and vans home to Buttevant so as to test drive them. On this particular day he had a small van with a split back door and he was taking me and a local girl home. The girl was already seated as Arthur slowed down to pick me up. He did not stop though, but slowed to a crawl. I ran along behind him, pulling open the back door and jumping in. Then Arthur, thinking I was inside, pressed his boot to the floor and accelerated off at high speed. I couldn't hold on, and fell out the back door straight between the wheels of an oncoming truck, which fortunately was not being driven by Arthur's brother. It screeched to a halt with onlookers almost fainting in shock. As I quickly got up from beneath the number plate, the driver, by then as white as a ghost, kept apologising and asking me if I was alright. I assured him that I was, but that I had now lost my spin home as Arthur was half way to Buttevant by then figuring I would be ok. I think the truck driver was so relieved that he had not killed me, he took me home that day, probably thanking God for the rest of the day as well. To me it was not even worth mentioning to Nannie, but I can still see the front of the truck's number plate.

As the years passed by I became really good at this television work, simply because I loved every second of it. My aim was always to get the mother out from under the stress of her TV rental payments, and the fear of its repossession. Eventually I made her a television set from scrapped bits I had gotten from Larry. This was a hybrid set. It was a concoction of lots of bits from various models of TVs. It had a Philips chassis, a Sobell transformer, and mainly a Pye body. It was so unusual that I could not get a back cover to fit it at all, so it was highly dangerous as well. Initially it sat on a wooden box on her kitchen floor, taking up precious space, but the father was over the moon, now owning his own set. The mother was afraid of her life of getting electrocuted, and she kept on at the father to 'sink it' in under the stairs where it would take up less space, and would be safer. I didn't want him to do this at all for two good reasons: one was that I used to steal the valves from it for my own growing private fixing jobs, and the second and more serious one was that the Sobell transformers were famous for going on fire for no reason, and I didn't want the house to burn down and confirm Nannie's belief 'that fire follows them Cahills'. I couldn't tell mother my fears though, as she would immediately get rid of my concoction, and father would be devastated. She got her way and for a long time I used to have nightmares, seeing her house and all in it going go up in smoke. These dreams got so bad that eventually I made her a better set, and the terrors stopped. At the start it was a real mystery to her how her TV set was even more unreliable than the rental ones, but she used to get consolation from the fact that her son John had made it for her, and she told everyone that too. The truth was that it was extremely reliable, but I was increasing my 'private customer' base, and stealing an ever increasing number of valves weekly. I'd sneak in and whip out a valve, and later mother would call me and say, "John, the old TV is gone off again. Any chance you'd fix it for us?" I know the father was not fooled by any of this, but he never let on. For a long time I managed to avoid being spotted, but in the end she caught me doing the robbing and the game was up. All she did then was laugh, proud that her son was becoming a business man as well as an engineer, but I never stole another valve from her after that.

Blessings upon you.

Like every town in Ireland in those days, there were always some really hard luck cases around. Poverty was the norm for the vast majority of the people, but some were far worse off than others, even us. I have a vivid memory of one of these poor people. She was a young woman of about twenty five or so, and I feel that there had been some awful trouble in her life before she arrived in Buttevant. This woman lived up at the top of our lane in an area known as New Street. I think she was called Mrs Flint or some such name. I don't think she was ever married and she just seemed to have arrived in the town overnight, or at least that's my recollection of it. It looked like she had no family, was totally alone in the world, and no one seemed to care about her.

I'm quite sure that she barely scraped by, living from day to day, eeking out a miserable existence in a town of little charity and no social welfare either. She had no income that I knew of, but I think initially she used to do a bit of house cleaning when she could get it. This continued until the moralistic hypocrites of the town saw to it that this work dried up, because they believed she had 'callers'; gentlemen of loose morals who provided her with some extra source of income, though I'd be loathe to believe it was true. I remember her as the most gentle of souls, so meek and quiet. She wore an old coat, sometimes a small shawl, and always she had a dark silky scarf tied round her head. For some reason, I have always felt that kind of a look signified dire poverty to me, I don't know why that is but it's always a picture of misery in my mind. She constantly bore a look of sadness on her face and she seemed to be lonely all her life, having few friends, but my mother was one of those few at least.

Despite the moralistic rumours, we never spoke ill of her at home, as neither the mother nor my father would have a bad word said against her. The mother seemed to have taken a liking to her from the beginning and to be honest so did my father. He was always a man who felt sorry for the less well off in our society, being a classic example of those people himself, and mother just saw her as yet another poor struggling woman, a bit like herself in those hard days. Mrs Flint was often talked about in Buttevant. I'm sure in those times its people were typical of those of any other small town in Ireland, no better or worse, with gossip being a kind of relief for those who have little, and Mrs Flint's 'profession' was juicy news. While playing handball with Hurley I often saw her coming down the lane with her little canvas bag, her old tweed coat and that haunted sad look in her eyes. Hurley would cat call and I would tell him to shut up, and once we almost came to blows over his insults to her. Even then as a so-called tough teenager, that sad look she bore always affected me, but some years later I was to see it at close range in an incident that was organised by my mother.

This event came about in a strange way, and it is one of the few deeds I did in my life which gave me a really great feeling inside. I don't know why, but I always seemed to have had a soft spot for this poor woman subconsciously, even though we never once spoke in a conversation. If she was passing by we might just say hello, or give a nod to each other as she shuffled down the ballalley lane. One day while visiting my mother, she asked me if I would do her a great favour and have a look at the old television set that Mrs. Flint had been given by the St. Vincent de Paul. She said that it had been broken for about a year, and there was no way she could ever afford to get it fixed. Of course I agreed to look at it and soon arrived up at Mrs. Flint's little house at the top of the lane. Her house which could be more accurately described as a hovel had a rusty tin roof with a small door and two small windows. One of them had a broken pane of glass in it and the frame was rotting. She had covered the hole in the glass with an old bit of cardboard and it stuck through the frame unevenly. The other window had an old lace curtain strung across it with two large holes in the lace, but at least it had glass and gave light into her tiny little bedroom. From the outside, her home looked like a picture of misery and belonged to the era of Charles Dickens and I did not like what was facing me at all.

I knocked at the door, which was a half door if I remember correctly, and when it opened in, she seemed very surprised to see me. I said I was there to look at her television because my mother had asked me to, and before she could protest I was inside in a flash. I didn't want to make a big issue of this job as I knew she had no way of paying for it, and so I had planned to pretend to be in a rush and fix it fast, then leave before she knew what had happened. Almost immediately she said that she couldn't pay me. I dismissed it as nothing of importance, saying my mother was looking after any payment needed. She was still protesting saying she didn't want my mother to be out of pocket either. But ignoring her protests I whipped off the back of the old set, telling her that I loved fixing things, and that it was she who was doing me the favour by allowing me have a go at such an old set. This was not going to be a fast fix however, as there was not even a spark of light coming from inside her television set.

My words seemed to pacify her, and as I examined the set she went off tidying and I got a chance to covertly look around at her house. She had a small table which was very clean, being covered with a cheap oil cloth. She had two old chairs and some kind of wooden cabinet, not too unlike my mother's one in our back kitchen, and that was it. I was embarrassed at this poverty as she was obviously way worse off than we had ever been. She seemed to sense my embarrassment as an awkward quietness descended upon us. Then, as if to break the ice, she offered me a cup of tea. I said I'd be delighted, and as she moved around I glanced across into her bedroom. It seemed to have had no door to it, and it felt dingy and cold looking. There were some old coats thrown on the bed and no blankets at all that I could see. An old bulb that was covered in cobwebs hung from the rafters, and I'm sure it had not shown light for years. Overall her little place did look tidy but was very, very cold. This coldness pervaded the whole house. I felt the damp clinging to my bones, and I shivered both inside and out.

I wondered how she bore such misery day after day, and what she did with her time. From my dimming memory, there seemed to have been a spark of a fire coming from some kind of fireplace near the television set. This fireplace was really just a group of old concrete blocks forming a grate, and a black chimney. The spark must have been only a small spark as the coldness was beginning to get to me, and I never suffer from the cold but I couldn't shake it off.

Her old television was even worse than the worst of crocks. Over the years I had seen all kinds of junky TV sets, but this was the worst I had ever seen. All its fuses were blown and it had soot all over it inside as well as outside, no doubt from its proximity to the spark of fire, the smoke, and the slab of stone it sat on. I couldn't fix it at all, and this was annoying me as each time I got one part going a new problem soon arose in a different part. She said in her gentle voice, "Your tea is ready," never calling me by my name, but perhaps she didn't even know it.

I sat at her little table and I wondered how I was going to tell her that I had failed. This failure was a big shock to me personally, as I had never failed to get a television set going up until then. Yet it was never going to be right and I knew it. The irony was that she needed a television set for company far more than anyone I knew, and she could least afford one.

She poured the tea from a very black pot which was battered with age. I watched the weak tea fall into a clean, white, chipped cup that had a flower painted on the side of it. A half empty milk bottle supplied us with milk and she began to pour her own tea into an even more chipped cup; the guest had been given the best china. Why I remember these little details has always puzzled me, yet I do. I looked around for a sugar bowl as I liked sugar, and realizing what I wanted, she said, "I'm sorry, I don't have any sugar tonight. Do you take it"? I lied and said I hated it, that it was real bad for you as it was poisoning half the country, and we were all better off without it. She gave me a knowing smile and sat down opposite me. I just could not tell her that her TV was never going to be right, so I said I'd have to take it away if she allowed me to, as it was very 'sick', and I tried to make a joke out of it. She didn't laugh though. I suppose she was wondering what else could go wrong for her, but again she asked me about the cost, saying she didn't want my mother to be paying her bills. She added the words, "Times are very hard these days, you know". I nodded in agreement, finished my tea and told her not to worry about the money. Then I left with her box of junk.

My mother was very upset when I told her that I could not fix Mrs Flint's television, as she believed that if I was able to make her a set, then surely I could fix anything. I tried to explain but it did no good. Then she said, "John, you'll do something for her for sure, wont you? You must, and I know you will. Sure she's worse off than ourselves, God help us".

I did do something for her. First thing I did was to dump the bloody set. I told Larry I needed to build yet another television set, and as usual he didn't give a hang what I did, even though I was using his parts, his time, and I was his workman. It was as if he knew I needed to do this and actually offered to help me if needed. It took me a full week, but I made yet another TV set. It had a small 'Sobell' body and mostly 'Sobell' parts inside it, but it was again a hybrid as usual, made from many different makes and models and bits and pieces. I figured that if the 'Sobell' transformer went on fire, it was already sitting in her fireplace, and at worst it would give her heat while it burned, as she sure had no possessions to worry about.

Looking back on it now, in today's days of mass production and high technology, it was a great achievement, but came easy to me then, as according to the mother, "Sure he's gifted". But I attributed it to my methods of 'doctoring' developed in her attic some years earlier.

On a bleak Saturday night I arrived back at Mrs. Flint's door. She welcomed me in, seemingly very happy to see me. Then I placed my new box of magic on her 'stone' table and turned it on. As it warmed up, I plugged in her dodgy looking aerial. The picture came on but it looked terrible. It was barely visible, flickering and rolling, but she got so excited saying, "Great, great, oh tis great and so bright too". I couldn't believe what I was hearing, as the picture was almost lost in the snow on the screen and no one could possibly watch it. Her aerial was useless, so I got some cable from the car and made my own version of a 'cats ears aerial'. Then she really did have a good picture. Mrs Flint became speechless - literally. It was as if she had never seen a real picture before in her life, and probably she hadn't with that useless aerial. She seemed over the moon with happiness, shaking and rocking back and forth in her old chair saying, "Oh my, oh my, it's so clear, so clear, thank you, thank you, thank you so much". She said these words without taking her eyes off the screen, the poor woman was actually hypnotized.

Then almost in a trance she became glued to the screen, gazing at the picture in silence as I tried to show her how to work it. It was like looking at a child receiving the ultimate gift from Santa. She was hearing me speak, but she only saw the pictures. I never saw anyone become so transfixed by a television picture before or since. It was amazing to see sheer and utter happiness and appreciation being displayed at something so ordinary. Suddenly, as if remembering her manners, she jumped up and offered me tea. As I was going out later that night with the lads and I hadn't much time, I politely said that I didn't want any this time, and before I got a chance to say why, she added quickly, "I have sugar tonight".

In spite of her poverty, in spite of her lack of money, somehow she had got me sugar. Who knows what she had to do, what she had to sacrifice just to buy that sugar, and she did it for me. It was her only way to say thanks. Obviously I hadn't fooled her one bit with my feigned hatred for the 'deadly' sugar. Still I had to go, as I was already late. She said again that she had no way to pay for this new television set, and that I was so good to do this for her. I brushed it off saying my mother was taking care of it all and that I hoped she liked it. Then as I was leaving for the door, a very strange thing happened. She stopped me and put her two hands gently on my shoulders, and standing there looking deep into my eyes she said, "God bless you, and may you always be blessed," still not saying my name. As I looked back in embarrassment into her dark pools called eyes, I am sure I saw tears forming there, but I quickly looked away saying, "Thanks very much Mrs Flint, and now I must go".

She had given me all that she could give me in this world: a blessing truly meant from her heart and Soul, and though I was very anti-religious at the time, I am convinced that I felt some higher goodness come from her blessing that night. I left her saying, "Be sure and tell my mother if anything ever goes wrong with it, as it's under guarantee".

I never heard from her or saw her again. I drove away from her house cursing a system that allows such things to happen to good people, and swearing as usual that I'd be rich one day. My mother was really delighted when I told her about the 'new' television. She said, "Son be proud of what you did, tell no one, and God will reward you". I left Buttevant that night with the lads, hell bent on adventure and feeling invincible.

In my years with Larry, I always wanted to rise above the mere fixing of television sets. Kyrle by then had moved into the broadcast side of things in Dublin, and I longed for that side of our business too. I felt that the real kings were those who made the television or radio signals, and sent them out to us viewers and listeners, and that's where I wanted to be. Larry never cared for that side of things, but he was ten years older than me with a family to support, so he could not afford the luxury of 'idle dreams' as he called them. Yet those dreams were to become a reality for me in the not too distant future, but before that day dawned I would have many more adventures with Larry, and later still his brother George, who joined us from England.

I could write another book on my escapades with George Anderson, Larry's brother. We got into numerous scrapes together, and every day with him was actually funnier than most days with Larry. 'Georgie', as we called him, had no clue at all about science and lived every day just for the moment and the sheer fun of being alive. He was a very big man, well over six foot tall, extremely good looking and reminded me always of Roger Moore. In spite of his size, I only ever saw him get really mad once. It so happened that we were to change an aerial for a farmer who lived out in the wilds of Mallow. The farmer lived alone, and no sooner had we arrived into his yard than he asked us, "Where are yer white coats lads". Georgie looked at me as if to say 'What's his game' and I had no idea either, so I said, "Why do we need them?" Our farmer replies, "Yerra no need at all, sure ye'll be alright I suppose", and in he goes to his dingy kitchen leaving us to get up on his roof. The house was a three storey affair with an old slate roof and I knew that getting onto that roof and chimney would stretch our ladders to the limit. I personally didn't want to do this job at all, and neither did Georgie, so we tossed a coin and he lost. Our extension ladder was out to the max and Georgie made off up it, pulling the roof ladder behind him with me helping. Georgie reluctantly got onto the roof ladder and made his way up to the chimney, where his usual method of removing the old aerial was to literally break it off, as he was as strong as ten horses. I was by then standing on the ladder at the guttering, ready to go up after him and help, but I got a feeling to stay where I was. I saw Georgie standing on the chimney with his legs spread across either side of the chimneypot, trying to break off the old aerial. All of a sudden I also saw the first line of bees come out of the pot behind his back. I shouted, "Bees, bees Georgie," and began my fast descent down the long ladder. As I'm heading down I hear a roar from on high and a thump, and I believed that I was going to see Georgie pass me out as he fell to his death. Thankfully, by the time I got to the bottom of the ladder his feet were crushing my fingers. As the bees had attacked him he had somehow got onto the roof ladder and scaled down so fast that he almost passed me out, and I was really moving, being terrified of bees myself. He leapt past me and we both ran into the house, slamming the door on the black cloud following us in. We beat at the bees with cloths and our hands, and the shouting and roaring soon brought the farmer out from inside his lair. He says, "What's wrong with ye lads, what's all the fuss about, surely yer not afraid of a few tame bees". I think this became too much for Georgie and the fright and the stings got to him. He exploded in rage. He made a drive for the farmer, had him by the throat and was pushing him up against the wall with one hand while he still beat at the bees with the other. He began calling him every name under the sun, and all of them were real bad. I tried to pull him off the farmer, all the time getting stung on my neck as I did so, and by then I'm also shouting out a string of curses as well. It was pure bedlam for a while. By then the farmer was also in a panic thinking that Georgie might really clatter him, and he croaks out, "Ye should have had the coats, they don't go near white coats. I told ye so". I thought I was hearing things. After a little while we killed the last of the bloody bees and tried to calm ourselves down. The old farmer had scuttled off again first chance he got, and Georgie and I stared out the window at the bees still flying in all directions outside. We agreed to make a dash for the car and escape, and this we did. Then I said to him, "What about the ladders". Georgie's answer was, "Fuck the ladders, I'm outa here, let Larry do it, and we wont tell him about the fucken bees either". Of course when we got back we had to tell him, and in the end he had to do that aerial job by himself as both of us flatly refused to go back. When he returned later that evening he told us that the farmer had called us 'townies' and 'cowards' and Larry laid it on thick, trying to make us feel like he was a hero and we were useless. Years later when I was doing calls to the same house,

I discovered that Larry had put the new aerial into the farmer's attic where there were no bees, and I saw Georgie's old aerial still hanging half way down the chimney. Larry was no hero either, but he pretended he was to us.

We played practical jokes on each other all the time in those days. It was a kind of tit for tat fun. Georgie had been tricking me into doing extra calls for a long time and I was planning some kind of revenge, but no opportunity seemed to present itself until one day we had to deliver a television to the badlands of County Limerick. This was a big sale for Larry. A farmer who apparently knew Larry's dad had decided to enter the television age, and no expense was to be spared. He was after buying our largest Pye television set, and we were to install a new aerial in his attic as well. The only problem was that we had no idea where he lived, and only knew that it was somewhere in the east Limerick direction. The deal had been done in a pub with Larry's dad, and Georgie and I were to set off into the unknown, loaded down with the gear and the television.

Larry's dad told us that the customer was 'well known', and that all we had to do was find any pub in the Kilmallock direction and ask for directions to his farm, so we set off. Georgie was driving as he insisted on using his car newly imported from England. There was no way he would let me drive it, and so I began to feel that this might be the day of my revenge. He also had a very bad hangover, having been drinking all the previous night while attending the 'Rose of Tralee Festival'. Still he insisted on driving and was as sober as a judge too.

We drove for hours, getting more and more directed up into the hills of east Limerick, and eventually we arrived in the yard. To say that this place was a farm was a gross exaggeration. The entire place felt like it had never come out of the dark ages. I was surprised they even had electricity because it was so remote and rundown. The farmhouse was a thatched two storey building that had seen whitewash paint about a hundred years previously. An old tractor acted as a prop for one of the walls, and hay was piled against another one. I thought we were in the wrong place and told Georgie so, but as he was about to turn to leave, a swarm of small children came running out to greet us. They were all smiles, laughing and as happy as can be, but they looked like they had never seen a bath or even water in their lives. Snotty noses and scabby elbows as well as wild hair were all the go on both the boys and girls. Yet it struck me as odd that they seemed incredibly happy children, and I filed that thought away in my mind for some reason.

The front door was open and the farmer's wife, a quite portly but friendly woman, greeted us warmly and invited us in. There was no sign of the farmer. The inside of her home resembled the outside of the farm. It reminded me of Nannie's home in Gortnabearna, but at least there it was clean and tidy, unlike this place. The front door opened into a huge kitchen area, where I believe they did all their living. It had a large table in the middle and half of the table was literally covered in unwashed dishes, books and cloths. I figured that they never used that half of the table at all. I did spot another table on the way in though, which had two or three oily looking fish spread out on an old newspaper. These may well have been there for a day, or a week, I did not know, but my plan for revenge began with their observation, and I was hoping that Georgie had also seen the same fish.

I said to him that we should do the aerial part first, and that he should do the attic bit while I did the wiring downstairs for the television. He fell for it, but before he did he says to me real quietly, "Did you see them fish, the heads are still on em. I almost got sick passing em in, did you see em". I said, "Yeah I did and I wonder who she's going to feed them to". Quick as a flash Georgie says, "The dogs of course boy, sure there's no way she'd give them to the kids," and he headed up the stairs with the aerial.

The kids have now become so excited that the noise level rises to fever pitch, but I noticed that some of them just stared at me as if I was from another planet, while some others run round and round the kitchen table playing some strange kind of game. The woman of the house says to me, "Ye'll be staying for the dinner lads won't ye, sure tis late as it is, and I'll be cooking a few fish. Do you like fish yourself?" Immediately the revenge plan crystallizes in my mind and I say, "God no maam, to be perfectly honest I'm actually allergic to all kinds of seafood, but I do love home baked bread. Do you have any?" I figured I couldn't get food poisoning from flour, no matter how old it was. She says, "And be God so you'll have plenty of it me boy, and what about himself upstairs?" Before I can answer she says, "He's a fine big man isn't he, God Bless him". I see my opportunity now and say, "I tell you what missus, he is a fine man alright, but he's a real shy one as well. What's more, he is always hungry and loves fish, but he will be too shy to ask for one. He will be saying no thanks all the time, but that's just an act. He loves fish". At that news she was ecstatic, "Be God he will have them fish so, and you'll have my best curney cake, is that all right". I tell her that's just perfect and go back to my wiring.

After about half an hour I can hear the fish frying away and see her moving her black skillet back and forth on an old stove. I go up to Georgie and set the trap. I say, "Georgie, she's insisting we stay for the dinner and that we will be paid by her husband after he finishes the dinner with us. It will be ready soon". He says, "Well I'm eating notten here, and I hope the husband or the dogs is getting them fish". I'm smirking away as he says it. I say, "Me too", and head off down again. The farmer arrives in smelling of drink, and he is like a king to the children, causing the laughter and merriment to double in volume. It's like a Christmas morning as he hugs and kisses his adoring children. I see the wife calling him aside and pointing to the skillet and nodding in the direction of Georgie upstairs. He is all happy in himself and says out real loud, "Yerra don't worry your head woman, sure I ate in the pub". With that bit of knowledge, I know Georgie is definitely getting all the fish.

"Come on down here now will you, the dinner's ready and I won't take no for an answer," she bellows up at Georgie. By then she has prepared the half of the table that's usable, and two white plates are placed in front of us as we sit down. Georgie immediately says, "Maam I'm not a big eater and I'll just have a mug of tea and a bit of your curney cake". Wise to his tricks she says, "You'll have no such thing, a fine big man like you. You'll have these two fine fish," and at that she turns around from the stove and brings the skillet to Georgie's plate. Then she scooped a fish right up and landed it on his plate. The fish still had its head on, and its eyes were staring back at Georgie. He lost it at that stage, jumping up from the table and running for the door clutching his face. I quickly apologised and ran out after him, followed by a line of the children and the farmer. There he was, up against the wall, puking his guts out. He was pale and in shock and could not speak, but glared at me as he vomited. I figured he knew I had set him up, but I could not hold in the laughter. I almost collapsed laughing and I simply could not stop. Then the kids all started laughing as well, and then the farmer began laughing. We were all in stitches except Georgie. The farmer says to me, "Jezus he got the gawks real fast didn't he. Was he on the piss or what?" I told him that the previous night he had been out celebrating at the Rose of Tralee festival, and with that important bit of news the farmer gave me a knowing look and disappeared. The rest is vague as I think he came back and gave Georgie a bottle of brandy to swig on to settle his stomach. We did finish the job but it was done in silence, and we did get paid as well, without Georgie speaking a single word to me for the rest of the work.

We left the farmer's home, and as we drove away I again exploded laughing. In rage, Georgie goosed the car, hitting a huge pothole and blowing out his tyre as he did so. Of course he had no spare wheel as he had got another puncture the previous night coming home from Tralee. I began to feel that this might be a very long and uncomfortable night indeed.

We were close to the village of Hospital and a pub that in another lifetime may well have been the one Nannie had worked in. After a phone call to Larry, where we told him about the wheel, he informed us that we should sleep in the car for the night. Georgie broke his silence in the pub and says to me, "I suppose its Lucozade you want, you ould bollix," and I think he ordered more brandy. We sat down and I stared across at him. Then he exploded laughing too, calling me the greatest bastard that ever lived on this earth and swearing revenge the first chance he got. More phone calls and hours later, Larry arrived with another wheel, which wouldn't fit, and after even more hours of boring the wheel holes with a brace, we managed to get the replacement wheel on the car, but it was on inside out and we could only get three nuts onto it. It was at that point that the two brothers got into an argument as to which of them had the fastest car. They decided to race home to settle it. We took off at high speed and then, literally travelling at one hundred miles an hour, I realised that I was in the wrong car.

Out of sympathy for Georgie for my tricking I had opted to travel with him for the race, and if any wheel was to fly off it would be his one, killing us both for sure.

We sped into Mallow at about four am and never heard from the customers again. Next day Georgie refused to go to work, claiming he was traumatised by my trick, and so I ended up doing his calls as well as my own. He had a minor victory after all.

I caught Georgie again on another day while we were out doing our television calls.   We were to call to a very rich and precise customer in the west end of Mallow. This woman needed to have an aerial cable tacked around the skirting board in her living room, and on that day I persuaded Georgie to do the tacking while I helped because I didn't trust myself to be neat enough for that woman.   I have always loved art and sculpture, and when we arrived to survey the room, I noticed a little, open, three-legged cabinet fitted into one of the corners of the room. This cabinet had three shelves full of ornaments, and one of them was the armless Venus de Milo. I knew Georgie wouldn't know the statue so I saw an opportunity for fun at his expense.   I stood in front of the cabinet so as to block his view of the statue, but I warned him about the 'valuable ornaments' in the cabinet behind me. As I'm doing this I removed the Venus and hid it behind my back. Then I suggested he remove the ornaments very carefully while I got our tools and cable from the car.

When I came back in he had removed the cabinet from the corner, and all the precious ornaments were laid out carefully behind him on the floor. I placed the statue under the lower shelf of the cabinet and said nothing. I told Georgie that I needed to go back to the car for more tools and left, knowing he would surely find the statue after I left and go into a panic, and that's exactly what happened. When I returned he was clutching the statue in his hand and searching all over the floor like a mad man. He looked ashen faced and says, "Jesus John, look at this. I must have dropped the statue and the arms are broke off and I can't find them. Help me find em will you". I go into 'shock' and say to him, "Didn't I warn you about these things, didn't I tell you she had valuable stuff? Now you'll have to pay for it, and I bet it's expensive; hundreds for sure". He swears he never even saw the statue, and I say it doesn't matter, we will be blamed for sure.   At that moment the woman comes back in to see the work, and Georgie quickly hides the statue behind his back like a bold child who is in trouble. When she left he says "I swear I never saw this bloody statue," and I tell him to keep looking around for the miniature arms as they must be there somewhere. In seconds he's back on his knees again looking everywhere, then all of a sudden he looks up at me and says, in all seriousness, "What will we do when we find em, Superglue is it?" At that idea I just can't hold it in any longer and I burst out laughing, telling him that in my opinion he is an 'ignorant philistine', and that this particular statue never did have any arms. Poor Georgie was so relieved he almost hugged me. It was pointless describing this fun to Larry as he wouldn't have known the Venus de Milo either, so I let it drop. Some time later, on a return call, I did tell the woman what I had done because I had a suspicion that she saw me hide the statue originally, and maybe thought I was going to steal it. She fell around the place laughing, and said that I should have let her in on it. Then she would have really made it worse for poor Georgie, before we left him off the hook of course. He took it well though and threatened revenge as usual.

Larry was no saint either, especially when it came to playing tricks on his brother. Every year at Christmas the Mitsubishi television company gave each of us a large bottle of Cognac brandy. At that time both Larry and Georgie were big into playing squash, and during a game both of them betted each other their bottle of brandy. Larry lost, and in typical form did not want to pay up, but Georgie basically took the bottle from him and left with it for his home, telling his wife Monica of his 'great triumph' over Larry. Next morning Larry told me of the game and his loss, and once again we felt Georgie should suffer at our hands, so we came up with a plan to get Larry's bottle back. As I didn't drink at all, I still had the dregs of the previous year's bottle in our cabinet at home and that was to act as the basis for our plan. Larry told me to fill it up with old tea or anything of the right colour, then seal it with the cork and covering from my new bottle. Then when I got the chance, I was to swap bottles when I was next in Georgie's house. Larry felt that Georgie was always getting up late in the morning, and that would be the best time for me to call and do the dirty deed. He even arranged for an aerial job to make sure it happened for me.

I had an old thermos flask half full of tea from a trip to the mountain, but it was about six months old, yet it looked perfect in colour, so I poured that into my bottle, added a bit of sugar, and felt that it would pass a cursory glance as brandy. Then I did a great job sealing the bottle, and all was then ready. I showed it to Larry, and even he was fooled, it looked so new. Next morning, as predicted, when I called for Georgie to do yet another aerial job, he was still in bed, and I exchanged bottles before he arrived downstairs. Later I gave Larry back his bottle and forgot about it all.

On Christmas Eve Georgie went to the pub and got sozzled. Arriving back home, he felt that a drop from Larry's ill gotten bottle would add to his Christmas cheer, and half pissed he opened the bottle and took a good swig. "That brandy is poor this year Monica, I'll have to complain. Then again twas Lar's, and I suppose I couldn't have luck," as he laughs out loud in triumph. Over the Christmas period the next door neighbour arrives, and true to tradition, Monica offers her a glass of the brandy. Oddly enough the neighbour woman didn't finish it either, and after taking just a small sip she beat a hasty retreat to her home. A few days later the coal delivery man arrives, and he too is offered a large glass of the brandy. He says, "Be God maam tis cold out there, and sure I'd love a drop just to keep the heat in me bones". Again Monica poured a large glass, which he gulped down in one big swig, and then immediately she noticed him turn pale. He too beat a fast retreat for the door. As he's leaving, Monica shouts after him, "And what about your helper, would he like a drop?" The coal man was already rushing up the pathway, waving his hand in some wild gesture of refusal while holding his other hand across his mouth. Still it did not dawn on Monica that anything might be amiss with the brandy.

Days later, and coming to the end of the season, Georgie was relaxing at home and asks Monica to pour him another glass of 'Lar's brandy'. He said he would start his New Year with one up on his brother. She does so, and after his initial swig, he spits the whole lot out into the fire, cursing and swearing at Larry. By then all of Monica's strange stories of drink refusals made perfect sense to him. The brandy was 'doctored'. There and then Georgie realized what I had learned the hard way, that Larry Andersen never once paid up on a bet. Georgie didn't speak to either of us for days, as I was blamed just as much as Larry for doing 'the dirt' on him, and once again he planned more revenge on both of us.

My Mallory days

I had been working for Larry for a few years when one day I got a call to go see a woman called Mary O'Mallory. She was the sister of a very nice woman who lived a few doors away from Gracie. Mary was married to John O'Mallory, known to friend and foe alike as Johnno. The Mallorys needed an engineer to fix televisions for their growing television rental business, and my reputation seemed to fit the bill. Mary asked me to go to a meeting in Charleville and see if we could agree a deal with her husband Johnno. My first impression of him was that he was a huge man with what seemed like a very gruff personality. This unnerved me a bit at the meeting, but somehow I felt it was just an act. Later I was proven right as we got to know each other better. He had a passion for fixing grandfather clocks and soon he and I were to become odd friends. I say friends, as I think in his entire life I was one of the few people who seemed to understand him, and we never had a cross word despite numerous disasters. He owned a TV shop like Larry, and was fast developing a growing business renting televisions to the people of Charleville town and the surrounding areas, which of course I knew well from my school days.

On the night of our first meeting, Mary struck the deal with me as Johnno kept out of it. In hindsight I realise that they were very badly stuck for an engineer as I'd guess Johnno had fought with the previous guy. Mary had probably warned him not to interfere in case his manner blew the new deal. I clearly remember that deal. I was to get seven shillings and six pence for each set I fixed, no matter how difficult it was or how long it took me, and they provided the parts. My job was also to do 'calls', which meant I journeyed all over County Limerick and North Cork at all hours of the night, fixing like a mad man. Some jobs were easy, some hard, and Mary and I did a balancing act on exactly what I earned at the end of the week. It was an unwritten rule that she wouldn't ever argue with my list of calls and repairs, and I would never 'do the dog' on what I charged her, and we both trusted each other. It worked perfectly, and I was soon earning real money as my Mallory wages were usually well over ten times what Larry paid me, but I was Larry's apprentice, and he too was just starting out.

I used to work five nights a week without holidays, and I did this for years. It was hard going, but I was young then and didn't have to drive, as I was still only learning in Larry's bomber. The Mallorys used to provide a driver for me. I was being chauffeured around and treated like a king as well as being well paid for my skill. Life couldn't be better. As my finances improved, so did the allowance I gave to my Nannie. Her lot in life was also improving, yet I have no memory of helping my mother financially at that time, and that has troubled me ever since. I started to save money like mad. My goal was for me to buy a motorbike that I had become determined to have so as take me off 'the thumb' and make me independent, but that purchase was still a long way off.

I had numerous adventures in my Mallory days, or should I say nights. I would start at about seven o'clock, having hitched a lift home from Mallow at six o'clock. Then I would eat my inedible dinner, which Nannie would have prepared four hours earlier, and which she kept hot over a boiling pot on top of her old black range. The minute I arrived in, she would have poor Eunice waiting on me hand and foot. "Make tea for John, Eunice, and be quick about it, he is going out earning money for us, the great lad. Sure we'd be lost without him". This would be a very pointed remark made to antagonise and belittle the one who really was providing for her, her son Michael. She did this most vehemently if he was in the kitchen as well at the time. It's amazing that Eunice or Michael didn't hate me in later life because of Nannie's obvious favouritism and jibes, which I didn't like or want either, but you dare not cross her.

Around seven, my chauffeur would arrive with a toot of the horn and I'd hop in, ready for another night's fixing. My night would usually begin with one of Johnno's sons acting as chauffeur, and proceeding to drive me at over ninety miles per hour to the Mallory workshop. This was located at the rear of their shop on the main street. It was guarded by about ten really dangerous Alsatian dogs, all vicious and all hating me, especially their leader and Johnno's best friend, a dog called Rommel. No amount of roaring or shouting by the Mallorys would quieten them when I arrived. Rommel, the fiercest, was nearly always chained or tied up, but sometimes he got loose and would make straight for me with jaws open. After this happened a few times I gave them an ultimatum, stating that unless the dog was chained up when I was around, I was not returning again. I told this to Mary and Johnno together after one awful scare, and they realized that I meant it as I was petrified of that dog.

From then on, I would be escorted by a Mallory to the workshop and literally locked in for my own safety. There I tried to concentrate on fault-finding while the bloody dogs barked for the first half hour or so. I had diagrams and valves and resistors and a big black Avometer, which I adored. That was the entire test equipment we had then. An oscilloscope belonged in the realms of the super rich, so to find any kind of difficult fault, one relied primarily on a totally unscientific technique known as 'intuition'. Larry and I had a saying about it. The saying went like this, "If in doubt cut it out".

I would be cutting away at the TVs while the dogs would be chewing away at the workshop door, and this continued for months. The constant barking would be just getting to me when my chauffeur would arrive to do the night's calls to the country. After my earlier frights with the dogs, my ultimatum, and not trusting Rommel to be always chained, I deemed it necessary to have a weapon to save me from his vicious teeth. I found a small hatchet after an intensive search, and I felt secure at last, but I decided to do some practice swings in the safety of the workshop. I swung back and forth, all the time adjusting my technique, and each night, just to annoy the dogs, I did this ritual almost taunting the bastards to attack. I'm sure they saw the shadows moving in the windows and it drove them berserk, but no one knew what was going on, only me and the dogs. It became a kind of game between us and I think they enjoyed it as much as I did.

One night though I became so engrossed with this fun that I forgot what I was doing and got a bit carried away with the game. Like an Indian in Big Kyrl's picture hall, I leapt about from place to place, lashing out here and there with my hatchet. The more I did this, the louder the barking became. Pretty soon all hell was breaking loose. Even Rommel had pulled free from his rope and I saw him leaping and clawing outside at the window. This huge dog was now snarling and foaming at the mouth, hell-bent on eating my throat if he could get at it. I lashed out at him in a kind of frenzy, and I don't know how he didn't come clean through the window, but I was ready for him if he did. Then I thought I saw a shadow move along the side window as well, and an attack from two sides seemed to be coming. It was dark, and with my adrenaline pumping I jumped up onto a chair and prepared for battle, hatchet at the ready. Just then Johnno's big head appeared in the window. He dragged Rommel off and came back inside. He was a smart man, and I suppose he believed that the pressure of fixing so many TV's without a break had finally got to me, as when he came inside, he asked me if I wanted a drop of the 'hard stuff'. He looked genuinely concerned. Johnno offering me drink was a sure sign that he was worried about me, as he knew I didn't drink at all. I tried to explain my madness, but he just dismissed it and asked if I needed a break. I never took the break as there was no one to replace me, and they would have been in a bad state coming up to Christmas. From then on, I think a strange kind of friendship developed between us. Maybe he figured his dogs had finally got to me, as I complained about them often enough. From then on, the dogs were somehow quieter, and I too gave up my Indian ways.

Johnno Mallory had TV sets rented everywhere in the county, and in spite of his manner, he was liked by almost everyone as he had a descent streak in him. I'm sure he often overlooked many an outstanding repair or rent bill. Sometimes Johnno would have to drive me around. Initially I didn't like this idea one bit, but later as we got more used to each other, I really began to like him, especially after the hatchet incident. We would discuss engines and mechanics and science as we drove along the winding roads of Limerick. He drove very slowly though in comparison to his sons, but I felt a lot safer with him. The down side for me was that I got very few of his sets fixed because he took too long getting me to them.

One night very late, as we arrived back at his shop, Johnno says to me, "John, when are you going to learn to drive?" Before I could answer he said, "No time like the present. Here take the car home, sure you know the basics". Then he got out and went into his house, leaving me in control of his huge Zephyr car. I was flabbergasted. I had never driven such a huge car, nor did I want to either, but he left me no choice, so off I went. I had no licence, no insurance, little or no experience, and as it turned out, no petrol either. I can still see myself passing the Garda station very slowly, almost running over a drunk who staggered out in front of me. Then as I got used to the sheer size of the car I became more confident, especially when I hit the open road. After about four miles I threw caution to the wind and gave her 'the gas'. This beautiful and mighty car glided forward and floated as if travelling on a cushion of air. I was in heaven for about five or ten minutes, then the spluttering started and very soon I came to a jerking stop by the side of the road. It was obvious then why Johnno wanted me to drive home. He knew for certain he wouldn't get back if he took me because he had left it run out of petrol. I was back on the thumb again, but by then it was well after midnight and I was back on a road I knew well from my bicycle.

I began walking, not feeling very happy with Johnno or myself, when with about three miles to go along came a farmer driving a tractor with no lights. He stopped and I ended up arriving into Buttevant on top of a cock of hay. This was some comedown from the dizzy heights of my gliding Zephyr. Johnno seemed to be missing for the next few nights, knowing full well that I was unhappy with him. In the end he said he was sorry, but that I had gained valuable experience for my own car whenever I got one, and that was the end of it.

In the course of my life there have been a number of times when, by all rights, I should have been killed in what would be called tragic accidents. Big Kyrl's driving us into the flood in County Limerick was one such incident, and yet another occurred also in County Limerick during my days with the Mallorys. It was wintertime and the roads had become very dangerous with black ice. This was one of the few occasions when neither Johnno nor his sons drove me, and I have the feeling that my chauffeur that night was called Jimmy. I know that he seemed to be very tired and I did not like the mood in the van at all. In a place called Bruree we almost hit the old stone bridge, which would have sent us into the flooded river, but my roaring of warning snapped Jimmy out of his daze, and instead we spun round on the road. I am quite sure that the river in Bruree is the same river Maigue that also tried to drown me earlier with Big Kyrl. We escaped, but that was not the end of our frights that night. Some hours later, after numerous cups of tea and coffee, Jimmy seemed to be more with it and the mood had greatly improved. Our last call for the night was to a farmhouse out in the wilds. The people were very pleasant, and even though it was late when we called, they also offered us tea while I fixed the old set. We left and by then it was really freezing hard. The uneasy feeling that had come over me earlier then returned with a vengeance, and I felt sure that something bad was about to happen, but Jimmy was not driving fast and he seemed fully awake by then. For some reason I propped my legs up against the dashboard and pushed my seat way back. I pretended that I was tired, but the real reason was that something inside me told me to sit like that. About a quarter of a mile down the road we came to a very sharp bend. The road was covered with leaves, and the next thing I remember was Jimmy cursing as we skidded on the ice under the leaves. We suddenly went careering across the road, clean through a small ditch and immediately began a freefall through the air, down to yet another river. When the van hit the ground it really gained speed, and even though this was all happening very fast, a kind of euphoria came over me and I felt like an observer, helpless and afraid, but not terrified. We then hit a tree stump so hard that it actually warped the chassis on the van, as we discovered in the 'post mortem' later. On impact with the stump, one of the smaller televisions in the back came flying forward, hitting me hard on the shoulder before going right out through the windscreen with a huge bang. I think it also hit Jimmy on the head and he fell forward. Then we hit the water with another bang and a big splash. My body shot forward, hitting my head on the roof where the glass had been. I felt a sudden and very sharp pain on my forehead and then nothing. I think I must have blacked out, and when I recovered it seemed like a repeat of Big Kyrl's headstone event. I again saw the steam, the front of the van under water, the eerie lights in the water, and felt our sharp incline as the van had nose dived into the river, but the river was just a very small one and was not in flood. I wanted so much to rest there, but

I wanted us out of there too. My door had swung open on impact and I pulled myself out and went round the back of the van to Jimmy's side to try to pull him out as well. He was moaning and kept on saying, "Johnno will kill me, the new van, the van". I got him out, and we began crawling and helping each other up the steep embankment to the road. I knew we were hurt, but I didn't think we were hurt badly as we made our way up the slope. After a terrible struggle, we finally got onto the road and both of us laid down across it to rest. The next thing I remember was looking up at the crystal clear sky, noticing how beautiful the stars were and feeling no cold at all as I believed I was dead, and it did not seem to be bad at all. Then I heard Jimmy moan out again, and saw that he too was stretched out across the road. Obviously we both had collapsed from exhaustion, and we were now in real danger of being run over by an oncoming car. The adrenalin kicked in and I hauled him to his feet saying that we needed to go back to the farmhouse and get help.

As we began to walk in the starlight I felt a warm liquid trickle into my eyes and realized that I was bleeding. We finally made it to the old farmhouse, and before I knocked on the door I washed my face in a barrel of freezing water to wash off the blood. Of course the opposite happened; the water only spread it all over me, and when the woman opened the door and saw the 'monster' before her, she let out a screech and then she fainted at my feet. Her husband ran out and, seeing us, he too almost went down with the fright. When they recovered we told them what had happened. The next part is a little vague. I do remember that we got a loan of a motorbike from the farmer and drove to a pub some miles down the road. Even that had to be insane as we must have still been in shock and I had a bad gash in my forehead. At the pub we got more tea, and I remember washing myself in an upstairs bathroom, preparing for the drive home to Charleville. We took off on the bike and somehow we arrived into Charleville, where someone else later drove me on to Buttevant.

My glasses were broken, my forehead had a deep cut which took years to heal and every bit of me ached all over. During the night my forehead again started bleeding and in the morning Nannie almost fainted as well when she saw the pillow covered in my blood. As if getting almost killed was a normal occurrence, next morning I got up and left for work on the thumb; no doctor's visit, no casualty visit, no treatment for shock, and no intention of ever making an insurance claim either. That evening I was again back at O'Mallorys, this time being driven around in an old van by one of the sons. In a time of incredible health and safety regulations, what we did then was sheer madness. It had no effect on me that I know of. I never had a single nightmare about that crash. I told Larry about it and he brushed it off saying we had a lucky escape and that I had nine lives for sure. Johnno's van was totally written off due to the warped chassis and damaged engine. As in my river incident with Big Kyrl, I don't know where exactly all of this happened, but I have always kept well away from the Maigue River ever since.

The experience I gained while working for the Mallorys was invaluable. I made a lot of money and I learned a lot, but it could not go on forever as I was becoming burned out. As soon as I bought my motorbike, I felt I had achieved my goal. I worked on for many months though, all the time telling Mary that she needed to get a full-time engineer as the business had grown and I could not keep doing the five nights a week. In the end she did and we parted great friends, and every time I pass their shop I smile and think of those happy days.

I had been working for Larry for a few years when one day a very distinguished looking man arrived in our shop. He was tall and very well dressed, and smoked what I'm sure was an expensive cigar.

This man seemed to me to be very friendly in manner, and chatted away about some problem he was having with his television set. I noticed Larry was being extra nice to him, and this was exceptional in itself, as he was nice to everyone. When the man left, Larry was all smiles and says to me, "Do you know who that was John?" I hadn't a clue as I never saw him before in my life. I said no, and then Larry says, "Well you should know, as that's the famous Jack O'Rourke. He owns the Majestic ballroom, and rumour has it that he's a declared millionaire".

I was immediately impressed for two reasons; first I had finally met an actual millionaire, and secondly he seemed to be a very ordinary and nice man to me. This was a shock, as in my very limited experience of wealthy people, they had all seemed obnoxious to me until then. Larry then says he is a new customer and we have got to look after him, so he was obviously impressed with Jack as well.

I was immediately dispatched to Jack's house to examine his television and see if I could sort it out. When I arrived I was let in by a maid who didn't seem to be very friendly, and before I actually got inside, I was nearly savaged by a couple of huge dogs. The TV set was a huge German Telefunken beast. After a lot of poking and head-scratching, I had no idea what was the matter with it. While I was thinking, Jack arrived in and welcomed me to his home. He was all chat, and I was now even more amazed at him as he wasn't just being nice, he was actually trying to help me solve the problem. In desperation I told him that I couldn't fix it, and his answer was for me to take it back to our workshop. We were supposed to be the best in Mallow at electronic repairs of any kind, and I should have been able to get it going, but he saw through my bluffing and made it easy for me. He helped me load the huge set into the 'bomber', and as I drove off, I again began thinking about his manner. I liked him immensely, and for some unknown reason that day I felt that he and I would somehow become friends in the future.

We did manage to fix the Telefunken, and when I delivered it back, I was again met by the maid and the savage dogs. This time there was no Jack to help me lift the monster inside. I struggled to get it out of the car, and even this was taxing all of my strength. That television was so big that I couldn't even see over it. I had to walk in a kind of sideways movement, trying to see around it. My arms were spread in a bear hug and the sweat was falling off me as I tried to ring the bell with my knuckles. As it happened, I didn't need a bell as the barking and growling told all inside that a stranger was at the door. The same maid let me in, and as she did so I heard a low growling from somewhere in front of me. In seconds I became petrified, as I was totally helpless at that stage. Suddenly I felt what could only have been a dog's snout shove right into my crotch. I got such a fright that I almost fainted and barely held onto the set. I let out a huge shout to the maid, who I couldn't even see. "Will you call off them bloody dogs for God's

231

sake, can't you see I'm scared of dogs". I'm frozen in terror on the spot, and there's no answer from the maid. I believe she had scurried off, just in case she might have had to help me. Jack's wife Mary heard all the commotion and arrived in the hallway. She was just as nice as Jack and tried to help me lift the set, but she didn't get rid of the dogs either. After a struggle we managed to get the monster up on the table, and then I suppose Mary realized my predicament and offered me tea, which I politely refused, both from my fear of the dogs, and more especially from the way they still kept sniffing my crotch. I couldn't wait to get out of there. When I got back, I told Larry all about my adventure and he just burst out laughing, praising me for not dropping the set in the panic. After he calmed down from his mirth, we agreed that any future visits to Jack would have to be two-man calls.

Over the next few years we did a lot of work for Jack. I got to know him a lot better, and it became quite clear to me that he was a very private and gentle man with a great charity in him, though he never preached it. Many people felt that he was a mean man, but I never saw that side of him at all. In fact he was just a very honest and honourable man, believing that when you made a deal, you stuck to it. He was a tough businessman though, well prepared to bargain and tangle for the last penny. In the end a handshake sealed the deal, and you could be quite sure that you would be paid on time, and get the exact amount you had agreed on; not a penny more or less.

For many years my only dealings with Jack were through Larry, but one day he arrived into our shop and started to chat to me about the new phenomenon called 'disco'. It was late summer and I wasn't busy, so we chatted away for a long while. Unknown to Jack, and by sheer coincidence, I was at that time developing an electronic form of light control which later became known as 'sound to light'. I know too that this work was quite unique at that time. My ideas had come from Kyrle, who had sourced a new device known as a 'thyristor' which I had managed to doctor in such a way as to make the light intensity follow the volume of the music. This was an unheard-of concept at the time, and I was within months of having a prototype working. I did get it working later, when it became known as The Liberation Mobile Disco. As we chatted I began telling Jack about this new idea of mine. He became totally fascinated with it and encouraged me to continue at speed and at all costs. A month or two later he arrived back in again and asked me if I could help him get some new disco equipment working in the Majestic. He had bought this equipment from an operation in Dublin that had failed to make a go if it and he felt that it would work in Mallow, but unfortunately no one had been able to get it working.

I was over the moon with delight at this offer, as his dancehall was a Mecca for all young people (myself included), and by then I had gone there many times with Hayes and Fowler. Now to be doing some actual work in the Majestic was an incredible honour altogether. I felt that I was surely on the way up because I was actually working for a 'millionaire'.

I arrived at the Majestic on a Thursday evening in late September on my motorbike, and met Jack and his entourage. Very soon I was shown the huge array of equipment recently bought by him. It was space age in design and I was blown away by it all. There were large boat-shaped speaker systems and a horizontal boat-shaped control unit for the DJ's to sit in. Equally amazing boat-shaped light units were spread all over the stage, and even though it was not working, I could imagine how it might look when it did work, and that was to be my challenge. Above all, the light units looked utterly fantastic. I doubted whether I could figure out how they worked, but I longed to see them going primarily because of my own light work at home, and secondly I was anxious to see my competition. I couldn't wait to get at it.

Jack carefully explained the problems to me. The sound section was working, but not the boat lights, and so far no one seemed able to find the problem. I said I would fix them no matter how long it took, or I would re-design the whole thing because I wanted to see this system working for myself. That seemed to really satisfy Jack. Then I asked him and his men to leave me alone as I needed to think. After a few hours I had the measure of it all, and realized that these lights were driven by simple relays in a huge box. I was on a cloud and waited for Jack to return as I had no music to play, and that would be the real test.

When he came back I said I was ready, and to just get me some music. I chose 'Cecilia' by Simon and Garfunkel and pressed play.

The very first beat of the drums caused the whole stage to explode into light of all colours and intensities. It looked absolutely amazing and the hair actually stood up on the back of my neck as I watched this happen. I was seeing the future and I had cracked it. Jack was beaming. He shook hands with me over and over and said, "Well done John, I never doubted you". Obviously he had bought this system as a gamble, which for a time looked doomed, but now it was working and we all loved it.

He was so excited that I just didn't have the heart to tell him that my electronic system had already made his relay driven lights totally obsolete. It would take me a year, but it was inevitable as I had seen and understood the relay design. Later that night too as I looked on at Jack's units, which were then 'state of the art', I became convinced that I should redouble my efforts on my own light unit, which I did. Pretty soon my lights were pulsing far better than Jack's, and me and my mad friends would soon be testing in Big Kyrl's hall, but that tale you already know.

Jack's discos took off and became a great success. Some time later I clearly remember giving him my bill as I entered his dancehall as a paying customer on a Sunday night. He nearly had a heart attack at the size of my bill. It must have seemed extraordinary to him, considering his entrance fee for a dance at the time was just five shillings, or one quarter of a pound, and I was charging him fifteen pounds. He always felt that I charged him way too much, and I still believe that I didn't charge him half enough. We had many a laugh about it in later years when we were both heavily involved in 'pirate radio' and had become fast friends.

Etta's years and our children.

Not too long after I started working for Larry, I was to meet my first wife Etta Butler. I used to hitch a lift home from work every evening, and at that time Etta was working in a sweet shop on the corner close to where I did my hitching. This intersection was known as the 'Bon Bon Corner', getting its name I suspect from the type of sweets sold in her shop, bon bons. I was to get my first whipped ice cream cone in that shop. It was called a 'ninety nine', and I discovered years later that these cones had been invented and used for the first time in St Louis, Missouri during a World's Fair being held in that city. Like much of my story, by a strange twist of fate St Louis and America were going to play a great part in my future life, but all of that was unknown to me on the day I wandered into Con Dore's sweet shop to buy a 'ninety nine' from the attractive shop assistant called Etta.

Etta did the making and selling of these cones as well as being the general money taker for sweets and groceries. It was summertime and I had spotted her earlier at work through the shop window. Her smiling face and happy personality seemed to hold a great attraction for me. I had never had one of these whipped ice creams and decided to try one, as I had seen a lot of people coming out of her shop with their tongues wrapped around them. Besides that, it would give me a chance to chat up the cone-maker and see what she was like as a person. The day I went in I didn't know what those cones were called, so I waited around keeping an ear open for the name of the ice creams while keeping an eye on the shop assistant as well. She didn't seem to notice me at all and I didn't know why that was, because you couldn't swing a cat in that small shop. Soon a customer uttered the magic words, "Ninety nine please," and I saw the whipped cream squirt out into the cone. Immediately I was at the counter asking for a cone, and as she made my ice cream I realized that Etta was as thin as a stick, and was way too thin for my liking. She wasn't a bit impressed with me either, but as she took my money she smiled, and there and then her smile got me interested again. I left with my ice-cream and ate it down, delighted at its odd taste. Next evening I was back again for more, and again she smiled. I was getting more impressed with her, and each day I tried to stay a little longer to chat her up. I was getting braver and more brazen too and it was getting to the point where I might ask her out, but to do that I needed an edge; something her many other admirers hadn't got. I had noticed that she seemed to have lots of other fellas who were interested in chatting her up too, and all of them were better looking and taller than me, so I had to come up with a good plan or forget about her.

I had been reading all the James Bond books at that time and I saw a few films too. I noticed that he always got the best looking women with no problems, so I'd model myself on James. From that bit of research I noticed that he had square shoulders and spoke with a real deep Scottish accent. This had to be the edge I needed. I dismissed the fact that he was a real good-looking Scotsman well over six feet tall as just a minor detail. Therefore all I needed was his accent and broad shoulders. I practiced my accent each day in Larry's shop, always pulling back my shoulders for better effect and doing my best to lower my tone of voice. Over a time I had dropped my voice an octave or so, and as my voice was always naturally deep, after weeks of this effort, it had turned out to be almost cavernous. I had deliberately kept away from her shop for a few weeks so as to get my voice perfected, and also to make it look like I wasn't interested in her at all.

I returned for a cone, asking the magic words in my now deep voice, "Can I have a ninety nine please," while squaring up my shoulders and smiling in Bond style at the same time. I tried to imagine that I was James with the girl already under my spell. The shop was crowded and Etta made a quick cone and seemed to be very anxious to be rid of me. I took it that she was busy and left, quite a bit deflated but willing to return the next day for another go at her. This I did, and again she got rid of me far too quickly I felt, so I tried to get my voice down even lower still the next day. I couldn't figure it out. The lower I got the faster she got rid of me. This was not the way it went for James Bond and I was in a quandry by then, as none of his charm was working for me.

Around that time I happened to be hitching home with a friend of mine known as 'The King' and I was telling him all about her, so we decided to buy some cones together. He had no money, and as I was not much better off, I bought one cone to share with The King every second lick. Etta served us as usual with a smile, but she went on to the next customer rather too quickly again with not a sign of her wanting to chat to either of us. Outside the shop The King wanted his lick of the cone, and when I gave it to him he took a large tongueful and immediately started spitting it out all over the street, saying, "That's gone off, that's gone off, you can't eat that, it's sour". I took a cautious lick and it seemed to taste the same as all the other cones had done, so I ate away. It took years before I realized that he had been right, and the cones she had made were often sour. As Etta never ate them herself, she didn't even know if they were okay or not, and customers were not going to complain to such a pleasant, happy girl in those days. After that failure I decided she was not for me. Some time later she left the shop and I forgot about her and her cones. Months later I met her in another shop and she told me she was a trainee nurse working in Dublin. Little did I know it, but she was actually working with my sister Lill in the same hospital, and Lill was about to set up a blind date between her friend Etta and her brother John. Life would then take on a whole new turn for me.

We began dating after our initial blind date, which took place on a St Stephen's Night in the Majestic ballroom, home to many of my earlier escapades. We got along great after a shaky start, and I suppose Lill painted me in such a good light that Etta was expecting a saint and found herself attached to a devil, or a madman at the very least. I wasn't long going out with her when her parents decided they were going to Youghal for a week on vacation. Youghal is a lovely seaside town, and in those days country people who could afford it would rent a caravan in Redbarn beside the sea, just outside the town. I was invited to join them because Etta would be made go there as well. I really did not want to do this as I didn't know them well, and the idea of being trapped in a mobile home for a week with strangers really scared me. In the end I agreed and we arrived in Redbarn. The only good thing about the place was that it had a big dance hall and it was close to the cinema in Youghal town, so we would be able to escape for some of the time at least. The other down side was that her brother, Anthony, was also there and he was only thirteen. He seemed quite wild to me and always wanted to hang out with us, which we didn't want at all.

When we arrived at the site, it was lashing rain as usual. This was a bad start off and I was already thinking this holiday was a very bad idea indeed. The caravan was a five-berth affair, and Anthony and I were given the inner bunks in the front, with Etta on the outermost side of the caravan. To ensure that no funny business happened, the parents shared the central part of the caravan, separating me and their precious daughter from any temptation. The real downside of all of this was that, if Anthony or I wanted to go out to the toilet, we had to pass through the parents' bedroom and Etta's room before you got to the door. I'm sure Anthony would be forgiven for passing on through, but I most definitely would have a devil of a job explaining my reasons for ending in the daughter's room. Her parents were very strict and left me in no doubt about their moral code, especially her father, who was particularly detailed in his objections to the funny business. From the first day I became petrified about having to go to the toilet in the middle of the night. So that a toilet trip didn't happen, I went to all kinds of lengths to ensure that I didn't need to go out at night. I would stop drinking tea after six o'clock in the evening, and refused all minerals as well. This, I'm sure, led them to the belief that I was a secret alcoholic and also very impolite when I flatly refused their constant offers of tea. I tried my best to counter these ideas, as I suspected they were getting wary of me after a few nights of this carry on because, before bedtime, I would be in and out like a man with a secret desire for drink. Etta of course knew all about my fears and saw the funny side of my predicament, but she did nothing to ease my fears. As the days wore on I got braver though, and settled into believing that her parents were nice after all, which they were, but it took many more years to find that out. Soon I was drinking tea, but no orange, as it always made me want to go all night long. Then one night the inevitable happened. We had been at a dance in the hall. I was drinking orange like a mad man due to the heat, and throwing caution to the wind, I continued drinking till the dance ended. We had a great night as we were all alone; no Anthony, no parents and great music. When the dance ended I went to the bathroom and made a real long piss and felt that that was it for the night - a wrong conclusion as it happened. By then it was way past bedtime and at the caravan I tried hard to go piss again one last time to be sure, but nothing was doing so I went to bed. I had to pass in through the parents' bedroom, and seeing them both asleep or pretending to be so embarrassed me to death, but I made it to our inner sanctum and got ready for bed.

Anthony wasn't asleep and was all up for chatting to me. I wanted to just collapse into bed, so I told him eventually to shut up or I'd throw him out the bloody window or I might just kill him and bury him in the sand. He took this rather too seriously I thought, and he started to threaten to tell his mother about what Etta and I got up to. I figured that he must have been out slinking around the campsite as we walked home and he had seen us snogging in the dunes. Eventually I fell asleep, ignoring his threats. It seemed only like an hour or so before the need to go to the toilet began. I am certain it was my imagination at first, but more and more it got worse. I was in a terrible state in a short time. I was clutching my mickey and tossing and turning all over the place, buy nothing did any good. Soon I resorted to pissing out my window. This was a window that opened out on a spring hinge, but it seemed to be stuck or the spring was jammed. Again and again I almost had it open, but it would spring shut again almost catching my mickey in this vice more than once.

Pretty soon I was so desperate that I had to wake up Anthony for help. He refused, telling me that he was no friend of mine. I offered him money though I had no notion of giving it to him. He must have suspected that, as he demanded it first. I actually hadn't got much cash, and in trying to find my trousers I felt the first drops of wee squirt out. Now it was time for real action. I told him if he didn't hold open the window I would actually piss on his bed and he would be blamed. That was a master stroke on my part and came from my Nannie's days of threats to kill me if I wet her bed. The new threat had the desired effect and he rushed to help. Between us we managed to get this big window open, where he held it for me to climb through. I actually fell out the window in the end and pissed all over the place; myself included. The relief was so wonderful I almost cried. Then I heard the window click shut.

Anthony, the little bastard, now had his revenge. He locked the bloody window and leered out at me. Here I was, outside in a caravan park, stark naked, and a foot from the window where his parents were asleep. I knew I was then in a fix for sure. I thought if I go around to Etta's window and I am caught I will be in real big trouble, as being naked outside the girlfriend's window could lead to only one conclusion. I started tapping the glass and calling to Anthony as quietly as I could, but he ignored me, having gone under the blankets pretending to be asleep, but I kept it up. I was nice at first, definitely guaranteeing money and friendship for life. When this didn't work I resorted to threats. I said I would actually kill him, that I was not joking, and I'd throw his body into the sea where the sharks would eat him. Then I said I might just half kill him so he would be alive when they ate into him. All this had no effect on him whatsoever. I threatened to put snakes in his bed, thinking of Lill and the eel, and how I would really do it first chance I got, as there must be eels in a sea port. This got him and he opens his window slightly and says, "You can't do that, there are no snakes here". Well it was a start. At least I had got his attention. I laid on a good story full of flaws, telling him how I planned to get a snake to bite him, but he was always countering my plans with real good arguments, so I knew he was biting, no pun intended. I was freezing by then, so I begged to be let in. He wouldn't let me in until I said I was sorry for threatening to kill him. Jesus, I says to myself, is that all he wants. Then I s wear I'll be his friend for life. With that he gives in and helps me in the window. This was very difficult for me as I am small and I had to get a bucket to help me up to the right height. Then I half jumped and half pulled myself up and tumbled into the room, hurting my mickey on the catch as I did so. Only for the pain of that I would have strangled the little rat in his bed. I was clutching myself with the pain and swearing I was leaving the next day, thinking to Hell with   Etta, her parents, and their son, I had had enough. Then sleep overcame me.

Next morning Etta's mother says to us all, but looking directly at me, "What was the racket going on last night between you two?" I tell her it's a long story, and at that stage I didn't give a damn if she found out or not as I was sick of the place by then. She didn't ask further and it was just as well. When I told Etta what had happened, she wouldn't believe me at first. Anthony denied it all saying I had imagined it all, but the bruise on my mickey was no imagination and the pain certainly wasn't either. We hitched back to Mallow and home the next day as I had had enough of the place. It was to be the only time I went away on holidays with her family, and it took some years and a lot of work on my part to convince them that their daughter wasn't dating a lunatic. How wrong they were on that one though.

As happens to most people who date, we had a big falling out and broke up. We went our separate ways, but I was missing her and heard she was due back in Mallow on a Saturday night, so I planned a visit to the town on the off chance that we might meet up again. Uncle Michael was reading meters for the Electricity Supply Board and he had bought himself a small Honda 50 motorbike as a means of transport. I had 'borrowed' this machine some months earlier to take Nannie for a spin to Kanturk, and I never had any luck with it. On that occasion we got punctured and walked ten miles home. Michael was gone to a meeting and I again 'borrowed' his Honda for the trip to Mallow. I met Fowler, who was dating his girlfriend in Mallow, and told him I'd give him a spin home when he was finished with his date. I never saw Etta that night even though I called to her house, so I decided to go pick Fowler up early and head back home. I drove around the town looking for talent and trying to look real cool on my Honda 50, not caring a damn that it was taken without permission, or that I had neither license nor insurance. I cruised around numerous times, making frequent sorties to St. Joseph's Convent where I knew Fowler was hanging out, but I had no luck on the talent front. It was time for food and after that I decided that if Fowler wasn't ready, I was going home without him. So back again to St. Joseph's I went, and he was there in a bicycle shed snogging with the girlfriend.

While I was waiting for him I started to chat up one of the girls from the convent and we were getting along fine. Every so often I'd roar in at Fowler to come on as it was getting real late, and always the same reply came back, "Fuck off will you, I'll be on in a minute". To be honest I wasn't too pushed as I was making progress with 'your wan' and I began to think of new possibilities with this girl.

So we chatted on for a little while longer. It was then getting really late and I wondered if there was enough petrol in the bike, as Michael was always running out of it, not wanting to overfill it in case it 'ever goes on fire' as he used to say to me often. He wasn't to be disappointed on that score, as I was about to prove shortly.

We were in the driveway of the convent. I was sitting on the bike and the girl was standing near to me chatting away, when I decided to check the fuel. The stupid thing for me was that there was a pole with a light literally six feet away from us and it would have been directly over me and the petrol tank if I had just moved that distance. But no, not me, I had to look into the tank in the dark. I couldn't see any petrol, so I stuck in my finger and I couldn't feel any petrol either. Now convinced that there wasn't even enough petrol to get me to a pump, I decided to see just how little I had. To this day it will remain the most stupid thing I ever did in my life; I asked the girl for 'a light'. All I had to do was move the bike six feet. She gave me her matches, I lit one and held the flame over the petrol tank. To my surprise initially, immediately followed by shock, a flame erupted from the tank. It wasn't a huge flame, but I was awe-struck. If I had put the cover back on quickly it might have gone out, but it wasn't to be. My potential new girlfriend started to scream and roar, and I became paralyzed. I am convinced that somehow I was sitting on the bike when all this happened, but I don't know how that could be. She ran screaming into the shed for Fowler, who was by then running out to meet her. When he saw his friend about to become a human torch, he dragged me away from the bike, and in so doing it fell over. This caused all the petrol to spill out. In seconds there was a real blaze going on with Michael's bike bursting into orange and red flames mixed with black acrid smoke from his tyres. I ran across the road to a house for some water and they called the fire service, but it was all too late to save the bike. In a matter of minutes it was all over; the bike was a smouldering black wreck and the road had actually been burned from the heat. For years afterwards I'd see that patch of melted tar and remind myself of the stupidity of my act. I'll not forget the feeling of loss that welled up inside me as I looked on at the black mangled skeleton that once was a shiny new Honda 50. I was also black from the smoke and in a state of shock. Fowler was trying to console me, but I was thinking of poor Michael's mode of transport now gone, and how was he going to earn a living again. I had taken it without his permission and I felt so guilty that night. I knew he would not give out to me as he was not at all like that, but I felt so ashamed that I had robbed him of the comfort of a bike that he loved so much.

We got to hitching a lift home, all the time Fowler saying, "It's an accident Cac," his nickname for me. But I knew it wasn't an accident, it was utter stupidity on my part, and I was supposed to be the one who understood physics: physics my arse. It was the act of a lunatic and no two ways about it. When I did get home eventually, I had a terrible sinking feeling in my heart. Michael was writing away in Nannie's kitchen when I went in home. He saw me black-faced, covered in dirt and without his bike. He quickly realized disaster had struck and I blurted out that it was burned and gone beyond repair. His only reproach to me was that I shouldn't have taken it without asking him, as he might have needed it that night. I asked him with sadness, "What will you do now for the meter reading Mike?" and all he said was, "Ahh tis all right Chicken, sure I'll just go back to me ould push bike". Those words were like a knife going through me, as he was no longer a young man, and cycling miles and miles was going to be very hard on him. Michael went back to the push bike, and in later years I bought my motorbike and he used to use it, but he never recovered from the loss of his Honda 50. I have become convinced that it was all just destiny and it had its place in the story of all our lives, though its one event I'd prefer to have missed. It made me again question Nannie's constant song that 'fire follows them Cahills'.

After some years, Etta qualified in the nursing business and she began working in Cork. After a major row at her home she left and got a little flat in the city. This was the first time I believe she was ever truly free to live her own life, as her parents were still terribly strict on her, even after she was qualified and obviously an adult. We began to date seriously then, and it became a very happy time for both of us. Even though we had little money, we seemed to be falling in love more and more as the months went by.

Bobo

One Easter weekend Etta and I decided to go to Tralee in county Kerry for the long weekend. I had my motorbike by then and I was still working in Mallow with Larry Andersen. We had decided to meet at Mallow Railway Station and take the train to Tralee, with my bike travelling along with us in the goods wagon. Why we didn't just drive the bike to Tralee beats me to this day, but that was the plan. I was also to book a bed and breakfast for an amorous weekend, and I was all set up for this as well. Before I got to do the booking however, Kyrle rang me from Dublin for a chat. I, like a fool, told him what we were planning to do, and he says to me,"Don't you do another thing, I'll arrange it all, I got good friends in Kerry". I knew he had, as he worked with some wild guys from 'The Kingdom' as it's known. I took him on his word and forgot all about booking any place. After some hours he rang back to say it was all arranged. I was to go to Howlins' Hotel where a room was arranged by a 'Bobo Boyle'. Being an innocent type, I never questioned this name as Kyrle always had crazies as friends, so I assumed Bobo was a genuine guy with an odd kind of name. Nothing could be further from the truth as Bobo did not exist.

We arrived in Tralee fully kitted out for a biking weekend, all bedecked with fur coats, helmets, gloves and food; well prepared for the icy weather of a Kerry Easter. We looked like people from another planet, or from Tibet at the very least. I decided on these clothes as it was an early Easter that year and a motorbike is a cold way to travel in our weather, so we came prepared for all eventualities. The train journey was uneventful, except all the time I kept getting this uneasy feeling about the hotel, not having booked it myself. When we drove the bike to the hotel I became even more uneasy. The car park was full and I began to wonder what was on in Tralee. Soon I realized that a huge car rally was on in Killarney and the overspill of people was also filling up every place in Tralee, twenty miles away. But I assured Etta there was no need for worry as Bobo had our room arranged and it was free as well. There was a queue for the reception desk and we had no choice but to join it and ask for Bobo, but it was obvious that rooms were really scarce that night. Still I was not too worried; ours was booked after all. As we stood in line, complete with our Himalayan garb, we began getting all kinds of condescending looks from the well-heeled customers who didn't arrive on motorbikes carrying large, cheap helmets, furry coats and bags of food. We were quite unconcerned at these scornful looks as Bobo had it all arranged for us, and I kept telling Etta that we were very lucky that Kyrle had such important friends. We slowly moved ever closer to the reception desk, holding our helmets, gloves, and coats, while the rich and famous politely moved their expensive suitcases along as well.

Finally we arrived at the desk and I saw the receptionist staring at us, her eyes travelling up and down our bodies as her brain began registering disbelief at the sight before her. Then she looked directly at me and began a long purposeful silence…. After she had done her best at intimidating me with the long pause, she goes, "Can I help you……. sir?" with another long pause before she says the word 'sir', and again she began staring me up and down. In my innocence I took this as possibly she had been told by Bobo to expect motorbike types as special guests, but alarm bells were tinkling nonetheless. Then in my best 'man of the world' accent, remembering how James Bond did things, I says, "Yes my dear, we have a reservation. Cahill is the name, it was arranged by Bobo,.. Bobo Boyle". As I started to speak she began to check the register, but the minute she heard the name Bobo her head shot up in amazement. I became sure then we were in for special treatment, as according to Kyrle, Bobo was a special friend of the manager. She coldly says to me, "No, we have no reservation, we are booked out, nothing at all, not a room left," and then she gives me another one of her special long pauses. Still it has not dawned on me that anything might be amiss.

I tell her that she's mistaken, that it's all been arranged by Bobo Boyle, a friend of the manager, and we have to have a room as we have no place else to stay. She becomes adamant that she hasn't got a room. The line of guests has now grown very long, and later I realized that we were quite the source of entertainment for all. This initial argument soon develops into a row, with me getting mad at her for her inability to read a register, and she threatening to call the manager. I tell her to go right ahead, as he will fix it being Bobo's friend. She picks up the phone and makes the call.

Within two minutes he arrives out of an office. He was a big man, not one to take on lightly, especially when you are weighed down with motorbike gear and your girlfriend is now bright red and tugging at you to leave. So I start to repeat the whole story again and as soon as I got to Bobo he roars out, "There's no Bobo here, do you understand English? No Bobo". His tone shocked me. This was not funny and I tell him so, then he says very firmly, "Look, we have no reservation for you two," giving us a rotten sneering look in the process and he continues, "You better clear off now and stop wasting our time or I'll have to call the Guards". That was too much for me. I then decided that with their kind of attitude I wasn't staying there no matter what they offered, so I say to Etta, "Let's get the fuck out of here, they are all only fuckers anyway. This place is full of em". If they felt we were tramps, we may as well speak like tramps. We gather our gear and slink out. By then I am raging, first in disbelief that Bobo let us down, then later Etta says rather quietly, "Maybe there is no Bobo, did you ever think of that?" The penny drops finally. We had been tricked, and I roar out, "That dirty rotten fucker, fuck him. He's the greatest bastard alive, I'll get him for this, no matter how long it takes".

By that time it had become really late on a Saturday night, and with every rat hole full, we hadn't a chance of finding a place to stay. It was now survival time. We went from place to place asking the same question, "Any rooms for the night?" getting the same answer, "No," and I becoming more and more desperate while cursing Kyrle all the time. We were eventually told of a woman called Mrs Kaner who was every person's last resort. We found her house, or should I say coven, in a narrow lane in the middle of Tralee town, and she arrived at the door as we knocked politely. She was a small, thin woman who kept coughing up phlegm into a dirty old handkerchief. I asked if she had a room for the night, and she looks us up and down slowly amid the coughing. There is no doubt but we must have looked a bit dodgy with all the gear, but she says, "Well I have only the wan room with two beds," and I say quickly, "That's fine, we'll take it". She says, looking at

Etta, "Are ye married?" I wouldn't lie about such things on principle alone and answer that we are not. Unknown to me, Etta was feverishly trying to change a ring to her married finger behind her back when it looked like I blew it. Mrs Kaner says, "Oh well sure I don't know about this at all. I can't have any of that ould carry on in me house, I don't go for it you see," while spluttering and hacking again into her hanky as she talks.

It's now time for quick thinking on my part and I resort to playing the religion card, having seen the many holy pictures in her hallway. I says, "Ah that's awright so, but would you know if it's too late for us to go to the midnight Mass?" We have no notion whatsoever of going to any kind of Mass, but I thought it might swing her around, and she mutters, "Aahh sure yer not too bad so, ye go to Mass do ye, and it's too late for the Mass now anyways, so come on in. Sure I'll keep an eye on ye meself in the night". So we do go in, glad to be out of the biting cold, but feeling we were not going to have a good night after all. I ask her if I can park my motorbike in her hallway, and she says okay but not to burn her house down. Secretly I was wondering if she had had a vision of my earlier bike burning incident in Mallow. After a short chat in her kitchen, complete with more coughing, she decides to show us the room. We make our way up a narrow little stairs along a creaking and creepy landing and arrive at the room with its two small iron beds. The room is freezing cold and we dare not ask for a heater. It was small and poky with a tiny window onto the street below. Then she said that she was sleeping in the room next to us, and she repeated this too often for my liking. With our room sorted for the night, things were looking a bit better and we ventured out for some food. Mrs Kaner warned us to be back by midnight or she'd lock the door and that's it. She opened it for no one after the "clock struck". She wouldn't give us a key either, and so we took off quickly trying to find a chipper before we fell down with the hunger. We got our food and I wanted to get to bed and forget that awful day, so we made our way back quickly. As we returned, we passed a pub on a corner where it had revellers literally falling out of it. It was also full of singers and dancers with a great buzz going on inside. It would have been great to be able to stay, but Kaner's curfew was close. I thought too that it might be a good idea to bring old Kaner back a little drop of whiskey to ensure we got a good breakfast, not the stale cornflakes I was expecting, so I tell Etta this plan. She agrees and we crush our way inside the pub. I eventually get to the bar and ask for whiskey in a bottle to take away. This must have been some kind of code word in Kerry because the burly barman looks at Etta and gives me a knowing nod, then he reaches under the counter, pulls out a large unmarked bottle and pours a clear liquid into another small bottle and tells me the price. I was surprised at how cheap it was, but obviously if you're brewing your own spirits, your costs are lower. He had given me Ireland's mountain dew known as poteen, and even I knew that. I really wanted whiskey, but there was no arguing with him, so I paid and left.

Just before the clock struck midnight Kaner left us in and says we were just in time, or we would be left on the street for the night, with no deposit back either. She keeps looking at Etta while we chat to her in her kitchen, making Etta feel uncomfortable because of the looks and the constant hacking into the dirty old cloth. She says, "You're very thin aren't you?" and pinches her. Etta is disgusted. I gave her the 'whiskey' and she says, "And what's this… is it the way yer trying to knock me out for the night? Well it won't work, coz I sleep light you see". I assure her that it's just a gift and she looks at it again and says, "Tis a quare class of a gift, isn't it," but she began to drink it nonetheless. I tell her it's just whiskey and I don't care what she does with it, as I was then tired out, still mad at Kyrle, just sick of the whole day, and her 'sleeping light' remark was the final straw.

By then it's way past bedtime and we go on up to our room. I soon realize we can't lock the bloody door either. I have visions of old Kaner rushing in through our door at the first sound we make, saying, "I'll have none of that auld carry on in me house". What's more, she had reminded me of someone all night long, and then it dawned on me that she looked like an old witch. I could almost see her flying round the beds on her broomstick in the middle of the night casting spells on us, so I knew I would not sleep a wink, and there was not even the remotest chance of any of her 'ould carry on stuff' happening either. We strip off for bed, and I ask Etta which bed she wants. She chooses the one by the window and we get in the beds. I hear Kaner coming up the stairs and snuggle under the clothes with visions of her broomstick swishing past the door, or worse still, coming in through it. After about an hour Etta whispers, "Are you asleep?" How could I be asleep with all the revelry going on in the street outside? With happy people having fun on the long weekend, and us two stuck in a coven with a witch six feet from my head while I'm laying in a bed as cold as the grave? She says she is cold and will I swap beds. I agree and in crossing the floor I make a grab for her, just for the fun of it. Etta lets out a laugh and leaps back from me, falling on her bed which flies across the floor and up against the wall. It makes such a racket that I have a vision of Kaner coming straight through the door right at that moment, so I leap into my bed, which also bangs off the wall, but she doesn't arrive in and we both fall sleep fitfully. Maybe the Poteen did work after all.

At about six a.m. I hear a car pulling up outside her coven, and the front door gets a few loud knocks. Thick Kerry accents were saying, "Mrs Kaner let us in, let us in will ya". I assume these were some revellers who didn't make her curfew and she was sticking to her rules, or else the poteen had worked. Later still they are back again pleading, but still no entry is allowed. Then there are peals of laughter from the callers and all goes quiet once more after their car drove off. In the morning I knew why. We are having the dreaded stale cornflake breakfast as feared, and I know the gift had failed when Kaner tells me that my bike is leaking water. I jump up, as there was no water in my bike but there was petrol, and I rush to the hallway not wanting a second bike conflagration. To my relief I found that the whole floor was covered in piss, not petrol, and then I knew why the peals of laughter took place; the revellers had all pissed in her letterbox in revenge. We finish our breakfast and as we leave she says, "Well ye had a fine time last night didn't ye, and be sure to return on yer honeymoon". Obviously the poteen didn't work for all of the night. I couldn't believe it. We had done nothing, and here is the old witch thinking we had sex all night long. I couldn't win, but I was sure of one thing, we wouldn't be going back to Kaner on our honeymoon or anytime else either.

The weekend's disasters didn't end there however. It was then Sunday and we spent a lovely day just driving around Kerry on the bike. It was gloriously sunny and we had such a good time that we decided to continue on to Killarney to see the car rally. This was uneventful and we drove all around the lakes and saw the beautiful scenery. We didn't notice the time passing until it was eleven o'clock at night, and then with drunks and revellers everywhere, we needed a place to stay once again, but none was to be had. I again raged at Kyrle and swore more vengeance on him, and as a last resort we headed for the railway station. I assumed it would be open and at least we would be in from the cold. We drove up and snuck in, trying to act inconspicuously, but we had just got in when a big fight broke out between a large amount of drunks who had had the same idea as us. We hurriedly left as the guards would be arriving, and even though it was freezing cold, a prison cell was not the ideal place to spend the night. I knew of the car park at the Three Lakes Hotel. It was somewhat sheltered on one side and we decided that was our spot. We sat on a wall inside it and tried to keep warm by huddling together. This went on for hours, but we couldn't sleep as I was certain we would freeze to death if we did sleep. Of course that was just innocence. Eventually we decided to sleep in an open sports car and we were just getting into it when the Guards arrived and told us to get the hell out of it. After an eternity, dawn broke and we saddled up and drove back to Cork. We crashed out on Etta's single bed, and even though it was a small bed, we were so tired that we would have slept on a stone that day. And so ended our terrible weekend. On the Tuesday Kyrle had the cheek to ring me and ask how Bobo was doing. I was so mad I called him every name under the sun before slamming down the phone on him. We naturally made it up later, but he probably thinks I have forgotten about the revenge. I have not. If he remembers though, it's got to be the worst kind of terror for him, not knowing when it will happen and the right opportunity just has not presented itself as yet, but it will.

We dated for about five years and then began living together, which was almost unheard of in those days. I had no interest in marriage and was quite happy with life. By then I had been working with my good friend Larry Andersen for years and time just drifted along. Etta would vaguely mention marriage, but I saw no need of it and would never have got married. However, after five years it became too much for her, and with Christmas approaching and no sign of a ring, one evening she just gave me an ultimatum: get married or shag off. During the row that erupted she simply pointed out to me that while a man can go on living like we did indefinitely, a woman loses her looks and then has to start to find a man all over again. It became crystal clear to me that she was right and I saw that we seemed to be happy, so decided to get married.

On the day of the wedding I had made the mistake of letting Hayes convince me that he would be my chauffeur; a mistake indeed, as he was always late for everything. In typical form for Hayes, on my wedding day Kyrle (my best man) and I had to walk to his house about a mile away, as there was no sign of him getting up. Jerry's mother had to drag him out of bed and then he managed to break all records getting us the seven miles to Mallow and the church, but we were late as usual.

Etta, knowing him well, made sure that she would be 'extra' late, but we still arrived after her and that was a bad omen for the marriage. The day became totally mad, with family and friends just having a great time. My father got totally drunk on poteen and that night he decided to have a row with the mother's kitchen table. He said the table 'had no clothes on' and it was naked. Everyone fell around laughing because he was sitting in his car seat chair in his nightshirt and nothing else. He looked like Ghandi on a bad day, and it was a classic case of the pot calling the kettle black.

I know that we went to Dublin on our honeymoon and Etta got the flu. After walking around Dublin all day and her getting worse, we went to a pharmacy and got tablets for the flu. The chemist warned us that they were strong and to take just two every four hours. I persuaded Etta to take four so that she would get better faster, and within minutes of taking them she conked out, sleeping for over twelve hours. It's a wonder she is still alive, but it cured her of the flu and so we began our turbulent married life.

The plan was to move to a little flat or apartment in Cork City, and this we did. I used to go to work in Mallow by train each morning and evening, and Etta worked in The Brothers of Charity home for retarded children. Being an inveterate practical joker all my life, I saw no reason to stop because of marriage, and many a joke I played on poor Etta. The worst or best of these jokes (depending on your point of view) was known to us all as the lizard incident. We were living in our flat in Cork City at the time on the Lower Road. This flat had paper thin walls and was not at all conducive to a tempestuous married couple. Our neighbours on the 'paper thin' side were Mick and Mrs Grimes. They were a lot older than us but were very nice people, keeping their distance, but being helpful if they could in a crisis.

Larry Andersen's son Lawrence was also a joker, and one day he arrived to our workplace with a huge rubber lizard. It was the most lifelike creature I ever saw in my life. He had a long, floppy jaw with red, bloody teeth and a real long tail. He would tremble at the slightest movement and was truly frightening to look at. I immediately saw potential for this monster and asked to borrow him. Above us in the flat was a real old busy body called Mrs Franklen. She knew everyone's business and took pleasure in spreading the bad word always. If it wasn't bad enough, she added her own version of things and suitably embellished the whole event. As I was travelling to and from work I had time to plan my lizard incident, but first I needed a test of its reality. The train journey was the obvious place to try out the lizard's capabilities, and so I placed him on the seat beside me and pretended nothing. Naturally he shook like a mad thing with the train's motion, and even I began believing that he could be real. I got such fun from seeing people on the train do a double take as they passed in the carriage. Their looks of shock and disbelief made me smile, as they thought they were seeing things. One old woman actually attacked my lizard with her walking stick, taking a swipe at it in terror. I had to rescue him from the beating saying he was a pet. She said, "You're a danger to society and I'm going to complain you". I was delighted as I took him home in my bag; my lizard had passed the first test.

Our bedroom was located in the front section of the flat, and you had to pass through it to go into the living room and kitchen. This bedroom developed out of a modification I had earlier made to the flat. To give us extra space I put up a wall and painted the ceiling black. I painted it black because I believed that it would make the ceiling appear lower and cosier. In fact it had the opposite effect, as after I finished it always appeared to be night there, and the room seemed more like a cave than a bedroom. There was war with the landlord when we left the place. Apparently it took them weeks to repaint the black ceiling and he threatened law, but we were gone and I didn't give a damn at that stage.

When I arrived home I immediately placed the lizard on Etta's side of the bed and covered him over with the bedclothes. Now it was time for the story to begin, me figuring on a repeat of Lill's snake incident. I knew Etta would be getting the dinner ready and never had much time to look at the news on TV, so I started to tell her that I was late because of all the activity down the road. When she asked what was going on, I slowly and nonchalantly told her that a really dangerous pair of green African Mamba lizards had escaped on their way to the Fota Wildlife Park due to a car accident. I thought the 'Mamba' word would signify danger for her, and it did. She was biting nicely at this news when I added that they had only caught one of them and were still looking for the other one. The road to Fota Wildlife Park passed right outside our front door. Then I dropped the subject completely for about half an hour. This was really working well. Soon she asks me to describe the lizard and I do a brilliant job of it, since he is sitting in her bed only ten feet away from us. After my detailed description she became really scared and was afraid to go out for her cigarettes, so I volunteer to go, warning her to quickly lock the door in case he should run in for 'the heat'. While I am out, Mrs Jennings arrives for a chat and Etta tells her the whole story, unknown to me. She tells it so well that by then Mrs Jennings is also scared, and she rushes off to her own rooms to tell her husband Mick all about the lizard. When I came back in, Etta wants to know if all is safe and I pretend it is, with me doing a real bad job of it. This so-called lying frightened her all the more. By then she wants me to completely check our flat. It was becoming an exact repeat of Lill's snake days, as she was then too scared to go to bed. So I do the checking. I make a big play of searching under and over and all around the bedroom and pronounce it all safe. Etta starts to ask what should be done if you're bitten and was it really that dangerous, and again I'm in like a flash with the bad news. I tell her that a lizard first trembles his tail like a rattle snake just before striking, then he spits poison and blinds you like the King Cobra snake does. While this is happening he goes for the throat with a sharp bite. A really agonizing death would usually follow soon after a bite, but again I advise her that he is not in our flat, and that we are near a hospital with an antidote, if they have one of course, but that's unlikely it being a 'Mamba lizard'. I know she has no idea about snakes or lizards, so I can lay it on thick and I'm loving it all.

By then I am almost in tears with the potential laughter, as she has fallen for this beyond all my expectations. She decided that she would go to bed and I say I'll follow later as I'm reading. I have my head down in a book to hide myself from exploding. She put on her nightclothes and pulled back the sheets, and then suddenly she sees the lizard trembling in the bed. She let out this huge wail and leaps clean into the air, totally terrified and stretched out against the back wall. She had literally jumped about four feet in shock and fell back against a cabinet on Jennings' wall, knocking it over with a huge crash. As things began to fall and Etta continues to scream, in burst Mick Jennings waiving a sweeping brush and shouting, "Where is he, where is he? I'll kill him, I'll kill the fucker". Etta is glued to the wall in terror and pointing to the bed where the monster had moved a foot or so. Then Mick starts to beat at the bed with the brush. As he beat at the bed the lizard leapt up in the air, and the more he beat it, the more it leapt. This was just awesome to see and my lizard looked really alive. I saw all this happen as I leaned against the wall trying to keep the laughter in but pretending I was petrified, just so that I could see all the fun.

Etta began running around the flat screaming as Mick flails away at the lizard. Then losing all control, I fall on the floor with the laughter. I literally collapsed; I was almost sick it was so funny, and even as I write I can still remember thinking that that was the best joke I had ever played on anyone. While still on the ground I looked up and there was Mrs Jennings peeping in around our front door while her husband, half in terror and rage, was still trying to kill the un-killable. After some minutes Mick noticed me laughing and realized it had to be a joke. I just couldn't speak I was so sick with the laughing and Etta was still shaking with terror. We all calmed down but she wouldn't speak to me for days over it and probably never forgave me for it either.

A few days later I happened to go into our local shop and was standing behind the upstairs busybody, Mrs Franklin, who had heard all the commotion that night. She was telling the cashier her version of events. She said she saw it all. Poor Mrs Cahill had been bitten by some class of foreign beast and had to be rushed to the hospital. She said that Mick Jennings had to kill it and rescue her as her no good, useless husband just fell on the ground in fright. Then she added quietly, "I never liked him anyways, he was always a bit strange if you ask me". All I could do was to pretend I hadn't heard her, and as she was leaving I said, "Oh hello Mrs Franklen, how are you today?" "Oh grand Mr Cahill, it's a great day isn't it", and as she's leaving she gives me a big smile heading out the door. The cashier, who knew Etta well, deserved an explanation, so I told her that it was just a practical joke and I described the events. We both laughed all over again, with her saying it was one of the best jokes she had ever heard in her life, and if I was her husband she would probably never speak to me again after such a shock.

The lizard met with an untimely end though. I played a good few jokes with him on other people, but when I took him to Mrs Connolly's butcher shop in Buttevant he finally succumbed to her son's meat cleaver. The shop was crowded and when no one was looking I placed him near a big lump of meat on the chopping block, and I started to chat to Mrs Connolly. Suddenly there was a scream from a woman customer who was near the block, and John Connolly, with the speed of a Samurai warrior, drew a massive swipe at my lizard with his clever, chopping the head clean off. The head flew into the air, landing on top of the woman's boobs and she immediately fainted. Consternation soon reigned, with customers fleeing out the door in panic. I had the devil of a job explaining to all that it was just a joke gone wrong, and that I was really sorry for making her faint. That ended the lizard's life, but he gave good service and travelled many a mile with me, giving me hours of laughter while he lived.

We lived on the Lower Road in Cork for quite some time, but in the end I succumbed to Etta's constant nagging that we should leave and find a nicer place. She found us another flat overlooking Cork city, and we began to move our stuff in dribs and drabs. By then I had bought the bomber off Larry for 20 pounds and it had got even more unique under my ownership. As a start it had a modified steering wheel which was now the size of a dinner plate. Hayes had convinced me that it gave better 'control' when driving fast, and by then he had infected me with his speed madness to the point of insanity. Next the doors were held in place by six inch nails acting as hinges, (I was keeping the father's nails tradition alive) and its brakes constantly leaked brake fluid, again nothing unusual in that as the Cahills' cars rarely had good brakes, and early on I learned to pump the brakes like someone stomping out a fire.

To add to its uniqueness, the starter key switch was also broken. This meant that the only way to start the car was to go out to the front and raise the bonnet a little, then carefully stick your hand in under the bonnet, press the manual starter switch, then rush back in before the car rolled off, as it had no handbrake either since Larry had broken it years earlier while teaching me to drive. This car-starting was Etta's usual job, and we just got used to people pointing and laughing at our novel way of starting the car. The car had numerous other idiosyncrasies such as no wipers, no locks on the doors, but it did have a 'racing' engine. At least it was built for speed. Its most endearing characteristic for me though was that I could just lift the seats right out onto the road if I liked, because they were never bolted to the floor. This was real handy for transporting our stuff.

On one particular Saturday I had made numerous transporting trips to our 'new flat' and I was completely sick of it in the end, so I say to Etta, "Look lets try and do it all in one last go this time". She wasn't for it at all and we get into a heated argument on the street in front of our old flat. I took out the seats and had them on the footpath, then filled the car to bursting point. I crammed in everything I could see; books, a small dresser, cups, plates, and clothes. Then I put a mattress on the roof, and then another on top of it. By then I was seeing the end in sight, so I persuaded Etta to help me load a wardrobe on top of the two mattresses. She did help, and then encouraged, I put all the cutlery, records and tapes into a drawer in the wardrobe. Finally I managed to string a bit of a rope all the way round this stuff on the roof. The plan was to pull the rope through my window and tie it to my seat before Etta got in to her side. My weight would then act as an anchor, and with the rope around the wardrobe, it would come in Etta's window where she would keep a strain on it. I believed that she could hold it all easily if I drove slowly. I had forgotten about the big hill though and the basic laws of physics. As we left we looked like a moving version of Leaning Tower of Pizza.

We took off down the road slowly with cars beeping me and making signs to get going faster, as we were holding up the traffic. Initially I ignored all of this, but then the hooting and shouting became worse, and then the on-lookers on the street began pointing as well. I was getting madder and more embarrassed at this and was blaming Etta for always being on the move, swearing she was secretly a gypsy. She was pulling hard on the rope and I had no choice but to speed up, as I couldn't take this racket to my rear any longer. We got to the place where the steep hill began and tempers were now high as I made a run at the hill. Suddenly she starts shouting, "Slow down, slow down will you for God's sake, I can't hold this rope". Her pride wouldn't let her say it earlier. "I can't hold on, tis gonna go, ahhhhhh". All I could now see was the wardrobe and mattresses begin to slide off the back of the car and hit the ground. Then I see all the spoons, forks, knives books, and records go flying in all directions as well. I screech to a halt. Etta's seat now topples over and she has fallen backwards into the clothes, becoming buried and cursing like a sailor. I jump out just in time to see a car roll over my favourite Pink Floyd album *The Dark Side of the Moon*, and then I become like a lunatic. I ran onto the road and started jumping up and down, screaming and roaring at the fucker who just drove over my pride and joy. By then there are cars whizzing around me in all directions, trying to avoid me and our stuff. It's a wonder the cops weren't called.

Etta is also raging by then, calling me stupid for ever thinking that she could hold that rope, and we became worse than any tramps at each other's throat. All the passers-by either make off quickly to avoid us, or fall around laughing at us. It took two further runs to recover our household goods. The wardrobe never recovered. We just left it by the side of the street in bits, and I was swearing I'd never again help her to move. The disaster was so bad that we didn't speak to each other for a few days. It made no difference to Etta though, as it wasn't long before she got the itch to begin the final exodus to our next flat in Mallow, and subsequently our new home in that town.

We finally left Cork for a flat over Larry Andersen's TV shop in

O'Brien Street. By then Larry had bought another shop across the street and this also had a flat over it like his original one. This newest move was Etta's idea as I was quite happy living in Cork, but in reality I didn't care where we lived as long as we were happy. She fortunately saw that the money we spent on rent could be put to better use in saving for a deposit on a house. I think she and Larry concocted a scheme together whereby he would let us live in the flat in lieu of no increase in my wages. The plan was that when we finally decided to move out, he would return every cent of the imaginary wages I was to get. Basically he was doing us the greatest favour possible and true to his word, when the time came to put a deposit on a house, he returned every penny, but that was still some years away in the future.

Our flat over the shop was something else. It had a tiny bathroom and toilet, which was shared. The bath was so old and rusty that I used to hate having baths in it. We had no shower so we just had to make do with the odd bath. The living room, which was on the first floor, looked out onto the street. It had two huge windows and I made a shelf unit to divide the room from the kitchen. The kitchen section had a counter top covered with linoleum for effect. It was never finished. The wiring was also never finished. A lot of the wires were left sticking out of the wall with no sockets attached. I was continuing in the well known Cahill tradition of 'doing it tomorrow'. We had started with a kitchen in the top of the building, but this soon came to a halt as I needed to have my own space for inventing things. We had our bedroom on the top floor facing the street, and in the night we used to hear cracks happening in the front wall. Etta began telling me that the wall would collapse one day and we would be killed. All of this I dismissed as her usual nonsense. She was far closer to the truth than she knew though, because while Larry and I were refurbishing the shop beneath us we sawed through a support beam that we were advised not to cut. When the building didn't collapse on top of us then, Larry pronounced it safe. Fortunately for us, one Sunday while we were out walking, the front wall did partially collapse bringing down the ceilings and filling the shop front with rocks from the wall. Larry had to have steel girders installed in the wall to prevent a total collapse, so Etta was right and once again we escaped an early demise. The building still stands to this day and seems to have changed little in thirty years; a tribute to steel girders and amateur builders.

The flat was a happy place in general, but I saw long term difficulties as we had to go through our TV shop below to get upstairs to our home. Taking shopping and coal up a steep stairs, as well as humping drums of gas, was very difficult, but all of this paled into insignificance compared to when our first baby, Adrian, arrived. The very large rats were a problem for us too, and Etta was scared to death of them. One day she was sitting on the toilet and on hearing a noise she looked across to the side of the bath where Larry and I had nailed a wide board to keep the rats in. We neglected to tell her that we had seen a large rat come through the wall there some weeks earlier. That rat had brazenly walked across the room right in front of us, so we took the easy way out and nailed an old board to the wall feeling that this would keep him at bay. As she sat on the toilet she thought she saw a rat out of the corner of her eye, but dismissed it as sheer imagination. After all, we had assured her there were no rats at all in the place. Then a rat's head appeared from behind the board. It seems that in the intervening weeks he had eaten through our defences. As she stared in disbelief, the rat got braver and eventually leaped out from behind the board, landing beside her with a thump. She took off out of the bathroom screaming, "Rat, rat, rat", trying to keep her jeans on as she did so. She dashed into the kitchen, slamming the door behind her. Larry's father, a man we called Kelly, saw her fly past and tried to console her by saying in through the door, "What's wrong with you girl, sure tis only an ould rat". Etta was not impressed at all and when I came in she was like a wild woman. She then demanded some solution, or she was moving again. My easy answer that time was to get a cat, but that solution turned out to be far worse than the rats ever were. We got a small female cat. Etta called the cat Kizzy after some character in an American TV series called Roots. Kizzy was a kitten and had this bad habit of deliberately finding my clothes and pissing on them. I am certain she liked my musk, as it was always my clothes she chose to piss on. No amount of booting her in the ass did any good either and I was going wild at the smell. She must have been pissing on the floor too because soon there was a constant smell of cat's piss around the flat, and as time went by it got stronger and stronger. Cat's piss is an amazing thing as it's impossible to get rid of it. I used to think that there was a definite invention in it if I could only turn it into a perfume of some kind as it would last for days, but I never had the time to investigate that idea properly.

After months we actually got used to this smell, and soon I ignored it. However, when our friends came to call they would almost get sick from the smell. Some were too polite to say anything, but usually never called again. My aunt May was not so polite though, and told me straight out to get rid of 'that stinking cat'. I was coming to the same conclusion myself, as it had pissed on my best jacket and absolutely no amount of washing would get rid of the smell. I had to just dump my best jacket in the end and I was savage, cursing both the cat and Larry's rats. That bloody cat was no use as a ratter either, as I was still seeing the furry fellas but not telling Etta about it. The cat never once caught a rat, and I used to say she was too busy eating, sleeping, and pissing on my clothes to be out catching rats.

One beautiful evening the cat began this violent wailing for no apparent reason. It went on and on and sounded to me like she was dying. We were so innocent then that we didn't know the cat was in heat. I was certain she had some bad pain, and as I believed brandy was good for all ills, I decided to get her some as a cure. I went across the road to the local bar which was crowded that evening. As I entered I got a lot of odd looks as I don't drink and most people knew me then, and knew this about me too. Mrs Duignan, the owner, looked very surprised also as she asked me what I wanted. I didn't want to be wasting my hard earned money on a useless cat, so I started to explain that I just wanted a half glass of brandy. She knew I didn't drink too and said, "John when did you start drinking the hard stuff? I thought you don't drink at all". I was quick to assure her that I didn't drink, and that this brandy was just for our cat. She exclaimed incredulously and loudly for all to hear, "You mean to tell me you're giving brandy to your cat, are you coddin me John?" I tell her I am serious, as our cat's in pain and brandy will cure it. Immediately all heads turn on me and I then became an instant talking point, with all the locals saying he's so crazy he's giving brandy to his cat. What a fool, wasting it. There were peals of laughter in the bar where everyone thought this was the funniest and stupidest thing they ever heard. I was being quizzed on all sides as to the reasons for this waste, and Mrs Duignan seemed to take ages giving me the brandy, hanging on every word that I spoke. She was having great fun at my expense. The more I recounted my reasons, the more laughter it caused. I still had no idea why they all laughed so much. When I had paid for the brandy, Mrs Duignan says to me, "Maybe the cat's in heat John, did you ever think of that boy?" More laughter came from the patrons and some even offered to help me hold the cat down, just in case some got spilled. I was the butt of numerous jokes for weeks after that incident, and every time I went to fix Duignans' TV, she always asked me with a smirk, "And how's the cat now John, still an alcoholic is she?"

I returned red-faced with my bottle to Etta saying it was nothing and that the damn cat was just randy, so I opened the back window to let her out for her fun, but she wouldn't go out. She was still screeching though with this awful moaning and after an hour of this I became convinced again that she was in pain and that the pub-goers were all wrong. It was time for action. Because it was so warm I had no shirt on when I grabbed hold of the cat. I told Etta to pour the brandy down her throat while I prized open her mouth. The cat was scratching and tearing at me when I turned her upside down on my lap, and she bit me when I tried to open her mouth. I persevered and Etta got the bottle ready. I got her mouth open again and shouted at Etta, "Now, now, pour, pour," and she did. The brandy went into the cat and onto me. The cat's paws suddenly shot out, with her claws becoming razors tearing my belly apart. I couldn't hold her as she seemed to have developed super strength and she escaped. She leaped up in the air and made a drive for the open window where she jumped clean out and we never saw her again. Now with no cat, plenty of rats, and Adrian a baby, Etta activated the doomsday scenario. We would be on the move again, but this time to our new house which was being built at a snail's pace in Avondale Park.

Before we could move in to our newly built house, we had to have the water main connected and this event was to set me off on a bad footing with the water section of the local authorities. I had been given a map which showed where the main water pipe for the whole estate was located. It was supposed to be about six feet outside our boundary wall on the road, and apparently it was my responsibility to dig to this pipe and have my house pipe brought out to it for connection by the official plumbers in the local council. I knew well that digging for this pipe by myself would be a terrible job, so I enlisted the help of my brother Hugh who was around at the time. It was a Saturday and we began digging around nine in the morning. After about four hours and four holes, all about three feet deep, we still had not seen the main pipe and we retired for the dinner almost dead from the exertion.

Etta kept asking me if I was reading the map right and this was driving me mad, as I was suspecting the map was wrong and that was our problem. At two p.m. we got at it again, this time digging between the holes in case we had 'missed it', and by about six in the evening we had one huge hole in the road and still no sign of the main water pipe. At that point Hugh decided he had had enough and was leaving, and in rage I took a lace at the ground with my pickaxe and suddenly we struck water. There was a huge jet of water going up about fifteen feet into the air, and we both stood awestruck gazing at it. I had inadvertently broken into the main water pipe for the whole area. People started to stop and look, and soon the hole in the road became a swimming pool full of murky brown water. If it had been a nice day we could easily have gone for a swim, but it was not. Quite quickly Hugh says to me, "We better cover this over and you'll have to call the council and tell them you have broken the mains," emphasizing the word 'you', adding, "Don't dare mention me in any of this". That sounded ominous and I didn't like it at all. What did he know that I didn't know. To stop the geyser from turning Avondale Park into New York on a hot summer's day, we got a sheet of iron from around the back and put it over the pipe. Then we added more sheets, rocks and a tar barrel to make a barrier around the 'swimming pool' and hoped for the best as the water continued to pour out from under our defenses for the rest of the weekend. By Monday a lake had formed outside our house. I called the council on Monday morning and told them that I had found the water pipe and had had a little accident. "What kind of accident Mr Cahill?" "Well actually I think I burst your main pipe". "What did you say.. you burst the mains is it? So you're the cause of no one having water all weekend, or those who did have it were drinking mud. You'll be paying for this....". I said, "If you had given me a proper fucking map I'd not have burst your bloody pipe," and hung up on them. An army of workers arrived and by dinnertime they had us connected, the hole was filled in and to their credit they never charged me a penny. My belief always was that anything outside my gate was their responsibility and so it was an accident with no one to blame, but Hugh was making sure he was not going to be tangled up in it.

Over the years that followed our move to Avondale Park, two more children would arrive in our lives; my daughter Lynda who I nicknamed early on as 'Lyndi the scientist', and our youngest son Kyrl named after my brother Kyrle. As the Cahills had already done before, we dropped the 'e' off the end of my son's name to distinguish him from my brother Kyrle. I could not say that we were great parents; far from it, because from an early age our three children had to become totally independent in mind and body. Each of them learned how to cook and survive by themselves because I was always out working, and Etta would often have to help me as no one else would. In hindsight, this survivalist thinking has been of great benefit to them as they are all now out in the world and well able to fend for themselves. I also believe honestly that Etta was a far better mother than I was a father, and to my great regret I spent far too much time working for others as by then I was not alone working for Larry, but I was also working for pirate radio. I could easily be out half the night or on weekends when I should have been spending that time with my most precious of gifts; my children.

As the years passed us by, Etta and I would go off on vacation abroad, usually to London for a week or less. Initially Etta's sister Helen was kind enough to take care of our children, and later still my mother and father stayed with them for the week that we were away. Then when Adrian became a teenager, we often took off leaving him to mind the other two all by himself. He did this with no bother at all and no disaster that we knew of ever happened. Helen was great and would still keep an eye on them, but he managed admirably, and despite how it might appear, I truly believe it made him a responsible adult and caused the other two to treat him with the respect an elder brother deserved. I'm very glad to say that that is how it has remained to this day.

On one of those trips we managed to get to the Costa del Sol and from there, in the company of a large group of other tourists, we took a day trip to Africa. I'll never forget the feeling I got as our ferry crossed over the Straits of Gibraltar coming in sight of the Atlas Mountains on the African coast. We landed in Tangiers where the police took all of our passports for safe keeping and soon we began a bus tour taking us all over northern Morocco. The heat was unreal, registering 40 degrees in our air-conditioned bus, and I loved it. We had dinner in the Kasbah in a clean but very old version of a restaurant. I had a belly dancer gyrating beside me for most of the meal, which put me off it completely. Then, during the meal, a real mean-looking photographer arrived carrying all of our pictures that he had secretly taken while our guide had made us go up a stone staircase passing a window and then down the other side for no reason. I soon realized that he had been hiding inside the window and snapped us all as we passed, and it was now time for us to pay for our unwanted photos. In his broken English he started pressing us to buy as he moved down the long table we all sat at. An American lady sat by us and felt intimidated by his looks. Very few bought the photos and he was getting madder and more desperate as he came to a German couple sitting beside the American. They flatly refused his demands, and as if to teach the rest of us a lesson he held up their photo, waved it around and then tore it to ribbons in front of us all, throwing the bits up in the air. The American lady was so scared that she bought hers immediately and I bought one too because I wanted it as a souvenir. Later still we were taken to a so-called 'shop of many floors' with each floor specializing in rugs and leather goods as well as brass ornaments. All the time we looked, but didn't buy. We all began to feel intimidated and the shop staff began to become worried too because we were not buyers. At about that time a large gathering of local sellers became convinced that our group must carry all the gold of China because they tried to invade the shop and get us to buy fake Rolex watches, hats and every other kind of portable junk imaginable. This annoyed the shop people so much that they threw out the locals, causing a mini riot at the front door before they slammed it shut, trapping us all inside. Our situation had become quite serious because we then had no passports and no idea where we were in the large Moslem city. We had no mobile phones either in those days, and our guide had also disappeared, leaving us to face the angry mob outside all alone. The hammering on the front doors scared the women even worse, and the shouts in Arabic from the insiders added to the increasing unease that we were all feeling. I knew that our ferry would leave on time, as we had been warned of that fact many times by the now vanished guide, and the time was passing too fast for my liking. With no more purchases likely and just before I myself was about to start panicking, the guide magically appeared from inside the shop and told us that we would have to make a run for the bus, which was parked some distance away in the middle of the square. We were warned sternly not to lose sight of him at any cost, and at that, the shop people flung open the door and the guide rushed out into the waiting throng of angry desperate locals. We followed quickly and then began a hilarious though very frightening event. Here were about fifty tourists of all ages and nationalities running through the streets of Tangier trying to avoid being robbed by the hundred or so local sellers brandishing their wares as well as their fists. It was both scary and exhilarating at the same time and I can see it all so clearly still. Etta ran along beside me, fighting off the hat and scarf sellers, while I kept refusing 'genuine Rolex' watches at a, "Good price for you kind sir". There were shouts of great bargains mixed with screams of insults in Arabic when we ignored the salesmen, and a kind of mad chaos reigned as we ran along faster and faster, all the time trying to keep the guide's fez in sight. When the bus came into sight we all redoubled our running so that it became a race to get inside the bus at all costs. We had no idea what would happen to any stragglers, but it would not be good, and none of us wanted to be left outside to the mob's anger. When the bus took off for the boat we all left out a huge cheer of relief and the guide even took off his fez and waved it about for us, but I think myself that he was in on it all and it may well have been a staged event. As the boat returned across the Straits, I sat on the upper deck bathed in the beautiful golden sunshine from a setting African sun and thanked God for the day while Etta calmed her nerves with some foreign liqueur mixed with coffee in the bar below me. The day was not over yet though, as when we finally arrived back at Torremolinos and went out for a very late dinner, the staff of the restaurant brought out a beautiful candle and placed it on our table along with the food. Etta said, "Isn't that the most romantic thing they just did, be sure to give them a big tip". I was about to agree with her when the whole candle literally exploded and splattered our food with all kinds of material. It was some kind of trick candle and our dinner was ruined. I nearly got a bloody heart attack as well while the waiters fell around the place laughing their heads off, but being Irish did we complain? No of course not, I just paid the bill and left, and the next day I believe the place was closed down for good. I think we were their last customers ever. They knew it and wanted to go out with a bang, or a tourist medical emergency. It had been a day to remember and I have never forgotten it. I'm sure neither has Etta. Years later, both Lill and Eunice went on that same trip. Lill hated it while Eunice loved it. Probably Nannie's rearing made us two impervious to the extremes of culture in that amazing place called Africa.

We went on numerous other trips to London as well, and on one of those I brought home one of the first computers ever made. It used to play a game where little alien ships were attacking you and Adrian, who was then about twelve, became so fascinated with it that I knew it was only a matter of time before he would want to programme his own game. That's exactly what happened, ultimately setting him on his own software career and taking him to Australia too.

North Cork Local Radio.

Around nineteen eighty or so, an old classmate of Kyrle from Pad's days walked into our shop in O'Brien Street. His name was Maurice Brosnan and he was working locally in the insurance business, and still does today as I write. Maurice and three other businessmen had decided to set up a radio station in Mallow after RTE, the national broadcaster, had done a very successful week's broadcasting, then left the area, leaving a radio entertainment vacuum behind them.

The group had decided to call their service NCLR or North Cork Local Radio. They had the right idea but lacked the technical expertise necessary to make it all happen. I found out later that they had a small homemade transmitter and were trying to make it heard all over the town, without any luck. Then I believe Maurice remembered 'the mad Cahills' blotting out Buttevant's radio service many years earlier with their own homemade transmitter, and he arrived in the shop to meet me and chat about their problems. He had been in the same class as Kyrle and I didn't recognise him at first, but when he mentioned Pad's schooldays, all the memories returned and we talked for a long time. In the end, Maurice told me of their predicament and asked if I would just 'look' at their setup. Kyrle was by then working for RTE, who hated the idea of any kind of illegal pirate radio service, primarily because they had a monopoly on the audience and did not want any form of competition. Obviously because of Kyrle's position, I knew that he would not be in favour of me going anywhere near such an illegal operation, and I told this to Maurice. Being the great salesman that he is, he convinced me to 'just have a look' anyway and maybe advise them on what they needed to do next. In the end I agreed to look. What was the harm in that? And besides, Kyrle was 'way up' in Dublin and would never find out about it.

After work on a Friday night I went down the street in Mallow and was taken in to see their little makeshift studio. What I saw there astounded me because they had an old 'disco deck' with a cheap microphone driving the transmitter, and that was basically it. The signal was then fed along a length of television aerial cable to a copper pole mounted on a chimney out the back of the building, and that was their entire radio station. It was no wonder the signal only went about a hundred yards before fading out. I examined the operation and discovered two major flaws which I doctored easily and quickly, and in less than fifteen minutes the signal suddenly covered most of the town. Then their phone started ringing with the good news. The radio group had been so impressed with my few minutes' work that they wanted me on board at almost any cost. As far as I was concerned I had done what they needed and I was about to leave when they asked me to come to a meeting the following morning at ten a.m.

Little did I know how my whole life would change as a result of that meeting. They told me that they had four thousand pounds to invest and were ready to spend all of it in any way I needed, if I took on the job of making them a 'proper' radio station. I had never even seen a 'proper' radio station by then, but I knew that Kyrle had, and my mind began to race at the challenge and excitement of a project like this. The fact that I would be paid only added to the excitement.

In nineteen eighty, four thousand pounds was a huge amount of money, and by way of comparison, I was earning about thirty pounds a week at that time. They had only one condition for the job; that I had to have the radio station on the air by the following Saturday. Yes, I had only one week to completely purchase all the equipment, get the desks made, install a transmitter on a new aerial system in a new location, cure any problems and be ready at ten a.m. the following Saturday. I asked for a fee of one thousand pounds of their four with half up front, and they agreed immediately on the condition that I could make it happen from the balance. Michael O'Sullivan, who was one of the four, said that the papers would carry the launch story on the coming Thursday and the whole town would be expecting it on air as agreed. Within minutes I proved just how insane I was then, as I took the job, accepting the conditions and the insane challenge involved. By Sunday afternoon I was on the train to Kyrle in Dublin, and designed the whole system on a notepad while on the journey. No laptops, smart phones or iPads then; the design would come out of my head and that alone. When I told Kyrle what I was doing and the timescale I had to do it, he actually fell off his couch laughing at the sheer impossibility of it all. Then as I told him about my commitment, true to form, and even though he hated the illegality of it all, he agreed to help me buy the gear in Dublin. By Tuesday I was on the way back to Mallow with a goods wagon quarter full of boxes of electronic equipment.

By Wednesday I had convinced Etta to leave me for some days so that I could have the whole house to myself. I had taken a week off work from Larry so that I could construct the studio, first in my kitchen, and if it worked, we would then transport it all to a place called 'The Willows', an area that is high above Mallow town. I got it all going, and on the Thursday night we were the talk of the town as we had to lift the finished desk in through the upper window in number four The Willows. It was a sight to see. Even the fire brigade people helped us, and there was a huge air of excitement and expectancy beginning. That day the local papers all carried the story of Mallow's impending new radio station and the pressure on me became immense. I had the studio done, but now the transmission had to be done in just one day.

I could easily write a book on the beginnings of that radio service, but it's true to say that it went right down to the wire for me, as by Friday night the transmission was still not working properly. Around ten p.m. that night, the four directors met in the room next door to our studio and obviously were very concerned that this might all fail, yet not one of the four ever said to me, "John will it be on air Saturday?" Noel O'Connor and Pat O'Brien, who were the other two directors, actually tried to encourage me on by saying with big smiles that they had their speeches ready and were going home to be up early for the first broadcast in the morning. Michael O'Sullivan also said the same thing, coming in to encourage me with kind words and then leaving Maurice Brosnan and I alone to deal with the technical problem I was still having.

It was a serious problem as when someone spoke into a microphone, a huge hum came across their voice and ruined it. Unfortunately this hum was intermittent, making it impossible for me to trace it. Numerous times I thought it was fixed but randomly it would reoccur. That night by eleven p.m. it seemed to be gone for good, and Maurice pressed me to go home and get some sleep. What he didn't know was that I had not slept for almost thirty six hours, surviving on coffee, catnaps, and buns. Today I believe that I was mentally cracking up under the strain of it all, but didn't see it myself at the time. Etta had called to see me and was also worried sick, as I wouldn't speak to her, but yet I seemed to be always talking to myself. In actual fact, that was my way of going over the problem in my mind, and all I wanted was for the radio to be perfect in the morning, and not let any of the four directors down.

I woke at eight a.m. and the transmitter was humming as bad as ever. I rushed back to the studio, locked the door, and began an emergency doctoring plan where I replaced a vital bit of gear as I prayed most sincerely for success. I was in uncharted waters now, and if this plan didn't work then all was lost for everyone. By nine fifty five, with five minutes to go, the signal became perfect and a huge cheer erupted from the room next door when I announced the good news. I think I went home and collapsed out of sheer exhaustion, but Cork, especially North Cork, would never again be without its own local radio service. I had pulled it off, and in my own little way, made history that morning. For as long as I live I will always be thankful to those four directors who, like Jack, never lost faith in me. Even when it looked like all had failed, they still believed in me and were sure I would make it all happen for them. I can thank my mother too for a philosophy that encouraged us to believe in ourselves, but the person who really kept me going was Big Kyrl with his philosophy of 'failure is not an option John', and 'the end always justifies the means'.

NCLR, the pirate radio station, began to take off and because it was local, carrying local news made by local people, the number of listeners began to grow very rapidly. We did many novel broadcasts in those days, and on one occasion it was decided to broadcast a special mass for the sick. This was to come from Saint Mary's Church in the middle of the town. Even though I was still working for Larry, he was good enough to let me troubleshoot the station in lieu of advertising, so I was dispatched to the church to scout out how this could be done. I saw a major problem for us, as our aerial cable for the second homemade transmitter was too short and there was no way to get another one in the time we had. While I'm wracking my brains as to what kind of miracle might be needed, in arrives the newly appointed Parish Priest, Father Denis O'Callaghan, and when he saw my gear he immediately christened it 'Steam Radio'.

I told him of the problem and without a moment's hesitation he says, "Sure can't you bore a hole in the window and get the wire out that way". These were beautiful new-looking windows and I just didn't feel right about it, so I asked him again if he was sure it was ok. "God save us man, sure I'm the Parish Priest. No one will say a word to you". I got my drill and bored a huge hole for the thick cable. The broadcast was a great success and we used that hole many times in later years for many a Mass. The sheer practical 'go do it' attitude of the Parish Priest was amazing to me and I loved it. I liked him immediately, and like Jack O'Rourke, we became great friends over the following amazing years. A few weeks later it was decided to broadcast the Angelus Bells at midday and I felt that recording a real bell would be the nicest way to do it.

I asked Denis if it was ok to record the bells in the bell tower in Mallow's Catholic Church, and he was so happy that he volunteered to help me with the job. We arrived just before midday and I climbed up the ladder with my equipment. He said he would pull the rope and ring the bell. Bong! Bong! Bong! After a large number of bongs I signalled to stop and he asked if I had been counting. I had not, and neither had he. This was a disaster as now we would have to return tomorrow, but Dennis would have none of it. He says, "We'll do it again". This time we both counted so intently that I had forgotten to press the record button, and once again we had messed it all up. "We'll do it again," was his mantra and so we did. This time we were almost done when the bloody rope broke. I was getting real embarrassed as well. By then the townspeople must have thought that some fiends had got at the bell, and it's a wonder the Gardai were not called. Not to be defeated though, Denis made off to the local hardware shop and arrived back with a new rope, and soon we were ready to try again. Bong, Bong, Bong, and that time we got it right. That sound used to ring out all over North Cork for years and years until, in the end, it too wore itself out and became just a memory of an earlier

271

wonderful era. Later on that amazing priest, as Chairman of our company, would guide us on to legality and ultimately ensure the radio service, which began in my kitchen, would become one of the most successful ones in Ireland, but that was still some years away.

Over the following years the local radio went through many ups and downs, both technically and financially. Always we were striving for more coverage, and in the end we decided to try and get a 'medium wave' service going along with our local FM service. To do this we would have to construct a large wire aerial and we simply did not have the room at number four The Willows for it, so I got a brainwave, or as it turned out 'a brain storm'. We would use a fibreglass pole about thirty feet long and wind all the aerial wire around it. In theory it was technically correct, but in practice the pole both looked like and acted like a giant fishing rod, which I could not keep up in the air. During my brainstorm I concluded that we needed to encase the 'fishing rod' in two twenty-foot sewer pipes connected together. These pipes were to be attached to a chimney on the roof of our two-storey house and held in place by numerous stay wires. Once again the local fire brigade came to our aid and what was once a new housing estate soon resembled Cape Kennedy. Despite this being a new estate, not one single person objected to this eyesore. The people were so good then, and we had no Health and Safety issues to worry about either. It was like being in our own Wild West and all one needed was imagination to succeed at anything.

The effort by all had been great, but still the aerial was a total flop. It could not be heard beyond Mallow town, but if you called any telephone in the area, you got a crystal clear signal from our studios. The joke in Charleville became, "Hey cove, if you want to hear NCLR, all you have to do is call someone in Mallow. You don't even need a radio at all". This was very embarrassing for me, but we just did not have the room to string up a two hundred foot wire, so I needed to rethink our situation.

Then a friend of Jack's, a man called Jim Sullivan, came to the rescue and told me to string up whatever I liked outside on his farm, as he had plenty of room.

Etta and I set off, complete with rope and wire, and arrived at

Jim's farm. I climbed up a huge tree of at least sixty feet high with my rope over my shoulder and began trying to tie it off on the tree. Then Jim's father arrived. He demanded that I come down immediately. Obviously Jim had neglected to tell him about us. Etta tried to explain that Jim had given us permission, but he ignored her totally, and I ignored him totally, as I did not want to climb that tree a second time. He got mad and went into the house, returning with a shotgun. He shouted up to me to, "Get down now I tell you, get down this minute or I'll blow you down", menacingly pointing the gun up at me. I came down figuring that no radio was worth getting killed for. We left and Jim later explained that his dad had thought I was trying to hang myself. We all laughed at it a lot later, and once again I climbed the tree, being like a bloody monkey in those days. That aerial did work, and for many years our medium wave service came from Jim's farm in Dromdowney, outside of Mallow. It never ceased to amaze me how good the farming community were to us in those days. They were always so helpful to me personally and Jim Sullivan was one of the best.

Some time later Maurice Brosnan and I climbed Mount Hillary, which is a mountain also outside of Mallow well over twelve hundred feet high. In the ongoing search for more FM radius, I knew that height is gold and we felt that if we could get on top of a real mountain, then we were made. We found the exact place, and on the way down we got completely lost. We arrived into a farmyard where we were warmly greeted by Gerry and Mary Lucy, also farmers who owned the land at the top. They could not do enough for us when they found out that we were with 'the radio'. It was decided to set up a transmitter on the top of their mountain and thus began a friendship that lasts to this day. Their daughter Deirdre had a best friend called Laurie O'Flynn, now Laurie Rickard, and that same Laurie is helping me proofread this very book. There are no accidents in life I feel. We got the site working after numerous trials and tribulations, and it became the cornerstone of the pirate radio service from then on. We would continue to use that site until legal radio began in nineteen ninety and we moved to the other side of the mountain, which was even higher.

In about nineteen eighty three we planned to build a new tower for the medium wave service on yet another farmer's land. He was a man called Jimmy Frawley and he lived in a place called Lisgriffin. The site was perfect and the tower was ready, but almost on the day when it was to be erected, a Gulf Stream Jet piloted by a South American Captain Ocana made an emergency landing in Mallow Racecourse. The plane's insurers decided to build a runway to get the jet off the ground, and over the next five weeks the captain became a regular contributor to our illegal radio. I know that on the day of the landing, our reporter was first on the scene and I arrived soon after. It was some sight to see. The plane had clipped the tops off of all the white racing posts, as it had literally run out of fuel as it landed. The captain had broken English, but he became an instant celebrity and we in the radio became his local newsletter.

The downside for me though was that the firm who were contracted to put up our tower now had a big contract to build a runway, and we had to wait our turn for the tower to be erected. It would have grave financial implications for NCLR as a company, as by then our costs had drastically increased and we needed the extra radius to make it work financially, and that never came because the tower was late. However, there was going to be a huge media event taking place over the next few weeks and we were right in the middle of it all, even though we were as illegal as it gets. I felt that somehow I was going to be a part of history, as a plane would take off against all the odds; its captain was a friend of ours and I would be broadcasting the whole event being watched by the world's legal media, RTE included.

Michael O'Sullivan and the captain would become great friends over the course of the next few exciting weeks. The town was buzzing with excitement as the runway neared completion, and then the question we all asked was, 'Did he have enough room for an actual take off?', because a line of tall trees marked the end of 'the runway'. The captain promised us an exclusive interview on the morning that he would leave, but more to the point, he promised to tell us when that morning would be. Secrecy was vital as the civil authorities did not want a huge crowd gathering to see a possible fireball if the plane exploded in the trees. We were sworn to secrecy too, but I had to get an 'outside broadcast' (OB) van lined up the night before and that gave the whole game away. The world's media, who were keeping a close watch on us, actually descended on the racecourse when they saw me at work that night. I had inadvertently given the game away and I got blamed as the one who blabbed, even though I had only told those I needed to help me rig the OB. By ten a.m. the next morning, the whole road was completely blocked with every kind of vehicle imaginable. Camper vans, horse boxes, old vans, cars, and even bicycles were parked all over the place, and thousands and thousands of people had climbed all over these vehicles for a better view. It was the most amazing sight to see and we had a prime view from the top of our broadcasting unit.

We had been on the air since early morning, and at the appropriate time the captain arrived into our unit and began thanking the people of Mallow for the great welcome they had given him. It was quite emotional listening to him in his poor English and knowing too that, unlike the other media, I had placed our van just yards from the trees where he might soon crash. For me at least, that possibility made it even harder to listen to him speak about how great we were, and how much he liked us as a radio station. Then he thanked us all personally, shook hands with us all, and promised to fly back over our unit if he made it, dipping his wings in a salute to the 'pirates' of Mallow. We were ecstatic, as to be given legitimacy by someone so famous and being recognized as part of a great media event by television and radio services from around the world, was almost too much to bear. We all wished him well, and he left for his jet. Within minutes we could hear the roar of the mighty jet engines in the distance. As it rapidly approached us we all held our breath and prayed for his success. I really did not think he would get the lift in time, he seemed too low and too slow to me, but he did make it with just inches to spare. I actually saw bits of leaves and limbs fly off the trees and I roared so loud with a cheer that I could hear myself over the engines. I jumped up and down with excitement as the plane became a dot, heading west for Mexico. Michael, who was describing the event live, looked deeply disappointed as he felt sure the captain would honour his promise and dip the wing to give us final legitimacy, but now he looked to be gone. As he was about to hand back to the studio I noticed the dot getting bigger and I shouted, "He's coming back, look, look, here he comes".

T he jet shot right over us, tilting the wings almost vertical while the whole crowd cheered so loud that our microphones were drowned out. The captain had honoured his promise, and that day I was on such a high that I took the rest of it off. Every person was talking about the event and the dipping of the wings for weeks and weeks. We in radio were stars for a day at least. Just recently a movie was made called *The Runway*, which is loosely based on that famous day. There is even a view that I figure as the pirate radio personality in the movie, but I have my doubts. Still, I did figure in the real thing, and that's good enough for a 'dunk' from Buttevant.

I stand to be corrected, but not too long after that day we got the tower up and the radios improved dramatically. By then it was all too late for NCLR, and the directors had no choice but to hand the whole operation over to the community at a public meeting held in Mallow. The station would from then on be called NCCR or North Cork Community Radio, and Jack and Father Denis would re-enter my story.

It is only fair to say that the pirate radio years would rob me and Etta of a normal family life. I was never at home, and when I was home, I was only half there. Usually my head would be glued to the radio in case it went off or sounded bad. All this stress was happening at the expense of my three children. By then my eldest son Adrian was about eight and Lynda, my daughter, would be about five years old. Kyrl, my youngest son, was still a baby, and so I think he escaped from having no dad, but the other two were truly reared by their mother, and all credit is due to her for how well they turned out. At the time of writing, Adrian has just immigrated to Australia, and Lynda is in the process of completing a Civil Engineering Degree, having already obtained a Marketing Degree in Dublin. Adrian has a PhD in Computer Science and my Kyrl is head of IT for Cork's 96fm and C103, as well as engineer for Limerick's Live 95 radio station. I am exceptionally proud of all three of them, and it never ceases to amaze me just how funny they all are and how different in personality each of them is. Even though I was missing for most of their rearing, when I was there it was usually a time of drama and fun. They often remind me of one occasion when we got the mad idea that we should buy a big tent and get into the camping spirit of things as a way of having family time, and it almost ended in an early divorce. We bought this huge and very expensive tent in Cork. It had no assembly instructions with it, or they got lost before we got to read them, and that would be typical of us anyway. Etta wanted to go off on a trip almost immediately, but not me. I felt we needed to assemble the tent as a test, and where better than out in our own backyard. I just wanted to get the feel for it before we got marooned in Kerry. This was an almost prophetic statement as it transpired. We set about this assembling on a warm Sunday afternoon, and after three hours we had constructed this God awful monstrosity. It leaned sideways and tilted down in the front, much like a Bedouin tent. We had started off assembling happily enough, but after an hour of confusion, the shouting began and all I wanted to do in the end was get it up somehow. I left it up for the next few days, being in no mood to even attempt taking it down. Then of course it rained, ruining the inside and outside, as it all fell over from a wind in the night. I was neither impressed nor surprised at any of this, not being a camping type at heart. Etta tried to dry it out over the next week or so, and even though we had made a total mess of our first attempt at assembly, she was determined that we should go to Kerry the following weekend. Myself and Adrian believed that we could make our own diagram based on laying out every single pole, bar, and peg in the backyard before we would commit to the trip, and this we did. It had all kinds of poles and bars and spikes, as well as a huge number of pegs and strings. It was a sheer nightmare just looking at all this stuff on the ground, but it was Saturday and Etta was hassling us to get a move on with the figuring. We tried for hours to make some kind of sense of it all, and finally we thought we had it solved and drew it all out on a bit of paper. Then almost on a whim, we set off for Tralee in the late evening sunshine. When we got to the Banna Strand campsite it was pitch black. We set about setting up the harem by the light from the car. This didn't go well for us, not well at all. Firstly we were all hungry and tired, and to make matters worse, I had forgotten the bloody drawing, so we were working off memory or guesswork again. Because of the rush leaving, we had decided on a barbecue for our food after the tent was up. This barbecue was to

277

be our dinner, tea and supper, and Etta was to do the cooking while we assembled the Bedouin tent. She had never done any barbecuing before and no matter what she tried, she could not get the charcoal to light. I had no idea either, but Adrian, Lynda and I were already fighting and shouting as to how to assemble the tent. By then it was really getting late, and we were all cold, hungry and still had no place to sleep. Unknown to us, we were the cause of much merriment from the other experienced campers on the site. We temporarily gave up on the tent and I took over the fire work, beginning by making balls of newspaper and setting them on fire, then roaring at Etta to blow the flames like mad under the coals. This was no good, as she smoked too much and had no breath at all. I was arguing with her about smoking and blaming the fags for all our ills as the kids tried to get the tent set up without me. I had a fallback plan for making tea. This was a small little gas ring that worked on a portable container of gas, and I had bought two of these containers, so we were set. I called a halt to all work, saying that we needed tea to think, and got out my gas ring. I had no idea how to connect this ring to its gas container, and on my first attempt it exploded, spewing liquid gas in every direction. It was a miracle the fire had gone out, or there could have been a real tragedy. I got such a shock that I threw it into a sand dune until it stopped hissing. In my ignorance I thought it was a faulty tank, so I repeated the exercise with the second tank, cautiously screwing down the ring. Once again it too exploded. Now I was really mad and threw the whole lot into the dunes again and left it there. No tea for any of us now by the look of things.

Tempers flew, and within minutes we were all screaming at each other, all well into the blame game. Camping was fast loosing its appeal for me. Eventually we calmed down and I said to Etta that I'd get the bloody fire going even if it killed me, and it nearly did. I decided that science and my knowledge of physics were the only answer, so I resorted to the one thing I could rely on to burn; I would use petrol.

I got under the car and siphoned off a bottle of it from the tank, swallowing almost as much in the process. Then in triumph I poured it all over the coals. These were still hot, and fumes seemed to be forming. I threw a bit of lighting paper at it, remembering the mother's 'lighter' and her gas incident, and suddenly there was yet another explosion. This time the whole area lit up. I remember nearby campers going, "Wow look at that fire", and heads popping out of tents on all sides. Even though the coals seemed to catch fire, they soon went out again, and even more petrol went in with the same result. By then we had an audience. One guy advised us to pull back the car, and others pulled their children to safety while my gang had yet another go at the tent.

I was now happy because at least we had heat, and to spur it on I added yet another dash of the petrol. This time the flash was way too close for comfort and I jumped back, spilling the petrol down the leg of the barbecue, which then caught fire, as did the ground underneath it. At that point the onlookers really became nervous. People pulled their cars way back and the fire brigade was even mentioned. After half an hour of this flame throwing, a nice English woman came across from the nearest tent and said that we were the maddest people she had ever seen in her life, that she and her husband hadn't laughed so much in years, so they offered to help us. She gave me the proper firelighters and we were off at last.

I became the chef and put on the sausages, burgers and rashers. They were not cooking fast enough for me, so when the rest weren't looking, I added the last of the petrol 'just to speed things up'. More flames followed, and I was spotted. The food was cremated, having turned completely black and looking like charcoal. Not to be defeated though, I got out the plates and dished out the cremated food, assuring my lot that this was what barbecuing was all about: roughing it with burnt food in the open air. Sure what could be better! Even though starved, the kids flatly refused to eat anything. Etta followed. I was facing a revolt on all fronts. They were all prepared to go hungry rather than eat this black meat, and a strike had happened. I couldn't let them get away with that, so I decided to lead by example and attacked all their plates, eating down this carbonized food by myself, all the time saying how wonderful it was. It was awful, but I couldn't give in at that stage. I encouraged them to just try it out and see what it tasted like, saying, "There's nothing like food in the open air when you're starved with the hunger". All of the rebels again refused, and I had to finish the food out of sheer spite. It was like a lump of lead in my belly. This lump seemed to get bigger and denser as the night wore on. Soon it was time to retire to the tilting harem, which looked even worse than it had done out our back yard, but by then I was wrecked and prepared to sleep on a stone.

About four a.m. the rumbling in my stomach began, and I had to get up really fast and make a dash for the toilet. It was locked of course. By then nature wasn't just calling, she was roaring. I ran to the dunes in the dark and fell over something, and couldn't wait any longer. There and then I did my business. In all of my panic I had forgotten the golden rule of camping which was to always have a toilet roll handy. I was then in a real fix. In the dark I reached around and tried to find a paper or some litter of any kind, but there was nothing, and I cursed the Kerry County Council for being too thorough with their cleaning. In the end I suffered the great ignominy of having to use grass to wipe my ass. That was the last straw for me; camping was out from then on, I was doing no more of it.

Morning dawned with the rain and wind lashing the tent from all sides. We looked out like a group of caged animals which were completely starved, (a truth in itself) and in very bad humour once again. I was worse than any of them, having had no sleep at all during the night from my many trips to the dunes. After half an hour of staring at the rain, I said, "That's it, we're fucking off from this place and don't mention camping ever again," so Etta says, "And how do you propose we do that? I'm not getting drowned in this rain". Another plan was needed, and Adrian had the perfect answer. We dispatched the others to the car, the two of us donned our swimming togs, and then we set about dismantling the harem and removing all the stuff. It lashed down on top of us but we didn't give a damn. We dismantled it all in a kind of mad dance, singing and laughing our heads off. Once again we had provided entertainment for the others on the site, and as we left Banna Strand, we still had our togs on. After a mile or so we changed and had breakfast, dinner, tea and anything else in a restaurant in Tralee. The lesson we learned from that experience was that if we ever became vagrants, we would surely perish.

My family not alone suffered from having no father, but they were all actually roped into helping me on numerous occasions. Always we strived for more and more radio coverage, which meant that I was always searching for more and more transmission sites. We had a site on the Galty Mountains which was accessible only by a three hour climb of over two thousand feet. It was the most difficult site we had and in hindsight it was a huge mistake to have put a transmitter there, but it covered hundreds of miles. I climbed this mountain with Etta twice on one day trying to fix a problem that was intermittent. It was heartbreaking having climbed it once, to arrive back down and realise that the problem was still there. Even though I was prepared to go back alone, she would not hear of it and back the two of us went for another three hour hike to the top. We had no food, no water and the only thing going for us was that we were both very fit then. On another occasion myself, Adrian, and a friend of his set off for that mountain to fix some problem. It started out sunny enough, and to reduce weight, all we took with us was my coat. On that journey we got soaked by sleet, a storm hit us, and finally it rained so hard that all three of us tried to hide under my coat as we squatted down and leaned against the wind on the open face of the Galty Mountain. Then when it passed we headed on up to the top. Adrian's friend never went with us again, and after a major storm when the whole site was almost blown away, I had had enough and we pulled it. Radios or not, without a road we were not going back there again.

No one would believe the things we did in the pirate radio days, or how much we suffered so that the listeners could hear us. I'm quite sure too that all the other engineers in Ireland who went through that phase have similar stories to tell, and the pity of it is that only their families know what we went through. While I am sure many of those engineers prospered, in my case I was not even being paid at that time. In the end the government, in their wisdom, would legalise radio in Ireland and grant licences to about twenty four of those radio stations.

I would say it was about nineteen eighty eight or nine when the community radio known as North Cork Community Radio would begin preparing for a legal licence submission, while still broadcasting away illegally. A subcommittee was formed to write our license submission. A great friend of mine and Jack's called DC Buckley would do the programming section, Donal Collins would handle the financial projections for us, and I would do the technical submission. In actual practice, DC and I actually wrote the whole document with Donal giving us the figures and acting as an unofficial editor. A book could be written about what happened next, but suffice to say that we were finally and almost reluctantly granted a licence to broadcast into North Cork by the IRTC. This Irish Radio and Television Commission were the government body set up earlier to oversee the advent of local radio in Ireland. Over the coming years I would develop many friendships with people in that body, but at the time they were seen as the most fearsome of civil servants, and nothing could have been further from the truth.

By then Jack O'Rourke had become a major player in the success of the community radio and he was the contact person for the IRTC on the day that the licences were awarded. I clearly remember the morning that the call came through to Jack's office. We became elated and I think I stuck a Christmas tree with lights on the roof of our studios, which by then were relocated to the Majestic Ballroom – Jack's old dance hall. Whatever about the pirate madness, we were truly then in the big time madness. We had no money, no official transmission site, and not one single bit of the old equipment that we could use. Despite this, some of the Board members believed that all I had to do was throw a switch and we would be back on air. In addition we had no CEO, but we did have a deadline that had to be met, or the licence would be revoked. What we did have though was a dedicated team of people who, having obtained the license the hard way, would not allow its revocation under any circumstances. It was my job to project-manage the operation while DC, Jack and the rest of the Board agreed to somehow find the money needed, and they did.

On January the 26th nineteen ninety NCCR, the original pirate radio station, began legally broadcasting under its new name of County Sound Radio, and yet another amazing chapter in my life would begin. Before leaving that period of illegal transmissions, it's only right that I recall a short-lived but hilarious period of illegal television broadcasting that I was involved in.

Local Television.

The video recorder machine had just been invented by both JVC and Sony and they were battling it out for supremacy in that new field of consumer electronics. To be able to record a television show at one hour, and watch it at a later time just utterly fascinated me. I know that both Larry and I had tried to invent this system years earlier and had failed, so when the machine was finally in production, I was determined that I would become a real expert on it. I studied everything that I could find about this new device. When on our trips to London I bought every video book I could find, and I specifically learned the mechanism and electronic circuits thoroughly. In a short time I really did become an expert and could fix almost any fault in any of them.

One day while driving along doing my television calls and thinking of these devices, I suddenly got a flash of inspiration. I knew without any doubt just how to turn a video recorder into a television station because I reasoned that there was a device inside the machine called a modulator, and it was in fact a very low power transmitter. All I had to do was to make its signal stronger, and it would travel a long distance just like a radio signal. Then if one plugged an actual video camera into the video recorder, you would immediately have live television. All of this came to me as I drove home to Buttevant for a visit with the mother and father, and I got so excited that I almost did not go home at all. I wanted to turn back to try it out, but I did go home and met up with my father. I told him all about my theory and all that he said was, "Jekus boys John, surely there's no way that will ever work because if it did, God only knows where it might end". The minute I got back to the workshop I proved that it would work, and I remember transmitting the science fiction classic *2001: A Space Odyssey* across the workshop. I felt like Marconi did when he sent a signal across the Atlantic, and I couldn't wait to tell Larry. He was less enthusiastic than I had expected, believing that I was already wasting enough of his time on a pirate radio, so a pirate television station did not appeal to him at all. However he did not completely veto the idea of me working on it, but it had to be on a separate business entirely. In any case I soon told Jack O'Rourke all about the new idea and convinced him that the three of us should become partners and set up Mallow's first ever local television station. He immediately agreed, and each of us invested a hundred pounds. I bought the amplifier that I needed and we began the project.

After all the years I can still see myself setting up the aerial on the very high roof of our shop, and beaming out a colour-bar test-signal secretly across Mallow town. The picture looked great and each of us became very excited at what might happen next. We saw ourselves needing programmes, doing recordings of matches and local events, and having commercials made for the business community. I was on a high all the time and never considered the illegality side of things.

Then Larry mentioned it to an amazing man called Alan Watson. Alan had a video production company and was a great success locally in that exciting field, but it was not live television. This is where a debate might begin, but in any case Alan stole a march on us and decided to do it all by himself. In fact I would probably have done the same thing myself, as he had every bit of equipment he needed except a transmitter. He did have one ace though; he knew a brilliant engineer by the name of Dessie Wallace who went off and secretly built him one in a few weeks.

The end result was that Alan made it public that he was going to be making a local television broadcast on a Saturday night. When I heard all about it, I went ballistic. Larry and Jack gave up on the project immediately, but I was dead set on revenge and the minute Allan's test card came on, I wiped it out with my transmitter. Dessie retuned his box, which took a few days, and the next week I wiped that one out as well. A tit for tat war then began, and Alan was in a pickle with egg on his face, so he called to see me in our shop. To say that we had an argument would be putting it mildly. I was shouting so much that even Larry told me to take the argument to the street, which we did. Oblivious to the many onlookers who knew us both, we shouted and cursed each other for a long time. I was screaming that he stole my idea and Allan was swearing that he got the idea at the same time and that it was pure coincidence. Then he said something to me which I cannot remember now, but it was so funny and crazy that it stopped me in mid curse, and I actually exploded with laughter. Then he started to laugh too, and within seconds we were both laughing so hard that we had to hold on to each other to keep standing. I'll never forget it; one moment we are ready to kill each other, and the next we were in a state of utter merriment. After we calmed down and passers-by realised it was almost normal behaviour for us, Alan said to me, "Johnny boy, I like you. Why don't we join forces and stop this arguing?"

If the truth be told, I had always liked and admired Alan, a Yorkshire man, as well, and we joined forces that day and became fast friends. With Alan's gear and Dessie's expertise we actually did set up Mallow's first ever local television service. It was also the first in the country I believe. Then the famous Chris Carey of Dublin's Radio Nova fame found out about it because I told him how to do it during a visit to Radio Nova, and he went into shock when he saw how easy it was. Within weeks Radio Nova had a test signal going out from Three Rock Mountain covering all of Dublin and it caused consternation in political circles. The Minister for Communications then made a statement in the Dail, our Parliament, saying that whatever about pirate radio being allowed, he would not allow pirate television. Almost immediately Nova's gear was seized, but strangely enough not ours, which only made us braver.

We called our station Channel 3, and our test card was made by having a camera pointing at the side of a video tape box. The box had the three colours red, green, and blue painted on the side of it and it looked nice. In those great days of pirate broadcasting, as I said before, you could do whatever your imagination brought forth.

Alan then had the genius of an idea to record the BBC in Cork City and re-transmit it an hour later in Mallow. Soon the whole town began to buy aerials and watch our channel. We then put my theory into practice and had a camera pointing at a chair where our 'continuity announcer' sat. Our announcer was Margot, Alan's wife, and she gave out the latest information about the night's viewing and any local news she could muster up. She looked brilliant and spoke with a naturally polished voice and attractive accent. She came across as totally professional in every way except for one rather important flaw. No one could hear a single word she said, because Alan had constant problems with the sound. This was due to the fact that, while Alan did have broadcast quality cameras, he had cheap microphones which were barely above the useless category. Margot got a lot of ribbing from friends and viewers over the days, but she forgave us the first few nights. Alan said it was 'teething problems' and he gave me a smirk when we were reviewing the broadcasts later. The problems continued though, with the odd word or full sentence being heard now and again. After a few weeks of good and bad sound, Margot called me in as the so-called sound expert from the radio. She told both Alan and me that it better be right 'tonight' or that was it for her, and she was out of it.

I was wanting to go over the whole system personally, but Alan would have none of it, assuring me over and over that all was ok, "Johnny boy, tis all perfect I tell you. I tested it meself earlier, so you can relax boy. She will be heard perfectly tonight". He seemed really sure, so I was about to leave when Margot arrived all done up and ready to broadcast to the town. She asked me to stay on, as she didn't trust Alan's assurances.

We agreed that I would stand off camera and nod to her, letting her know that she was being heard. For me to hear her, I had to rely on Alan giving me the nod, as he had concocted some system for him to hear her while he was working the camera. Still he assured us both that all would be perfect, as he had 'personally tested it'. Margot's retort was, "And that's why I'm worried Alan".

The broadcast began with Margot speaking to camera, but also looking at me and expecting the nod. I was looking at Alan waiting for his nod, but he began fidgeting and ducking down behind a large television monitor. I saw him feverishly twiddling the volume control, and when I looked directly at him he had this hilarious look on his face as he began to shake his head from side to side. Margot could see none of this as he was using the monitor as a shield. I knew then that once again there was no sound and Margot was moving her lips with nothing coming out to her viewers' ears. She continued to speak as a professional would, but she was developing a look of concern. I could not look her in the face any more either because by then Alan had completely submerged himself under the desktop and I saw him holding his hand across his mouth to prevent his laughter from being heard by

Margot. So in solidarity with him, and out of sheer embarrassment, I too began to slowly sink down behind my monitor and almost exploded laughing myself. Then with both of us gone and Margot left alone, she realized the game was up. We were peeping up from below the table top and saw Margot jump up and throw her papers away and shout, "Allan". Then she stormed out of the studio slamming the door so hard that I think she might have broken it. We collapsed on the floor in total stitches. I could not stop laughing because Alan had the face of a schoolboy in big, big trouble, and he reminded me so much of how my old friend Joe Hurley looked in a scrape. After we finally stopped laughing Alan said to me, "Johnny boy, she's fairly pissed at me tonight. Is there any chance I can stay at your place mate?" More peals of laughter followed, and while I knew Margot was always a gracious hostess, often filling me with tea and cakes, that night I felt that it was safer to avoid the house, so I left. I think my good friend and 'sound expert' may have slept in his mobile home that night. It was one of the funniest incidents that had ever happened to me in my life, and to this day, whenever I meet Alan, it's as if it was just yesterday we made that broadcast, and I can still see him in panic, then holding his hand to his face in laughter.

We continued without our 'continuity announcer', and the whole idea began to take off. Soon big business began to notice our venture and we met a group in Millstreet town who were prepared to heavily invest in the project, but wanted 'live' BBC for racing and matches. We concocted a plan to transmit the live BBC by microwave link from the top of Sliabh na mBan in Tipperary to the NCCR site outside Mallow, and then on to Kerry, where it would ultimately cross the Shannon and end up in Galway City. This idea was light years ahead of its time, but such was the vision and confidence of Alan Watson. It would have been an incredible engineering feat had we pulled it off. Then instead of Ireland having just the two television channels provided by RTE, rural Ireland would suddenly have had at least four more. We decided to run with the plan and had Italian transmission people building the equipment. After some kind of survey was done, the initial safe estimate suggested that we stood to make about three million on the venture: a million a man. I had almost become a millionaire at the young age of thirty six. When Alan phoned me with that great news I got cold feet, feeling that the government would never allow this to happen, especially because of its illegality. Unfortunately I was proven so tragically right. Within weeks, and with work ongoing on the gear in Italy, Alan's studio was raided by the Department of Communications and his livelihood was confiscated. It was a tragic and terrible loss for him, and a very sad day for both of my good friends. Our whole dream quickly fell apart and the money evaporated. I believe Alan eventually did get his video equipment back, but Channel 3 was dead. Some years later another friend called Paul O'Sullivan and I did transmit the early satellite service called Super Channel into Mallow. It too folded from lack of support in the town, and after that I decided to never again put any kind of television service into the town, nor have I.

Just last week I met Alan by pure accident and he told me that the previous night he had been dreaming of Channel 3, and the fun we had in those wild days. By sheer coincidence I too had been dreaming the same dream on the same night, and we met a day later. There are no accidents in life, and it's completely possible that Alan did get the same idea as me at the same time all those years ago, possibly because we are all connected in Consciousness. Even now as I write of Alan, Margot, and Dessie, I am smiling broadly and remembering the last night Channel 3 had its silent announcer.

Legal radio the fun ends.

We had hardly begun broadcasting as a legal entity when it dawned on us all that this was a very different kind of environment to the one we were used to in the pirate days. From the beginning I worried about our ability to continue in business at all. We had found an excellent CEO, Colm O'Connaill, who had put together a great broadcasting team, but we only transmitted to a small area i.e. North Cork, yet we had the costs of a very large radio station. Our Board was equally concerned for our future, and then one day while driving along perusing the problem, the answer came to me. We were supposed to be a radio for the people, so why not get the listeners directly involved in keeping us alive. To do this I came up with the idea that we should start a small local lottery, and have collectors selling books of lottery tickets to the listeners. We would then do a draw every day and announce the numbers at regular times. This idea would later become known as 'Radio Bingo' and it still goes on today. Anyone having matching numbers would then get a real good cash prize, and the whole idea would get us both listeners and revenue. It was without a doubt one of my best ever ideas, and I remember the night I proposed it at a Board meeting in the Hibernian Hotel. It was not hard to convince our Board that we should give it a try, and it was agreed to put it in train. Then having come up with the idea I dropped out of the administration of it completely, and concentrated on doing my job which was engineering the station.

We were very fortunate in having a brilliant legal advisor on the Board who formulated the court application, which was later granted. Now we had hope at last. The money began to roll in, and so did the listeners. I was secretly delighted that my idea had worked because I had given up my own successful video repair business at home to become a full-time engineer with the station, so I had a vested interest in its success.

We were still small, but at least we had the potential to grow. Then, at a crucial time and by a total accident, we had a great stroke of good fortune fall in our lap. A major publicity coup would happen for us.

At that time our government was formed by a coalition between the larger Fianna Fail party and a smaller party known as the PD's. It was a very rocky government indeed and the head of it was Mr Albert Reynolds, who was a business friend of Jack's from their dancehall days. He had kindly agreed to be interviewed by us in a hotel near Kanturk, in County Cork. Mr Reynolds gave a very pleasant interview to our Head of News, John O'Connor and I engineered the recording. Then later in the night, John and I were sitting in the public bar having a drink and simultaneously Mr Reynolds was giving a private speech to his Fianna Fail faithful in a different part of the hotel. Unknown to him, his private speech had become a very public one as it was inadvertently piped into the hotel's public address system, and as such it became available to everyone sitting in the bar. We had been given a copy of his speech and the loudspeaker carrying that speech was situated right above my head. As we sat having a drink, I realised quite quickly that Mr Reynolds' speech was becoming excited and he departed from it almost immediately. As we listened in, I recorded it on John's advice, never thinking that it would soon contain the political bombshell that it did. Mr Reynolds assured his faithful that the coalition with his partners the PD's was, "Just a temporary little arrangement," and our Head of News almost knocked over the table when he heard it. Within hours it was released into the newswires and the government almost fell as a result of it. Our recording became immediate national news. It launched us into the spotlight with the national media and immediately gave us a credibility we did not actually deserve at that time. The 'temporary little arrangement' is now so commonplace as to have its origins almost forgotten, and I only write it for the posterity it deserved because it helped make our radio station a huge success. On a personal level I felt really sorry for the problems it had caused for Mr Reynolds, who seemed to be a really nice man. He had been kind enough to give us a very valuable interview, and as far as I was concerned we had stabbed him in the back, but all seems to be fair in love, war, and politics. By comparison to what goes on in the media today, it was a very mild accident of good fortune for us, and Mr Reynolds was a tough businessman and a well seasoned politician. The government survived but only barely so, and we were launched at last. Now we had recognition, we had a cash flow that was the envy of everyone, and we had a CEO who wanted to take out his main competitor: 96fm in Cork City. In time he did just that, and also added another licence to our little group; the combined licence for West Cork and Cork City, probably the second most valuable one in the country.

Over the next ten years this fledgling radio station, which had begun in my kitchen becoming known as County Sound, and later 96FM and C103, would grow beyond all expectations. Over those years I was directly involved in many worthwhile schemes to help people through the power of the radio medium. The one I am most proud of happened as a result of a terrible famine in Somalia when millions of people were dying of hunger. I was asked if I could set up a system which would allow for a joint national radio appeal by all of Ireland's local radios. Mick Mulcahy, one of our DJ's, was the driving force. He and I were good friends, so having seen the terrible images on television and knowing Mick's sincerity, I agreed. We got fantastic co-operation from the IRTC, particularly Michael O'Keeffe the CEO, and every one of the local radios got involved for that famous one-day appeal. The hub was a studio that my son Kyrl and I set up in a warehouse in Cork, and on that day I believe we raised over one million pounds nationally. I was presented later with a certificate of thanks by the little committee, and it means more to me than all of my technical certificates to date. To this day it gives me great pleasure to know that my work, in conjunction with that of the many, many others, helped save the lives of people I will never even meet. That radio appeal, which was started in a pub in Cobh by a group of ordinary people, showed me that each of us can make a difference in our world, especially when the motivation is sincere. On that morning, as I sat at the sound desk listening to a nurse describing how their work had saved the life of a little boy in a mud hut in Africa, for some unknown reason it brought tears to my eyes, but I hid them well. I knew for sure in that moment that Nannie was smiling at me and saying, "Sure I knew the senna would give you brains one day".

My pen chance for practical joking would reach a peak during the early days of our new legal radio, but I was not the instigator just a pawn in the game. My birthday is the day before 'Fools Day' and it was traditional for radio people to try and fool the public on such a day, or at least way back in those days we tried to, before it became uncool. My radio friends and Etta had secretly combined my birthday party with a big Disco gig that we were holding in a hotel in Mallow, and the place was packed. The atmosphere was great and during the celebrations the Radio Talk Show host, a man by the name of Derry O'Callnan came up with the idea that we should try and convince our listeners that the Blackwater River was drying up. This river flows through Mallow, and most of the towns in our listening area are located along the river. It's also a famous fishing river with anglers from all over the world trying their luck along its banks every year, so a dried up river would have dire consequences for our area. Derry convinced me that I should be his 'reporter' along the river due to my travels to mountains as part of my job, and in a moment of weakness I had agreed to be part of the broadcast. The gig and my party went on all night long and about four in the morning I fell into bed happy in the knowledge that I was supposed to be off all the next day, and I planned a late snooze. My phone rang about ten and it was Derry asking if I was ready to go 'on air' with a report. I woke from a deep sleep and could not even remember what day it was, let alone do a live link, so I told him to call me back in ten minutes when I could get my thoughts together. I switched on County Sound and heard him talk up the river disaster so convincingly that even I almost believed it myself. He had so called experts from America who knew all about climate change, a man from Arizona I believe, and also he had some local politicians in on the act. It became very real even before I added my bit. Then the phone rang. "And we go over now to John Cahill who as you all know is always out and about in our area, what's the story John". I got into my imaginative mode and said, "Well Derry, I am out and about, but what the listeners don't know about me is that I studied weather patterns for years as a hobby, and specifically the critical factor of water shortages in Africa, and I am sad to say, and I don't want any panic, but the Blackwater is actually four feet lower than normal". Derry questioned me more and I added more and I thought that would be the end of my part in the show, and so I got back under the blankets. The phone rang again with Derry on the line all excited. "John, John boy, you have to do another broadcast, you were brilliant, the phones have all lit up and people are now ringing in confirming your belief that the end is near for our river, you have just got to come back on again later". I was flabbergasted, as I thought I only spoke to the people as if it the event was real, and now it seemed that my words were making magic happen, so I agreed. In the meantime, Derry took callers from all along the river and each one convinced him and the listening public that it was all true the river was indeed lower. Soon we would have only a dry riverbed and no fish. Then he added his ace card and brought on the local politicians, who each blamed the other for not draining it, or for building on it, and they had a field day slugging it out. All were in on the gag of course so it was great fun, and then the phone rang again.

"You ready John; its going great beyond my dreams boy, sure the whole place is listening".

In preparation and so as to add realism to my location on the river, I had put an extension cord on my phone, those were the days before mobiles and I had the bath taps running full belt and I was standing in the bath as well. "Over to you John".

"My God Derry, I can only say that I am seeing a terrible thing, there is a fissure in the ground right before me now and thousands of gallons of water are pouring into it every second, can you hear it" I put the phone down near the water and Derry assures me that he can almost see the water it's so clear. "I think we are done for with the river Derry, what are the listeners saying to you in the studio". Derry then took another few reports from the public, one was in Castletownroche and one in Fermoy and they both confirmed that the Awbeg River, as well as the Blackwater was indeed drying up, because they could see how much lower they were now. Then he began getting calls that people were lined all along the bridge in Mallow staring in at the little island which I had earlier confirmed was 'way out' of the water. Being a true professional Derry took me back on and this time he was playing the skeptical card and he says, "John I know you know about this stuff, but could it be imagination at all boy, could you be wrong it's very serious". I tell him that I have had 'measuring sticks' in the river for the past two years, and the water is definitely two feet lower than ever before. Then I add that I have also had friends in

Youghal who tell me that the river is only flowing through two of the eyes on the bridge, when it was normally going through six. That was it then he hung up and I thought it was all over for the day, not so. In five minutes he was back telling me that he had some official from the fisheries board on the line going mad about it and would I talk to him. In my innocence I thought that Derry had made him wise to the prank, but he had not, and so I once again got into my disaster mode. The man was really going wild. He attacked me saying I was a fool that the river was tidal and what qualifications did I have to make such a serious allegation, and I defended myself getting more and more heated, but all the time I believed he was in on it. He got so mad that he said we would hear more about this, and he hung up on me as did Derry. The broadcast ended around midday with Derry in hysterics telling the listeners that they could relax it had all been an April Fools Joke. The next day we got a demand for the broadcast logs of the show because it had not gone down well in 'official' circles and a court date looked likely. I was all for my day out in court, as I believed no harm was done and a Judge would see the funny side of things for sure and it ended at that, but a week or so later the Phoenix magazine carried a story on Fishy Business in Mallow, fame at last I believed and for years people would meet me in the street and laugh at the prank we had pulled on them. I heard too that one of the other bridges was blocked up with onlookers trying to see the water dropping and arguing about it all. I still laugh at how innocent good people are, and even today a convincing liar will make believers out of almost anyone, sure politics is based on it.

Under a great management team led by Colm O'Connaill, with a great group of broadcasters and professionals, County Sound and 96FM grew and grew. We built new studios into Jack's old Majestic dancehall, and I designed them in a way that the staff would be bathed in both light and good energy every hour that they worked there. I had a vision that if the broadcasters felt happy in their work environment, then they would come across as happy to their listeners, holding them for longer, giving the advertisers statistically a better chance of having their adds heard. The buzz word for this holding is known as 'market share' and we have one of the highest in the country. This vision was brought into reality by two of the most brilliant people I ever dealt with; John Mullane the engineer and Mick Sheehan, a builder and craftsman of immeasurable vision and talent. Above all, those two people not alone saw what I was trying to achieve, but they both also enhanced it, while still surmounting every obstacle that came in their way. Today I am very proud of the edifice we all created together in Mallow. I get a great sense of pride when a new staff member tells me that they love the building, and the feeling they get while working there, not realizing that I had anything to do with it.

As time rolled on we had an ever-increasing pot of money, and pretty soon the station that the IRTC believed would be the first to fail, became one of the strongest stations in Ireland. Some years later this Cork consortium would make a bid for the National Radio Licence, and almost succeeded before finally being sold for over thirty million pounds to the huge media provider, Ulster Television Plc. Unlike so many of the greed-driven corporate companies we see today, our consortium gave one million of their thirty millions back to their staff as a gesture of thanks. I may be wrong, but I believe this was unprecedented at the time, and I know of no other case still where it has happened. In a time when workers are not even being paid proper redundancy, there are many who could well take a leaf from our guys' books. The pirate radio that began with an idea from four local businessmen in Mallow, and that was first built in my kitchen, had succeeded beyond all expectations, and in line with my madness, instead of owning a quarter of the company I had just ten shares in it. These I had actually bought years earlier unlike other engineers who had argued for, and got, huge share options in similar situations. It was at that stage that I began to question what my life was all about, and how badly I had treated my own family, because of my addiction to radio. Only I was to blame though, as when I had only asked for a penny, it would have been foolish of me to expect to be given a pound. Guard Ryan's slap in the face was still affecting me, but not alone me, it affected my family as well. It was long past the time for a rethink of my whole life and that I began.

As I write, we are now entering a completely new age. This is fast becoming the age of the iPads, iPods, Podcasts, and Apps. It's actually easier for my son Adrian to listen to us now in Australia than it is to hear us in some parts of our licensed area, and I predict the demise of FM radio transmissions as we know them. It will soon become both uneconomical and unnecessary for a company to keep an FM transmission system operating, when the internet will offer a much bigger audience at a tiny fraction of the cost. The new kings in broadcasting are now the IT people of this world, and I believe proof of that fact is not far away. I am immensely proud that our internet radio services are now being sent out into the world by the IT skills of my youngest son, Kyrl. He has persistently followed me into this radio work, despite my warnings against it. At this time he is both the Chief Engineer of the Limerick Radio station Live 95, and Head of IT of the very radio stations that started in his kitchen when he was but a baby. No one could possibly have foreseen such an event. Colm O'Connaill has long since left us and his protégée, Ronan McManamy is now in overall charge of the UTV Radio sector in Ireland. We in Cork are still fortunate to have both Ronan and an excellent CEO in Kieran McGeary guiding our great team of radio fanatics. Kieran, a Waterford man, has continued the growth of our radio stations despite savage new competition. He continues to see the value of close co-operation with our listening audience because he was instrumental in bringing about yet another amazing radio appeal. This time it was for the cancer services in the Cork Hospitals. I am very pleased to say that once again our radio work has eased the suffering of numerous children and adults from cancer, and over the past years we must have raised close to two million euros to help combat that terrible disease. I have always maintained that the best radio people in Ireland are in Cork, though they are not necessarily Cork people, and the best team in radio is ours, but of course it is true to say that I would be biased. Commercial radio has been very good to me over the years, and it was while setting up a new radio station for Limerick that I began my Internet chatting and ultimately found my second wife, an American called JoAnn Elms.

JoAnn. Dream Maker.

So as to explain how my life was to take on a new and dramatic turn for the better, I need to return to Buttevant and the year nineteen sixty five. I was then about fifteen years old and I had an extraordinary thing happen to me during a trip down the castle. This castle was owned by the Barry Clan in past history, and the town of Buttevant had been named after their war cry of 'Boutez an Avant' meaning 'push forward'. If you were trying to 'get off' with a girl, you took her on a trip down the castle, and when I was fifteen it was then a Mecca for teenagers. Getting off with a girl covered a multitude of possibilities, and ranged from holding hands to sex in various forms. I can say straight up that I never experienced the latter, but I did have some nice experiences there.

On the day in question my two friends, Hayes and Fowler, were heading down the castle because they both had girlfriends then. As we were all good friends I was asked to tag along for part of the walk at least. Unfortunately I did not have any girl on my arm and I remember feeling a bit odd in myself all that day. It had nothing to do with my lack of female company, or so I thought, I just felt strange.

It was a most beautiful summer's day with bright blue skies and a blazing hot sun warming our barely clad bodies. We were all so happy in those days with the hippie era beginning. All of our friends were avid supporters of The Beatles, The Stones, long hair and tie dye shirts, with the girls doing their best to defeat the rules and practices of Catholic Ireland.

Quite unlike what was believed of us at the time, none of us ever took drugs or drank alcohol. We were a very strange bunch of hippies indeed, but we rebelled in every other way we could, including the dress code, and our long hair was considered the worst in the town.

As we slipped through the old iron gates, I began to get an even stranger feeling about the day. A kind of sadness and yet elation began to come over me. First I thought it was because the lads had women and I did not, but that really was not it. I just felt more and more odd with every step we took. We walked and laughed and the lads hugged the girls and winked at me. By then we had reached the actual castle. This was where we were parting as I was no longer welcome for the rest of their adventures; an understandable and accepted fact by me. I would kill the time somehow while they had their fun with the ladies. Pretty soon they disappeared into the privacy of rows of very large and very old trees still there today, and I would not see them again for a long time.

I resigned myself to waiting at the actual castle, and decided to sit on a large windowsill which was big enough for me to comfortably stretch out on and enjoy the beautiful sunshine. After a time I began to feel real sorry for myself, especially in relation to the women situation, and my lack of them. It had been some time since I had a girlfriend, and even then she hadn't lasted very long because I was more into electronics than women in those days, and I probably didn't treat her right.

I believe I drifted off into a half sleep or into some strange trance-like state, but I know I was neither fully awake nor fully asleep. While that feeling has often happened to me since, on that day I had never experienced anything like it before, and it felt really weird but also fascinated me.

Still in the trance-like state I became more and more miserable and depressed in myself, feeling that I might never find a nice girl. I don't know how long I was feeling sorry for myself, but I clearly remember feeling a kind of soft thought begin inside me and it said, "It's all right John, don't be upset about not having a girlfriend". This was not an actual voice but seemed more like some kind of feeling inside my head, yet it did not seem to belong to me. I think I argued with the thought in my mind, becoming resentful at the intrusion, just wanting to be allowed to wallow in my own misery that day.

In hindsight, it felt like I was stuck between two different realities and time did not exist for me right then. It was easy to feel two versions of me existing at the same time that day. One of me was laying across the window sill in a gloomy black state, and the other me was a softer, gentler version that seemed to be trying to help the one on the window sill.

Suddenly, right before my eyes and crystal clear, and just as solid looking as myself, I saw this image of a beautiful girl with long hair and a very broad smile. She was obviously not Irish and looked Indian, and I had never seen anyone like her in my life. She smiled at me and then quickly vanished. This image lasted just fractions of a second and I got such a shock that I actually fell off the window ledge in fright. I know I stared for a long time across at the Protestant Church, as that was the direction I was looking at when she appeared, and I so longed for her to come back. I was still there staring and begging for her return when the lads came back, but she never did.

On numerous trips to the castle later that summer, and over the following years, I would try to see her again, but she never came back to me. I never told a soul either about that apparition because I felt I would be mocked to death by my friends, and it would confirm the local belief that we three were weirdo's, and I was definitely on hallucinating drugs.

From that day on a kind of deep longing began in my heart which I was not able to shake, but I hid it well. I could not get this girl out of my mind no matter what I did. Every dance I went to I would search for her, and every film I saw I would do the same. I clearly remember thinking that Ingrid Bergman was the closest the cinema ever got to her, but even she was not fully like her. At the time that incident made no sense to me, yet I knew that I longed to see her again.

Some years later I began to have a recurring dream where I was a very young Indian boy of about nine or ten. In this dream I played in a rock pool in among the trees, trying to catch minnows. The sunshine gleamed in through the woods and sparkled on the water now and again, and the whole place seemed magical. A large, round, domed rock lay on the edge of the pool and a young Indian girl dressed in a long dress with moccasins looked on, and she seemed to be my girlfriend of the same age.

I would see myself trying to catch the tiny fish in my hands so as to give her one, but they always escaped, and she would laugh out loud each time I failed, especially when I fell over and got soaked in the stream. In the dream I would get mad, and cupping my hands I'd shower her with this very cool water. Then laughing and screaming, she always ran off into the forest being closely chased by me. I always saw the sun's rays streaking in amongst us as we ran and laughed, and then there would be a sudden flash of very bright, white light just before the dream would abruptly end. For years and years this dream would happen to me randomly. It was not a nightmare, just a kind of friendly dream and I got quite used to it, almost expecting it. I knew it meant something but I had no idea what that dream was about.

The years rolled by. I was working in radio and married with three teenage children by the time the internet began. I was not keen on the idea of getting the net at the start, as I couldn't type, and I just did not see the point of typing a conversation that you could easily have had on the phone, even with the savage cost of phone calls. Adrian, my eldest son, became an avid chatter though, and would be out in the shed at home for half the night talking to women in America because of the time difference. I would say at least a year went by before I gave in and decided to use this net for radio, space, and electronics information.

On Christmas week nineteen ninety six, I bought the 'Golden Pages of the Internet', an amazing reference book with hundreds of thousands of web links, and descriptions as well. We had no Google in those days. It was a gold mine for me, and for a long time I used the book purely for research and loved this new information source.

One day, quite by accident, I came across a website called Powwow. The name intrigued me as all my life I had loved the Native Americans and innocently I thought this might be a website made by such people. A further thought crossed my mind that someone on the site may be able to throw some light on Uncle Johnnie's famous Cahill from the Little Big Horn Battle.

I had no experience of any kind at this chatting though, and so I registered on the site with my real name and real address, even putting down our phone number. This was insane of course, but I knew no better. I remember so clearly the night I first got on Powwow. No sooner was I registered than I started to get chat requests from Americans, and in particular from American women.

Everyone seemed very friendly and nice, but I was surprised at their fake names known as handles, and I also found out that none of them were Native Americans. Months went by and I developed a good friendship with a lady from Florida, who seemed to be wanting more than chats. When she suggested that I leave my wife and go live in America with her, alarm bells rang and I felt we should end our chatting. Before she did though, she told me how to search what was known as the 'white pages'. These pages were a directory of those who were on line at any one time. I had never been a searcher, as all the requests kept coming to me, so after ending with the Florida lady, a vacuum existed and I quite missed the chats. I decided to search for the Native Americans on the white pages.

Powwow used to have about half a million people on line at any given time, and I'm sure the night I began searching it was no different. The first thing I noticed was the really weird names people were using on these pages like Cyber King, Sex Goddess, and even more explicit names as well. Then the penny dropped as to why I was always getting so many requests. It was because I seemed normal in comparison to most others, especially with an Irish name like Cahill, an address and even a phone number. How stupid can one get?

I n a very short time, almost within minutes of my search, I noticed another normal name; it was JoAnn and Jessica Elms. I felt this might just be a mother and daughter looking to chat to other people from around the world, and according to her profile she was a 'domestic engineer'. I figured she fixed washing machines, such was my ignorance of the net. Her profile also showed that she came from a small town in Missouri in the Mid West flanked by Huck Finn's Mississippi. This had to be a good sign, so I sent her a chat request. Nothing happened, so I did it again, as it was her or the Cyber Kittens, and I was wary of that lot after the Florida woman. About to give up, I sent her one last request figuring that three requests were enough. Ping went the little sound and her screen comes alive with the words "Hi" and a smiley symbol. Immediately I felt some kind of an affinity with this person. I did not know why, at the time. We began to chat and laugh, and talk about our towns and our lives, our kids and partners, and hours went by in a flash. Before we said good bye, I asked if she would chat again tomorrow because I liked her so much, and I felt she was very normal and friendly. By then I had wormed out of her what a domestic engineer was, and it was her term for a housewife.

She said it entailed mending socks not washing machines. She agreed to chat again, and over many months we began to develop a strong bond of friendship and only friendship at that stage.

Neither of us had still seen a picture of the other, both being too shy for it, but in the end we e-mailed a scanned photo to each other. I got such a shock when I saw her that I thought it was her daughter's photo she had sent to me by accident. But when she sent me another one, a distant shot by a swimming pool, I realized that she was a very beautiful woman indeed. Still I had no close up of her and the curiosity was beginning to kill me.

As months went by we chatted away, each of us getting closer in spirit though never admitting it, nor daring to even think that we might be falling in love, as both of us seemed to be happily married at that time.

After seeing her pictures I did feel that she seemed familiar somehow, but I could not place it. I found her very attractive and it turned out that she was part Native American. I had made no connection to my castle vision until one day she sent me a black and white photo of herself as a young girl, and there before my very eyes was the girl from my apparition. She was identical to the girl I saw in Buttevant all those years before, who had vanished before my eyes. I was in a state of shock and didn't know whether to tell her or not. That day I clearly remember staring at her photo in disbelief for a long time. Finally I asked her what age she was in the picture, and she was about seventeen years old. I then told her about my strange experience, but she did not seem a bit surprised. She told me of her lifetime longing for Ireland and an Irishman that she too was searching for all her life. She said that she knew what the Irish mist felt like, how she would sit in a tree as a young girl wondering about it, and how it felt so familiar to her. Later I told her about my recurring dream of the rock pool and the Indian girl, and almost on cue she told me that she knew exactly where that pool was, as she knew it well. It was located in the woods just behind her grandmother's house, and finally as if to complete the circle, she said that both her grandmothers had Native American blood in their veins and that they lived very near the famous Cherokee Trail of Tears. It was no wonder that all of my life I was fascinated by Native Americans, and the Missouri and Mississippi

Rivers.

How could all this be? No one would believe it, yet it was all completely true. That single incident of my vision, and the photograph associated with it, started me on a quest which is still ongoing. I began to question life; what it is, and who I am. I think sooner or later we all ask these questions, but for me, a person who loved science above all else, they were very challenging indeed as I had no concept of metaphysics then. However I was sure of one thing; JoAnn was the cause of it all, and to make sure she never vanished again, I still keep that picture in my wallet, and give a sneak look at it now and again just to remind me that miracles can and do happen.

Over the next year or so it dawned on me slowly that this person whom I chatted to almost every night was beginning to mean more to me than just a very good friend. Of course my wife Etta was aware that we were very close, and I'm sure JoAnn's husband John also knew that we were real good friends, and that was the truth of it. We had never met, we almost never spoke on the phone due to the cost, and yet I believe we were both falling in love with each other without ever admitting it.

We would chat for hours about all kinds of events of the day, music, my work in radio, as well as the many inventions I would be attempting to make or build. Early on, during one of these chats, JoAnn persuaded me to begin writing a book about my life, saying she would act as my editor and critic. She felt that I had a way of writing that made her 'see the scenes' and she said that I had led a very interesting life, especially in my youth. She became fascinated with how we grew up in a small town, how we managed the poverty, and how good my mother was to us. We used to compare our individual lives growing up just for the fun of it, as she came from a small town too, but while she was not rich she was not poor like us ever, her dad being a Deputy Sheriff.

So I did begin the book, and this version is my fifth and last go at it being ten years in the making. Unknown to me at the time, the genius Frank McCourt from Limerick, just thirty miles away, had written his masterpiece *Angela's Ashes*, and by a strange twist of fate, I got to know of it while standing inside a building he was well familiar with; his school I believe.

I was at that time project managing the setting up a new radio station for Limerick city, and our auctioneer and I were scouring the inner city for a suitable building to house the new studios. The auctioneer took me to see a building on the Crescent, or near it, that was up for rent or sale, and it was owned by a religious order in Limerick. We were ushered into a large, beautifully decorated room to await the arrival of a senior Brother who would 'discuss the lease' with us. As we stood in the room the auctioneer said to me, "John, I bet you don't know that you are standing on very hallowed ground". "No," I said, "I didn't know, how come?" "Well, a Limerick man who emigrated to America has written a book which looks like it's going to be a huge success, and he is talking about this very room that you are now standing in". As I was weighing up this titbit of information against the room's use technically as a radio studio, the senior Brother arrived. I never forgot what happened next.

His manner was obviously unfriendly, and we were never even asked to sit down to discuss the details. The meeting lasted less than ten minutes, with the three of us standing in the middle of the room. The minute we told him why we wanted the building, his answer was, "No, no, that would not be appropriate.... good day," end of conversation, and he left us to find our own way out. I never forgot that incident, but I did forget about the book until months later when my brother Kyrle rang me from Dublin, and he was genuinely all excited. "John, you just have to buy a book called *Angela's Ashes*. It's all about growing up in Limerick, but it's just like it's our story too". He said he was laughing constantly as he read it, and while the boys in it were not inventors like us, the rest of the story was very similar and I had to buy the book. I still did not buy the book though, and I think it became a world famous movie before I finally got my own copy. Then like Kyrle, I too laughed constantly as I read it. Later the film came out, and the moment I saw it I immediately saw the similarities between their story and ours, especially the father's plight in it, and the long-suffering poor mother. By then JoAnn had also read the McCourt classic and immediately saw the similarities too. She again began encouraging me to continue with my book of my life in Buttevant.

Unfortunately I'm no Frank McCourt, and over the next twelve years I would write and re-write this book with JoAnn criticizing it so much that in the end I gave up out of sheer frustration, and the years went by. Still I could never fully shake the feeling inside of me to give it one more go.

So once again I decided to write it just for me, and for better or worse, you are now reading our story and I hope you are really enjoying it.

Though JoAnn will dispute this, I think it is possible to love two people at the same time. Then over time, as one love grows stronger, the other weakens. I think this was happening to myself and Etta, and I still had not met my American, though I chatted to her online each night.

Fate stepped in though, and by a minor miracle I was provided with the money to fly Etta and me to America to meet JoAnn and her husband.

We had never been to America before and I was really looking forward to seeing a country I had loved all my life, but I was also incredibly nervous at meeting these Americans, and Etta felt exactly the same way.

We were going to be staying with them for two weeks as their guests. I had never been on a two-week vacation in my whole life, let alone be living with people from a different culture. I was quite terrified at the prospect, but equally so I wanted to meet my American in person.

Before we met we had agreed that no matter what we thought about each other physically, we would remain true friends forever. We hoped everyone would all get along very well and there would be no 'funny business' between us.

I still wear glasses, and the morning we drove to Shannon Airport, I was so nervous that I kept fidgeting with the leg of my glasses on the journey. In typical form, as I drove into the airport, the leg broke off and my glasses fell right onto my lap. This was a real disaster, as I could not see much without them and I was then going to America for two weeks.

There was nothing for it but to go back to my old school days with Pad and solder the leg onto the frame, which I did, with Etta holding a magnifying glass so that I could see what I was doing. All this was taking place in the parking lot of Shannon Airport. I

305

was very glad that I had brought my tool case with the gas soldering iron in the car that day.

This was the start of a long trip that got more and more nerve wracking as we got closer to St Louis in Missouri. On the way into Newark the pilot announced the time change, and as I reset my watch to American time I determined there and then that if I liked America, I would never reset my watch again, nor have I. To this day it's always on American time.

The US Customs official asked me why I had put down on my customs card 'goods to the value of two thousand dollars.' I told him that it was for my laptop and camera as well as gifts and cash. He asked if I was writing a book (a sign in itself) and I told him maybe. Then he put out his hand, shook mine and said, "Welcome to America, enjoy your stay". That handshake and those wonderful words confirmed for me what I had always suspected about the country, it would be a great place to live and work.

However, we were still going on to St Louis and the nerves were getting even worse for both of us by then. It did not help when I spilled coffee all over Etta's cream-coloured jacket, and the fact that she had not smoked for hours was driving her mad as well. The tension between us was really rising.

The muggy heat was also getting to me and my new shoes were literally cutting into my leg. In Newark Airport I spent my first US dollar buying sticky plasters for my heel, which was bleeding by then. I did a job on it in the men's restroom, much to the surprise and astonishment of the cleaners. I stood with one bare foot raised backwards on the washstand and laid on my plaster. I bet they never saw that done before.

We had a long stopover in Newark and my nerves were growing worse. It was a combination of butterflies that JoAnn might not like me, mixed with the sheer amazement at all that I had seen so far of America. After landing at midday, we eventually took off around ten pm on our last leg of that fateful journey. I was within three hours of seeing my apparition in the flesh.

As the jet began its decent into Lambert Airport, I looked like a tramp. My hair was all matted, my shirt was all open and wrinkled, my tie was loose and over to one side, and my glasses were barely hanging on by the bent leg. I looked so bad that even Etta was demanding that I fix myself up before we were met by our hosts. I told her that I planned 'a complete overhaul' in the restroom in the airport before we met them, and that she should do the same as she looked no better. The butterflies were now wildly dancing around inside of me as I knew I was just minutes away from meeting JoAnn for the very first time.

Then the plane landed. The two 'tramps' from Ireland walked up the connecting ramp, and as we came through the security door, there stood JoAnn and John Elms. I nearly died of embarrassment at the state of us meeting our hosts. I will never forget her amazing shy smile, and I could feel a gentleness coming off her that felt very familiar to me. I knew immediately that this girl was the one I had seen in my vision and she was the one I had been waiting for all my life. With that knowledge I realized immediately that I was in a real fix, secretly hoping that JoAnn felt the same about me, and if so, what was going to happen to us all in the future. In that moment I put all thoughts of a future aside and decided to try and flow with the situation as best I could and all I could do was hope for a miracle.

That same night, my first impression of John Elms was that he seemed like a very hard working, good-looking man with bright, sparkling, blue eyes and a warm, friendly manner. I liked him immediately, which made it all the more difficult later for me and him as the inevitable happened, especially when he and JoAnn bitterly arrived in a divorce courtroom. Etta on the other hand, having the benefit of a woman's intuition, told me much later that she knew the moment I saw JoAnn that night that our time together had ended. While she resented it, she said there was no point in making life miserable for either of us, and subsequently she was as good as her word and did not contest our divorce.

We all hugged, or shook hands, and we were made feel so welcome immediately by both of our hosts. That night, virtually straight off the plane, we were taken to a wedding. Then, later still, we went on to have breakfast in a truck stop. After travelling and visiting for about twenty four hours, I was still full of energy, and I had fallen totally in love with America.

From that moment on, we began a whistle stop tour of beautiful Missouri. We were introduced to JoAnn's family; Jessica, Justin,

Julie and Johnnie. We met her parents and sister, Wanda, and numerous other family and friends.

Our hosts treated us so well, I have to say. They took us all over Missouri. I got to go to a place called Six Flags, which is a huge theme park outside St Louis. There I was persuaded to ride my first roller coaster. To say that I nearly died is an understatement. When I staggered off of it I went into shock, getting pale, shivering and feeling deathly cold despite the summer heat. I was afraid I would ruin everyone's night, so I asked to be allowed to lie down on a bench and try and sleep it off for an hour. I believe I was feeling better after half an hour when once again I felt the motion under me and began to get queasy all over again. When I opened my eyes I discovered that John and Etta had been lifting the bench and swaying it from side to side. They collapsed laughing and I think they were both getting revenge on me for the future ahead. Then on another special day they took us to my most favourite place in all of Missouri, the Lakes of the Ozarks. Here we got to go for a trip on a paddle steamer called 'Tom Sawyer' and another childhood dream was lived out by me as we sailed across the lakes just like Mark Twain had described on the great Mississippi in my youthful readings.

The longer I was there the happier I felt, and I never wanted our trip to end. In contrast, Etta became more and more unhappy, probably picking up on my longing to be in America with JoAnn, and she could not wait to get home. In hindsight, while it probably was one of the best times of my life, it was probably one of the worst times for her and I'm sorry for that.

During a shopping spree in JoAnn's town, I ventured into a place selling Indian bows. Within minutes I was captivated by a most beautiful five-foot handmade hunting bow. I pulled its string back and could feel the power of this amazing weapon. I became an Indian for a few minutes and just had to have that bow. I was going to buy it, but JoAnn put me off it saying it was way too expensive. Her vehemence surprised me at the time. Later on she would secretly buy it and present it to me on the day we were leaving, as a parting gift. I just did not know what to say to her. Full of emotion, I decided there and then that on Christmas day from that day on I would take it to a mountain and shoot it in memory of her and our time in America. Every year since then I have taken my bow to Mount Hillary just outside Mallow, and shot it on Christmas day just before dinner as promised. It's a tradition that started with my children, and now continues with my JoAnn. We shoot it together in thanks for all that we have been given, for what we mean to each other, and every year I lose an arrow. We laugh and say the year we lose the last arrow is the year I go to America for good. As of last year I'm down to one arrow.

The holiday did finally come to an end, and at the airport JoAnn and I agreed at a minimum to remain friends forever, but hoped for a lot more when the time was right. So the die was cast, and we would do our best to hurt least our children, and those we had once loved in the past.

There is no doubt in my mind that over the next number of years, our falling in love did cause great hurt. We severely hurt our partners and our children, especially JoAnn's younger children, who were not even teenagers. Mine were a little older, but completely unprepared for a divorce and a huge upheaval to the crazy lifestyle they knew as home. Obviously, hurting all those people was never our intention, but I honestly believe that we were powerless to change what I'm sure was our destiny. Over the coming years, in the eyes of the world, we began having an affair, but that was actually not true at all. I hate the term 'affair'. It always smacks of torrid, illicit sex coupled with secret meetings and a lot of lies. In our case we never had sex, both believing that if we did, then we would have to immediately leave our partners and start a new life together because we both believed that the act of sex would seal our love, and we just could not do it at that time. It was patently impossible anyway, as even though JoAnn could divorce her husband, I could not divorce my wife because we had no divorce laws in Ireland. Concern for our children was also a huge factor in any future we might have.

In spite of that, we grew closer and closer in mind and spirit, and just trusted in the love that was developing between us by then. With no other option, we began subconsciously believing that a miracle would somehow happen and allow us to marry, despite the obvious obstacles before us. Concluding that part of my life, I

309

know that I am truly sorry for any hurt that I caused, as I'm sure JoAnn is as well.

Then the first of the miracles happened. Ireland passed a Divorce Bill after two goes at it, and secondly, I found a book for ten euros that would show me how to do a DIY divorce for virtually no cost. This type of divorce, which was almost unheard of in Ireland then, was conditional on it not being contested, and to Etta's great credit she agreed not to contest it. I began to study the book and drafted the legal papers all by myself. I studied the law via the internet, and finally when I was ready, I got a lawyer to check the paperwork. He charged me two hundred and fifty euros, and eventually Etta and I ended up in a divorce courtroom in Cork. We had no legal counsel, nor did we need one. The judge gave me a fair grilling because we had no lawyers, but I knew the law stated that we did not need them. I was ordered to the witness box, took the oath, and the grilling began. He questioned me on our settlement and the ages of our children, and pretty soon I got the impression from him that he felt I was either tricking Etta into this divorce, or I was coercing her into it. Neither was true of course, but it looked very bad for me for a while until Etta realised the same thing, and from the floor she spoke up. "Do you mind if I speak your honour?" The judge looked down at her and said, "Madame, I would be very delighted if you would". Then in great detail she told him that it was a completely amicable arrangement, and both of us were happy with it. She explained the financial deal and answered his questions better than I did, and he believed her. He said, "I have to say that I am very surprised at all of this. If more people could agree like you two, then all our lives would be easier. Ye came in married, ye now leave divorced". We all went off and had tea to celebrate the end of twenty seven years of marriage, and we parted with no bitterness whatsoever. The entire cost of the proceedings was two hundred and fifty euros, compared to our original legal quotation of eighteen thousand. It would be wrong of me not to mention the great help and kindness shown to us by the court staff. They could not have made it any easier than they did.

Etta has since found happiness, and John Elms too is happily married. Our children have come to accept that we meant them no harm, and we did our best to hurt them the least of all.

Two real miracles had actually happened. The first was divorce legislation had finally passed in Ireland (almost an impossibility I would say), and the second one was that I saw a book for ten euros in Waterstones book shop in Cork which called out to me to buy it, and which saved me eighteen thousand euros that I did not have.

In two thousand and four JoAnn and I got married in Jamaica all alone, without family or friends, but that was our choice. It would have been far too expensive to be dragging people across the world, and besides that, I personally hate large weddings with loads of fuss and stress. The only sadness I felt that amazing day was for JoAnn, who had to make the little walk up the isle all alone. She gave herself away to me willingly, and a large black preacher married us in a civil ceremony on the edge of the Caribbean Sea.

When I kissed my bride, to our great surprise, a lot of clapping went off from the many strangers who, unknown to us, had been onlookers at this unusual wedding of no guests. Looking back on it today, it's quite likely that our wedding went into the record books as the smallest wedding ever celebrated on that romantic island. The only people at it were us and two strange witnesses. It's no wonder we had onlookers.

The night before our wedding I awoke from a deep sleep with a strange feeling. I felt that we should have a little ceremony that would release us both from our past, and that we should each write a private and personal letter to our previous spouses and then burn it. I don't know where or why I was given this feeling, but it felt so important that we agreed to act on it.

We did not read each other's words, nor did we discuss our thoughts ever afterwards, but as the sun set we walked out hand in hand to the edge of the warm blue waters of the Caribbean Sea. There on the sand we set fire to our letters, and later the ocean consumed the ashes of our past. From the morrow on, JoAnn's pet name for me, which was 'Punkin', could be honestly spoken. A new and wonderful life was about to begin for me, but getting there had been a very long tough road for JoAnn, and it had taken one real miracle after another to bring about the day we could truly be free.

The long lonely years.

It took every bit of willpower I had to prevent me from getting up and leaving the plane on that first parting in St Louis. I'll never forget the longing in my heart. I came back home a changed man, feeling both distraught and elated at the same time. On one hand I knew for certain that I had found my vision, and on the other hand I had also lost her again.

The real killer for me though was that I had no idea when I might see her next, and this was troubling me greatly. I did have one little link to her every day and it was my watch. I had secretly made the pact with myself that if I liked America and JoAnn, I would never again change my watch back from Missouri local time, nor did I. This watch became my lifeline, as I could guess in an instant what she was doing, or where she was at. At work it became a friendly joke and I would notice my colleagues taking sneak looks at my watch, just to see if I had gotten over my American infatuation, but because I never shut up about the place, they finally gave up looking.

I think the next time we met was when my son Kyrl and I went to see her. Kyrl was my chaperone to ensure no funny business or temptation, and we had a great time. He got his first chance to drive in America, and actually JoAnn helped him obtain a legal permit at sixteen so that he could drive there. We decided to drive to Hannibal and see the home of my hero, Mark Twain. Then later, in a beautiful town park on the banks of the Mississippi, we decided on a picnic. We tried to light a little fire because, even though the sky was deep blue, the temperature was minus fourteen and a strong wind blew across the river. Kyrl took his chance to drive around the empty car park and experience driving on ice patches, while I worried sick that he would soon sail into the nearby unprotected river. JoAnn would not hear of me stopping him, and she kept egging me on to get a fire going for us. It was so cold that the lighter would not work, and I almost gave up when I managed to set fire to a little cardboard box, which I dropped onto a pile of tinder dry leaves. As they caught fire there was a danger that I would once again prove Nannie right about fire following them Cahill's but instead we just sat and picknicked on the banks of the Mississippi-Missouri in the town of my boyhood hero Huck Finn. It was a great great day and we would return again in the future.

During that trip to America, one day we visited a shop selling Native American artifacts, and as I came in the door I saw this most amazing picture high up on a wall. It was a copy of a famous painting of the Battle of the Little Big Horn, and it clearly showed a white man in buckskin firing on Custer. I stared and stared at that picture knowing that I was seeing the Cahill from my Uncle Johnnie's story, told to me in his attic years earlier. Then a most amazing thing happened. Kyrl insisted on using his very limited few dollars to convince the shop owner to sell the picture to him. It was not actually for sale, more a shop decoration, but somehow Kyrl convinced him to sell it, and then he gave it to me as proof of Uncle Johnnie's amazing story. When I returned home from that trip, once again I developed a terrible ache in my heart, and I was really sad, both inside and out. I believe only Kyrl saw it though, as by then both Adrian and Lynda were living away from home, and rarely saw me.

Since meeting JoAnn I had begun reading a different kind of book. I had begun my search for 'who' I am, and how to become rich, because I felt that large amounts of money might be the only way we could get together. My favourite book then became the Napoleon Hill classic *Think and Grow Rich*, so on arriving home I redoubled my reading of that and a growing number of inspirational books in the hope that some kind of miracle would bring JoAnn and I together, and it did happen, even if only for a brief length of time.

One day in July of 1999 I believe, I got a phone call from JoAnn at home. That in itself was very unusual, as she never called me, but the news she had for me that day was quite startling. She said that by a pure fluke some friends of hers had decided to come to Ireland in a week or so, and they had asked her to accompany them on the plane trip. JoAnn had never flown in her life and was always petrified of it, but now she had a chance to live her dream,

313

which was to see Ireland, and seeing it with me would be a real bonus. She asked excitedly if she could come to stay with us for about two weeks. I nearly collapsed at that great news it was so welcome, but Etta was still living in our house at the time even though we were living separately, and it would be very difficult for both women to be together. I knew they would all be ok as long as it was just a visit to Ireland with, as usual, no 'funny business' going on, so I told her she would be more than welcome.

We found out that, all going well, she would be landing in Dublin on a Saturday, so Kyrl and I went to pick her up. We stayed with my brother Kyrle in Dublin on the previous night, and then got totally lost going to the airport the next morning. I was in a huge panic trying to make sure that we were there before she got off the plane, and we barely made it. We were running into the arrivals hall as she walked out the door, looking both tired and beautiful. I was not as nervous as I had been that first time in St Louis, but still I was in a very excited state. After saying good bye to her friends, we set off for Dublin. My JoAnn from the Midwest of America was about to achieve one of her secret lifetime dreams; she was about to see her misty green Ireland, and feel our Irish mist too because it was raining as we drove into the suburbs of Dublin. She was in a trance looking for castles and faeries and green fields, but still in the Dublin suburbs she marvelled at how the Irish must love their plants so much, because they planted them in the chimneypots and on the roofs of their homes. Kyrl and I just looked at each other and almost burst out laughing. She was from the Midwest alright, and had never seen an ill kept flatland before, but I didn't want to disillusion her so early in her trip, so I kept quiet and just smirked at Kyrl.

The sun eventually came out and we parked and began our tour of the capital. I showed her the General Post Office made famous from our 1916 Rising, and the bullet holes associated with that few days of struggle against the British. Then later we shared an orange bought in Moore Street, completing a promise made a year earlier that some day I would buy her an orange in Ireland. When we entered the Garden of Remembrance and began to walk around it, all of a sudden Kyrl said to me, "Da isn't that Jerry Adams over there?" To my astonishment it was indeed that famous Irishman, who was at that time walking a political tightrope. We stopped and

314

looked while I explained who he was to JoAnn, and what was going on in our politics at that crucial time in the North of Ireland. With that news, she insisted on meeting him and wishing him well. He was almost alone that day, with maybe three people beside him, and even from a distance I felt that we would be intruding, as he looked quite downtrodden and not at all the television icon we were used to seeing. Still she insisted, so over we went.

"Hi my name is JoAnn, I'm from America and I hear you're a famous Irishman, so I want to shake hands with you," and out went her hand. I think Jerry Adams was totally surprised and shocked, but with his distinctive northern accent, and a broad genuine smile, he said, "Well I'm Jerry Adams. I'm not sure about being famous, but you are very welcome to Ireland JoAnn, from America".

I introduced myself and Kyrl, and told him that we were very surprised to see him in Dublin. He said that he had come to 'The Garden' for inspiration because he was at a crucial point in the talks and facing a very important meeting in the coming days.

It seemed wrong then to take up any more of his time, so we wished him well and left. I believe we saw him on television in the White House the very next evening, meeting with President Bill Clinton. He had met one American in Dublin, and was meeting a much more famous one in America the next day. Having met such a famous Irishman that day, JoAnn became even more interested in Irish history, Michael Collins, and the bullet holes in our GPO in Dublin.

As we got nearer to Mallow I could feel the anxiety coming off my American, and we tried to assure her that she would be made welcome by my estranged wife, which she was. From that meeting onwards her days in Ireland went by in a flash. We showed her what we could in the time allotted, and in early August I took her back to Dublin and parted with her once again, both of us hiding our tears. I drove home in a daze, reliving the two magic weeks we had just spent together.

Then began a time of great partings interspersed with joyful happy meetings, when I and one of my children, either Lynda or Kyrl, would go to America on vacation. At other times JoAnn would come to Ireland with one of her young children, and as the years passed by we just made the best of our lot together.

In order to complete a promise made earlier that somehow I

would see in the new Millennium with her, and despite the idiotic warnings of planes falling from the sky, Kyrl and I travelled to America on the day that no one wanted to fly. It worked in my favour as the tickets were very cheap, and we did get to see the Millennium arrive together, even if it was with her husband and his friends. I didn't like it, but there was nothing we could do about it, and we made the best of it. A new era had arrived in human history, but our personal situation seemed to have gotten worse. Later I left for Ireland feeling even more depressed and almost didn't make it back. In Lambert Airport our plane sat on the runway while the captain and his senior engineer got into a dispute over the refuelling documentation. According to the paperwork the plane was full of fuel, yet the gauges said it was almost empty. In typical engineering form, the engineer blamed the gauges saying they were faulty, but fortunately the captain insisted the tanks were dipped, and after the long delay he announced, "Well it's lucky for you lot that I am the captain and not my engineer. If we took his advice I would just have got you up before we all fell back to the ground. We are late now, but we will get to New York in one piece not pieces". Then he chuckled as if this was an everyday occurrence. We took off, but that was not the end of that journey. As the plane gained altitude, I began to think on what might have been; a quick and dramatic death. I was so low I didn't care about me, but thanked God that my son had been spared.

We were just flying into Newark in low cloud when suddenly our plane went into a really steep nosedive and veered off to the side before correcting itself. Once again the captain is on the blower telling us, "Apologies for the sudden manoeuvre ladies and gentlemen, but a small plane almost collided with us. It should not have been in this airspace. We will land in five minutes". A large round of applause went up from us all for our brilliant pilot. We crossed the Atlantic and this time landed in London's Heathrow. Tired and still feeling sorry for myself, we boarded the plane bound for Cork Airport and then more consternation broke out. We could see people on the tarmac running around our plane in a kind of organised panic. I was too miserable to care, but the guy in front of me rang his wife in Cork and told her the plane was delayed because they had spilled aircraft fuel all over the baggage section inside the plane and they thought it might go on fire. Then he calmly hung up.

We were all being told of the delay, but not the reason. Obviously he had overheard the cabin staff talking, and it turned out to be the truth because when I finally got my bag delivered to me as it had 'vanished' in the transfer, it smelled of fuel and all my stuff inside of it was destroyed. Somehow I feel that I was not supposed to leave America after the dawn of the new era, but I had to, and with Kyrl's help and encouragement I convinced myself that a day would come when this would all be a memory, or more likely a nightmare.

After 2000 it became more and more difficult to afford to go to see JoAnn. I did manage to go with Lynda, and we returned to Hannibal on that trip. I know that we surely had a great time, but it's a blur to me now. I am sure that the next time we met was on my brother Kyrle's fiftieth birthday in June of 2001. We decided as a family to give him a great party, which was to be held in Glasgow, Scotland. Here, for the first time, JoAnn would finally meet all of the mad Cahills in one place, including my mother. She managed to bring her eight year old daughter Johnnie Rae to Ireland, and subsequently we flew on to Glasgow for the party. Hugh had flown in from Australia with his wife Celestine, and Eunice and Lill had arrived from the Isle of Man with their two husbands Seamus and Philip. My sister Tishie and John her husband arrived last, even though they only lived down the road in Dalkeith. The birthday boy and his wife Emer were already holed up in the hotel we were all using as a focal point, and around five o'clock in the evening we all finally met. JoAnn was scared to death that my family might not like her, but she need not have worried. She was a big hit, as was her daughter. It became a great weekend. We ate and drank, and chatted and argued, and mother just loved everything about this beautiful American from the Midwest. Hugh tried to get her into an argument about some ecological issue, but she gave as good as she got, and out of fear, or sheer politeness, he pulled back from making her really mad. Later I was codding her about taking on the smartest Cahill in a heated argument, and she confided that, while she did not doubt that he was the smartest, she also felt that he was the softest; a point well proven to me often over the years.

317

On that same weekend I saw a hilarious thing happen with Johnnie Rae. This little chubby girl had a very pleasing round little face with eyes that seemed to draw you into them. She was also as innocent as they come, and when we were shopping in Glasgow's High Street she spotted a set of toy bagpipes and believed they were real. Nothing would convince her otherwise, and she began pestering and pleading with her mother to buy them for her. Eventually this pestering won out, and she got the toy. Almost immediately she began to blow into it and a God awful squeaking noise came forth. We could not get her to stop it. The noise was so bad that JoAnn asked me to take her outside into the street so that she could continue without embarrassment. I took this American bagpipe prodigy outside and parked her in front of the shop, telling her to be quiet, but she flatly refused. Then as she continued her squawking, and fearing a migraine, I put some distance between us and I sat on a waste paper bin nearby. Johnnie became lost in the awful sounds she believed were music, and she played and played until she got tired from standing. Eventually she sat down outside the shop, putting her purse beside her, and played her little heart out. It was both sad and wonderful to see her try so hard, to bring music from a toy, and as I stared at her so did some others.

After a while an old lady and her husband began to look lovingly at her, and felt she was an orphan. "Och eye isn't she a darling Hamish, give her some money, poor thing". He dropped a few coins onto her purse and a big smile came forth from Johnnie Rae, and she blew even louder. Shortly after that another few people stopped by to look, smiled and passed on, throwing in another coin or two. I was flabbergasted at the generosity of the Scottish people, especially the old people. JoAnn finally arrived out from her shopping and Johnnie Rae, by then all excited, jumped up with her coins in hand, and with a huge smile she said to her mother, "Look mom, I can play, and I got money. From now on I'm playing all of the time". I nearly fainted with that news, and as more noise emanated from the pipes I felt that I might have to resort to serious measures later that night and puncture the bag, but I didn't. Today that prodigy still remembers that day, and now has two very small prodigies of her own, so as soon as possible I'm buying both of them a set of toy bagpipes in revenge. Let Johnnie Rae beware.

Once again JoAnn had to return to the USA, and a new ray of hope for my millions began with Hugh finding the solution to the deadly condition known as Deep Vein Thrombosis or DVT. This invention was beginning to look great. We had formed a company and a prototype was under construction, when later that September '9-11' hit the world, and the big airline companies had other things to worry them besides passenger health issues. It looked like JoAnn and I were destined to remain apart forever. Then in desperation, and with her marriage finally over and becoming bitter, she left home for good with the help of a shelter group for women. A turning point had arrived in JoAnn's life. She had little money and decided to rent a small house on the edge of town. She also got a job to support herself, as I was also struggling at that time.

She began working in a factory that made leather goods, and her job was terribly hard on her hands. This woman, who had almost everything in her life before, now had to give up her children, and she was reduced to doing factory work that was killing her hands from a condition known as carpal tunnel syndrome. I felt so helpless and guilty about it all. The only ray of light was I do remember her telling me that she loved her little house. She had taken little from her previous home, and as her parents were feeling that she had made a terrible mistake, they were no help at all at the time, and they used to pass her door almost every day without calling to see her. JoAnn was then virtually alone in the world at a time when she needed support most of all, and worst of all, it would be almost a year before we could meet again. With no choice, JoAnn continued to work and to damage her hands, and I began both my divorce proceeding and my house refinancing.

During those days I came to believe that the only way we could ever be together was if I could somehow become incredibly rich suddenly, and while the search for millions has always been an ongoing part of my life, it took on a new urgency especially in those days. Today I don't care about millions because I have learned life's great secret, but back then I was almost frantic with the searching.

A Buttevant girl called Martina Coughlan used to work with me in the radio station, and she always impressed me with her drive and sheer go-ahead attitude about life, and over time we became good friends. She was also a very well educated girl and at that time I was after writing the third version of this book, complete with a zillion spelling and grammatical errors, and you might think its bad now, but you have no idea how bad version three was.

One day while having tea in our canteen at work, I was telling Martina about some story or other about our hometown and she fell around laughing so much that she said" John, you just have to write a book". I said that I had written one, but it was going nowhere because I could not correct it, nor could I afford to have it professionally edited either. To Martina's great credit, she said "I'd be glad to correct it for you for free, I have time at night to do it and I would hear more stories", and so I agreed to give her my manuscript. After a week or so Martina rang me and said we needed to go over the book, as she was both constantly laughing and crying, and having to explain this to her little daughter. When she would tell her child some story from the book the little girl would demand she take her to see the places in the book, and in a joking way she said I was costing her a fortune. I arrived at her house and she made coffee and we chatted for a long time fixing and arguing over how I write things. It was getting late and there seemed to be little progress made so we agreed to meet once a week and progress the book properly, as Martina utterly believed in it.

During these winter nights we shared both of our ideas for millions as she had the same drive for them as I did, and then one night right out of the blue Martina says to me, " John I have an idea that I cant shake from my mind". I said tell me and she went on to describe her belief that it has to be possible to use a 'beer mat' for advertising or giving out information. She said that if you watch people in bars, especially when they are alone, they are always twirling and turning the beer mat. It's being read over and over, with people tearing it and playing with it, and surely that's got to be 'in your face advertising'. Martina was a marketing expert and I don't think either of us realized it then.

I got an inspiration immediately and said "Why don't we design an electronic version of a 'beer mat' and sell it to the breweries for millions". I remember Martina just holding the kettle in mid air as the idea flew around inside her head, and she said that's it, that's how we will become rich. An air of total excitement took over the two of us, and our minds went into a kind of overdrive. The electronic mat would have a small screen, be connected to the bar computer for updating, and it would constantly display messages advertising interesting facts and bar games, as well as promotions. Martina saw it being used on airplanes when they bring you the little drink and it would carry their specific promotions and flight information. She saw it used as a novel promotional idea for car launches where it could be given out as a timer which would be blank initially, but on launch day, it would suddenly come alive in the hands of the winner of a new car. She had a hundred great ideas, and my job was to design it. The best I could do back then was to do the conceptual design, the Chinese would do the manufacturing, and a Cork company who were far better than me, would do the complete prototype designs. To say that we were on a high was a great understatement, because we could see the millions as clear as we could see each other. We put a patent on the idea within a week and Martina came up with the brilliant name 'Infomate'.

Our device would be simple and beautiful and above all friendly, and I met the Cork engineers to go over the design. The unit cost was always the problem though and we had no money to develop a prototype. The banks were no use at all either, and all we could do was to try and market the concept to possible investors. We both passionately believed in the idea and I still do, as I'm quite sure Martina does too. Martina was by then working in the print business and she designed a fantastic brochure to be sent out to anyone we thought would come on board with us, and we began the posting. The Irish magazine Business Plus did a full article on us and our Infomate, to our sheer amazement, and I think the national Sunday papers carried an article or two as well. We did meet some people and even tried to get the Enterprise Ireland on board but we were two unknowns with no money and just a wonderful dream.

One night Martina said why we don't send our brochure and a letter to Richard Branson, surely he might be interested and he has the money to make it fly. We wrote a simple and honest letter to that great man, and months passed by without hearing from him, and we became very disappointed and low. We met regularly once a week and tried to 'push forward' the idea but still nothing from Mr. Branson or anyone else either.

I was driving in West Cork to a transmitter site and I heard the song 'The Living Years' by Mike and the Mechanics come on the radio. I have always associated that song with my father who had passed away, and I think of him when I hear it. Usually when I think of my dad he will send me a 'double rainbow'. Hard as that is to believe, it is completely true and has happened to me hundreds of times since his passing. As the song played away, I got sad and wondered about life and if my dad was able to connect with me still and was he ok, so I said "Father if your there and happy, send me a really big sign today not just rainbows". Then the skeptic in me kicked in and I said, "Send me a sign that will be so awesome, so impossible that I will not be able to doubt it". I drove on thinking what sign I could ask for that would be meet my criteria, and then it hit me. I wanted to hear from Richard Branson before the day was over. I told father that I didn't care if he wanted our Infomate idea or not, just a letter of acknowledgment would do.
The phone rang shortly after my chat with my dad, and Martina told me that she could not make our meeting that night because her child was sick, and of course I said no problem the next night would be fine. I thought no more about my dad, having handed him the job he was to do, and I did my work for the rest of the day on the transmitter site.
Driving home east in a day of showers, I began to see the sky brighten and my mind returned to my father and his task. Almost immediately I saw a rainbow form to my right, but its brightness took my breath away. I started to smile both inside and out as the second one formed around it. Then as I drove it moved right in front of me and literally went over my jeep, but as I stared in amazement the impossible happened. I saw the rainbow surround and cover the complete bonnet of my jeep, and I got such a shock that I screeched to a halt and dialed America.
JoAnn answered and she knew by my voice that an amazing thing had just happened to me, and the rainbow was still there though

fading fast now. We talked briefly and said it was a great sign and I clicked off and thanked my dad for the sign, but it didn't end there.

By then it was about five thirty in the evening and I seemed to be driving on autopilot. I was going over and over what I saw and tried to use science to explain what had just happened but there was none. Then the phone rang again and it was Martina apologizing for not making our meeting, but then she dropped the bombshell, she said. "Hey John, are you ready for a surprise". After my day of surprises, nothing would have surprised me by then or so I thought. "John I am holding in my hand a letter from Richard Branson". She said he thanked us for our letter, but at that time it was not a project he would be interested in, but he wished us luck with it. She was disappointed but I was elated. Far more important to me than millions then, was the knowledge that my dad was very much in communication with me that day. Later I told Martina all about it and she too took comfort from such an event but she said, "I believe it John because it has happened to us, but no one else will".

Maybe even today, no one will believe me, but I'm sure she still has that letter. Time passed by and our idea got shelved and Martina moved to the UK, where I am sure she is prospering, the millions were not coming from that idea but I had many more.

Seville

During my many chats with JoAnn over the years, I often described a day trip I had taken to Seville. This city seemed to fascinate her so much that I promised to return there one day in the future and marry her in the cathedral, even if it was only a personal ceremony. Like most of the things that meant a lot to me, it seemed like an impossible dream at the time, but I held fast to my promise. Time moved on, and after JoAnn had left her husband, she was free to do what she liked. However money, or the lack of it, was the great limiting factor, and many months went by without us meeting.

One evening, as I was having a bath, I got this powerful feeling that we should just go to Seville and get married, even if it was just in our own personal ceremony. I could ill afford it and she could not afford it at all, but I had this crystal clear vision in my mind of us both in Heathrow heading for Seville, Spain.

Exactly as I had seen it in the bath, down to the smallest detail, it all came to pass some weeks later. To this day I do not know how I got the money for it, but it came. Within a day of JoAnn landing in Shannon, we were in Heathrow holding hands as happy as could be and heading for Spain, where we did marry in our personal ceremony. In the days before she arrived I made out a 'charter of marriage' with little things we would agree to try and do for each other, such as always to say I love you at least once a day, among others. I had left places for us to sign our charter when our little ceremony was over in the cathedral. All this we did in the sight of God in that church, and to this day I still believe we were first and truly married on October thirty first, long before any legal ceremony in Jamaica.

Later that day as we took a boat trip on the Guadalquivir River, an Italian man came and sat right down right in front of us. The back of his shirt showed a map of Old Route 66. The town in the middle of his back was Cuba, Missouri, nine miles from where JoAnn had lived all her life. As we disembarked from the boat, a happy young couple stood kissing each other beside us. The girl was wearing a beautiful golden Cladagh ring. Missouri and Ireland became linked by total strangers on the day we had married in Spain. We took this as another great sign for our future, and this type of link has been repeated over and over since then, with more and more strange synchronicities happening all the time. Then after our Seville week, JoAnn had yet again to return to America and we parted once more.

Almost exactly six months went by, and with my birthday near, I was missing her terribly. On a mad whim I decided to go meet her in New York for a weekend. I had always wanted to see New York, especially the Statue of Liberty and the Empire State Building. Despite the cost, I would get to see my JoAnn on my birthday, always assuming she could get time off from the factory, and she did.

I landed in Newark first, and as I had bought a Paul Brady album in Shannon, I almost wore him out trying to kill time while waiting for the woman I loved to arrive from St Louis. Eventually I saw her on the escalator and we began a most awesome few days in New York City. When we got to the Statue of Liberty, as if by an unknown instinct, both of us rushed forward and put our hands on the plinth at the same time, then looking up at the outstretched arm I asked God to bring me back again soon. I had booked us a cheap hotel and on arriving, our little room was so small that we had to step over our suitcase to even get to the window. Despite all this, as I slept on the morning of my birthday, JoAnn rose early and secretly decorated the whole room. She had filled it with balloons and decorations, and gave me my gift. It was a small, metal red Corvette, the car of my dreams. She said one day the real one will come too, and I know it's just waiting for me to pick it up. We had a most wonderful few days that ended all too soon, and yet again we parted.

Over the next few years we would visit New York two more times, and on the last trip with my finances improving and a glimmer of hope in my heart, I bought her our engagement and marriage rings. Later that day we were walking around Chinatown, and in a small shop window I spotted a most unusual glass ornament. It was a beautiful cut-glass piece with a drawing of three Spanish galleons engraved on it, as well as a strange Chinese inscription. I fell in love with it instantly and decided to see what it might cost, so in we went. The old Chinaman told me the cost, and I was in two minds, thinking it had been an expensive day. Then I asked him what the inscription meant.

He tried to explain in his poor English that it meant 'push forward'. I thought I was hearing things, so he repeated them again, this time with his elaborate hand gestures of pushing forward.

We had just bought our wedding rings, and though four thousand miles from my home town of Buttevant, the glass ornament I was holding had a Chinese inscription written on it that had the words 'push forward'. Only I knew that those words were the war cry of the Barry Clan, on whose castle window I sat on the day I first got sight of JoAnn. Was it just a coincidence that I looked in a window and saw that ornament on the very day we had officially committed to marry? I was absolutely astonished at the sign presented to me, and took it as the greatest of all good omens for our future. I bought the glass ornament, and it's sitting in our house in America now as I write. When the day comes that we return to America for good, then our amazing circle of life will be completed. In the meantime JoAnn had to return to the factory, and with her hands failing, she was eventually told to go. So much for corporate America, and thank God for trade unions.

With no job and no way to work, life then became very hard for my American. Anxiety hit her as well as a deep depression, then finally her husband filed for a divorce. Almost a year had passed by since I last saw her, and those last months had been the worst ones in her whole life. It was long past the time when she should come home to Ireland for good.

Ireland. A new beginning

In 2003, after an eternity of partings, I finally picked JoAnn up in Shannon Airport, bringing her home at long last. Having had some idea of what she had gone through over the previous months, I didn't expect a model to arrive out the gate, but the person who did come out was almost unknown to me. She looked terrible, and as she took my little bunch of flowers, the first thing I noticed about her was how cracked and broken her fingernails were. The second was that she had trouble even holding my flowers, as her poor hands were bent inwards and it was very painful for her to grip anything, even my few roses. I was deeply shocked, feeling in some way responsible for what had happened to this once beautiful woman that I had met in St Louis not too many years earlier.

She began to shiver physically as we left the terminal, and even though it was a cold, damp, dark morning, I believe the weather was not the reason for her discomfort. I am quite sure that on her sleepless journey across the sea, she had asked herself a thousand questions, and every answer must have filled her with self doubt, and an anxiety for what might lay ahead for her.

My JoAnn had left her two small children, her two older ones as well, her family and numerous friends for a man she barely knew who was living five thousand miles across the ocean. She had no idea when, if ever, she would see her family again, and as well as all that, she was then immersed in a bitter divorce with her husband. As if that was not bad enough, she had no friends to turn to here if it all went wrong between us. Nor had she any money, and finally, she could not even drive here. She sat into my car and began to cry uncontrollably. Nothing I said or did was of any help to her, and between sobs and tears we drove home to Mallow to begin our new life together. As we drove, it dawned on me very quickly that the woman I had planned to marry loved me far more than I had ever imagined, and as a result of that love and the terrible sacrifices she had to make, she had become a physical and emotional wreck. I believed too that I was responsible, in part at least, if not in full, for it all. There and then I made a promise to love her even more, and so as to show her I meant it, I would give her a little flower every single day for the rest of our lives. I have kept that promise, never missing a day in years. When she is abroad I draw squares on a sheet of paper, adding my flower and my thoughts for the day to the square. Then when she returns she has my flowers to help her get over the homesickness.

An hour or so later we drove into Mallow, and I soon put her to bed where she slept for almost a day. Next day she rose up, transformed. It was as if a long dark dream had ended. While there was still a very long way to go, especially in overcoming the pain of missing her children and her homeland, she began to transform another woman's house into her very own little home in Avondale Park.

By 2004, with both our divorces finalized, we were at long last free to marry. We decided to wait no longer and got married in the Caribbean island of Jamaica. It would be just the two of us. All we wanted was a simple ceremony, and a break from all the stress of the past number of years, so we set off in late April for Montego Bay, Jamaica. The first person we met outside of the airport terminal, and even before we got on the transit bus, openly offered us drugs. I almost fell over with surprise, but politely refused. That night we went to bed early and slept through one of the worst tropical storms ever to hit the area, and we never even heard a sound. Next day the roads were all gone and the beach was deserted as a cleanup began. This was a stormy beginning to one of the most amazing holidays I have ever had in my life.

We hired a driver and a car, and he took us to see Kingston, New Seville, and Rick's Café, one of the most famous bars in the world. There, every evening, thousands of tourists come to see the cliff divers who are insane enough to dive from death-defying heights into the sea for money. I saw some Americans do it as well, and figured that the only way they were mad enough to try this stunt was because they too had met the same guy we did, and did not refuse the drugs. It was wonderful to sit in the sun, hear the Bob Marley music playing and just chill out, then ultimately buy the t-shirt.

Our wedding day came and was as simple as it could be. The

hotel presented us with a bottle of champagne and a complimentary horse and buggy ride along the torn up roads. After a bit of unnerving driving, the Jamaican driver, probably also on the ganja, decided that he and the horse had had enough, so he tried to wheel the horse around in the middle of the main road and return home. This was almost the end of us, as none of the cars would stop for him, so he had no choice but to make a mad burst across the road, whipping and shouting insults at the poor horse, who was surely as scared as we were. In this mad lurching forward we almost fell out the back of the buggy, ending our honeymoon, but we just collapsed laughing. I gave him the bottle of champagne as a token of our thanks for the ride, and he almost hugged me, probably believing we too were as high as he was and didn't know the value of the drink.

Next day we headed off for an amazing adventure to a place called the Dunns River Falls. Here you hired river shoes, and if you were 'quite mad' you entered a waterfall under the strict supervision of a local guide, and began your ascent about half way up the falls. From that point on, you literally climbed your way to the top of this huge cascading waterfall which is at least two hundred feet above the sea floor below. The challenge is to do this climb from within the actual waterfall, carefully picking your steps, and trying not to slip to your death way down in the sea. It is an exhilarating experience and everyone should try it at least once in their lifetime.

When I looked at how all this was done, I felt that we should do it 'right' and literally climb these falls from where they enter the open sea. Unlike the others, we would begin in the waves and climb up out of it. No one was doing it this way and I felt that they were a lot of 'ould women', and we would do it the way Irish men did it. There was no need to bother with an expensive guide, and of course I'd ignore all the warnings about drowning and falling hundreds of feet, or slipping on rocks like glass. All of that was for wimps and old people, and against her better judgment I persuaded my new wife to follow me upwards. We would scoff at the millions of gallons of water pouring down upon us and climb like the Irish did; we would climb from the sea up.

It was an amazing experience to walk out across a beach, then into the sea, and start where this torrent fell down upon your head.

I'll never forget it. We climbed and slipped and laughed and held each other close and almost suffocated often. I believe I drank well over a gallon of water that day but cared nothing, and feeling quite invincible, I pushed and pulled JoAnn up through the Dunns River Falls. After an hour of struggling we got to the area where the 'quite mad people' used to begin their trek. By then we, the certifiable lunatics, were seasoned veterans, well over the worst of it and we almost flew to the top. I was exhilarated it was so exciting and dangerous, and I wanted to redo the whole thing again, but JoAnn began shaking in terror when she looked back down and saw where we had come from, and she flatly refused. Aside from the wedding, that falls adventure was the highpoint of our holiday for me, and even though we did do a lot more fun stuff, nothing could compare to the sheer terror of possibly drowning or falling from a great height into the sea below.

We reluctantly left that wonderful romantic island of Jamaica, and on landing in Cork, we discovered that once again my bags had gone missing. When they were finally delivered, all our clothes were ruined because we had bought some bags of Blue Mountain Coffee in those same mountains, and I believe they showed up on the x-ray machines as drugs. It's quite likely that the security services just stabbed our coffee bags to see the contents and didn't bother to reseal or bag them, so we had no coffee and no clothes, but we were married at long last and who cared about clothes after that.

In the mid nineties Ireland had spawned a Celtic Tiger that we now know was fuelled by a combination of political corruption from the highest level to the lowest, and a banking business that thrived on pure greed. Our little country was booming. U2 were the best band in the world, becoming Ireland's musical ambassadors, Riverdance and Michael Flatley's dancing phenomenon had captivated the whole world, and being Irish was just about as great as it could get. JoAnn and I partook in this great wave of prosperity, and we went on many trips abroad, as well as her going back to the US frequently. Fortunately we did not go into the insanity of the property boom, but at the time all boats were rising, including ours, and we spent our extra cash on creating memories stored up for the future.

I had always longed to see Rome, and for our first wedding anniversary I had secretly planned to take JoAnn there and show her 'the angel pictures'; her strange name for the Sistine Chapel. This was supposed to be a great surprise, and I had it all booked with a travel agent in Cork. Not having heard from them as the day approached, I rang them to discover that they had got the month wrong. All they could then offer at such short notice was a trip to Malaga in Spain. I was really annoyed and disappointed, but it was either we take it or got into a long battle over money. By then our day would have passed. Besides, I had got a feeling to just run with it, so somewhat disappointed we landed in Malaga and began a weekend break in the sun.

With nothing planned and time to spare, we decided on a whim to cross Spain to Seville for a day, revisit the cathedral and marry each other all over again. When we arrived there the beautiful church was being refurbished, and the day we arrived turned out to be quite special. The cathedral had been closed to tourists for the previous weeks and would be closed again for a similar time from the next day onwards, but by some unseen power it just happened to be open on the one day we got there to remarry, so we did, and thanked God for all that we had. Then we returned to Malaga excited and exhausted.

Our hotel was outside Malaga and had a beautiful beach at the end of its grounds. We loved our time there laying in the sun, reading books and eating their strange foods. On the night before we returned home, we took a taxi into the centre of the city for a last look and got lost right away. It was wonderful to walk around that ancient Roman city and feel the atmosphere of bygone days. We took in the sounds and the smells, and the smiles from Spanish people who could see we were very happy to be there. Then one of the many really strange things that happen to us happened that evening. We were walking along as lost as could be, when all of a sudden I got a really strong feeling of certainty inside me that I would be guided to what I used to call 'my window'.

This was the front window of an art shop located down a small back street somewhere in the city, and I have no idea where it is still. However, fifteen years earlier I had been walking alone in Malaga one evening and came across this particular art shop window. It had nothing special in it at all, neither did anything unusual happen there, nor did I go into the shop, but that day for some reason I had stared at the window for a long time, memorizing every detail. It had an easel with a blank canvas, a stick figure, paints and brushes in a pottery jar, as well as some drawing books on small shelves over to one side. For years after that day and quite at random, this window would return to my mind in perfect detail, but I never knew why. It was as if it had some great significance that I was not being allowed to forget.

I suddenly stopped in the street and told JoAnn that I would now describe a window to her that could not possibly still exist after fifteen years, but that I was sure we would see if she followed me down some nearby alleyways. JoAnn listened without comment, and then I began walking, being guided purely by instinct. After only five minutes or so we arrived at 'my window'. It was exactly as I had described it, down to the smallest detail. We both stood looking on in total amazement at this incredible sight. No one would expect that a window would remain unchanged in all those years, but it had. I still do not know what the significance is, but I am sure it was no accident that the travel agent got my dates wrong, and we were meant to remarry in Seville and see my window.

Over the next five years we went on holidays all over Europe. Courtesy of Ryanair we saw the UNESCO city of Carcasonne in France and the Alhambra Palace in Granada, Spain. We went to Amsterdam in the winter, deliberately missing Anne Frank's house, but taking a boat trip beneath it, and going to the red light district, which was heavily populated by Japanese tourists with a zillion flashing cameras. They seemed to travel in groups of twenty or so, for 'moral protection' no doubt. I think we both loved the place. There was a great sense of freedom in the city, but also what appeared to be a great drug problem too, especially late at night. My lasting memories from that trip were twofold: one was the amazing chocolate sweets they gave you after a meal, and the other was a visit we made to a sex museum, which literally was an eye opener for both of us. The only downside was that JoAnn bought about a hundred tulip bulbs in a market and not a single one became a flower. I think they saw us coming.

On another one of our trips JoAnn's twenty-something year old daughter Jessica, a beautiful tall girl, arrived for a holiday in Ireland and I decided to show my guests the city of London, one of my all time favourite places on earth. I booked us a triple room in North London, and that's where our first troubles began. We had taken the bus into central London and made our way to 'Paki land' only to discover that the room I had booked was a small pokey pigsty. My Americans were used to a very high standard of room, and the place I had booked online bore no resemblance whatsoever to the thumbnail pictures I had squinted at on my laptop. They were shocked at the size of the room and how dirty it was. The only place I had ever seen that was smaller was in New York, but that room had been spotlessly clean, unlike our 'Indian or Paki' abode. I think the managers of that excuse for a hotel deliberately spoke poor English just in case we might complain, and JoAnn did want to leave immediately. I tried my best to assure my guests that all we would be doing there was sleeping, but my words were of little comfort and fell on at least one set of deaf ears. I couldn't help notice the ancient, stained and mouldy bedspreads. They were so nasty that they could easily have passed as Afghan rugs which had once been used by goat herders, until the goats had refused to sleep on them any longer, and their owners had then sold them on to our Pakis. Even I, who came from the era of hairy blankets and savage fleas, became scared to pull back the sheets, just in case some uncatalogued insect bit me in the night, and I never woke up again. But all we could do was make the best of it, and we hit the town, taking a Red Bus tour of central London to get our minds off the filthy place. The bus tour was brilliant, and while on it, Jessica found a brochure.

She had always been interested in the spooky side of London, and after she read the brochure describing 'A Jack the Ripper Tour' I knew that we were going to be going on it one way or another. By pure luck we got a cancellation, and even though it was going to cost each of us about a hundred dollars in English pounds, we decided to do it as a once in a lifetime adventure. The brochure had painted this amazing picture of a three hour tour. It included a guided coach tour of old London, with the highpoint of the tour being a sunset cruise along the River Thames. Then after this cruise the whole group would be taken to see some old dungeons, and finally we would all end in a real English pub, frequented by the Ripper and many of his victims. Jessica became very excited as we drank high tea in a posh hotel, known to be the last pickup point for the tour. While still drinking our overpriced brew, in runs a small man shouting, "Ripper Tour, party of three, where are you? Ripper Tour, come on will ye, we're late". He repeated this a few times as he ran up and down the foyer before we realized he was talking about us. My laidback Americans sauntered over to him while I tried to find a waiter to pay for the tea. Our tour guide was in a panic as he tried to rush the ladies to the door, then hardly gone but a minute he ran back inside to tell me, "If you're not out in ten seconds, we're leaving. We're late, can't you see that". It was at that point that I realized he was as Irish as I am, and knowing how we treat time, I decided to wait for my change rather than leave the expected tip of a 'tenner' to the snotty waiter.

I'm running down the foyer when our tour man once again pokes his head in the foyer and shouts, "Bus is going, NOW", so I dashed for the door almost knocking over some old codger coming in. The little coach was full up in the front, and when I arrived out I saw our guide wrench open the back door and begin pushing JoAnn and Jessica into the back of his minibus. I asked if I should pay him now, and then he realized I was one of his own kind and says, "Yerra not at all boy, you can pay me later. Sure we're late, hop now will you, or we'll miss the ould ship". I hopped in and he slammed the doors. Then he ran round to the front shouting, "On Cedric, on, and don't spare those English horses". Cedric the driver gunned the engine, and we shot out into London's rush hour traffic. Instinctively I felt it was going to be a very interesting evening.

All this excitement has been great for us so far, and the three of us began to laugh at this poor man with his distinctive Dublin accent in the middle of London. Soon I noticed two really sour-faced, middle-aged Americans sitting in the seats next to us. They made it very clear too that they didn't like us at all. We were probably too happy for them. "Well some people can never be on time for anything…No they can't dear, and now we are all going to be late because of them. This is not good enough". This remark was pointedly aimed at the three of us, who then laughed even more just to annoy them. By then Cedric was stuck in the crawling traffic, and our guide, who was probably called Paddy, began his touring spiel. He told us about London's history, alluding quite often to England's many 'conquests'. I soon got the impression that he didn't like the English one bit. He showed us the Tower of London, describing the many heads lost there, and some Roman ruins, but much of this we already knew from our earlier Red Bus tour, so we talked and laughed, ignoring him completely. This laughter and talk was maddening the two sourpusses beside us even more by then, and every time I took a sneak look at them, they were glaring back at us. Taking the odd break from his 'conquests', our guide began taking a shine to a much nicer American lady who was sitting beside him up front. He started to chat her up with his old Irish Blarney. However, unknown to him, or maybe he didn't care, he had left his microphone turned on, and between his outbursts on the 'English oppressor', we got to hear him try and make a date with the American woman. It was simply hilarious listening to him making his play for this nice lady. "And where are you from dear lady? Oh New York is it, sure I know it well". While Paddy was making good progress, we seemed to be making none, so he announced that it was not looking too good for the Thames River Cruise, simply because we were stuck in the "bloody English rush hour traffic". Paddy assured us all though that he could give us just as good a tour on his bus as you'd get on any ould English ship on their river. At that news the sourpusses went ballistic, shouting out loud enough for all to hear that the Thames River Cruise was the reason they took the tour in the first place. As expected, some others began bitching as well, and Paddy soon came under severe pressure to get us to the boat. His next announcement was that Cedric, our driver and his very good friend, would now take drastic action. Then suddenly our minibus almost flipped over as Cedric made a sudden and very sharp illegal U-turn in the middle of London's traffic. This had to be illegal, and to escape detection he drove up over a footpath, landing back on the road with a loud bang. Then he headed off down a narrow street at high speed. As we flew down this street, Paddy, who was by then really agitated, added a new titbit of information telling us that the house we had just passed was the home of the ex British Prime Minister Margaret Thatcher, and he offered a reward for anyone who would do him a favour and shoot her. I nearly fell out of the seat at that shocking news. Obviously he had no love for the British, and despite our traffic problems, here he was preaching terrorism against a famous English politician who actually was ill at the time.

Leaving us to think about his reward, Paddy soon returned to his future date, but every so often he gave us an update on our progress, which was that it was too slow. The noises from the sourpusses grew ever louder and people started to really pester Paddy with questions, interrupting his potential night of pleasure. In desperation he announced that he would make a call to the Captain of the ship, who just happened to also be a very good friend of his, and as a special favour he would try and get him to hold the ship for us. I thought it rather strange that from the start he constantly referred to our boat as a ship, and even though I knew better, I could not shake the idea of a sailing ship from my mind.

He made the call and triumphantly announced that the ship would be docked at the London Eye, and that it would wait as a favour to Paddy, but only for five minutes. He stood up and announced that we could still make it, provided we followed him precisely through the crowds milling around the Eye, and we were to not delay the moment Cedric stopped the bus. By then I had decided that we must not lose sight of Paddy no matter what, and as he and I were both small, I wanted to be right at his heels the minute we stopped. So I told JoAnn and Jessica that I intended to be out the back door the minute Paddy went out the front door, and to be right on my heels as we raced for the boat.

I believe the two sourpusses must have overheard this advice, and feeling that the Irish would know their own, they too planned to be out as fast as us and follow me and Paddy to the boat. Paddy shouts, "Nearly there, be ready now. I'll hold up me hand so ye can see me". The bus suddenly stopped and Paddy shouts, "Out, out, follow me, and keep me hand in sight as ye head for the Eye and the ship. Don't delay," and at that he leaps out the front door, quickly followed by myself and my gang out the back door. As usual I lost Paddy immediately, and I couldn't see a sign of him. Figuring the boat had to be on the water somewhere, I took off in the direction of the river. My Americans were chomping at my heels, but I didn't know that. So too were the sourpusses, as well as some Germans, Italians, and about six or so others. Apparently I was running like an ostrich, with my head stuck out in front and tail to the wind, and I had a look of sheer determination engraved on my face. The Ripper Tour group were by then reduced to a bunch of lemmings, all following an Irish ostrich heading for the Thames River. When I did arrive at the wall overlooking the dock, to my surprise, and to the shock of the others, we saw our cruise boat heading out into the current with Paddy's people all waving back at us. In rage the sourpuss began to shout at me, "He specifically said follow him to the Eye, and you led us all astray". He seemed to be furious. It was about then that I saw Jessica pull her hood up around her beautiful face, and she said to me, "I think its time we disappeared". It was good advice, and the three of us took off running once more, this time directly into the middle of a million tourists at London's famous Eye. We had escaped the wrath of my followers. When it seemed safe we stopped and broke into tears of laughter, recounting over and over 'my famous run' for the boat. Then it dawned on me that we had not paid a cent, but the others had paid a fortune, and must be totally lost in London with no cruise, no Ripper pub and no Paddy to entertain them.

We ran the many scenarios of what might happen to Paddy when he found out that he had lost half his tour. JoAnn suggested that we should go on by taxi to the Ripper pub, and when Paddy arrived we should ask him what kept him. This brought more peals of laughter, but I felt sure that, being a Dub, he would blame the whole thing on a fellow Irishman from Cork, and that he was sure to be fired the next day. Poor Paddy had become a victim of a typical Cahill experience.

The evening did turn out to be great for us though as we got to see a huge Mardi Gras and food fair travel along the riverbank. It was a warm beautiful evening as we looked on at the riverboats cruising up and down the Thames. We had no way of knowing that the next day, while visiting St Paul's Cathedral, we would see the world's banking system crash with the shock news of the Lehman Bank collapse. On that day I clearly felt it was going to be very bad news for us all in the long run, but I had no idea that it would kill our Celtic Tiger, and end the run of prosperity sweeping through Ireland and the world in general.

Of all the pain JoAnn went through, the worst has always been the missing of her children. Jessica came to visit as did Johnnie and finally her other daughter Julie came to see us as well. She was a young and beautiful teenage girl full of adventure but very shy around me I felt. She had done amazingly well in her graduation and a trip to Europe was her promised reward by her mother. So we picked her up in Shannon and whisked her off to Seville for a few days break in the sun. Julie had already been to Paris with us some years earlier and now it was Spain's turn and she loved it all except for the jellyfish incident.

We had gone on a day trip to Tore Molino's and were laying in the beautiful sunshine looking at the clear blue waters and the swimming urge was getting to my Americans, both expert swimmers. Far be it from me to dissuade such desire, so I told them to go for it. I had an uneasy feeling though, because some geezer beside us kept trying to give us some kind of warning but we just smiled and ignored him, then in they went. I lay and soaked up the rays not being a good swimmer. I saw the huge waves toss them around and they laughed and screamed with delight. It did seem a bit odd that the water was not full of people, but my lot did seem to be having great fun. After a while they arrived back out and lay in the sun. Pretty soon I saw Julie whisper to her mom. "What,…a jelly fish, did you say a jellyfish stung you". I sat up concerned and sure enough the huge red marks began to show all over Julies thighs. My science kicked in and I suggested the only obvious answer, which was that I pee all over her thighs and that would fix it. I said sure you can keep your eyes shut and it will make you better. Kyrl Cahill's mantra was at work once again, but no, absolutely not, they would not hear of it. Julie would suffer before I could pee on her, I suppose it was an understandable protest from a teenager to her step dad so she suffered in silence until we got some stuff from a local drugstore. Later that day, I took them to see the zillion shops and once a buying frenzy took over, all pain soon vanished. Later Julie left and JoAnn again was alone and went into a deep sadness. I don't know how she has ever kept doing it, all I can say is she must love me a lot. Her son Justin has never seen Ireland as yet, and one day soon I am sure his turn will come, but of this I am sure, we won't go swimming in Toro Molino's.

We always tried to go away someplace nice for our anniversary and one year I got a feeling that we should go to Venice. Going anywhere in Europe was ok with JoAnn as she loved to travel, so Venice it was. The money seemed to come for it easily; I don't remember how, but we landed in Treviso, courtesy of Ryanair. The airport shuttle bus dropped us off in a small square, definitely not San Marco's Square. It was late at night and I had booked our hotel in a place called the Lido because it had a great review and was real cheap for a four star hotel. What I neglected to find out though was where it was. The hotel was not in Venice at all but on another island across from it, and when we got off the bus, all we had was an address and not a word of Italian, except 'scusi'.

The night was warm and we found our first water bus. After a lot of head scratching and guide book reading, the location of our hotel dawned on me. Then after two hours of getting lost, and in total confusion, we finally arrived at the hotel. The receptionist was a very weird man. He reminded me of the Maitre D in *Pretty Woman,* having exactly the same looks and mannerisms as he had. I did not know whether to laugh or thank him for his style, so we did neither and just went to bed exhausted.

Next day we rose early and took the waterbus across to San Marco's Square in beautiful sunshine, and began our three day vacation in the absolutely amazing city of Venice. JoAnn quickly discovered the fake Gucci, Prada and other expensive fashion bags, and she fell into the bargaining mode immediately. We walked for miles and miles that day, lugging our bag of bags and loving every sound and splash of that place.

At dinner a waiter insisted on dancing in the street with my American, much to the ohh's and ahh's of the onlookers, while I ate his pizza.

We did the typical walk around San Marco's Square, which was actually floating beneath three inches of water. The inventive Italians had built wooden walkways to provide access to their shops for the thousands of tourists. Venice is really sinking, of that I am now quite certain. We took thousands of photographs and saw a film crew making a movie while travelling on our waterbus. I'm sure JoAnn is in it as an unpaid extra, because she stuck her head in their camera often enough. The Rialto Bridge was one of my favourite places, and it was great to stand there and watch the world go by. Later that night of our anniversary, after an awesome evening meal and as we water bussed back to our Lido, we noticed that the moon was totally full. It shone across the water in a way that was too beautiful to describe. We stared at it in awe and felt incredibly close and happy. As we looked at the moon and thought of its romantic implications in poetry and stories, I remembered another moon incident I had with JoAnn some years earlier. She had not been living in Ireland long and was feeling very homesick. We had begun a clean out of our house, dumping of all things, an old mirror. This was out in the back yard with other stuff waiting for the skip to arrive. During the night I had got up to go pee and saw that the whole back yard was lit up by a full moon, but the moon was right above our house. It was about two am and I got the mad notion that I could do a really romantic thing for my new homesick wife, if I could just give her the moon.

Out I went in my nightgown and bare feet and I got a stepladder from our shed. Then I tied the mirror to the ladder and kept adjusting the angle until the moon shone directly into our curtainless bedroom, right above the bed. I snuck in and woke JoAnn up saying, "Sit up Punkin". She did so suddenly saying, "What's wrong," and as she sat up she was blinded by the moonlight. I said, "Nothing is wrong love. I might not have got you millions yet, but I give you the moon to show you how much I love you". JoAnn almost burst into tears. She stared and stared at it saying it was the most romantic thing anyone had ever done for her. After a while Kepler's laws of planetary motion pulled my moon out of range of the mirror and soon it was gone, but the memory remained and it was easy for us to go back to it that night as we sailed across in the moonlight to the Lido Island and our bed.

Next day we headed for Verona, the city made famous by Shakespeare's play *Romeo and Juliet*. I was really after the coliseum though; the second largest one in Italy, being just beaten by the one in Rome. I had always wanted to see this place, having seen it on television when the rock band Simple Minds played an amazing concert there. We travelled by train and crossed beautiful Italy at a great speed, arriving in the station quite early. The day was wonderful. We went to the markets, saw museums, and the famous window in Shakespeare's play. We took a zillion photos and finally arrived at the coliseum.

I'll never forget it. The sheer wonder of how it was built blew me away. I could not wait to get inside and walk around the upper rim so that I could say I did the rim. JoAnn was petrified. The building was so well designed that every onlooker had a clear view of the sport below, if it can be called sport. The only problem they would have had was that the sunshine would have killed them as they sat. We had a most wonderful day in Verona and I absolutely loved Italy. The train headed back to Venice.

About a mile or so out from Venice station, we heard the announcement that we would soon be at our final destination, so we got up and were waiting in the exit area beside the doors. I saw the yellow buttons come on and knew these were to open the doors when it stopped. As we stood there I got a crazy idea. I had always wanted to jump off a moving train and always tried the buttons when they came on, but they never opened for me. I was telling all this to JoAnn as we stood, and we decided to check our buttons on the off chance, so I pushed and whoosh the door shot open with a gush of wind coming inside. With that I saw my chance and said to JoAnn, "Well here goes, I'm off," and I jumped right out the door. This happened so fast that she could not even stop me, and as I sailed through the air I realized the bad news. We were not actually travelling as slow as I thought, nor were we near the platform. Then bang; I landed hard on one leg and crumpled to the ground, rolling over a few times on the hardcore, three or four feet below the level of the train. The pain then hit. My knee seemed to be stabbing me and I hobbled along to the platform to be met by a very annoyed wife. She said the train announcers were screaming abuse and all kinds of Italian gibberish and was I ok. I pretended I had no pain and that I was fine. Inside I was over the moon with happiness as I had achieved the lifelong dream of jumping from a moving train, and in Venice too. I ignored the pain and we proceeded to get totally lost in Venice as the evening closed in. We learned a very good lesson that night. It appears that virtually the whole city closes down after nine pm. To make matters worse for me, we got on a waterbus which landed us on a remote island and we were on the last bus to it. After pleading in gestures, the driver agreed to land us back in Venice, but in his zero knowledge of English he was trying to tell us that we were on the very opposite

341

side of the city from San Marco's Square which had the bus to our island, the Lido. It got totally dark, very foggy, eerie, and quiet. We were trying to find anyone who could guide us in a direction of people. JoAnn informed me that she took an intense dislike to the idea of being mugged or worse, and what were we going to do. My answer was to hobble along faster than ever, getting us even more lost. Finally we came across a young couple out walking. The man had perfect English and told us the news that we were on the wrong side totally. He proceeded to draw a line on our map that we were to carefully follow. This would get us to the square and off he went. Pretty quick I saw a new problem, as he had drawn the line across the street names on our tiny map, and after five minutes we were again navigating by the 'force' and it was letting us down. The pain in my knee by then was becoming very uncomfortable and yet we began to run along aimlessly, hoping for a sign saying San Marco. It was getting so late too that if we didn't make the square by midnight, we would have no boat to our hotel, and that would be a disaster. I think we must have crossed a hundred bridges that night, but eventually we did run out an alleyway into the square to the strains of a Beethoven symphony being played there. It was five minutes to midnight and our bus was about to leave. JoAnn wanted to stay on, but I dashed for the boat and by one a.m. I was laying in bed with a bandage around my knee. Thank God for first aid kits. JoAnn persuaded me to take some aspirin for the swelling, and by the next day I was considerably better. Just as well too, as we left Venice that morning. My stupidity could have gone very wrong, but like my Seville incident it didn't, and now it's a dearly held memory that always brings a smile to my face. Kyrle, my brother, may have jumped off a train in Buttevant while drunk, but I did it in style while sober in Venice. JoAnn has said many times that I should tell no one of my train jumping escapade as it was clearly the act of a madman, and I take that criticism as the ultimate compliment for a Cahill, as we were all supposed to be mad. In truth I suppose by all rights I should have been killed many times in my life, but had that tragedy happened to me, I would never have experienced the truth inherent in Eleanor Roosevelt great saying:

"The future belongs to those who believe in the beauty of their dreams".

This inspiring quotation was given to me years earlier by my son
Kyrl, who noticed my sadness and despair after I returned from a
particularly sad trip to America. Even though I myself could see no
way to happiness then, he believed in the power of my dreams for
me, and I end this account of my life with the proof of that power,
when we finally took my journey of dreams.

Dreams do come true.

America has always attracted me. This attraction began with me reading about Huckleberry Finn and his adventures along the great Mississippi River. As I grew a little older and read more about America and its vast land mass, especially the Western part of America, I began to develop a longing to see certain parts of that country, especially the area around the Midwest and the great Mississippi. Later still, when we began to get free entry into Big Kyrl's cinema, the Wild West became an area I deeply longed to see 'before it was gone' according to Kevin Costner in *Dances with Wolves*, my favourite film of all time. But above all, there was one area that had a really powerful draw on me spiritually, and that was the Monument Valley area on the Utah-Arizona border.

We have all seen this amazing place in numerous films, especially the cowboy films of John Huston and John Wayne. The movie *Stagecoach* is one of the most famous early ones, and *Back to the Future* a later one. There was never a time when I saw that vista, composed of the tall Buttes and the Mittens set against the backdrop of a deep blue sky, that my heart did not skip a beat, and it still does even today. I simply love the place. My only explanation for this longing is that in some past life I think I must have lived there. A psychic once told me that I had lived many times with the Bird Tribe. Every chance I got to see a picture of that area I took it, and I would just stare at it forever, hoping to someday go there. One of the most famous road photographs in existence today is the view from North to South, looking into that famous valley on Highway 163. It was there that Forest Gump stopped running, and I wanted to stand where he stood, and have my photo taken on what I believe is one of the most historic roads in the world.

For as long as I can remember this was a secret dream of mine that I kept to myself, believing that if I told people they would say it was totally impossible, and in so doing somehow make me believe they might be right. However, I kept it alive within myself, and daydreamed of going there a thousand times as the years passed by. About twelve years ago I began a dream journal; not a journal of dreams but a secret journal of my most hoped-for desires. In this journal I placed a picture of a man in a blue shirt and black pants walking on that famous road in Monument Valley. This would be me some day, I hoped. I had found the picture in a magazine and I studied every detail of the picture, even down to the tumbleweed that was blowing across the man's path. I made up my mind that somehow, someday I would be the man in that photo. I had no idea how it might happen, or how long it would take, but I kept the dream alive all the same. Then almost ten years ago I began to think that it might happen for real because of JoAnn being an American.

Since meeting JoAnn, and probably because I was growing older, I drifted away from reading electronic books to reading a more spiritual type of literature, and my whole outlook on life has begun to change. I began to study more and more about who we are, and what we are, and I came to the conclusion that the whole area of Sedona, and especially Monument Valley, had some spiritual significance for me.

I started to make my computer screensavers show different pictures of Monument Valley and Arizona, as well as my dream car; a red Corvette. This area of America was becoming my obsession. I studied the maps, studied the satellite images, drove the valley from space (thanks to Google) and I saw the rock formations known as the Mittens from a hundred angles. I read all about Goulding's Lodge and Harry Goulding who built a famous trading post, and who later convinced John Huston to begin the whole movie business in the valley. Then later still I read about a new Native American hotel known as The View. It's an eco friendly hotel, and orientated so that every room faces east. This beautiful building is owned by the Navaho and is built on their sacred grounds. I wanted to stay there.

Almost every week in some guise or other I would do some research on the internet and learn a new tit bit of information. As my knowledge grew, so did my desire to be there. Even though I had been to the USA many times since meeting JoAnn, we had never ventured south of Missouri. When I finally told her of this place that I so wanted to see, she said it was just a desert, and who wanted to see a desert, preferring the beautiful lakes and forests of her home state, but I longed to be in that desert, and I knew that we would go there together.

The big problem had always been my belief that the cost would make it impossible for me, and rather than be crushed by a confirmation of my fears, I always chickened out when it came to just checking it out. I dearly wanted JoAnn to be with me on that trip, desert or not, and so for years more I continued to dream as life passed me by. One day I woke up and I was sixty years old.

Every year JoAnn returns home to her family for some months, and this parting is always very hard on us both. Usually within a week or so I get terribly lonely and long to be with her in America. It was during one of her extended visits, when I was feeling very low, that once again I returned to my computer and the Valley.

I had been reading one of my many spiritual books that were all beginning to point me in a particular direction. I was learning about consciousness, and how powerful this kind of thinking could be for us all. The teaching seemed simple, yet very hard to put into practice. It basically says that in order to achieve our dreams, all we need to do is to first develop a burning desire for our wish to be fulfilled, then imagine as often as possible, especially before sleep, how we would 'feel' when we realized our desire. Consciousness, or the Universe, or the God that created us then takes over and handles the details of how it will manifest into our reality. The guarantee for success seems to be that our desire must benefit all that it touches and be love driven, while the guarantee for failure seems to be a belief in fear and a doubting mind. To take this kind of teaching on faith is incredibly hard to do at any time, but for someone coming from a logical and scientific background, it's almost impossible as it smacks of being a daydreamer, not a doer. To even begin to grasp the concept had taken me well over ten years, and I was still somewhat skeptical about it until recently.

So on a beautiful summer's evening while sitting alone with my laptop, and missing my Punkin, I decided to test out the teaching.

In complete faith I returned to Arizona in my mind and turned on my laptop. I decided to dream big, and re-read my dream journal, which I had a devil of a job finding. As I read it, I realized that not alone had I wanted to walk in the Valley, but I also wanted to see the town of Williams on Route 66, and have my photo taken beside the train that took tourists on to the Grand Canyon. I found that I had drawn two stick figures standing on the platform on a photo of the train station. On a whim, I decided to include the town and the train and the Grand Canyon in my big dream. And if I was going to go mad with the dreaming, I may as well do it in style, so I also included a trip to Meteor Crater where thousands of years ago a vast explosion took place as a result of a meteorite strike. I felt that we should also go to Sedona, and Flagstaff on Route 66, and to top it all off, we would return to Missouri by sleeper train, crossing America in the style of rich people. All of this just came to me as I let my imagination run wild.

The more I imagined about this amazing trip, the more I became convinced that we just had to do it, but not in a rushed way. We should take our time, at least ten days, and stay in old Route 66 motels whenever we could. I just knew too that we would stay in Goulding's Lodge where the movie stars had stayed, and I was equally sure that somehow we would sleep on the rim of the Grand Canyon, ideally in a log cabin.

Of course this was all just a massive daydream on that evening, but I did get a map drawn out, and began to make a plan, all the time assuming that money was not a problem, which it clearly had to be. In line with the teaching, I ignored the financial problem, trusting in a power within me, or beyond me, I cared not which. After hours of fun, playing with every kind of possibility, it became clear that the best way to have this grand adventure was to fly to New York, and then on to Phoenix. There we would hire a car at the airport, and drive the rest of the trip, using Flagstaff as a kind of base. On the last day we would drop off our car, and get a taxi to Flagstaff train station early in the morning for our twenty three hour sleeper train journey back to Kansas City, Missouri. Then after spending a day exploring Kansas City, we would take yet another train on to Washington, Missouri, and there be picked up by JoAnn's family, and be taken home to Steelville.

I became quite sure that it could now be done physically; financially was another matter entirely, so I decided on a 'feeling' to challenge my fears and cost the whole trip.

The internet is the most amazing invention. I was able to find out quite quickly that this dream trip would cost about three thousand five hundred euros all in, plus about five hundred was needed for food, and that cost seemed a lot less than I had ever imagined it would be. There was never any doubt in my mind that my dream trip was worth the money, but I still could not contemplate the idea of going into debt for my dream, and I had many more pressing calls on that kind of money. Yet I remained faithful to the teaching, and adopted an air of 'I don't care, if it's to be, then it will be' and that night I went to bed on a high.

During the night I woke from a dream where I saw JoAnn and I sitting on the road, watching the morning sun rise slowly over the Mittens.

When I switched on my laptop at work I was greeted by my screen saver of Monument Valley, the road, and those beautiful Mittens. I clearly remember thinking I dreamed of this place last night and 'I'm going there this year'. I was feeling a kind of certainty, the same kind of feeling I had felt before our Seville adventure. This feeling was very strong and reassuring, yet gentle. Then the phone rang and I began my day's work.

Lunchtime came round. I went home for my bit of food and saw my post on the floor. There was a letter from the taxman, as well as a few bills which I decided I would not open till later, not wanting indigestion for the rest of my day. I ate my sandwich and sat in the sun, and then on a whim I opened the tax letter. To my absolute astonishment, disbelief and shock, there was a cheque inside it. It was made out to me for the huge sum of..... three thousand, seven hundred euros approximately. I had to check and double check that it was an actual cheque, not some kind of tax demand. It was indeed a cheque, and it was for the exact amount I needed to comfortably pay for my entire dream trip, with some money to spare, as if the taxman had said, "By the way, have a drink on me".

The tax letter explained that I had been overpaying tax in the Tiger Economy times, and to their great credit they had reimbursed me. This refund came at a time when everyone feared clawbacks of every kind, and we were in the middle of the worst recession in history.

I'm not ashamed to say that I thanked God over and over, as well as the taxman. I thanked my spiritual books, and the Universe, and everyone who had passed over in my family. Once again I experienced yet another extraordinary miracle. All I needed then was to find the spending money and food money, and suddenly I remembered that earlier in March my wonderful colleagues at work had made a collection for my sixtieth birthday. They had very kindly presented me with five hundred US dollars, and had written on my birthday card the words 'for your next trip to America'. That money was still in its envelope in a drawer beside my passport. At the time of their presentation I had resigned myself to the fact that an American trip was impossible that year, and I had totally forgotten all about the money. Now the icing had just been poured all over my cake. I became very excited and just wanted to spread this great news, so ignoring the cost, I called JoAnn in America and told her to 'prepare for the desert', that we were going on the trip of all trips. When she asked me how we planned to pay for it all, I just said that a miracle had happened, then I hung up and went back to work on a cloud.

For the rest of that day everything went extraordinarily well. It was as if I was in a kind of crystal zone, and that evening I booked our flights, our car, and the great train journey across America. When I checked on availability for Goulding's Trading Post, it seemed that they had a long waiting list, as did the brand new View Hotel. For us to stay in the middle of Monument Valley, we had to stay in either one and it looked impossible. Then on checking availability for the Bright Angel Lodge in the Grand Canyon National Park, I also discovered that they too were booked out for the days we planned to be in Arizona. In spite of the seeming impossibility of sleeping in my dream places, I had no worries at all, especially after the earlier events of that day. I became relaxed and sure in my mind that somehow we would be staying in Goulding's Trading Post, and we would be sleeping on the rim of the Grand Canyon. Like the funding for our trip, I was happy to leave the Universe or Consciousness to handle the sleeping details as well. Quite certain of it all then, we would be heading to America at the beginning of October in 2010, the year I turned sixty years of age, and I couldn't wait for JoAnn to come home and begin the packing.

She returned home and both of us decided that in order to do justice to this adventure, we should both lose weight and become fit. The plan was for us to rise every morning at seven thirty, and walk for about an hour or more along the bank of the Blackwater River. We began immediately, and soon we were becoming so fit that we could jog part of the way. This walk took us through the woods and along a narrow ledge, and in places it went right down to the water's edge before rising and falling again for much of the journey. It was muddy in many places, and quite dangerous in places, and all the time we did this JoAnn began telling me that she didn't like this walk as she felt one of us would get hurt in this place. I ignored all of this, as I knew it was working and we were definitely fitter. About six weeks before our departure, on a beautiful sunny morning, JoAnn was proven right. She had been trailing along behind me when suddenly I heard her scream out. When I turned around she was lying on the ground with her leg all twisted behind her. She was crying and scared, believing her leg was broken. We were a long way from our car, and after doing my best at first aid, I became her crutch, and somehow managed to get her home. Then the 'ice pack' days began.

I had hoped that in America JoAnn would do all the driving, as she loved it, and I was scared of it. Now she could not even walk let alone drive, and we were only six weeks away from departure from Shannon Airport.

Rest and ice packs, as well as bandaging were all we could do, and instead of getting fitter, we both actually got fatter. It was definitely my fault as I should have taken her advice, but dismissed the Indian ways in her as just unnecessary fears. Weeks of suffering went by, with her slowly improving, but she was always in pain. With a week to go, we decided to visit a healing area in West Cork, and on the way back she got a feeling that something very bad was going to happen in America. It was not that we would die in a plane crash, but she did not know for sure what would happen. This time I believed her, and was half thinking of cancelling the whole trip.

From deep inside me though a kind of gentle voice said over and over, "It will all be wonderful and ye are protected. Go ahead, as I have provided the way". This was not a voice inside me, but a kind of feeling in words; a 'word feeling' is the best way I can describe it. In any case we decided to go ahead.

On the day we were leaving, my son Kyrl drove us to Shannon and everyone wished us so well. JoAnn's foot was not better yet, but she could walk for short periods, and then rest with her ice pack.

From the moment we left Shannon I began to feel wonderful. The journey of my life had begun, and was uneventful until we were flying into Phoenix Airport in the late evening.

The plane had gone into a holding pattern and slowly circled the airport. Then I noticed a violent thunderstorm with fork lightning in the near distance. The plane could not land because the airport was under the weather, and we were flying around it. Every so often we would hear the announcement that 'soon we should be able to land'. Our jet was hanging in the sky, and even though it had to be travelling at well over a hundred miles an hour, it just seemed to be stationary. JoAnn read and I looked at the storm as some passengers became edgy. Then my wife from 'Tornado Alley' said, "This feels like a tornado to me. It's got that kind of feeling in the air". She was overheard by the old ladies sitting near us, and they vehemently disputed this, telling her, "We are in Arizona now. We rarely if ever get tornados". JoAnn said, "I come from Missouri, I know what a tornado feels like, and this has that feeling". The plane began its decent. Suddenly there was a massive bang. It sounded like a huge hammer had violently hit the entire plane. The shuddering travelled all along the fuselage, scaring the hell out of us all - me included. The whole plane shook terribly and suddenly went into a steep nosedive. Some screaming began, and JoAnn dug a hole in my hand with her nails, feeling it was all over. In that moment I too questioned my inner voice, wondering if she had been right about the bad thing happening in America being our untimely death. Then I distinctly heard the 'word feeling' say, "No, you are protected and all will be fine". In that minute the plane leveled off and we landed soon after. By sheer coincidence, the day before we had left I had been reading all about wind shear and how dangerous it is in the West. It had brought down a number of cargo planes before they finally figured out how to deal with it. The symptoms were identical to what had just happened to us. As we left the plane the captain was standing at the exit, and I said to him, "Thank you for your skill. Wind shear I think". He smiled

351

with a knowing look and said, "It was a close one". After surviving that incident, I told JoAnn that no matter what happened next, we would be safe for the rest of the adventure. From then on I was prepared to enjoy every second, and care nothing for my safety either.

By the time we collected our hire car it was about ten thirty at night, and JoAnn very nervously got onto Hway 17 heading north, as I did the navigating. We came to a roundabout and she had her first of many panic attacks, stopping right in the middle of the road in a multi-lane roundabout. No one honked, or got annoyed, and after the initial screaming and panicking, she got round it. We drove on for an hour or so, and then well outside of the city we found our first motel. The room, which was awesome, was incredibly cheap due to some deal going on, and the manager told us that his people all came from Ireland, and he wanted to go there so badly.

When I awoke next morning I was greeted by a deep blue sky and a huge cactus just outside the window. I had only ever seen a huge cactus in the movies as a child, and now I was in the desert looking at thousands of them.

Soon we were back on the road, always heading north, and loving every minute of it all. The desert was quite beautiful, filled with cactus and brush, and covered in a kind of red clay. The roads were straight, had little traffic, and it was easy to navigate using a GPS and the maps I had printed months earlier on my day of decisions.

Hours later we arrived at a little town called Camp Verde and decided on coffee. In the café, while waiting at the counter, I overheard a woman ordering a slice of cheesecake. Then out of the blue she told the assistant that her favourite cheese of all time was Dubliner Cheese. I had not even said a single word, and here was a stranger beside me talking about Irish cheese. When I made my order with my Irish accent, the assistant almost fainted. I smiled at her and took it as a sign, so I immediately persuaded JoAnn to call the Bright Angel Lodge in the Grand Canyon Park to see if she could magic a room for us, and she did. We got a 'cancellation' at a reduced price in a private log cabin, some forty feet from the rim. The Universe had come good as I suspected, and we booked the cabin immediately. Everywhere we went for the rest of the day, we met people who loved Ireland, who wanted to go there, or who had ancestors from there. That in itself was not too surprising, but while in the heritage centre outside of Sedona we bought a famous local chili jam, and its manufacturers were Cahill's from Arizona. What were the odds of that?

Another thunderstorm hit us. Then as we entered beautiful Sedona, the most incredible sunset shone through the windscreen as the storm cleared. It left behind a rainbow of such intensity that numerous people ran out into the street to see it. I felt we were being welcomed to Arizona by my dad who I always associated with double rainbows, and this was the brightest one I had ever seen.

The journey to Sedona had eaten into our time, and next day we had to leave early, as by then I was beginning to feel a great urge to get to the Valley. We did see Bell Rock and Cathedral Rock, as well as a most beautiful church built into the mountains. The Church is called the Chapel of the Holy Cross and no photo can possibly do justice to this church. It has to be seen and experienced, and the designer no doubt was influenced by Frank Lloyd Wright. I sat alone in the peace of that place and thanked God for all that I had, especially for my American wife. She was trapped way below in our car, as we could not drive to the doorway, and the steep walk seemed out of the question for her.

The view from the church was beyond description and I so wished for JoAnn to see it. As I turned to leave, there she was slowly making her way up the ramp to join me. The pain in her foot seemed to have been overcome by her longing to see this wonderful place too. I felt incredibly happy as we both sat and just looked out at the view. This area of Arizona is supposed to have places of high energy, good energy that helps heal people mentally and physically, and we saw people climbing way up on the rocks, no doubt searching for these energy centres. They are called vortexes, but we never felt anything during our brief stay there. Perhaps at a future time we might be luckier.

The sheer distances we had travelled so far, and the time it was taking, was amazing to me. The scale of America has always impressed me, but after driving and driving we seemed to be making only slow progress. We had certain deadlines that were unchangeable such as the Grand Canyon arrival date, and the day we had to leave on the train journey, but all the rest was flexible, so north we went again.

Entering Flagstaff I looked up at an intersection sign and saw it say Route 66. We were driving the most famous road in the world in a city basically founded by three brothers with the name of Riordan. They had come south from Chicago, either as Irish emigrants or with Irish parents as emigrants. There in Flagstaff they built up a huge lumber business, a dam, the Lowell Observatory, hospitals and churches, finally bequeathing their home to the state so as to help the tourist business. Even though I knew none of this at the time, I felt instinctively welcome there, and would now love to see their home and get to know more about these three brothers. With time catching up on us, we just drove on through the city, still heading north on highway 89, all the time inching closer to my dreams. At Cameron we arrived at the junction for the Grand Canyon, but that was for another day. Today was the day we would first set foot in Monument Valley and I could not wait to get there.

We left the Native American trading post of Cameron, and after about ten minutes driving I noticed, by pure accident, that JoAnn was driving with the wrong foot. Obviously the pain had finally won out and she had been sneakily driving our little automatic car very dangerously for hours. I had no choice but to become the driver and put our lives in my hands. The last time I attempted to drive an automatic was in a state park in Missouri, and that time we both painted our faces on the dashboard. I was a disaster with automatics. As well as that, my brain could not get used to the 'wrong side of the road' driving, so when I nervously pulled out in front of a huge speeding semi, JoAnn nearly lost her life. "Speed up, speed up will you, before we are run over. You're not in Cork now," she roared at me in fright. The car was small and sluggish, and the semi bore down on us so fast that again I thought we were gonners. Then with its horns blaring and slipstream tossing us all over the road, he passed us by. It was a scary, bad start, but based on our earlier frights, I felt we would be ok no matter what came at us, so I relaxed and began to just drive. After half an hour I was a 'seasoned veteran' and from then on I drove most of our journeys.

When we took the fork for highway 160, I knew we were getting really close at last. We sailed along now in the sunshine, with a big storm away off in the distance, but the evening was closing fast, and I really wanted that day to end with me seeing the Valley. I began to have inner panics when suddenly, away off to my left, I got the first glimpse of Monument Valley. We shot into Kayenta, and there in a McDonald's restroom I changed into my blue shirt and black pants, just to keep the magic on track and authenticate my dream journal picture.

Turning left onto highway 163 I sped forward, feeling the adrenalin rushing through every cell in my body. Then a kind of euphoria started to flow through me as well. The first mountain came into sight and I swung over for a photograph. As I did so, JoAnn pointed to a single tumbleweed that blew right across the road in our direction. There was no wind and no reason for it to move at all, yet on it came as my dream picture was completed in minute detail. Then in a fever and with the light fading fast, I drove like a demon to get to the Forest Gump spot on the road. We drove and drove and passed the Mittens, and just as I did so, my wonderful American wife pressed a button on the dash and out came U2 from the speakers. Months earlier she had secretly created a CD of my favourite music, and somehow managed to get it into the player while I was in McDonald's changing. This was the most wonderful thing she had ever done for me, and I fought back tears as we drove on to the Forest Gump spot on the road.

With the sun setting in the west, and while watching the sky change into colours of unimaginable beauty, I had arrived. I spun around on the road so as to face in the direction of that famous photograph, and jumped out of the car. I had no words for a long time. After a lifetime of dreaming the impossible dream, I was standing on the road, on the very spot I had imagined, wearing a blue shirt and black pants, and was driving a car of the exact colour as my dream picture back in Ireland. The photo was now complete in every detail. Again I thanked God for that day, for the miracles, and for all that we had in life. All too quickly the sun set and darkness fell almost instantly. We sat and savoured the dusky, starry sky, and felt the energy in that awesome place. We had somehow lost a day, and we had to register at the Grand Canyon within thirty six hours or lose our cabin, yet I just could not leave Monument Valley like this. I needed to see it in the sunshine, like I had all those years before in Kyrl's cowboy films. I needed to see where John Wayne stayed, and where he worked. I needed to see the movie museum in Goulding's, and right then we both needed to find a place to sleep. We decided to return to Kayenta, find a motel and return next morning before dawn to see the sun rise over the valley. As we drove back, we passed the entrance to the Goulding's Lodge, John Wayne's favourite place. On a whim JoAnn decided we should go ask if they had a room, despite my assuring her that they did not.

At the reception desk we were told that they were fully booked up except for a complete chalet, which came with an exorbitant price tag. There was no arguing about the cost of it either; the price was fixed and that was that. We left and drove off down the road, but again JoAnn persuaded me to go back, feeling that she could still get it. After all I had seen happen in recent days, I was not going to argue with her, and I really did want to stay in the valley, so back I drove. The receptionist was surprised to see us back and JoAnn arguing began in earnest, but it did no good. Finally, as if wanting to really get rid of us, he assured us that there was no way it was within his power to change the rates. Only the manager could do that, and she was away for the day. We turned to leave and in walked the manager. She was a nice-looking lady, but had the air of a tough businesswoman. JoAnn explained our situation; how I was from Ireland, wanting to stay in John Wayne's hotel since childhood, she told of our limited budget and embellished nothing. The manager looked at us both for a while. Like many others, she was puzzled with our personal story; an Irishman and an American together. Then she said, "Ahh ye have caught me at a weak moment, give them the chalet at whatever they can afford," and that was it. She left, and we were staying in the famous Goulding's Trading Post with free entry into their John Wayne Museum next morning, and all of this at a rate which was less than half the nominal price. Yet another miracle had happened.

We can't say for sure, but I believe I slept in the same room as my cowboy idol did, and that night I dreamed of Big Kyrl smiling at me a lot. Was all of this a simple coincidence, or is there much more to our lives than we have ever imagined? I believe there is for sure, but no one has told us about it.

We rose before dawn and sped off to our spot on the road. Then as the sun came up, we were bathed in the most beautiful light I had ever seen in my life. The whole area became magical. Reds and golden rays flooded that incredible place, and I could clearly feel the good energy known best to the Navaho Indians. We took picture after picture. JoAnn photographed me in my many poses, especially my dream one of me standing in the road in the sunshine with the Mittens spread out behind me. At long last I could say that my American dream was complete. We sat on the road and shared our breakfast; a banana, a muffin and water. We were about five thousand miles from home, and forty five years away from Kyrl's movie hall. I longed to stay longer, but we could not. We rushed back to Goulding's and saw the museum. I saw just how small I was, and how tall my idol was. Another photo kept this memory alive for posterity, and we headed across the road to the View Hotel in the Navaho Reservation.

The Hotel is aptly named, as without a doubt the view from any part of that hotel is spectacular. We were unable to stay at The View on that trip, but it would be a terrible shame if we could not at least have lunch in their restaurant. This beautiful glass-enclosed eating area had been chosen so as to give their patrons a spectacular view of the entire Monument Valley vista. We ate almost in silence, taking in the surroundings and reveling in the atmosphere of a place I had dreamed of seeing for so long.

Then it began to rain, an unusual event in a desert, and like Forest Gump, it was time to turn back. As we headed south my heart became deeply sad inside, and I felt a terrible longing to stay just a little bit longer, but we could not. We had reached the turning point of that amazing journey, and a peak in my life had occurred. Now my return journey had begun in the rain, and it felt like Ireland was calling, reminding me of my homeland and my roots. When I finally dragged my soul away from the Valley, I could not bring myself to look back, it was too hard. We began heading back to Flagstaff and the Grand Canyon in yet another violent thunderstorm, and even though deeply saddened inside, I still loved it all.

We drove for hours and hours in a kind of downpour that I had never seen before. The lightning flashed and struck things at random some miles away, but it never once occurred to me that we might be in any danger. We hit old Route 66 on the outskirts of Flagstaff and found an old 66 motel where we decided to stay for the night. It had clean rooms and a bar which doubled up as their restaurant. After some food, we decided to attempt to play pool in the bar. This little bar had its locals sitting around drinking beer, and when we set up the table and I explained to JoAnn that I never played pool before, my strong Irish accent became the centre of attention. I could not help noticing people nudging and nodding in our direction, and a kind of quietness descended on the place. I played like a mad man, hitting the wrong balls into the wrong holes, and at such a speed that the first game ended very fast. JoAnn declared herself the winner by default due to my cheating, so another game was soon set up. There was a look of astonishment on one old guy's face near the door as he took a great interest in us and in our 'story', and most especially in this new version of pool, but he never said a word. A rather portly lady of mixed blood, mostly Navaho I believe, took an even keener interest in me, even though it was obvious to all that I was there with my wife. She soon began a slow belly dance while standing facing me, and was giving me the Navaho version of 'the eye' or a 'come on look'. I ignored her, but that only seemed to challenge her more, and then she swayed even closer to both me and JoAnn's beer. To this day I'm still not sure which she was really after. However, I concentrated on trying to play pool by my wife's complicated rules, and this time the pool game went on a bit longer, with JoAnn trying in vain to teach me how to play pool properly. Impatience got the better of me again, and I began potting every ball I could see, irrespective of its colour or number. I just loved the potting stuff and wanted to put every ball into any hole. This was causing amazement and entertainment for the growing number of onlookers, as well as the belly dancer who smiled all the time. JoAnn had laid her beer on a table beside us, and as if to make some kind of play for the drink, our belly dancer then placed her empty glass right beside JoAnn's almost full one. Trouble was brewing, and as if to give her a clear 'hands off' signal, my beloved wife gave her a deadly black stare of 'don't fuck with me bitch', and dramatically moved her beer to another table. It made no difference at all. The swaying only momentarily slowed and began again in earnest, while the onlookers all smirked with the knowledge that a 'fight' might be the night's real entertainment. Taking the challenge, my groupie then sidled right up to the table and stared drunkenly across at me, totally ignoring JoAnn's jet black stares back at her. At that point my groupies' few girlfriends, fearing a real scrap, took her outside, and I continued to pot balls like a man possessed. With the excitement all over, JoAnn once again declared me a cheater and claimed the game, getting some applause from the onlookers.

It was time to leave, and as we did so we got nods of appreciation, or maybe admiration for my new form of 'Irish' pool, and a shake of the head from the old geezer at the door. I loved that place. It was real America, exactly what I had seen in the movies. No pretentious wealth, no falseness, just ordinary people living an ordinary life in a city built by the Riordan Irish. I could easily live there, but JoAnn had other ideas, and didn't like it at all. Later that night it would be hit by five tornados while we slept.

We returned to our room, and being tired out from the days adventures, we both fell fast asleep, leaving the television set turned on, tuned to CNN. Around five a.m. I was awoken in terror to a constant blaring sound screaming at me from the television set. It was a tornado warning being transmitted by some kind of early warning system. JoAnn jumped out of the bed and ran to the window and looked out. She said excitedly, "That noise is a tornado warning, and it does feel like a tornado is near. Can't you feel it?" I could feel nothing, and I could see a repeat of the plane incident was on the way, but at least we were on the ground this time. I threw on my pants and ran outside only to discover that a huge limb had been blown off a tree, landing beside our car. Another foot and our driving days were over. There were bits of trees and debris scattered all over the car park, but I could see no real property damage, so I dismissed all the panic as media exaggeration. I did notice however that the sky looked very peculiar. It was a strange colour, and the clouds were rolling by really fast. Rain was lashing the area now and again, but to me this was the kind of storm we had seen almost every day since arriving in Phoenix.

The newscaster on CNN was describing the damage done by the 'five tornados' that had hit the Flagstaff area during the night. Trains had been derailed, campers overturned, some trailer courts were totally destroyed, and whole streets were hit in the Flagstaff suburbs. We were in the suburbs, and had slept through it all. I sat on the bed transfixed as I watched the reports coming in. This was all so new to me, but very common to a woman from Tornado Alley, and she seemed to be hurriedly dressing and gathering our stuff. All the warnings were suggesting that new tornado cells were forming in our area, and would be slowly moving north of Flagstaff. This was exactly where we were heading on our way to the Grand Canyon. Months earlier I had figured out a short cut from Flagstaff to the Grand Canyon, and from the weatherman I could see that the cells seemed to be forming along the road right on our path.

Then the argument started. I was all for heading off there and then, before anything worse happened, and to hell with the warnings. I didn't want a repeat of Monument Valley where we ran out of time. Besides that, we were booked into the Bright Angel Lodge that night. JoAnn was dead against it, telling me that she could 'feel' the tornado in the air. Not me though. The television reporters were dishing out warning after warning for our area, and then we compromised. I agreed to get a disk for the camera, and that would take less than an hour, and surely all would be ok by then. We headed for Wal-Mart. Though she denies this, I believe that JoAnn deliberately got us lost, despite my GPS directions. After almost two hours of shopping, we were again heading north, this time with me doing the driving, and of course we didn't bother listening to the radio for weather updates.

The sky got darker and darker. We were also climbing rapidly into the mountains, and I could see the temperature falling with each mile we drove. Suddenly a huge flash of lightning struck the trees on our left only a short distance into the forest. Then it really began to storm. More lightning began flashing and striking all around us, and it seemed to be getting closer, so much so that poor JoAnn became concerned that we might be struck and completely annihilated. I assured her in my best 'science voice' that we were in a 'Faraday Cage' and perfectly safe from lightning, but I secretly wondered about falling trees.

The number of cars approaching us soon dwindled down to a trickle, and finally stopped all together. The only cars then on the road were ourselves and a big four by four jeep travelling just behind us, with possibly a family inside it. Like us, I believe they were on the way to the Canyon also, and the driver was now tailgating me, much to my annoyance and growing concern.

Almost too suddenly it became as dark as night. I had the lights on full when the sheets of rain turned to sleet, then to hail, and then to snow, all within minutes. By then we were driving through a big forest, and we started to notice that trees had just been torn up from the ground, and there were freshly mangled limbs strewn all over the roadside.

In shock and amazement I braked hard and had my first skid, as the road had become both a skating rink and an obstacle course. At that point even I became scared, and began looking for someplace to pull off the road before we slid off, possibly into a deep ravine. It was almost impossible to see anything though, and I was afraid my tailgater would run right into me if I slammed on the brakes again. Our situation was fast becoming very serious. I think the jeep driver must have somehow believed that if a tiny car like ours could drive in this weather, surely so could his jeep. Through the blizzard I spotted a kind of lay-by up ahead, just as another huge fork of lightning struck close by. Our car veered into the lay-by, and we slid to a halt in among the trees. I was very relieved. The jeep sped on past us, and my tornado woman announced, "That's a very stupid thing to do. He has no clue at all. We may well find him up the road in the ditch," prophetic words indeed.

The storm moved on to the north, and after about ten minutes we headed off again. As we rounded the first bend, and literally a hundred yards from where we had stopped, we saw the first of the many big trees almost blocking the road. I swerved to avoid a smash, and in panic slowed to a crawl on the ice and the snow. The destruction in the forest was like nothing I had ever seen in my life. Just feet in from the road, and spread along the roadside, were huge trees, twisted and broken like matchsticks. It was a kind of random destruction. A clump of trees here and there were totally destroyed, then a foot or two away, there was no sign of damage. Without realizing it, I had been driving us inside, or very close to the edge of one of the worst tornados ever seen in the area. I saw our exact tornado later on You Tube, and became mesmerized at how near we had been, through my ignorance, to tragedy. Only minutes had separated us from who knows what. JoAnn still says it was the act of a mad man, so at least I was keeping that tradition alive.

About half a mile down the road we saw the jeep. It was turned upside down and lying on its roof inside in a field. As we passed by we could see no one in it, but all their belongings were strewn all over the road and a police car was just arriving at the spot. JoAnn had been right after all, and I felt so thankful for our safety. My dream trip had almost cost us our lives. If we had not pulled over, we would have been that family in the jeep, and I still wonder what became of them.

Having survived our ordeal, once again I felt sure that we were being protected by a power beyond us. With that comfort in mind, I drove on in bright sunshine to the Grand Canyon. One of the Seven Natural Wonders of the World was awaiting our arrival.

Miracles we are....

It took some considerable time to reach the Grand Canyon Village and the South Rim Visitors Centre. We spent time inside and got to know the ideal way to see this wonder of nature. The whole viewing experience is top class and designed for the visitor to see this awe inspiring place at its best. The thing I liked most was the free bus transport to every possible viewing point. You parked your car and took the shuttles everywhere after that.

I will never forget us walking through the little trees and shrubs as we headed for the rim, full of expectation, but nothing can prepare you for that first sight. When at last we came through to the rim, I froze in awe. It was the most breathtaking sight I know I will ever see for the rest of my life. We stood and stared in amazement and silence. Both of us became overwhelmed by the grandeur and spectacle, and I said, "No matter who we tell about this, or what photos we take, nothing will ever be able to do it justice". JoAnn agreed. It would be a total nonsense for me to try and describe what we were looking at. It has to be personally seen to be experienced fully, and that is the truth. I think my mind simply could not take in the sheer size of the valley laid out before us. This canyon had a myriad of rock formations constantly changing colour before one's eyes. Everyone around us seemed to be feeling the same awe. We stood transfixed, looking down for a mile into the brown Colorado River. Then as if to welcome us again, a most beautiful rainbow formed right before our very eyes. People pointed and clicked a thousand cameras. To add to the magic of that moment, an eagle with huge wings outstretched glided gracefully into the canyon, bringing gasps of excitement from all those who saw it.

The Bright Angel Lodge is located further along the rim, and we finally checked in and got our chalet. It was wonderful; a log cabin situated on the rim of the Grandest Canyon in the world. It is beautifully decorated, spartan and old, but just wonderful all the same. We were in Heaven and we were so happy. We returned to the Bright Angel and had a most wonderful meal. We also bought books, souvenirs and a DVD called *The National Parks, America's best kept secret* by Ken Burns, my favourite director. I had been looking for that DVD forever, and I just knew it would be there. The evening was closing in and everyone wanted to see the sunset change the canyon into a million different colours, including us, and we were not disappointed. We travelled along the rim until we could see no more, and then arrived back to the little train station which took people to and from the town of Williams. I had wanted to travel on that train to the Canyon, but changed my mind later as we had the hired car. Another time perhaps. Thousands and thousands of people from every nation on Earth were visiting that beautiful place, and many of them were travelling in style on that train. Thousands more came by bus and by car, and even by helicopter. JoAnn walked and walked, and here we got the first sign that her foot may finally be getting better. We loved the place. Our senses went into overdrive at each new viewing point, and after the day closed and we lay in bed chatting, we came to the conclusion that the only thing left was to see the dawn come up over the rim in the morning. It had been one of the most exciting and exhilarating days of my life, and sleep overpowered us. I clearly remember thinking just before I succumbed to the blackness that, 'we are sleeping on the rim of the Grand Canyon. I hope I don't sleep walk tonight'. Then darkness fell both physically and mentally. I cuddled up to my wife and told her I loved her, but she was already in dreamland.

JoAnn dragged me reluctantly from the bed before five a.m. because we had planned a complete series of viewings, chasing the sun as it travelled across the Canyon. With coffee in hand we made off into the stinging cold Arizona air and saw the dawn break. Hours went by, and at each new spot I thought I had seen the best I could see, but it was as if the place was taunting me with its beauty, challenging me to mentally judge the infinitely beautiful, a task I finally gave up on. By day's end we had both concluded that our minds were numbed with the sheer beauty of it all. My favourite viewing place was Powell Point. There I ventured so close to the edge that JoAnn could not hold our camera steady because she was so scared that I might fall over the edge. As if to taunt her, I sat on the edge and dangled my legs over the rim. Then later on I stood on the edge and winged my hands out like a human

364

bird.

I could see for hundreds of miles, but I wished we were way down below, drifting along on the Colorado River in a canoe in the sunshine. JoAnn finally became enraged with my antics and threatened all kinds of punishment if I didn't come back from the rim, and in the end I did. But the memory of that sheer drop is burned into my mind forever more. I doubt if we will ever see a more beautiful place on this Earth, but for all its beauty, I did not feel called to it spiritually like had happened to me in Monument Valley. There was no sense of sadness either as we left and headed for the town of Williams, our next stop.

The town of Williams is located right on old Route 66. It was the staging point for the Canyon for all those tourists en route to California on that famous road. My purpose in going there was to authenticate the drawing I had made years earlier in my dream journal by having us stand on the train station platform, and have our picture taken in front of a choo choo train.

By the time we arrived into Williams, evening was fast approaching and the sky had once more become a multicoloured spectacle, changing minute by minute. We rushed to the station and had our photo taken in the last rays of the sun. JoAnn snapped my picture as I pointed up to the Williams sign, and I felt wonderful. This photo was just another proof that the journal had worked. Night fell and we drove around the town just like the tourists had done in the fifties and sixties. All that was missing was our red Corvette. The people of Williams are very proud of their 66 heritage, and virtually every shop had some connection to the famous road. The neon signs and artwork adorned the shops and cafes, and it was so easy to feel that we had gone back in time. That night we slept once more in a Route 66 motel, this time without the groupies or the pool tables.

The next day we headed back for Flagstaff, and by then we were truly on the return leg of our trip, but there was still one more wonder to see.

When I was mapping our trip months earlier, I felt that the icing on the cake for me would be a visit to the Meteor Crater. It would be a huge bonus if we could manage it, and on the second last day we felt that we still had time for one more visit before we returned our car. We drove east, heading for Winona and Wilmslow, both towns made famous by songs of Route 66, and the Eagles' song about standing on the corner. Pretty soon JoAnn turned off the highway, and we crossed the desolation to Meteor Crater in beautiful sunshine. It was our last day in Arizona and the only one that we didn't have a thunderstorm. Meteor Crater was formed when a small meteorite hit this remote area fifty thousand years ago, and it obliterated the whole place. The Crater is an amazing sight. I loved being there because when I was a young boy in Buttevant, I had read all about it in Uncle Michael's little encyclopaedia, and wondered if I might ever see it one day. Today was that day. It's a great facility and well worth a visit. They have a museum there, and while JoAnn studied inside, I got to walk on the outside with a guided tour and take many amazing pictures. It truly was the icing on the cake for me on the trip. Now all that was left was for us to be sure to wake in time for our early morning train and begin the journey back to Missouri, but the day was young yet and Flagstaff nightlife was calling me.

We dropped off our hired car at the local airport and got a taxi back to our original motel, famous for Navaho groupies, and the new ball game known as 'Irish pool'. Then we headed out on the Flagstaff town. At the bus stop we were joined by two 'down and outs' who helped me figure out the local bus timetable. Quite early on they told me of the amazing news that a dollar bus ticket got you almost anywhere in Flagstaff. It was no wonder I loved the place. During our chat, the more talkative one was amazed that I was a genuine Irishman, and he proudly informed me that he too had Irish blood in him, due to his red hair and red beard, but I saw no red in either of them. As if to banish my obvious scepticism, he told us that his people had all come over from 'Liverpool in Ireland' many years earlier, and settled in Arizona. I didn't have the heart to tell him that Liverpool was in England, and so we chatted away until the bus finally arrived. Sure enough one dollar did get you right into the centre of town, and as we were parting, 'Redbeard' gave me this parting advice, "I hope ye have a wild night in the pubs. You know what us Irish are like with the drink," and with a wave of his hand, he and his silent friend disappeared down an alleyway.

We did end up in an Irish bar that night, but the only wild thing that happened was my shock at the size of our bill for the food.

Next morning at five a.m. a taxi took us to Flagstaff train station, and by five forty we were on board the South West Chief, saying good bye to Arizona. I was too tired to be sad, and by some mix up our pre-booked sleeper car had been given out to someone else. We sat in the dark while our room was being cleaned, and saw the sun come up over the western desert for one last time. JoAnn just loved it all, as did I. Eventually our room was ready, complete with refreshments and privacy. Included in the deal were all of our meals, which turned out to be amazing. We were crossing America on a journey that would take over twenty three hours, travelling thousands of miles and stopping only once in Albuquerque, New Mexico. We met some wonderful people at meal times and became mini celebrities. Everyone seemed to be curious about 'our story' and how we had met. Some came right out and asked, and some hinted around it, but all were even more curious about Ireland. I'm happy to say that I did my bit for our Irish tourist industry, and I welcomed everyone to Ireland, as did JoAnn.

During the evening meal, a discussion began at our table about the power of the media and how it can influence our lives. This became so vociferous that soon we were righting all the wrongs of the world, and saving the oil for future generations to come. It did not take long for those at the tables nearby to join in, and before long almost half of the dining car was in high spirits. Even the concierge, a huge African American, had become infected, and he became quite friendly. This was in contrast to his earlier five a.m. manner when he commanded us all to, "Sit down together and shut up complaining", breakfast would arrive when he was good and ready. I told those others at our table then that my aim was to wear him down with kindness before the journey ended, and by eight p.m. that evening he was a changed man. It's possible that my little financial token of appreciation given to him at the Albuquerque stopover may have helped, but that night those at our table all had prime rib and his personal service with a broad smile, while the less fortunate may have been told their steaks were all gone. Big Kyrl's mantra of 'the end always justifies the means' was proven correct once again. Later on in the evening, as the staff were encouraging the listening people of our dining car to leave, the man in command went to great pains to assure our group that there was 'no rush', and 'did we need any more of anything?' Kindness had won out in the end.

It was late when we all said good bye, and we retired to our beds. I had the top bunk and felt claustrophobic, falling asleep eventually, but JoAnn was so enthralled and excited by her experience that she didn't sleep at all, and kept looking out at the cities and towns of her homeland as they rushed by in the dark. In the early morning we arrived into Kansas City. Confused by the time zones, and having got no warning from our concierge, we almost stayed on the train and would have ended in Chicago. Perhaps he was planning on another financial incentive at the Kansas City stopover, but we never saw him again.

We spent a day exploring Kansas City, and around four p.m. I heard for the last time that famous train call, "Board, all aboard". We were then just hours away from our family and home in Missouri. The train travelled along a track running parallel to the mighty Missouri River, and as darkness fell, I slipped into a deep and dreamless sleep. Hours later our Amtrak train pulled into the Washington Missouri station where we were excitedly greeted by JoAnn's daughter Jessica, and our granddaughter, Paige. With the bags quickly stowed away, we headed for home, with me in the front, and JoAnn and Paige in the back. Paige soon fell sound asleep, and after an initial burst of talk, it soon subsided.

We turned south onto I44, a road that parallels the old Route 66, and in my mind I began to relive our amazing trip. But after days and days of fulfilled dreams and miracles of all kinds, I was totally exhausted and drifted into a kind of strange trancelike state, neither awake nor asleep. In the distance I could still hear the soft southern accents, and I felt comfortable and safe with Jessica doing the driving.

JoAnn was asking Jessica if there was any news from home. Then I heard her say, "Well, Grandpa Earl is not doing so good".

"What's wrong with my dad?" concern immediately apparent in JoAnn's voice. "They don't know yet. He has to go into hospital next week for some tests". That news unnerved me, and in my half state of consciousness, I began to go back in time to my first meeting with JoAnn's father.

I remembered how this ex Deputy Sheriff had cautiously, but

warmly welcomed me into his home many years earlier. How he took such pride in showing me all of his guns, especially a gun that he had handmade. Some friend of his had argued that a gun could not be made from bits and pieces found around the house, and Earl took up the challenge as a bet with him, and he won that bet.

As he showed me this beautiful hand carved pistol, he could clearly see that I fell instantly in love with it, and then he promised to give it to me 'before he passed away'.

I remembered his humour and what we called his 'Earlisms'. These were sayings he had that were unique to him. One time I had thought about buying a ticket for a local car raffle, and Earl gave me this advice. In his slow southern accent he said, "Well John…if I were you I would save my money because those people are so crooked that when they die, we will have to screw them into the ground," an 'Earlism' I'll never forget.

Over the following years on my many visits to America, we had become great friends, and sometimes I felt that he thought of me as the son he never had.

As I thought of those days, for some strange reason my memory returned to an earlier day in West Cork just before our Arizona trip, when JoAnn had told me that her hands were hurting. She said that whenever her hands hurt, it was a sign that bad news was coming, and that something would happen in America. Could the bad news be Earl's illness? I brushed off my forebodings by thinking of Earl's wife Georgia, and how she reminded me so much of my own mother because both of them smoked like chimneys and had an infectious laugh. I felt that Georgia and my mother would have become great friends too because of their common addiction to cigarettes, and their love of cooking. Today as I write, both of them have since given up cigarettes. Miracles are still happening.

Had my mother ever made it to America, I could easily see us all sitting around a barbeque in the warm evening air, laughing and joking, with mother telling everyone her numerous stories about her Henry, while all the time keeping the mosquitoes at bay with the clouds of smoke from her fags. It was a magical vision warming my soul with sheer happiness, but unfortunately it was never to be.

,gan missing my own mother, and still in that dreamy
,ssed over the ocean and saw her smiling and welcoming
m.   her room with a big Irish hug. In my mind I sat down on
her bed and began telling her all about the wonderful dream trip we
had just completed. She listened carefully and looked so very
happy on hearing all of my news, and was just about to say
something really profound when I was gently but firmly pulled
back into reality by JoAnn shaking my shoulder.

"Honey, wake up, you're almost at home. Do you know where
you are now Punkin?" Reluctantly I focused my eyes on the road
ahead, and immediately knew exactly where we were. We were
driving through the town of Cuba, Missouri, crossing a junction I
knew very well indeed.

"Of course I know where we are," I said rather gruffly, still
wanting to hear what my mother was trying to tell me.

"Jessica has just crossed over old Route 66, where you gave me
my first driving lesson here in America, and it was in this very jeep
too. Now will you let me go back to my dreams, please". I tried
hard to return to my trancelike state, but then almost at home,
JoAnn was determined to have more fun at my expense, and so she
started to rise me again.

"You were snoring loudly too, did you know that Punkin? And
what were you dreaming about anyway?" Peals of laughter then
followed my vehement denial of my snoring faux pas, though I
secretly suspected it might be true. "Ahh come on now, tell us
what you were dreaming about. What was so very important about
it?" Again I said gruffly, "Well, if you must know, I was dreaming
of my mother, and I was telling her all about our great adventure
when you shook me awake". More laughter then followed from
the two Americans. They saw right through my veiled pretence at
being annoyed at them. "And what did she say, Irishman?" I
paused for a while, and in my mind I returned to my mother where
I heard her clearly speak. Smiling, I turned round in my seat and
looked back at my beautiful American wife. "Well if you must
know, my mother just said, 'John, you've come a long way from
Two Walls and a Roof, haven't you'."

I thought about it for a moment and said, "Yes mother, but it's not
over yet".

In memory of Earl Garms, who passed away from us all on December 3rd 2010.

About the Author John Michael Cahill.

Born into poverty in a house that used to be an alley, in Ireland, in 1950. I was stolen by my grandmother at three months and never given back to my parents who lived across the street. It broke my father's spirit and he took to the drink. From then on my other five siblings and I were destined for a big fat nothing, and three of us were even told we would be blind before becoming teenagers.

In our little attic my brother and I made gunpowder, talked on a beam of light ever before fiber optics was even heard of, and among numerous other inventions we blotted out the whole town's radio service for weeks.

As a teenager while sitting on an old castle window sill, I saw a vision of an American girl appear before my eyes, and I spent the next thirty years searching for her despite being married with three children. Eventually I did find her in Missouri in the USA, then a whole new life began for me, culminating in a trip to Monument Valley and this book, but it's not over yet.

I work in Radio broadcasting, own my own Video Production company, and with my brother and his partner we also own two US Patents that will cure the killer condition known as Deep Vein Thrombosis. My life so far has been one amazing journey driven always by Hope for a better day tomorrow. This Hope was given to all of us by an extraordinary mother, in between Two Walls and a Roof.

372